AF837620

Maike Gossen, Laura Niessen (eds.)
Sufficiency in Business

New Economies | Volume 2

Editorial

Our current economic systems are not geared towards the satisfaction of needs and the care for our environment and our fellow human beings, but solely towards growth and profit. The consequences of this are a constant reproduction of social inequalities along the axes of class, *race* and gender as well as the isolation of individuals and the destruction of nature.
The **New Economy** book series provides explanations for these multiple crises of our time and opens up possibilities for a sustainable, solidarity-based economy. It provides an editorial space for heterodox empirical research, paving the way for pluralistic, interdisciplinary and self-reflexive economics.

Maike Gossen (Dr.) is as a post-doc researcher at Technical University Berlin, Germany. Her research centers around sustainable consumption, sufficiency, sufficiency-promoting marketing and digitalisation.
Laura Niessen is a doctoral researcher at the Maastricht Sustainability Institute at Maastricht University, the Netherlands. She works on sufficiency-based business models and on how companies can promote sufficiency practices amongst their customers.

Maike Gossen, Laura Niessen (eds.)

Sufficiency in Business

The Transformative Potential of Business for Sustainability

[transcript]

We acknowledge support by the Open Access Publication Fund of Technische Universität Berlin.
This work was supported by the European Union's Horizon 2020's European Research Council (ERC) funding scheme [grant agreement No. 850159], as part of project Circular X.

Bibliographic information published by the Deutsche Nationalbibliothek
The Deutsche Nationalbibliothek lists this publication in the Deutsche Nationalbibliografie; detailed bibliographic data are available in the Internet at https://dnb.dnb.de/

First published in 2024 by transcript Verlag, Bielefeld

Cover layout: Maria Arndt, Bielefeld
Cover illustration: Isabella Krzyscik (IZAIZA)
Printed by: Majuskel Medienproduktion GmbH, Wetzlar
https://doi.org/10.14361/9783839469101
Print-ISBN: 978-3-8376-6910-7
PDF-ISBN: 978-3-8394-6910-1
ISSN of series: 2942-1489
eISSN of series: 2942-1497

Printed on permanent acid-free text paper.

Contents

Part B –
Experiences of Sufficiency in Business

Part C – Transformative Changes for Sufficiency on Political and Societal Levels

Appendix

Foreword

Nancy M. P. Bocken

Sufficiency is a concept that is becoming ever more important in developing nations to come to sufficient levels of health, education and nutrition for all, and in developed nations, to start addressing unsustainable levels of consumption. In this way, sufficiency is at the heart of sustainable development. However, the world is on fire, and at the time of writing in autumn 2023, 6 out of 9 planetary boundaries have been crossed (Richardson et al. 2023). And still, we do not yet have a concrete plan to break through business as usual.

The way in which products and services are produced and consumed drives our global footprints. From a business perspective, this can be captured conceptually in a "business model", which provides an overview of how a business proposes value; creates and delivers this value and captures financial and other forms of value, preferably in a sustainable way. The business model lens therefore has the potential to break through unsustainable production and consumption patterns.

In the now popular area of the circular economy, we coined the resource strategies of narrowing the loop (using less resources per product and using less in general), closing the loop (in essence, recycling), slowing the loop (extending the life of products) and regenerating loops (improving natural resources). While the closing the loop model is still the most common circular business strategy, ample research has shown that we cannot recycle ourselves out of the environmental crisis, as recycling uses energy, exacerbating carbon emissions and cannot continue perpetually because of material degradation.

One solution would lie in pursuing a *sufficiency-driven business model* – the ultimate type of business model to counteract unsustainable consumption. This idea emerged from the observation that not all businesses had the typical "take-make-waste" linear model based on planned obsolescence but quite the opposite. Mark Adams, Managing Director of furniture company Vitsœ talks about his company enabling: "Living with Less that Lasts Longer". Outdoor company Patagonia asks us to not buy stuff at all or to buy second-hand where possible. Inspiring examples led us to conceptualize a sufficiency-oriented business model.

Sufficiency in business might sound like an oxymoron but there are many opportunities to create value in a more *sufficient* way. These would include longer lasting and durable products, offering quality over quantity, designing for upgrading and multiple life cycles, offering second-hand or vintage marketplaces, frugal innovations, offering alternatives to materialistic consumption and services rather than products.

While this idea of *sufficiency in business* stimulated discussions on desirability, feasibility and viability, on top of the long-term concerns about *the economy* if we were to consume less, I am happy to see that Sufficiency in Business is now an important theme in business and academia.

The editors of this book have taken on the challenge to bring together different perspectives on Sufficiency in Business. It is almost impossible to do this type of research without a personal conviction to make a change in the world. Maike Gossen and Laura Niessen have created their own strong voices in shaping the *sufficiency debate* and how business could play a role in this. Sufficiency in Business is no longer a term to shy away from but a topic to investigate, debate and put in practice. On the macro-economic scale, debates about degrowth and alternative forms of valuing the world around us, beyond the economic, are continuing to take shape.

Some final words from others that find themselves on a sufficiency journey and feel insecure about the future – a word of wisdom borrowed from American computer scientist Alan Kay: "The best way to predict the future is to invent it!" So let us all try and contribute to this positive future.

References

Richardson, Katherine/Steffen, Will/Lucht, Wolfgang/Bendtsen, Jørgen/Cornell, Sarah E./Donges, Jonathan F./Drüke, Markus/Fetzer, Ingo/Bala, Govindasamy/von Bloh, Werner/Feulner, Georg/Fiedler, Stephanie/Gerten, Dieter/Gleeson, Tom/Hofmann, Matthias/Huiskamp, Willem/Kummu, Matti/Mohan, Chinchu/Nogués-Bravo, David/Petri, Stefan/Porkka, Miina/Rahmstorf, Stefan/Schaphoff, Sibyll/Thonicke, Kirsten/Tobian, Arne/Virkki, Vili/Wang-Erlandsson, Lan/Weber, Lisa/Rockström, Johan (2023): "Earth beyond six of nine planetary boundaries." In: Science Advances 9/37. https://doi.org/10.1126/sciadv.adh2458.

Introduction

Maike Gossen and Laura Niessen

The cover of this book shows a tree in a much smaller flowerpot. Why might this image seem strange to observers? The tree is green and thriving, even though it feeds off little soil. For us, this is an analogy of sufficiency in business. Sufficiency in businesses is about strategies that reduce production levels, curb sales and promote lower consumption with the aim to stay within ecological planetary boundaries and ensure well-being. This is at odds with current economic thinking and, like the tree in our image, does not yet stand firmly on solid ground. However, the growing interest in research and practice in sufficiency-oriented businesses promises a blooming future. This book is a contribution to present some of the latest work and provide an interdisciplinary perspective on this innovative field of research.

What is sufficiency and how does business relate to it? There is no generally agreed definition of sufficiency but the idea is intuitive: "It is the sense that, as one does more and more of an activity, there can be enough and there can be too much. I eat because I'm hungry but at some point I'm satiated. If I keep eating I become bloated." (Princen 2005: 6) This is similarly logical at the collective level, because it is recognized that sufficiency is not an individual responsibility but a collective endeavor. In the context of ecological overshoot, this commonplace principle of sufficiency has been revived to represent an ecological principle: when does too much resource and material use threaten social well-being and ecological boundaries?

Sufficiency in the sustainability context thus is a response to two major challenges: First, it addresses environmental degradation, with its accompanying effects, such as the extraction of more resources than can be replenished and the emission of more greenhouse gases than can be absorbed. Here, it is often understood in a triad with efficiency and consistency. Efficiency means using fewer resources to produce the same amount or even more. Consistency refers to producing in accordance with nature: designing products that are not harmful or closing the resource cycle, such as in a circular economy. Sufficiency complements these two principles by reducing the overall consumption of resources.

The second major challenge that sufficiency addresses is to secure human needs and social well-being. Many humans struggle to meet their basic needs, while the wealthier sections of society consume far more than is necessary for their basic well-being. A particularly striking example is that in 2018, one per cent of the world's population caused 50 per cent of CO_2 emissions from commercial aviation, particularly private aircraft (Gössling/Humpe 2020). This contrasts with the estimate that 89 per cent of the world's population did not travel by air. Similar examples can be found across sectors, where the excess by some groups is mirrored by the scarcity of others. Sufficiency addresses this inequality, as it proposes to reduce overconsumption in affluent communities so that resources are left for communities that are struggling. As such, it aligns with the goals of a Doughnut Economy (Raworth 2017), where the social needs of all should be met within the ecological boundaries of the planet.

Sufficiency has seen increased interest both in academic research (Sandberg 2021) and in the real world. Global events such as Russia's invasion of Ukraine in 2022 and the following energy crisis increased public awareness in Europe of the need to reduce resource and energy consumption. While it is still the "ugly duckling" of sustainability principles and often left aside next to its more popular siblings efficiency and consistency, sufficiency is starting to step out of the shadow as a real necessity for a sustainable future.

One highly under-researched question is: what role can businesses play in driving sufficiency? As a central decision maker in processes of production and consumption, businesses are increasingly called upon to take responsibility in a sustainability transformation (Hoffman/Ehrenfeld 2017). Businesses can create new demands and wants, with mainstream marketing and advertising practices stipulating that people keep buying new products. As such, the node of business is a potential transformation point in spreading the sufficiency principle across society. The field of research on sufficiency-oriented companies can be traced back to the 1990s, when Wolfgang Sachs (1993) defined four dimensions of a sufficiency economy: less clutter, less speed, less distance and less market. Dyllick and Hockerts (2002) also introduced sufficiency as a fundamental element of a sustainable company. A few years later, Bocken and Short (2016) used practical examples to demonstrate how companies can develop sufficiency-oriented business models. Niessen and Bocken (2021) built on earlier work and provided an overview of strategies that companies can use to promote sufficiency. The most common strategies originate from the marketing toolbox (Gossen et al. 2019): Sufficiency-oriented product strategies that focus on the development of durable, high quality and repairable alternatives to conventional products, as well as extending the warranty period and offering repair services. These strategies are often complemented by communication measures such as anti-consumerist messages, raising awareness of the impact of consumption on the environment and humans and challenging the materialistic norms of a consumer society.

This book is a snapshot of the growing interest and community around sufficiency-oriented businesses. With ecological and social challenges becoming ever more pressing, it is necessary to imagine alternative forms of business and explore real-world cases of courageous frontrunners. The book is structured into three parts. It combines contributions from academics and practitioners, some of which are based on empirical data and some of which are conceptual in nature.

Part I introduces sufficiency in business more broadly, through presenting different viewpoints. Julia Bruckner gives an overview of the existing academic debate on sufficiency-oriented business. Christel Maurer then looks at strategies that businesses can pursue for sufficiency. This is followed by a chapter by Maren Ingrid Kropfeld and André Reichel on transforming into a purpose-driven business. Part I also includes an exploration of what sufficiency in business means through the lens of critical realism by Iana Nesterova and Hubert Buch-Hansen. Finally, Laura Beyeler connects sufficiency to the principle of care.

In Part II, experiences with sufficiency in business are explained using empirical examples. The chapter by Jana-Michaela Timm and Michaela Hausdorf deals with community-supported business models in various sectors. Jessica Jungell-Michelsson and Iana Nesterova explore the process of embedding sufficiency in the food business. The chapter by Joshua Hurtado Hurtado, Heini Salonen, Tina Nyfors, Pasi Heikkurinen and Kristoffer Wilén stays in the food sector and looks at cultures of sufficiency in business. Beatriz Garcia-Ortega, Javier Galan-Cubillo, F. Javier Llorens-Montes and Blanca de-Miguel-Molina then provide an example from the fashion sector: they examine social media communication of a sportswear brand for sufficiency. The chapter by Maëlle Soulis and Oksana Mont explores how the sufficiency-oriented business model is applied in French fashion SMEs. Then, Viola Muster and Marlene Münsch examine the role that minimalism can play in hindering sufficiency. The next chapter by Laura Niessen, Nancy Bocken and Marc Dijk gives an example of how sufficiency-oriented efforts can influence users in the mobility sector. Then, Isabelle Dabadie reports on her experiences with sufficiency in the ICT sector. Finally, Jana Gebauer, Laura Niessen and Maike Gossen look at how sufficiency can address the rebound effect in a steel and metal processing company.

Part III goes beyond businesses and deals with the necessary changes in broader society. Isaac Arturo Ortega Alvarado critically reviews the role of the market in social transformation. Maike Gossen, Josephine Tröger and Vivian Frick discuss economic and societal barriers that still stand in the way of sufficiency businesses. The broader part of the transformation is then linked to politics with the chapter by Jonas Lage, Benjamin Best, Tobias Froese and Carina Zell-Ziegler, who examine the interplay between business action and policy for sufficiency.

References

Bocken, Nancy M. P./Short, Samuel W. (2016): "Towards a sufficiency-driven business Model: Experiences and opportunities." In: Environmental Innovation and Societal Transitions 18, pp. 41–61. https://doi.org/10.1016/j.eist.2015.07.010.

Dyllick, Thomas/Hockerts, Kai (2002): "Beyond the business case for corporate sustainability." In: Business Strategy and the Environment 11/2, pp. 130–141. https://doi.org/10.1002/bse.323.

Gössling, Stefan/Humpe, Andreas (2020): "The global scale, distribution and growth of aviation: Implications for climate change." In: Global Environmental Change 65, 102194. https://doi.org/10.1016/j.gloenvcha.2020.102194.

Gossen, Maike/Ziesemer, Florence/Schrader, Ulf (2019): "Why and How Commercial Marketing Should Promote Sufficient Consumption: A Systematic Literature Review. In: Journal of Macromarketing 39/3, pp. 252–269. https://doi.org/10.1177/0276146719866238.

Niessen, Laura/Bocken, Nancy M. P. (2021): "How Can Businesses Drive Sufficiency? The Business for Sufficiency Framework." In: Sustainable Production and Consumption 28, pp. 1090–1103. https://doi.org/10.1016/j.spc.2021.07.030.

Princen, Thomas (2005): The logic of sufficiency, Cambridge: MIT Press.

Raworth, Kate (2017): Doughnut Economics: Seven Ways to Think Like a 21st-Century Economist, London: Random House Business Books.

Sachs, Wolfgang (1993): "Die vier E's. Merkposten für einen massvollen Lebensstil." In: Politische Ökologie 11/33, pp. 69–72, 6.12.2023 (https://epub.wupperinst.org/frontdoor/deliver/index/docId/66/file/66_Sachs.pdf).

Sandberg, Maria (2021): "Sufficiency Transitions: A Review of Consumption Changes for Environmental Sustainability." In: Journal of Cleaner Production 293, 126097. https://doi.org/10.1016/j.jclepro.2021.126097.

Part A –
Viewpoints on Sufficiency in Business

Towards a Characterization of Sufficiency-Oriented Businesses

Enhancing their Understanding and Identifying Key Dimensions

Julia Bruckner

Abstract *This chapter examines the prevailing understanding of sufficiency-oriented businesses and identifies their (ideal) characteristics along six dimensions according to the current state of knowledge. Based on a systematic literature review and expert interviews, it offers a conceptual basis for future research and provides guidance for the integration of sufficiency in businesses.*

1. Introduction

In response to the current environmental crisis, the sufficiency approach, which seeks to align current production and consumption levels with planetary boundaries while ensuring a decent standard of living for all, is gaining scholarly interest across various academic domains (Sandberg 2021; Jungell-Michelsson/Heikkurinen 2022). For businesses operating within the current growth-oriented economic system, sufficiency seems to represent a comprehensive and far-reaching concept that necessitates a fundamental shift in traditional business logic (Jungell-Michelsson/Heikkurinen 2022). While existing publications on corporate sufficiency have discussed the concept mainly with regard to specific sufficiency-oriented business models (e.g., Bocken/Short 2016), business strategies (e.g., Freudenreich/Schaltegger 2020) and corporate marketing (e.g., Gossen et al. 2019), the need to incorporate sufficiency as a holistic principle throughout the business has been emphasized for effective implementation (Bocken/Short 2016; Gossen et al. 2019; Beyeler/Jaeger-Erben 2022; Niessen et al. 2023b). Recent studies have begun to take initial steps towards a more comprehensive approach by empirically examining the constituent elements of general sufficiency-oriented business practices (Beyeler/Jaeger-Erben 2022) and of entire businesses driving a sufficiency-based circular economy (Bocken et al. 2022).

However, as the prevailing conceptualization of corporate sufficiency reveals contradictions and ambiguities (Jungell-Michelsson/Heikkurinen 2022), a comprehensive and systematic characterization of sufficiency-oriented companies is warranted. A pressing need has emerged to advance our understanding of sufficiency-oriented businesses, including their partly distinctive conceptualizations, and subsequently to identify their characteristics based on the existing state of knowledge. This would provide a crucial theoretical foundation for future research and guide companies in embedding sufficiency throughout the business.

To address this research gap, this chapter aims to both enhance the general understanding of sufficiency-oriented businesses and to provide a systematic synthesis of their (ideal) characteristics according to the current state of knowledge. Hence, the following research questions are investigated: (1) How is corporate sufficiency currently understood and conceptualized in research? And (2) which characteristics constitute or should constitute sufficiency-oriented businesses? For this purpose, a systematic literature review was conducted to identify prevalent themes in the understanding and common characteristics of sufficiency-oriented businesses. Additionally, semi-structured expert interviews with corporate sufficiency scholars were employed to validate the findings and obtain deeper insights into their understandings, complementing the findings from published work.

2. Method

2.1 Systematic literature review

As systematic literature reviews (SLR) aim at assessing the existing knowledge of a research field and identifying research gaps (Tranfield et al. 2003), this method was used to investigate the general understanding and (ideal-typical) characteristics of sufficiency-oriented businesses. This study followed the recommended procedure of Snyder (2019) for SLR in business research.

The SLR included articles published before May 2023 and used the Web of Science, ScienceDirect, Emerald, Wiley, EconBiz and WISO databases. Initially, the search strings "sufficiency" and "business", including synonyms and wildcards in English and German, were used in the "title" and "abstract" search fields. Since this yielded an unmanageable number of results given the ubiquitous applicability of the term "sufficiency", the search strings were further restricted by using "sustainability" as an additional keyword and excluding the term "self-sufficiency". To restrict the search string as much as necessary, but as little as possible, these two additional keywords were only applied to the search field "abstract", as the results of the "title" search field were still manageable with the initial search string. Consequently, the following search string was used:

Title = sufficiency* AND (business* OR compan* OR corporat* OR firm* OR enterprise*) OR
Abstract = sufficiency* AND (sustainab*) NOT self-sufficiency AND (business* OR compan* OR corporat* OR firm* OR enterprise*)

Articles were selected by screening abstracts to make an initial selection, followed by in-depth reading of the articles to ensure that they fulfilled all determined criteria (see Table 1). Papers published in non-peer-reviewed journals and book chapters were deliberately included since this would otherwise limit the sample size and prevent a comprehensive approach to understanding sufficiency-oriented businesses, as recommended by Jungell-Michelsson and Heikkurinen (2022) for SLR on sufficiency in specific contexts.

Table 1: Inclusion and exclusion criteria for the SLR

	Inclusion criteria	**Exclusion criteria**
Language	English or German	All other languages
Search parameters	Search string keywords in title or abstract	Search string keywords in other search fields
Source	Scientific journals or book chapters	Other sources, e.g., dissertations
Meaning of sufficiency	Sufficiency in the sense of reducing or changing consumption/production or ensuring a minimum level of consumption/production	Sufficiency with a different meaning, e.g., as a general expression for "enough" or as part of the Thai "sufficiency economy"
Business context	Discussion of sufficiency in the business context	Discussion of sufficiency in other contexts, e.g., politics
Notions of sufficiency-oriented businesses	Author-made conceptualizations or descriptions of existing/ideal-typical characteristics of sufficiency-oriented businesses	Other statements on sufficiency-oriented businesses

The articles of the initial sample were further complemented by six articles that were known to the author but were not found via the search strategy. In total, 39 relevant articles were identified. Figure 1 presents a summary of the search process. An overview of the final sample is provided in Appendix A.

Figure 1: Overview of the search process.

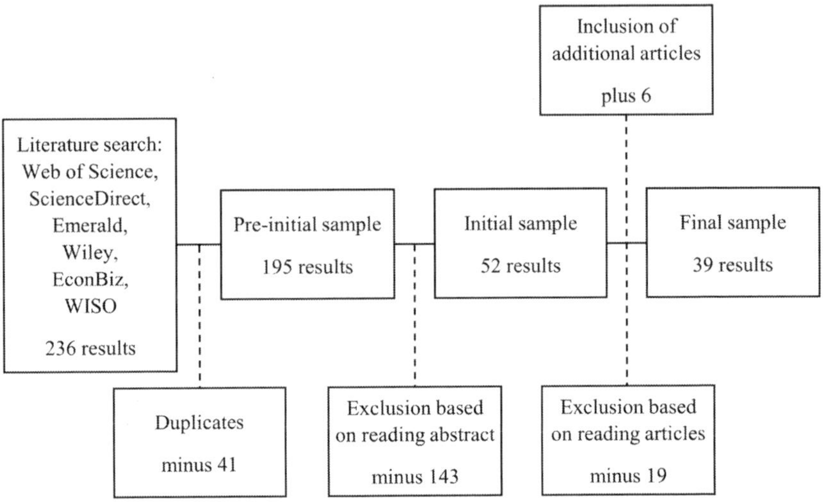

The distribution of the publications on corporate sufficiency until 2023 is shown in Figure 2. The first year that the term "sufficiency" was used in the business context was 2002 and in the subsequent years, only a few articles were published. Since 2013, publications have mostly remained at a modest level. From 2019 on, the number of publications on corporate sufficiency has risen considerably.

Figure 2: Distribution of publications across time.

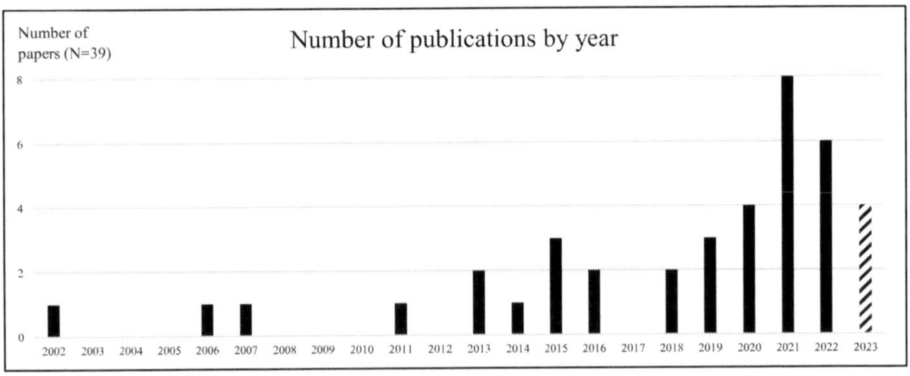

After the final sample was determined, qualitative content analysis according to Mayring (2015) was used. Categories were built inductively and were thus directly derived from the material. On that basis, the publications were analysed line by line and all complete and generalizable statements by the authors on the understanding or characteristics of corporate sufficiency were coded.

2.2 Expert interviews

Explorative expert interviews assist in organizing research and gaining orientation in novel or unstructured research fields (Bogner et al. 2002). Semi-structured, explorative expert interviews were thus employed to validate and complement the findings of the SLR.

The interview participants in this study comprised current or former researchers possessing a record of publications on corporate sufficiency. These experts were particularly qualified to validate the findings and supplement essential information to the research field, as they possessed a comprehensive and systemic understanding of corporate sufficiency that went beyond the firm level. In total, 14 experts were identified and contacted. Additionally, the request was published on the mailing list of a sufficiency research network. This resulted in seven experts participating in the interviews of this study (six based in Germany, one in the Netherlands). Table 2 provides an overview of all participating researchers, their main research focus and the abbreviations assigned to them for presenting their statements in the results section.

Table 2: Sample of the expert interviews

Expert	Main research focus	Abbreviation
Prof. Dr. Niko Paech	Post-growth economy	A
Dr. Maike Gossen	Sufficiency-oriented consumption and marketing	B
Prof. Dr. Uwe Schneidewind	Sustainable transformation processes	C
Prof. Dr. Alexandra Palzkill	Sustainability transformations	D
Laura Niessen	Sufficiency-oriented businesses/business models	E
Laura Beyeler	Sufficiency-oriented businesses/business models	F
Prof. Dr. André Reichel	Post-growth economy	G

The interviews were conducted between April 2022 and May 2022. All interviews took place online in German or English and were recorded and transcribed. The interviews lasted between 43 and 70 minutes. Since explorative expert interviews are guided by an open interview style, aimed at generating a wide range of knowledge rather than closing knowledge gaps in an exhaustive and standardized way (Bogner et al. 2014), the focus was on gaining in-depth insights versus extensively covering all interview questions.

Similar to the SLR analysis, qualitative content analysis according to Mayring (2015) was used while the two data sources were analyzed separately. In contrast to the previous procedure, deductive categories, i.e., pre-determined categories based on the SLR findings (ibid), were built first, enabling a broad initial categorization of the material. Subsequently, additional categories were built inductively.

3. Findings

This section presents the findings of the SLR and the expert interviews and is structured according to the research questions outlined in the introduction. For better readability, the references of the SLR are presented as numbers in line with the table of the final sample in Appendix A.

3.1 General understanding of corporate sufficiency

Corporate sufficiency as a principle for absolute reduction of environmental impacts

In the current debate, corporate sufficiency is mostly conceptualized as a principle for addressing issues of overconsumption and overproduction. The primary goal of sufficiency strategies according to the literature [7; 11; 12; 15; 19; 21] and expert interviews (B, C, D, E, F, G) is hence the reduction of environmental impacts in absolute terms to comply with maximum limits defined by planetary boundaries. References to minimum-level considerations, i.e. acknowledging and addressing the lack of basic needs satisfaction experienced by economically disadvantaged individuals, are only made sporadically, either by advising sufficiency-oriented businesses to ensure that reducing consumption does not push people below the poverty line [12], or by referring to business models that enable the fulfillment of basic needs by offering simplified products in low-income contexts [7]. Hence, the literature [33; 35] and expert interviews (D, E, F) emphasize the importance of a comprehensive understanding of corporate sufficiency, which considers both environmental and socio-economic concerns.

Conceptualizations of corporate sufficiency

The early corporate sufficiency discourse primarily framed sufficiency as an issue of consumers, who were expected to drive sufficiency in the business sphere by putting external pressure on companies through, for example, consumer boycotts [1; 2]. In contrast, current publications acknowledge the active role of businesses in driving sufficiency. However, when it comes to the attributed scope of action and the actual nature of sufficiency-oriented businesses, the contemporary literature shows ambiguities [34]. Building on the distinction between externally-oriented and internally-oriented corporate sufficiency strategies according to Maurer [17], three conceptualizations of sufficiency-oriented businesses were identified: (1) externally-oriented, (2) internally-oriented and (3) integrated.

(1) Externally-oriented conceptualization The most prevalent notion in the literature [3; 5; 6; 7; 11; 13; 19; 20; 29; 33; 36] and the expert interviews (B, C, D, F) is that sufficiency-oriented businesses support consumption reduction or shifts towards sufficiency-oriented consumer practices. This conceptualization makes consumers the primary object of performing sufficiency and involves both the quantitative dimension of reducing consumption and the qualitative dimension of promoting shifts towards sufficiency-oriented consumption practices. However, it was cautioned that narrowing the focus solely on this conceptualization exceedingly shifts the responsibility to the consumer (F, G). As Reichel[1] expresses:

> It is pretended that consumers have to save the world. But how can they do that if they are part of a political-economic system that doesn't actually allow them to do that, or if they do, it breaks down. That's why you have to think about production […] and the political-economic environment (G).

(2) Internally-oriented conceptualization Since sufficiency does not necessarily imply "doing things differently, but simply doing less or not doing more" (A), corporate sufficiency does not automatically imply supporting customers' sufficiency-oriented practices, e.g., by realigning the business model with sufficiency (A, D). Rather, some scholars apply the principle of sufficiency to the business itself and its activities, which can include limiting production volumes, employee numbers, profits or the geographical scope of action [9; 17]. This conceptualization would thus imply proactively serving less demand than would otherwise be attributed to the business (A). It was stated that this type of sufficiency is often applied in owner-managed businesses to maintain quality, sustain corporate culture, or increase resilience (A). However, applying the sufficiency principle solely to the business carries the danger of not delivering any environmental benefits, as this may not prevent consumers from buying products from competitors who will accordingly serve the unsatisfied demand [15; 17]. Hence, these businesses "are then sufficiency-oriented,

1 All original quotes from interviews that were conducted in German were translated into English.

but sufficiency unfortunately does not have the overall effect, in macroeconomic terms, of contributing to a smaller economy and thus to sustainable development" (A).

(3) Integrated conceptualization Conflating the previous conceptualizations, some publications state that placing limits on production and business activities independent of demand stimuli *along with* supporting sufficiency-oriented consumption is the ultimate aim of sufficiency-oriented businesses [12; 15; 18; 21; 22; 35]. More generally, sufficiency-oriented businesses have been recommended to apply the sufficiency principle to all internal processes as well as external strategies [35], determining at which point enoughness is achieved and further accumulation would serve abundance (F). Thereby, the suggestion has been to limit the number of products and services to the extent that human needs as opposed to wants are met [21; 35]. This conceptualization was partly deemed essential (C, F), since businesses were considered responsible for proactively limiting production (F).

Corporate sufficiency frameworks

To operationalize corporate sufficiency, various frameworks have been developed and used to investigate how businesses can promote sufficiency (see Table 3). While these frameworks predominantly focus on describing externally-oriented strategies for business model innovation, they also sporadically include internally-oriented strategies, such as regionalising supply chains ("less distance" as part of the four lessens) or limiting production ("less clutter" as part of the four lessens) [4; 8; 11; 18; 19; 24; 33]. Only one publication predominantly applies the framework to internally-oriented sufficiency practices [9].

Table 3: Sufficiency Frameworks

Framework	Strategies	Sources
Four lessens	Less clutter, less speed, less distance, less market, (less dependency)	[4; 8; 9; 35]
Higher levels of the waste hierarchy	Avoid, reduce, reuse	[11; 19]
Management and use perspective framework	Extended use, reuse, partial reuse – less clutter, less speed, less distance, less market	[18]
Business for sufficiency framework	Rethink, reduce, refuse – less clutter, less speed, less distance, less market	[24; 33]

3.2 Characteristics of sufficiency-oriented businesses

Six dimensions were identified which businesses should realign as part of their pursuit of sufficiency. Several interdependencies between the different dimensions and their characteristics were found, demonstrating that the holistic integration of sufficiency into the business is crucial. For instance, effective business model innovation is indicated to require aligning marketing, corporate growth, incentive systems [7; 11], governance and corporate culture [11] with sufficiency. Also emphasized was the necessity of guiding principles to ensure that sufficiency is considered in all decision processes of the business model [12]. Conversely, to increase effectiveness and avoid greenwashing when pursuing sufficiency-promoting marketing, all business activities must be compatible with sufficiency [16], including the purpose [28; 30] and the business model [25; 30].

Purpose

The significance of sufficiency-oriented purposes, i.e. explicit reference to the idea of sufficiency, is highlighted in the literature [21; 28; 33; 35] and the expert interviews (C, F). A sufficiency-oriented purpose not only serves as a fundamental guidance for all business actions (F) and a transformative narrative can even steer established companies towards sufficiency [10], but it also shifts existing customer preferences towards sufficiency more effectively (C).

Nevertheless, most sufficiency-oriented firms examined in the literature refer to sustainability-oriented purposes, i.e. addressing social and/or environmental challenges [11; 19; 30; 33]. Sometimes, neither sustainability nor sufficiency concerns are explicitly articulated in the companies' purpose, making sufficiency an indirect consequence of their operations, as exemplified by the purpose of delivering high-quality products [33].

Guiding principles

As described in section 3.1, sufficiency-oriented businesses aim towards reducing absolute environmental impact to contribute to operating within the biophysical limits of the earth. Hence, sufficiency-oriented business activities are guided by their quest to satisfy needs while respecting ecological carrying capacities [12; 15]. Their scope of action is thus defined by the businesses' impact on planetary boundaries [12] and sufficiency-oriented companies must determine how to conduct their activities within these carrying capacities and contribute to restoring them (G).

A closely related guiding principle for corporate sufficiency is to move away from profit maximization [12; 21; 27; 28; 35]. Sufficiency-oriented companies are reported to still be profitable, but they do not make "profit for the sole sake of profit maximization" [28: 169] and profits are primarily reinvested to further promote sufficiency [35]. In this context, the notion of profit sufficiency has been introduced, which means that businesses generate profits that are merely sufficient to sustaining the company in the long term [12; 28]. However, profit sufficiency may be applicable to owner-managed firms but not to shareholder businesses due to their obligation to increase shareholder value (E).

Moreover, creating a learning environment for sufficiency, i.e. providing opportunities for stakeholders, like customers or employees, to learn sufficiency-oriented practices while constantly learning and receiving feedback from them, is essential for sufficiency-oriented businesses [18; 28; 30; 35] and ensures effectiveness of sufficiency practices [35]. Sufficiency-oriented businesses can thus be understood as communities of practice where members learn from each other by sharing experiences and building competences related to sufficiency [28; 30].

Business model

The value proposition of sufficiency-oriented business models refers to supporting sufficiency-oriented consumption [7; 13; 27; 33]. The frameworks presented in section 3.1 show various ways of providing this support. Instead of serving or even creating insatiable consumer wants, sufficiency-oriented businesses aspire to satisfy basic needs with their offerings [18; 29; 35; 38]. Hence, the question "why and for whom do we produce and consume?" [38: 12] arises. However, the challenge of adequately defining needs has been emphasized [19; 35].

Value creation of sufficiency-oriented business models involves aligning practices of the business and its stakeholders with sufficiency in the sense of the proposed value [7]. According to some authors, this requires the active involvement of the consumer in the value creation process, shifting the role of consumers to prosumers [27; 28].

Value capture of sufficiency-oriented business models goes beyond the economic value generated and the company boundaries and refers to generating ecological and social value alongside economic value [7; 13; 27; 28]. While ecological values can include generating more ecological equity [27; 28], societal values can refer to the fulfilment of basic needs or sufficiency education [7; 8; 13; 28]. Economic value for the business itself is captured, for instance through enhanced customer loyalty, positive reputation [7; 13; 24; 28] or increased resilience to macroeconomic fluctuations [31].

Business infrastructure and operations

Several publications highlight the critical role of a sufficiency-compatible legal structure and governance in facilitating corporate sufficiency [4; 11; 16; 33; 35]. Sufficiency-oriented companies are predominantly privately owned [33; 35], which enables autonomous decision making in the sense of sufficiency [4; 33; 35]. Nevertheless, there are empirical examples of sufficiency-oriented stock corporations [33], which have the advantage of owning the necessary capital to drive transformative processes [4]. However, some experts emphasized the inherent conflict between sufficiency and the growth paradigm within shareholder companies (A, C, E). Hence, it was questioned whether sufficiency could be embraced solely by small, owner-managed companies, where the owner can independently influence the entire corporate strategy towards sufficiency (A). Lastly, collaborative business forms [4] and involvement of stakeholders into ownership structures and corporate governance [33; 35] are viewed as predestined to foster sufficiency, although autonomous decision-making by organizational members has also been identified as a potential barrier to the adoption of sufficiency [21].

Furthermore, sufficiency-compatible financing with an investors' focus on driving sufficiency, such as crowdfunding, has been shown to be pivotal for sufficiency-oriented businesses [33; 35]. This is because traditional financing requires high growth rates, which contradicts the logic of sufficiency [11; 24; 33]. Empirical evidence has demonstrated that traditional financing can be the predominant factor impeding the adoption of sufficiency strategies [32]. Nevertheless, the study of Bocken et al. [33] revealed that the majority of a sample of 150 sufficiency-oriented companies relied on conventional financing.

The need for sufficiency impact accounting, i.e. measuring the impacts of sufficiency strategies, has been highlighted to inform target setting, design incentive systems [33] and evaluate performance [24; 33]. Quantifying sufficiency impacts is hence seen as a key factor for facilitating businesses' transition towards sufficiency and provides the basis for understanding which business activities should be expanded and which should be reduced (G). However, the lack of unified metrics for assessing actual impacts of sufficiency offerings has been emphasized [33; 37]. Hence, the field of sufficiency impact measurement merits more research (E, F). A major challenge lies in quantifying purchases that have not yet been made [24; 30] and determining the causality between a company's sufficiency strategies and changes in consumption patterns [24]. Bocken et al. [33] suggest defining product category-specific target values for sufficiency-oriented consumption as a baseline and then establishing metrics such as repair rates. Initial empirical assessment approaches include surveys on customer behavior [24; 33], some combined with interviews [37] or downloads of repair guides [30].

Sufficiency-oriented supply chain management is another characteristic of sufficiency-oriented businesses, which entails limiting production systems [4; 9; 18; 20; 35] and consumption space [9; 35] to local or regional settings. This involves shifting focus to primarily serving local needs rather than catering to distant commercial markets [20; 35]. Shortening production systems has been found to improve transparency [18; 35], while proximity to customers strengthens relationships with consumers and local communities, which is vital to, for example, provide direct access to repair services [35]. Still, most of the sufficiency-oriented companies in Bocken et al.'s study [33] operated at the national or international level.

A holistic sufficiency strategy additionally involves sufficiency-oriented human resource management (F, G) and a corporate culture oriented towards sufficiency. The strong internal drive for sufficiency is mentioned as a crucial prerequisite for the implementation of sufficiency given the demanding enforceability of this approach [11; 24]. Accordingly, top leadership promoting sufficiency [11; 19] and ensuring that every employee is committed to sufficiency [19; 24], for instance, by intensively communicating corporate values [11; 19], becomes essential. Moreover, as building internal expertise on sufficiency is decisive for sufficiency-oriented businesses, companies should strategically hire individuals with respective qualifications and provide targeted training on sufficiency (G). Since employees are consumers themselves, businesses should also facilitate their adoption of sufficiency-oriented lifestyles (F).

Lastly, corporate sufficiency requires sufficiency-promoting marketing and sales [7; 33]. The goals of sufficiency-promoting marketing are supporting consumption reduction in the first place [14; 16; 23; 25; 30], enhancing well-being [16], valorizing sufficiency-oriented lifestyles [14] and conveying sufficiency-related knowledge and competences to customers [35]. The experts further stressed the role of marketing in communicating the significance of sufficiency-oriented lifestyles, supporting the development of skills (G) as well as identifying and appropriately serving stakeholder needs (D). Concerning sales, establishing internal incentive systems that are aligned with sufficiency is essential [7; 11; 13]. This could, for instance, include incentivizing sales staff to undersell products [11].

Corporate growth

Suitable growth strategies for sufficiency-oriented businesses are generally assessed based on whether they induce a decline in aggregate output on the macro-level (A, C, D, G). Hence, high growth rates while substituting less sustainable alternatives is the predominant growth strategy attributed to sufficiency-oriented businesses in the literature [11; 17; 19; 24; 25; 33; 35] and expert interviews (C, D, F, G). The decisive factor is whether businesses reduce environmental impact by crowding out the market share of conventional companies in a way that the demand reduction induced by the sufficiency-oriented firm is higher than its own growth rate in the long term [11; 33]. Thus, the rationale for growth aspirations becomes the scaling of sufficiency-oriented production and consumption practices [35], and growth becomes part of a process for positive change (G). It was argued that high growth strategies are particularly important for businesses with sufficiency-oriented offerings that fulfil basic needs such as food or education (C). However, this growth strategy should also be examined critically due to the uncertainty regarding whether and how substitution will occur (B, C, E), since determining these market effects is exceedingly complex and lacks data (B). For example, competitive dynamics within a segment could imply that the growth of one sufficiency-oriented business could be accompanied with the decline of another sufficiency-oriented company, preventing market shares of other segments from changing (C), or the growth of companies with sufficiency-oriented offerings could lead to additional consumption and production (B). Hence, high growth rates can scale adverse impact [33] and are subject to undesirable systemic impacts such as rebound effects [17] or the erosion of a firm's sustainability orientation [19; 24].

Another common strategy of sufficiency-oriented businesses is to moderate growth [11; 33] or to not actively pursue growth due to the priority of qualitative over quantitative aspects [35]. Benefits of moderate growth include maintaining sufficiency-oriented corporate culture or value chains [11; 35]. However, it has been emphasized that relying on sufficiency-oriented companies to grow organically would not lead to a significant system-level change in due course and could additionally endanger the businesses' viability [11].

While only a few companies have already set absolute limits to growth [30; 35], envisioning a limit to growing to the point where they have enough power to influence structures is common for sufficiency-oriented businesses [35]. Particularly for companies offering conventional products, absolute growth limits could trigger reassessing how wants can be better met with reduced production volumes (C). However, defining appropriate limits to corporate growth is challenging according to the literature [35] and experts (D, G). Moreover, it was noted that sufficiency-oriented businesses must be at least profitable to be viable and hence probably need to grow (E). More investigation is needed on how political regulations should be designed to support non-growing companies (B).

Collaborative advancement of sufficiency transitions

It is considered crucial for sufficiency-oriented businesses to strongly engage with customers [7; 11; 13; 18; 27; 28; 33; 35]. This can result in a notably closer customer relationship compared to conventional businesses (C, D). Reasons include the necessary feedback from customers for improving sufficiency-focused offerings [35] and the continuous support of customers in fostering sufficiency-oriented practices [18; 35]. As a sufficiency orientation of customers does not often exist from the outset, businesses take individuals on a "customer journey towards a sufficiency-oriented lifestyle" (C). Hence, sufficiency-oriented businesses aim to transform existing preference structures (C) and establish new meanings for sufficiency-oriented practices, which may ultimately trigger irritations in the mainstream in the direction of sufficiency (D). Consequently, sufficiency-oriented businesses are constantly considering the socio-economic structures in which they are embedded and work towards transforming them: "Thinking within sufficiency categories automatically means understanding the company in its socioeconomic context and the impact of its products and services in the context" (C).

However, as sufficiency-oriented businesses are still part of the current socio-economic and political system, a sufficiency-oriented business' scope of action and the effectiveness of its actions are highly constrained by these boundary conditions (G). Effectively fostering sufficiency transitions requires structural changes at the policy level [26; 33; 35; 37; 39]. Hence, to drive substantial change, lobbying for sufficiency-oriented political changes is proposed [15; 35; 37; C, D, E, F]. An alternative option is to support customers to advocate for political changes towards sufficiency (C). If successful, businesses would have a competitive advantage themselves [15].

Moreover, sufficiency-oriented businesses typically collaborate with businesses and other stakeholders to initiate change towards sufficiency [28; 33; 35], which is decisive to effectively advance sufficiency transitions (F). Collaborating with various stakeholders helps to create acceptance for implementation [5] and can increase credibility and know-know [33]. Examples include transferring practices and know-how to other entrepreneurs [35] or participating in joint campaigns to increase customer awareness [28; 33].

4. Discussion

This chapter sought to provide insights into the characterization of sufficiency-oriented businesses according to the current state of knowledge by providing the first systematic literature review and conducting expert interviews with leading scholars in the field.

The findings yield significant implications concerning the current understanding of sufficiency-oriented businesses (see Table 4). Firstly, they underscore that the prevailing understanding of corporate sufficiency primarily focuses on aligning production and consumption with planetary boundaries. However, sufficiency also encompasses ensuring a minimum level, i.e. providing a social foundation for all (Spengler 2016; Gossen et al. 2019; Spangenberg/Lorek 2019; Jungell-Michelsson/Heikkurinen 2022). Future research should thus systematically explore the potential social implications of corporate sufficiency strategies. For example, strategies involving the provision of durable or second-hand products that satisfy basic needs could give economically disadvantaged individuals permanent access to essential products. However, other sufficiency strategies, such as premium pricing, pose the risk of limiting access to sufficiency-oriented offerings to affluent individuals (Gossen/Kropfeld 2022; Niessen et al. 2023b). Meriting further investigation is also how businesses can systematically support individuals to move from a state of deprivation of certain basic needs to their adequate supply while respecting planetary boundaries.

Secondly, recognizing distinct conceptualizations of corporate sufficiency (internally-oriented, externally-oriented, or integrated) is essential as they substantially influence the expected scope of action attributed to sufficiency-oriented businesses. In practice, most cases will exhibit a mixed type, such as an externally-oriented conceptualization with some internally-oriented elements (e.g., limiting supply chains to a regional level). These conceptualizations should therefore be viewed as points along a continuum, with externally-oriented and internally-oriented approaches at opposite ends and the integrated notion situated in the middle (see Figure 3). This continuum perspective provides a pivotal analytical foundation for future research.

Thirdly, it became apparent that a purely internally-oriented conceptualization and hence solely applying sufficiency to the business itself seems to lack effectiveness as customers will likely satisfy their demand through other firms in competitive markets. Conversely, purely externally-oriented conceptualizations supporting customers in adopting more sufficiency-oriented lifestyles could reduce overall consumption and production but also carry the risk of adding to material-energy throughput. The effectiveness thus depends on the reactions of other market actors in terms of actual changes in consumption or production patterns and levels, which is why sufficiency-oriented businesses will have to continuously and carefully adapt their externally- and internally-oriented activities to align overall practices with sufficiency. Hence, an integrated perspective, considering both customers and businesses as objects of corporate sufficiency, may be most effective. This could extend to limiting production quantities and forgoing profits if their externally-oriented sufficiency strategies would likely lead to an increase in energy-material throughput in the long term rather than its reduction. Where exactly in the continuum sufficiency-oriented businesses should be positioned to be most effective may greatly depend on contextual factors, such as the sector and type of sufficiency (as categorized by Sandberg 2021), and thus requires further investigation.

Figure 3: Overview of the understanding of sufficiency-oriented businesses.

Understanding sufficiency-oriented businesses			
Aim	Sufficiency-oriented businesses aim for the absolute reduction of environmental impacts		
Conceptualization	Externally-oriented	Integrated	Internally-oriented
	Customers as the primary object of sufficiency		Businesses as the primary object of sufficiency
	Supporting consumption reduction and/or shifts to sufficiency-oriented consumption practices		Limiting production and applying sufficiency to business practices
Frameworks for operationalization	Four lessens [4; 8; 9; 35] Higher levels of the waste hierarchy [11; 19] Management and use perspective framework [18] Business for sufficiency framework [24; 33]		

Turning to the second research question, the findings propose a set of (ideal-typical) characteristics of sufficiency-oriented businesses that provide guidance for businesses to implement sufficiency (see Figure 3). It should be noted that these characteristics are compiled based on studies that assume either customers, businesses or both as objects of corporate sufficiency, which is why certain contradictions could be observed. For example, shareholder-oriented businesses and those reliant on traditional, growth-driven financing, while offering access to substantial capital for sufficiency, may struggle to pursue sufficiency of profits and the logic of satisfying needs rather than wants may become increasingly difficult. Similarly, a trade-off exists between leveraging growth to reduce environmental impact by replacing other offerings, which cannot be guaranteed and risks eroding sufficiency values, and constraining growth, which may endanger viability and impede opportunities to scale sufficiency. As discussed earlier, the relevance of the characteristics depends on the context, underscoring the importance of empirical investigations into the circumstances in which specific characteristics hold greater or lesser importance.

Other areas warrant further scholarly attention. These include establishing guidelines for business actions, e.g., for determining appropriate limits to corporate growth, assessing the impact of sufficiency-oriented business actions and distinguishing between actual needs and wants. Additionally, empirical studies on the implementation of sufficiency in human resource management or supply chain management would be beneficial. Another neglected area concerns the application of sufficiency principles to production processes.

The findings underline that sufficiency, due to its radical nature, requires anchoring in the entire company, which could necessitate a comprehensive reorientation of businesses. Yet, the adoption of a holistic approach towards corporate sufficiency can pose significant challenges for companies given the prevailing growth paradigm and consumerist culture (Bocken/Short 2016; Gossen et al. 2019; Niessen/Bocken 2021; Gossen/Heinrich 2021). This situation poses a complex dilemma: While sufficiency-oriented businesses aspire to reshape existing socio-economic and political structures, they still operate within the prevailing system, which significantly influences the possible extent and effectiveness of their sufficiency actions. Future studies should explore strategies to mitigate this dilemma, including how varied framework conditions could widen businesses' scope for sufficiency action.

Finally, the characteristics reveal striking similarities of sufficiency-oriented businesses with other business types. For example, degrowth businesses aim to benefit the environment and society instead of maximizing profits and growth while fostering sustainable consumption and advancing systemic change (e.g., Hankammer et al. 2021). Equally, strongly sustainable businesses prioritize creating positive environmental and societal impacts over maximizing profits while permanently recognizing systemic embeddedness (e.g., Upward/Jones 2016). A systematic analysis of the differences and similarities between these related business types could greatly enrich the corporate sufficiency debate.

Table 4: Overview of the characteristics of sufficiency-oriented businesses

Characteristics of (ideal-typical) sufficiency-oriented businesses	
Purpose	– sufficiency-oriented purpose – sustainability-oriented purpose
Guiding principles	– satisfying needs while respecting ecological carrying capacities – moving away from profit maximization – creating a learning environment
Business model	– value proposition: supporting sufficiency-oriented consumption while satisfying basic human needs – value creation: aligning practices of the business and its stakeholders with sufficiency – value capture: generating ecological, social and economic value
Business infrastructure and operations	– sufficiency-compatible legal structure and governance – sufficiency-compatible financing – sufficiency impact accounting – sufficiency-oriented supply chain management – sufficiency-oriented human resource management – sufficiency-promoting marketing and sales
Corporate growth	– high growth rates under substitution of less sustainable alternatives – moderate growth rates – absolute limits to growth
Collaborative advancement of sufficiency transitions	– strongly engaging with customers – collaborating with businesses and other stakeholders – lobbying for sufficiency-oriented political changes

5. Conclusion

The central aim of this chapter was to advance the understanding of sufficiency-oriented businesses and investigate their (ideal) characteristics through a systematic literature review and expert interviews. Next to demonstrating the prevailing focus of sufficiency-oriented business research on ecological considerations, this study proposes a nuanced understanding of corporate sufficiency conceptualizations along a continuum between externally-oriented and internally-oriented notions. The various characteristics identified provide guidance in implementing sufficiency into businesses and assessing the general orientation of businesses towards sufficiency along six dimensions. While the actual scope and effectiveness of corporate sufficiency will always be contingent upon the socio-economic and political context in which businesses operate, this study shows that corporate sufficiency can serve as an overarching principle for companies that build on an alternative way of doing business.

One major limitation of this study is that the SLR relied on specific search strings conducted in a restricted number of databases. Including non-peer-reviewed articles decreased the risk of missing relevant articles but added less sophisticated and academic publications to the sample. Moreover, due to the literature and expert sample, the study applied a European (particularly German) perspective to sufficiency and business. Further research is thus needed to examine cultural differences, including, for example, the Thai conceptualization of sufficiency-oriented businesses. Finally, the experts who participated in the interviews were exclusively scholars, implying that the assessment of the characteristics is primarily theoretically-driven. Hence, empirical studies should delve into the contextual factors that determine the varying relevance of these characteristics.

References

Augenstein, Karoline/Palzkill, Alexandra (2015): "The Dilemma of Incumbents in Sustainability Transitions: A Narrative Approach." In: Administrative Sciences 6/1, pp. 1–23. https://doi.org/10.3390/admsci6010001.

Bauwens, Thomas/Hekkert, Marko/Kirchherr, Julian (2020): "Circular Futures: What Will They Look Like?" In: Ecological Economics 175, 106703. https://doi.org/10.1016/j.ecolecon.2020.106703.

Beyeler, Laura/Jaeger-Erben, Melanie (2022): "How to make more of less: Characteristics of sufficiency in business practices." In: Frontiers in Sustainability 3, pp. 1–25. https://doi.org/10.3389/frsus.2022.949710.

Bocken, Nancy M. P./Niessen, Laura/Short, Samuel William (2022): "The Sufficiency-Based Circular Economy – An Analysis of 150 Companies." In: Frontiers in Sustainability 3, 899289. https://doi.org/10.3389/frsus.2022.899289.

Bocken, Nancy M. P./Morales, Lisa Smeke/Lehner, Matthias (2020): "Sufficiency Business Strategies in the Food Industry – The Case of Oatly." In: Sustainability 12/3, 824. https://doi.org/10.3390/su12030824.

Bocken, Nancy M. P./Short, Samuel W. (2016): "Towards a sufficiency-driven business Model: Experiences and opportunities." In: Environmental Innovation and Societal Transitions 18, pp. 41–61. https://doi.org/10.1016/j.eist.2015.07.010.

Bocken, Nancy M. P./Short, Samuel William/Rana, Padmakshi/Evans, Steve (2014): "A literature and practice review to develop sustainable business model archetypes." In: Journal of cleaner production 65, pp. 42–56. https://doi.org/10.1016/j.jclepro.2013.11.039.

Bogner, Alexander/Littig, Beate/Menz, Wolfgang (2002): Das Experteninterview, Wiesbaden: Springer.

Bogner, Alexander/Littig, Beate/Menz, Wolfgang (2014): Interviews mit Experten, Wiesbaden: Springer.

Borrello, Massimiliano/Cembalo, Luigi/D'Amico, Valentina (2022): "Redefining Wellbeing and Normality: Circular Consumption Beyond the Low Hanging Fruit." In: Resources, Conservation and Recycling 179, 106034. https://doi.org/10.1016/j.resconrec.2021.106034.

Colombi, Chiara/D'Itria, Erminia (2023): "Fashion Digital Transformation: Innovating Business Models toward Circular Economy and Sustainability." In: Sustainability 15/6, 4942. https://doi.org/10.3390/su15064942.

Csutora, Maria/Harangozo, Gabor/Szigeti, Cecilia (2022): "Sustainable Business Models – Crisis and Rebound Based on Hungarian Research Experience." In: Resources 11/12, 107. https://doi.org/10.3390/resources11120107.

Dyllick, Thomas/Hockerts, Kai (2002): "Beyond the Business Case for Corporate Sustainability." In: Business Strategy and the Environment 11/2, pp. 130–141. https://doi.org/10.1002/bse.323.

Freudenreich, Birte/Schaltegger, Stefan (2020): "Developing sufficiency-oriented offerings for clothing users: Business approaches to support consumption reduction." In: Journal of Cleaner Production 247, 119589. https://doi.org/10.1016/j.jclepro.2019.119589.

Gebauer, Jana/Mewes, Heike (2015): "Qualität und Suffizienz in stabilitätsorientierten KMU: Unternehmensansätze für die Postwachstumsgesellschaft." In: uwf UmweltWirtschaftsForum 23/2, pp. 33–40. http://doi.org/10.1007/s00550-015-0352-9.

Gossen, Maike/Heinrich, Anneli (2021): "Encouraging Consumption Reduction: Findings of a Qualitative Study with Clothing Companies on Sufficiency-Promoting Communication." In: Cleaner and Responsible Consumption 3, 100028. https://doi.org/10.1016/j.clrc.2021.100028.

Gossen, Maike/Kropfeld, Maren Ingrid (2022): ""Choose Nature. Buy Less." Exploring Sufficiency-Oriented Marketing and Consumption Practices in the Outdoor Industry." In: Sustainable Production and Consumption 30, pp. 720–736. https://doi.org/10.1016/j.spc.2022.01.005.

Gossen, Maike/Schrader, Ulf (2018): "Welche Potenziale die Digitalisierung für ein suffizienzförderndes Marketing bringt." In: Ökologisches Wirtschaften 1/33, pp. 8–9. https://doi.org/10.14512/oew330108.

Gossen, Maike/Ziesemer, Florence/Schrader, Ulf (2019): "Why and how commercial marketing should promote sufficient consumption: A systematic literature review." In: Journal of Marcomarketing 39/3, pp. 252–269. http://doi.org/10.1177/0276146719866238.

Griese, Kai-Michael/Halstrup, Dominik (2013a): "Suffizienz in der Unternehmenskommunikation: Zur Wirkung von suffiziensorientierter Kommunikation." In: Ökologisches Wirtschaften 4, pp. 40–43. https://doi.org/10.14512/oew.v30i4.1314.

Griese, Kai-Michael/Halstrup, Dominik (2013b): "Umsetzung einer suffizienzorientierten Unternehmenskommunikation und die Bedeutung der Stakeholder: Ansätze und Empfehlungen." In: uwf UmweltWirtschaftsForum 21, pp. 59–64. http://dx.doi.org/10.1007/s00550-013-0287-y.

Griese, Kai-Michael/Wawer, Tim/Böcher, Robert (2016): "Suffizienzorientierte Geschäftsmodelle am Beispiel von Stromspeichern: Zukunftsfähige Ansätze in der Energiewirtschaft." In: Zeitschrift für Energiewirtschaft 40/2, pp. 57–71. http://dx.doi.org/10.1007/s12398-016-0175-6.

Gunarathne, Nuwan/Lee, Ki-Hoon (2021): "The Link between Corporate Energy Management and Environmental Strategy Implementation: Efficiency, Sufficiency and Consistency Strategy Perspectives." In: Journal of Cleaner Production 293, 126082. https://doi.org/10.1016/j.jclepro.2021.126082.

Hankammer, Stephan/Kleer, Robin/Mühl, Lena/Euler, Johannes (2021): "Principles for organizations striving for sustainable degrowth: Framework development and application to four B Corps." In: Journal of Cleaner Production 300, pp. 1–20. https://doi.org/10.1016/j.jclepro.2021.126818.

Heikkurinen, Pasi/Young, William/Morgan, Elizabeth (2019): "Business for Sustainable Change: Extending Eco-Efficiency and Eco-Sufficiency Strategies to Consumers." In: Journal of Cleaner Production 218, pp. 656–664. https://doi.org/10.1016/j.jclepro.2019.02.053.

Jungell-Michelsson, Jessica/Heikkurinen, Pasi (2022): "Sufficiency: A systematic literature review." In: Ecological Economics 195, 107380. https://doi.org/10.1016/j.ecolecon.2022.107380.

Kelleci, Alpaslan/Yildiz, Oğuz (2021): "A Guiding Framework for Levels of Sustainability in Marketing." In: Sustainability 13/4, 1644. https://doi.org/10.3390/su13041644.

Konash, Anastassija/Nasr, Nabil (2022): "The Circular Economy and Resource Use Reduction: A Case Study of Long-Term Resource Efficiency Measures in a Medium Manufacturing Company." In: Cleaner Production Letters 3, 100025. https://doi.org/10.1016/j.clpl.2022.100025.

Kropfeld, Maren Ingrid/Reichel, André (2021a): "Das Geschäftsmodell des Genug." In: Ökologisches Wirtschaften 36/3, pp. 30–34. https://doi.org/10.14512/OEW360330.

Kropfeld, Maren Ingrid/Reichel, André (2021): "The Business Model of Enough: Value Creation for Sufficiency-Oriented Businesses." In: Annabeth Aagaard/Florian Lüdeke-Freund/Peter Wells (eds.), Business Models for Sustainability Transitions, Cham: Palgrave Macmillan, pp. 163–189. https://doi.org/10.1007/978-3-030-77580-3_6.

Maurer, Christel (2019): "Unternehmerische Suffizienz, persönliches Glück und ökologische Verantwortung." In: Peter Buchenau (eds.), Chefsache Zukunft, Wiesbaden: Springer, pp. 385–405. https://doi.org/10.1007/978-3-658-26560-1_18.

Mayring, Philipp (2015): Qualitative Inhaltsanalyse: Grundlagen und Techniken, Weinheim Basel: Beltz.

Niessen, Laura/Bocken, Nancy M. P. (2021): "How Can Businesses Drive Sufficiency? The Business for Sufficiency Framework." In: Sustainable Production and Consumption 28, pp. 1090–1103. https://doi.org/10.1016/j.spc.2021.07.030.

Niessen, Laura/Bocken, Nancy M. P./Dijk, Marc (2023a): "The impact of business sufficiency strategies on consumer practices: The case of bicycle subscription." In: Sustainable Production and Consumption 35, pp. 576–591. https://doi.org/10.1016/j.spc.2022.12.007.

Niessen, Laura/Bocken, Nancy M. P./Dijk, Marc (2023b): "Sufficiency as Trend or Tradition? – Uncovering Business Pathways to Sufficiency through Historical Advertisements." In: Frontiers in Sustainability 4, 1165682. https://doi.org/10.3389/frsus.2023.1165682.

Paech, Niko (2007): "Unternehmerische Nachhaltigkeit und die ungelöste Wachstumsfrage: Von der Funktionsorientierung zur Bedarfssubstitution." In: uwf UmweltWirtschaftsForum 15, pp. 86–91. https://doi.org/10.1007/s00550-007-0025-4.

Palzkill, Alexandra/Wanner, Matthias/Markscheffel, Florian (2015): "Suffizienz als Geschäftsmodell: Die Bedeutung von Social-Entrepreneurship-Initiativen am Beispiel von Utopiastadt Wuppertal." In: uwf UmweltWirtschaftsForum 23, pp. 69–76. https://doi.org/10.1007/s00550-015-0353-8.

Robra, Ben/Heikkurinen, Pasi/Nesterova, Iana (2020): "Commons-Based Peer Production for Degrowth? – The Case for Eco-Sufficiency in Economic Organisations." In: Sustainable Futures 2, 100035. https://doi.org/10.1016/j.sftr.2020.100035.

Roman, Philippe/Thiry, Géraldine/Muylaert, Coralie/Ruwet, Coline/Maréchal, Kevin (2023): "Defining and Identifying Strongly Sustainable Product-Service Systems (SSPSS)." In: Journal of Cleaner Production 391, 136295. https://doi.org/10.1016/j.jclepro.2023.136295.

Sandberg, Maria (2021): "Sufficiency Transitions: A Review of Consumption Changes for Environmental Sustainability." In: Journal of Cleaner Production 293, 126097. https://doi.org/10.1016/j.jclepro.2021.126097.

Schneidewind, Uwe/Palzkill-Vorbeck, Alexandra (2011): "Nachhaltiges Ressourcenmanagement als Gegenstand einer transdisziplinären Betriebswirtschaftslehre – Suffizienz als Business Case." In: Hans Corsten/Stefan Roth (eds.), Nachhal-

tigkeit – Unternehmerisches Handeln in globaler Verantwortung, Wiesbaden: Springer, pp. 1–22.
Snyder, Hannah (2019): "Literature Review as a Research Methodology: An Overview and Guidelines." In: Journal of Business Research 104, pp. 333–339. https://doi.org/10.1016/j.jbusres.2019.07.039.
Spangenberg, Joachim H./Lorek, Sylvia (2019): "Sufficiency and Consumer Behaviour: From Theory to Policy." In: Energy Policy 129, pp. 1070–1079. https://doi.org/10.1016/j.enpol.2019.03.013.
Spengler, Laura (2016): "Two Types of 'Enough': Sufficiency as Minimum and Maximum." In: Environmental Politics 25/5, pp. 921–940. https://doi.org/10.1080/09644016.2016.1164355.
Tranfield, David/Denyer, David/Smart, Palminder (2003): "Towards a Methodology for Developing Evidence-Informed Management Knowledge by Means of Systematic Review." In: British Journal of Management 14/3, pp. 207–222. https://doi.org/10.1111/1467-8551.00375.
Upward, Antony/Jones, Peter H. (2016): "An Ontology for Strongly Sustainable Business Models: Defining an Enterprise Framework Compatible With Natural and Social Science." In: Organization & Environment 29/1, pp. 97–123. https://doi.org/10.1177/1086026615592933.
Yip, Angus W. H./Bocken, Nancy M. P. (2018): "Sustainable Business Model Archetypes for the Banking Industry." In: Journal of Cleaner Production 174, pp. 150–169. https://doi.org/10.1016/j.jclepro.2017.10.190.
Young, William/Tilley, Fiona (2006): "Can Businesses Move beyond Efficiency? The Shift toward Effectiveness and Equity in the Corporate Sustainability Debate." In: Business Strategy and the Environment 15/6, pp. 402–415. http://dx.doi.org/10.1002/bse.510.

Appendix A: Final sample of the systematic literature review

#	Authors	Year	Title	Source
1	Dyllick, T., Hockerts, K.	2002	Beyond the business case for corporate sustainability	Business Strategy and the Environment
2	Young, W., Tilley, F.	2006	Can businesses move beyond efficiency? The shift toward effectiveness and equity in the corporate sustainability debate	Business Strategy and the Environment

3	Paech, N.	2007	Unternehmerische Nachhaltigkeit und die ungelöste Wachstumsfrage: Von der Funktionsorientierung zur Bedarfssubstitution	uwf Umweltwirtschaftsforum
4	Schneidewind, U., Palzkill-Vorbeck, A.	2011	Suffizienz als Business Case: Nachhaltiges Ressourcenmanagement als Gegenstand einer transdisziplinären Betriebswirtschaftslehre	Hans Corsten/Stefan Roth (eds.), Nachhaltigkeit – Unternehmerisches Handeln in globaler Verantwortung, Wiesbaden: Springer
5	Griese, K.-M., Halstrup, D.	2013a	Suffizienz in der Unternehmenskommunikation: zur Wirkung von suffiziensorientierter Kommunikation	Ökologisches Wirtschaften
6	Griese, K.-M., Halstrup, D.	2013b	Umsetzung einer suffizienzorientierten Unternehmenskommunikation und die Bedeutung der Stakeholder: Ansätze und Empfehlungen	uwf Umweltwirtschaftsforum
7	Bocken, N. M. P., Short, S. W., Rana, P., Evans, S.	2014	A literature and practice review to develop sustainable business model archetypes	Journal of Cleaner Production
8	Palzkill, A., Wanner, M., Markscheffel, F.	2015	Suffizienz als Geschäftsmodell: die Bedeutung von Social-Entrepreneurship-Initiativen am Beispiel von Utopiastadt Wuppertal	uwf Umweltwirtschaftsforum
9	Gebauer, J., Mewes, H.	2015	Qualität und Suffizienz in stabilitätsorientierten KMU	uwf Umweltwirtschaftsforum
10	Augenstein, K., Palzkill, A.	2015	The Dilemma of Incumbents in Sustainability Transitions: A Narrative Approach	Administrative Sciences
11	Bocken, N. M. P., Short, S. W.	2016	Towards a sufficiency-driven business model: Experiences and opportunities	Environmental Innovation and Societal Transitions

12	Griese, K.-M., Wawer, T., Böcher, R.	2016	Suffizienzorientierte Geschäftsmodelle am Beispiel von Stromspeichern: zukunftsfähige Ansätze in der Energiewirtschaft	Zeitschrift für Energiewirtschaft
13	Yip, A. W. H., Bocken, N. M. P.	2018	Sustainable business model archetypes for the banking industry	Journal of Cleaner Production
14	Gossen, M., Schrader, U.	2018	Unternehmerisches Marketing für Suffizienz: Welche Potenziale die Digitalisierung für ein suffizienzförderndes Marketing bringt	Ökologisches Wirtschaften
15	Heikkurinen, P, Young, C. W., Morgan, E.	2019	Business for sustainable change: Extending eco-efficiency and eco-sufficiency strategies to consumers	Journal of Cleaner Production
16	Gossen, M., Ziesemer, F., Schrader, U.	2019	Why and How Commercial Marketing Should Promote Sufficient Consumption: A Systematic Literature Review	Journal of Macromarketing
17	Maurer, C.	2019	Unternehmerische Suffizienz, persönliches Glück und ökologische Verantwortung	Peter Buchenau (eds.), Chefsache Zukunft, Wiesbaden: Springer
18	Freudenreich, B., Schaltegger, S.	2020	Developing sufficiency-oriented offerings for clothing users: Business approaches to support consumption reduction	Journal of Cleaner Production
19	Bocken, N., Morales, L. S., Lehner, M	2020	Sufficiency Business Strategies in the Food Industry—The Case of Oatly	Sustainability
20	Bauwens, T, Hekkert, M, Kirchherr, J.	2020	Circular futures: What Will They Look Like?	Ecological Economics
21	Robra, B., Heikkurinen, P., Nesterova, I.	2020	Commons-based peer production for degrowth?—The case for eco-sufficiency in economic organisations	Sustainable Futures

22	Gunarathne, N, Lee, K. H.	2021	The link between corporate energy management and environmental strategy implementation: Efficiency, sufficiency and consistency strategy perspectives	Journal of Cleaner Production
23	Kelleci, A., Yildiz, O.	2021	A Guiding Framework for Levels of Sustainability in Marketing	Sustainability
24	Niessen, L., Bocken, N. M. P.	2021	How can businesses drive sufficiency? The business for sufficiency framework	Sustainable Production and Consumption
25	Gossen, M., Heinrich, A.	2021	Encouraging consumption reduction: Findings of a qualitative study with clothing companies on sufficiency-promoting communication	Cleaner and Responsible Consumption
26	Sandberg, M.	2021	Sufficiency transitions: A review of consumption changes for environmental sustainability	Journal of Cleaner Production
27	Kropfeld, M. I., Reichel, A.	2021	Das Geschäftsmodell des Genug: eine praxistheoretische Perspektive auf suffizienzorientierte Unternehmen	Ökologisches Wirtschaften
28	Kropfeld, M. I., Reichel, A.	2021	The business model of enough: value creation for sufficiency-oriented businesses	Annabeth Aagaard/Florian Lüdeke-Freund/Peter Wells (eds.), Business Models for Sustainability Transitions, Cham: Springer
29	Borrello, M., Cembalo, L., D'Amico, V.	2021	Redefining Wellbeing and Normality: Circular Consumption Beyond the Low Hanging Fruit	Resources, Conservation & Recycling
30	Gossen, M., Kropfeld, M. I.	2022	"Choose nature. Buy less." Exploring sufficiency-oriented marketing and consumption practices in the outdoor industry	Sustainable Production and Consumption
31	Csutora, M., Harangozo, G., Szigeti, C.	2022	Sustainable Business Models-Crisis and Rebound Based on Hungarian Research Experience	Resources

32	Konash, A., Nasr, N.	2022	The circular economy and resource use reduction: A case study of long-term resource efficiency measures in a medium manufacturing company	Cleaner Production Letters
33	Bocken, N. M. P., Niessen, L., Short, S.W.	2022	The Sufficiency-Based Circular Economy—An Analysis of 150 Companies	Frontiers in Sustainability
34	Jungell-Michelsson, J., Heikkurinen, P.	2022	Sufficiency: A systematic literature review	Ecological Economics
35	Beyeler, L., Jaeger-Erben, M.	2022	How to make more of less: Characteristics of sufficiency in business practices	Frontiers in Sustainability
36	Colombi, C., D'Itria, E.	2023	Fashion Digital Transformation: Innovating Business Models toward Circular Economy and Sustainability	Sustainability
37	Niessen, L., Bocken, N. M. P., Dijk, M.	2023	The impact of business sufficiency strategies on consumer practices: The case of bicycle subscription	Sustainable Production and Consumption
38	Roman, P., Thiry, G., Muylaert, C., Ruwet, C., Marechal, K.	2023	Defining and identifying strongly sustainable product-service systems (SSPSS)	Journal of Cleaner Production
39	Niessen, L., Bocken, N. M. P., Dijk, M.	2023	Sufficiency as trend or tradition? – Uncovering business pathways to sufficiency through historical advertisements	Frontiers in Sustainability

A Taxonomy of Corporate Sufficiency Strategies

Exploring Driving Factors for Sufficiency in Business

Christel Maurer

Abstract *This chapter develops a systematic approach to corporate sufficiency. It emphasizes purpose-driven sufficiency approaches beyond sustainability, as well as the role of entrepreneurs. It turns out that the literature contains inconsistent examples of sufficiency and that the range and intentions of sufficiency strategies that are not based on sustainability is underestimated.*

1. Introduction

This chapter is written from a practitioner perspective. It is based on a methodological premise: Certain questions within sustainability-oriented business studies are dealt with in the context of theoretical or social-empirical research, which can be usefully supplemented by systematically evaluated practical experience. Complete perspectives on ambiguous phenomena, such as entrepreneurial sufficiency, can only be developed through combinating scientific methods and practical experiences, a combination that resembles a transdisciplinary approach. Contrary to what is presented in most of the literature, the ambiguity of the sufficiency principle results from the fact that the underlying intention can be more or less independent of sustainability concerns.

The sufficiency debate in the corporate sector is still very young and incomplete. At the corporate level, the literature primarily justifies sufficiency with pressure for change towards sustainability (Jungell-Michelsson/Heikkurinen 2022). This focus is derived from measures based on efficiency and consistency not being sufficient to lessen the burden on the ecosphere, making sufficiency essential (see, for example, Beyeler/Jaeger-Erben 2022). The latter thus becomes part of sustainability management (Bocken/Short 2016).

Considerable definitional ambiguities are conspicuous here. Sufficiency strategies in companies are often classified according to the categories proposed by Sachs (1993) or Schneidewind/Palzkill (2011): decluttering, decelerating, disentangling and decommercialization. Decelerating and decluttering are difficult to distinguish since the deceleration of a process also reduces output, i.e. deceleration only represents another perspective of decluttering. Furthermore, disentangling does not necessarily have to lead to limiting activities because local/regional supply chains can also be geared towards maximizing surpluses. Moreover, decommercializing is more likely to be associated with subsistence than with sufficiency and, in the literature, sufficiency often covers phenomena that can hardly be distinguished from efficiency aspects.

This efficiency aspect has been covered in many ways in the literature. For example, sharing (see, for example, Schneidewind/Palzkill-Vorbeck 2011, Bocken/Short 2016) does not reduce transport demand but merely leads to more efficient satisfaction. Freudenreich and Schaltegger (2020) point out that "consumers using carsharing services do not necessarily drive fewer miles but that about a quarter sell their personal vehicles and about half avoid an intended car purchase" (2). Further examples in this vein are energy-contracting services considered as sufficiency by Schneidewind and Palzkill-Vorbeck (2011) and Beyeler and Jaeger-Erben (2022) and open source services classified as sufficiency by Niessen and Bocken (2021), which are all efficiency measures that can even lead to an increase in demand and thus in output under certain conditions (rebound effect). Moreover, the purchase of eco-friendly products and services associated with sufficiency by Bocken et al. (2022) corresponds either with efficiency or consistency solutions. Niessen and Bocken (2021) refer to (sustainable) awareness-raising and Bocken et al. (2022) to corresponding rethinking as sufficiency, presupposing that it could be ruled out that both only lead to efficiency or consistency measures.

Without a plausible demarcation, the potentials of sufficiency cannot be fathomed because they do not extend beyond a relabeling of efficiency or consistency measures. The example of car sharing is instructive here: If an annual mileage of 10,000 km is travelled by car sharing instead of with one's own car and this is described as sufficiency, how should the halving of the mileage – regardless of the means by which the 5,000 km are travelled – be classified? This far more purposeful potential, reduction instead of pure optimization, would then not be included although it is precisely where the core of the sufficiency principle should lie.

The sufficiency principle cannot be specified without emphasizing its reductive character. For this reason, sufficiency is defined in this book chapter as "targeted and substitution-free omission" (Folkers/Paech 2020: 143), which can take effect at three levels:

- Self-limitation of an achieved level of supply, although options for its quantitative or qualitative increases would be available and fundable [...],

- Reduction of a certain level of aspiration, without completely eradicating the activity in question [...],
- Complete renunciation of an option [...] (ibid: 143).

The fact that sufficiency has so far been dealt with primarily in the context of sustainability gives rise to a second problem, which is the focus of this paper: Motivations for corporate sufficiency strategies beyond ecological concerns (see, for example, Bocken et al. 2022, Gossen et al. 2019) are generally neglected. This disregard does not change the fact that differentiation of sufficiency strategies in companies is increasing (Jungell-Michelsson/Heikkurinen 2022 and, for example, Beyeler/Jaeger-Erben 2022). Sufficiency measures can enable the pursuit of a specific purpose or patterns of action that are perceived as meaningful without directly aiming at sustainability (Maurer 2019). Scherhorn (2015) and Princen (2003), among others, have already pointed to sufficiency logics that are not necessarily located in the sustainability context. These remarks give rise to the following questions:

a) At which levels in companies are sufficiency strategies applied and how can the latter be systematized from a business management perspective?
b) What sufficiency strategies beyond ecological sustainability can be identified?
c) What role do entrepreneurs play in the use of corporate sufficiency strategies?

The chapter is structured as follows. In the following (2), possible goals and motives for sufficiency strategies in companies are presented and then (3) the role of entrepreneurs and the purpose of sufficiency in companies are discussed. In (4), the empirical approach is described, and based on that, in (5), a taxonomy of entrepreneurial sufficiency is presented together with some selected business cases of sufficiency strategies that can be classified as purpose-motivated. The chapter concludes with (6) a discussion and (7) a conclusion.

2. Possible goals and motives for corporate sufficiency

Sufficiency in business can be attributed to different motivational situations: Scherhorn (2015) does not speak of motives but mentions economy-, ecology-, society and quality-related goals with regard to limiting growth. In a systematic literature review, Gossen et al. (2019) distinguish "a societal demand to pursue sufficiency as an external perspective for companies, and a company-internal perspective on altruistic and strategic motives" (7) for sufficiency-promoting marketing. Jäger (2022) differentiates between motives of sufficiency "in three dimensions of sustainability: ecological motivation, social motivation and economic motivation" as well as "ideals as normative attitudes of companies" (35). Economic constraints can also lead to sufficiency strategies. Schneidewind and Palzkill-Vorbeck (2011) describe how the Danish logistics company Maersk extended the duration of transport by sea in times of declining turnover and, at the same time, reduced fuel consumption, thereby reducing CO_2 emissions and allowing this entrepreneurially critical situation to be overcome. Paech (2016) points out that sufficiency strategies can increase resilience. In addition, Folkers and Paech (2020) emphasize a time-economy aspect and thus "sufficiency as a prerequisite for successful consumption" (168). Using a time-economical approach, they explain that sufficiency can protect against overstimulation and excessive demands.

Often it may be a combination of different motives that leads to sufficiency in entrepreneurial activities. Sufficiency may be a consequence of an entrepreneur following his or her purpose, which can also be understood as an expression of inner abundance on the part of the entrepreneur (Maurer 2019). This aspect raises the following question: How can the management of a company be combined with a lifestyle that is not fed by material abundance or the maximization of surpluses but rather derives from a wise desire (Reheis 1998) and leaves out the superfluous in order to concentrate on the essential?[1] This lifestyle has the potential to increase "life satisfaction and meaning through focusing on non-material aspects of life" (Gossen et al. 2019: 2). To do justice to the diversity of possible (goals and) motives for sufficiency, the following categorization is suitable. It can also be found in a similar form in Gossen et al. (2019):

- Ecological sustainability;
- Economic factors (quality of products, services and corporate culture, employee satisfaction, resilience);
- Exogenous factors such as reactions to crises, political interventions, or social demands;
- Individual inclinations or a preference for extended scope for development that cannot (or need not) be justified either ecologically or economically, which does not rule out the possibility that this development may also have ecologically positive side effects.

3. The role of entrepreneurs and purpose for corporate sufficiency

One premise of this chapter is that the actions of entrepreneurs – especially in the case of owner-managed firms – cannot be represented exclusively as classic ratio-

1 Also interesting at this point is the concept of eudaimonia as formulated by Aristotle, a state that is inadequately described as bliss (Ryff 1989). "Eudaimonism refers to a person's efforts to recognise and live in accordance with the 'true self'[...]" (Waterman 1981: 764).

nal behavior. The motivation of entrepreneurs is not limited to striving for surplus maximization: a rich scene of purpose-oriented corporate models has been emerging next to the models of the market-dominating corporations (Zeyen/Beckmann 2019).

Schumpeter (2006 [1912]) distinguishes different motives of entrepreneurial activity. One is to strive for prestige and profit and is thus related to the classic idea of rational behavior. Another, which he considers no less relevant, is the motive to create something new and be active "for the joy of creative design" (138). He also presents this form of entrepreneurial action as "creating for the joy of what is created" (142). In a similar vein, Sennett (2008) describes how some people are devoted to their work for their own sake and measure their success by the quality of the values or objects they create, instead of seeing their activities only as a means to the end of achieving the highest possible market value.

Recent approaches, such as "soulful entrepreneurship" and entrepreneurship that focuses on purpose – the raison d'être of an entrepreneur and his or her company – describe how this orientation is changing the way companies are managed (Bruce/Jeromin 2020; Maurer 2017). At the same time, a distinction must be made between a person's personal purpose and a company's corporate purpose. The personal purpose can be described as a specific type of vocation – or calling – toward which the individual's actions are oriented. This purpose can manifest itself in individuals feeling a pronounced desire or strong inner drive to dedicate themselves to a particular idea or task and to implement it. Hirschi (2012) outlines vocation as "a consuming, meaningful passion for a particular career domain or work that a person perceives as her or his purpose in life" (479). Zeyen and Beckmann (2019) have elaborated on the significance of vocation for purpose-oriented entrepreneurs, who, on the one hand, pursue economic goals but, on the other, attach a greater meaning to their actions that sometimes also involve taking on societal responsibility.

In science and in practice, no uniform definition of corporate purpose has emerged. Here, I rely on the definition by Bruce and Jeromin (2020), according to which "the corporate purpose is the higher purpose of a company that goes beyond the sole profit orientation" (23). This definition is used here to define and deliver on a long-term value-creating promise, either in the company's local environment or in the global market environment directly related to the company's value creation. I posit that owner-managed companies and their entrepreneurs, can reach their potential if the corporate and personal purpose are identical. Ideally, even in non-owner-managed companies, the personal purpose of the management should be in harmony with the corporate purpose so that the people involved, and thus also the company, can develop and use their potential to the greatest extent. This relationship also applies to the employees of a company.

If the position of Bruce and Jeromin (2020) were to be followed, indicating that corporate purpose should have a greater influence on corporate governance than financial figures, there would be a turn-around in the means-purpose relationship in terms of why a company was founded and how it is managed. A conventional entrepreneur implements a business idea in order to make a profit. A purpose-oriented entrepreneur is primarily concerned with placing a purpose that goes beyond profit at the center of entrepreneurial action. The profit that results from any business activities is used to further the purpose-based business idea rather than to maximize profit. The related actions mean that, for entrepreneurs, intrinsic motives can play a more significant role than extrinsic ones based on economic incentives.

Life and work satisfaction is higher among entrepreneurs who follow their vocation (Zeyen/Beckmann 2019). It can be assumed that this satisfaction is accompanied by a sense of fulfilment in the face of meaningful activities beyond pure profit maximization. Finding fulfilment or self-efficacy in the pursuit of higher-level goals means not needing compensatory satisfaction in the form of economic or consumerist goals. Gronemeyer (2009 [2002]: 20) argues for distinguishing between "true" and "false" needs. It could be that entrepreneurs face this tension in order to follow an independent preference that can be classified as an individual vocation. The related decision-making and patterns of actions can be so satisfying that they replace – or at least reduce – conventional material desires. This satisfaction point is precisely where a gate towards entrepreneurial sufficiency opens (Maurer 2019), which is perceived not as a sacrifice but as inner abundance, life satisfaction and the creation of meaning (Gossen et al. 2019).

It is not surprising that, in their analysis of 150 companies that applied sufficiency strategies, Bocken et al. (2022) found a great number of family businesses, while large companies were significantly less represented. This difference may be due to large companies being subject to greater constraints to orient themselves towards short-term profit orientation. However, it is also not insignificant that, in such companies, where CEOs often change frequently, there is a lack of a personality that pursues and implements a pronounced purpose orientation. The example of Patagonia shows how things could be different in that the founder still shapes the company's direction.

In recent years, a reorientation of the role of companies in society can be observed. In 2019, for example, the Business Roundtable, an association of large companies in the USA, announced a move away from focusing solely on shareholder value, intending to focus additionally on stakeholder value in the future (Murray 2019). As Murray notes, even if it is debatable how serious these proclamations are, they nevertheless send a signal. At the same time, purpose orientation is gaining in importance. Even Fink (2018), CEO and Chairman of BlackRock, states:

"the public expectations of your company have never been greater [...] every company must not only deliver financial performance, but also show how it makes a positive contribution to society. [...] Without a sense of purpose, no company, either public or private, can achieve its full potential, if the corporate purpose is based on the personal purpose of the owner." (1).

The Enacting Purpose Initiative[2], founded in 2020, aims to "establish best practice purpose governance, globally" (Enacting Purpose Initiative 2021) and works together with numerous companies to this end. These remarks raise the question of how consistently the alignment with a higher corporate purpose is pursued or whether it is a case of purpose-washing in the sense of a marketing strategy (Willan 2020). Nevertheless, it is to be expected that pioneering companies, investors, customers and employees will increasingly influence companies to align themselves towards a higher purpose. In this context, the question of how the purpose orientation of a company is measured, in terms of indicators and reporting, is also gaining in importance (Barby et al. 2021; Stroehle et al. 2022).

4. Method

The method of this study approach comprises two stages, the first of which consists of an identification of corporate sufficiency measures, taking into account the definitions and extensions of possible motivations presented above. This first stage of analysis results in a taxonomy, which is presented in the next section. In the first stage of the analysis, there were indications for some of the identified business cases that the motive of individual inclinations plays a relevant role. These cases are examined in more detail in the second stage of the analysis.

Selection of companies (Section 5.1 and 5.2)

The practical perspective, especially in the field of management consultancy, not only provides insights into phenomena that often remain closed to distanced scientific observation. It has network structures through which special cases can be recognized in the first place. The cases presented come from the business environment of the author, who works as a management consultant. Further cases were identified through research (available documents, company websites), a literature review and, in one case, through a suggestion from someone else[3]. In section 5.2, only busi-

2 "The Enacting Purpose Initiative is a multi-institution partnership between the University of Oxford, the University of California Berkeley, BCG BrightHouse, EOS at Federated Hermes and the British Academy" (Enacting Purpose Initiative 2021).

3 The business case Schatzalp Slow Mountain was pointed out by Jonathan Eiser, together with fellow students of business administration, on the course at the University of St. Gallen

ness cases that correspond with motive category d) have been selected as described above, i.e. are based on individual inclinations or preferences of the management for extended scope for development that cannot (or do not have to) be justified either economically or ecologically.

Data collection for selected business cases (Section 5.2)

The results were obtained through guideline-based expert interviews (Helfferich 2011) conducted with the entrepreneurs, with the exception of Elektrizitätswerke Schönau, as sufficient information is available for this case. In addition, there was correspondence with one of the managing directors. The expert interviews took place between winter 2014 and autumn 2016, with further interviews in autumn 2018/winter 2019 and spring/summer 2023, also to update previously collected data.

Evaluation of selected business cases (Section 5.2)

The interviews were digitally recorded and transcribed. Subsequently, they were analyzed inductively in four steps using "thematic analysis" (Braun/Clarke 2006; Braun/Clarke 2021). First, codes were generated from the transcripts of the interviews. These codes were then categorised and themes were formed on the basis of the categories. In the final step, the themes were checked for content consistency. In this way, three themes were generated on which the description of the business cases is based. Before these themes are applied to analyze a selection of business cases (section 5.2), an overview of the entire range of sufficiency strategies will be provided.

5. Empirical results

5.1 Taxonomy of sufficiency in business

The following is a taxonomy of corporate sufficiency strategies. Corporate sufficiency involves not only measures to limit capacity but also measures to limit monetary demands. Both can have a direct or indirect impact. Corporate sufficiency can lead to a reductive impact directly via certain target variables (e.g., profit) or indirectly via certain levels of action (e.g., legal form).

'Transformatik – Grundlagen einer neuen Lehre des Wandels' (Transformations – Foundations of a New Teaching of Change) by Prof. Dr. Jörg Metelmann and Dr. Björn Müller, where I gave a lecture in the winter semester of 2022/23.

Figure 1: Taxonomy of corporate sufficiency strategies.

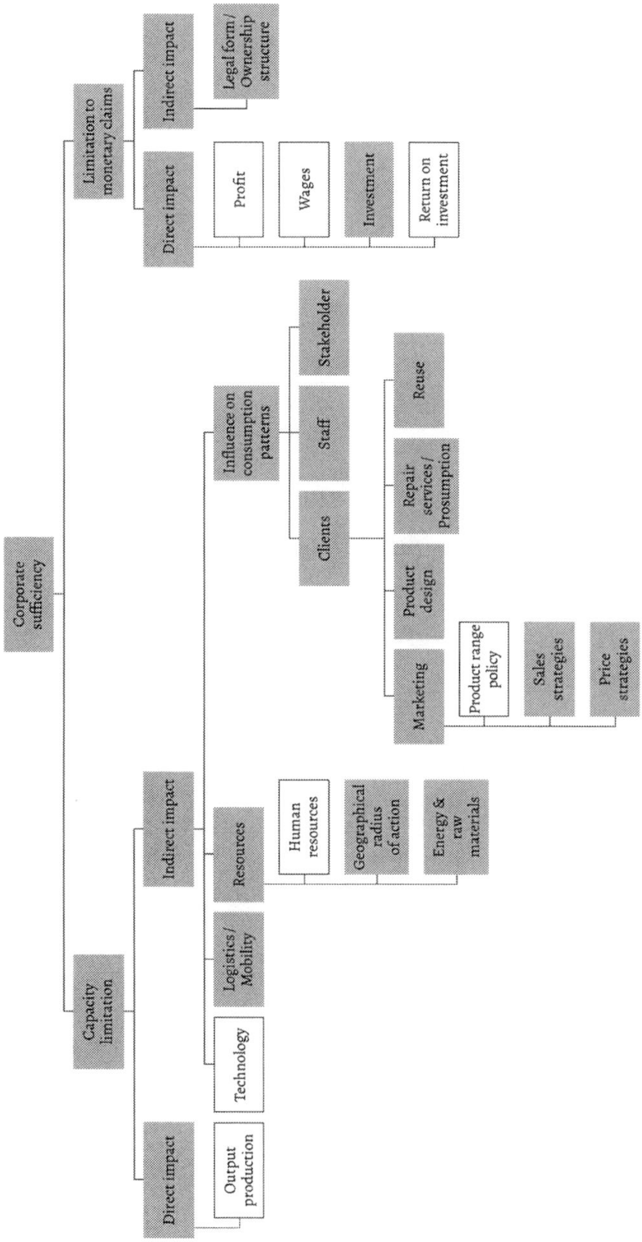

Figure 1 shows all the identified targets and levels of action for sufficiency in companies, which are based on the four motive levels described above. The white boxes indicate the target values and action levels that are described in more detail in the business cases with the corresponding sufficiency strategies from section 5.2 onwards.

Table 1 shows all the target values and action levels shown in Figure 1 with the identified sufficiency strategies and the companies that apply them.

Table 1: Overview of the aims or actions in sufficiency strategies

Target values or action levels	Sufficiency strategy	Associated business case
Production	**Limiting output**	Neue Holzforum AG, CH
Technology	**Limiting technical means**	Schatzalp Slow Mountain (Berghotel Schatzalp AG), CH
Logistics/Mobility	**Limiting logistics & fossil fuel-based mobility**	Teikei Coffee, GER
Human Resources	**Limiting the number of employees**	Ruprecht Möbeldesign GmbH, CH
Geographical radius of action	**Limiting the geographical operating area**	BBO Bank Brienz Oberhasli AG, CH
Energy & raw materials	**Limiting consumption of energy and resources**	Schweizerische Bundesbahnen AG, CH
Marketing	**Limiting marketing**	Bio Company SE, GER
Product design	**Using product design measures**	Grüne Erde GmbH, A
Product range policy	**Limiting product range policy**	Karl Siegel Vertriebs-GmbH & Co.KG, Brand Rymhart, GER
Sales strategies	**Adjusting choice of sales strategies**	Vitsœ Limited, UK (Bocken/ Short 2016)
Price setting	**Using pricing measures**	Vitsœ Limited, UK (Bocken 2017)
Repair services/Prosumption	**Using repair services and/or prosumption**	Nudie Jeans Marketing AB, SWE (Bocken et al. 2022)
Reuse	**Using reuse**	Revendo AG, CH
Staff	**Promoting sufficiency practices among employees**	Standort Achim, DE, of Norsk Hydro ASA, NOR

Stakeholder	**Promoting sufficiency practices by collaboration with stakeholder**	Ebay Inc., USA, with iFixit, USA (Bocken/Short 2016)
Profit	**Limiting profits**	Premium, GER
Wages	**Limiting entrepreneurial wages**	Länggass Tee AG, CH
Investments	**Limiting investments**	Elephant Box Stainless Steel Limited, UK (Bocken et al. 2022)
Return on investment	**Limiting shareholders' profit expectations**	EWS Elektrizitätswerke Schönau e.G., GER
Legal form/ Ownership structure	**Adjusting choice of legal form or ownership structure**	Patagonia Inc., USA

5.2 Business cases

For reasons of space, the business cases described in more detail only deal with those cases that can be associated with motive category d) described at the end of section 2 (i.e. with individual inclinations or a preference for extended scope for development that cannot (need not) be justified either economically or ecologically, which does not rule out ecologically and economically positive effects occurring as a side effect).

For the following case analyses, the method described in section 4 was applied. The description of the selected cases is based on the three extracted themes, which are formulated as questions in the following:

a) On which of the three sufficiency levels mentioned in section 1 can the effect of the measure be located?
b) Can the main motive be assigned to category d) described above?
c) How do the companies manage to remain economically viable and stable in the long term?

5.2.1 Sufficiency by limiting output

(Capacity limitation with direct impact)
Business case: Neue Holzforum AG, Bern, CH

The company is considered a pioneer of modern timber construction in Switzerland. The buildings, designed using digital planning technology, are erected using a timber frame construction.

A) Markus Mosimann, owner of the company, distances himself from the prevailing growth paradigm, which he considers problematic due to his own experience with the bankruptcy of his first company. With his company, founded in 1998, he has not aimed for any further quantitative growth since completing a start-up phase, which corresponds to a sufficiency strategy also described by Beyeler and Jaeger-Erben (2022), namely to "produce less by choice" (ibid: 12). In the spirit of self-restraint, an upper limit is set on the number of houses produced each year, which corresponds to the sufficiency level of self-limitation.

B) Markus Mosimann states his intention is to develop an "optimal house". He voices three entrepreneurial goals, first, to constantly increase the quality of his products and services, especially through developing an "optimal house"; second, to create above-average working conditions for the current 13 employees; third, by limiting his output, to hopefully achieve a lifestyle that meets his needs for personal development and his convictions (Mosimann/Lettau 2012).

C) The intensive focus is on quality results and high customer satisfaction. The resulting reputation effect is reflected in recommendations, which lead to a stable order situation. Furthermore, financial and organizational risks are avoided through self-limitation.

5.2.2 Sufficiency by limiting technical means

(Capacity limitation with indirect effect)

Business case: Schatzalp Slow Mountain, Berghotel Schatzalp AG, Davos, CH

The entrepreneurs Pius App and Erich Schmid opened the Schatzalp ski area as a 'slow mountain' area at the end of 2009. This comparatively high-altitude and relatively snow-sure ski area is run in conjunction with a hotel that has been acquired by the entrepreneurs. Schatzalp Slow Mountain is frequented mainly by families and older people because the slopes are skied at a slower pace and there are only as many accidents during a season as there are elsewhere in a single day.

A) The company renovated the existing chairlift and one draglift without replacing them with more modern and faster gondola lifts. They also refrain from using artificial snow from snow cannons, which is why the lifts may open later in the ski season and/or close earlier if the amount of snow available is not sufficient for operation. In this way, profit losses are consciously accepted in order to offer, as Pius App puts it, "... a contemplative counter-model [...] to the 'ever faster', 'ever more hectic' and 'ever more crowded' of today's winter sports arenas – a ski area in which sport and recreation can be combined" (Fitzthum 2020: 1), which corresponds to the sufficiency level of reduction.

B) The company strives to create a ski resort where winter sport enthusiasts find natural snow on slopes that are less frequented due to the lower capacity of the lifts (Schatzalp 2023).

C) Through the unconventional business model, the ski area achieves awareness and covers a niche need. In addition to the high altitude and snow-sure location, other factors are relevant for survivability. For example, the hotel and the ski resort are aimed at the same target group, which makes both more attractive. According to one of the founders, alternative skiing areas are also important for securing survival, making it possible to use a combination of conventional slopes and those of the Slow Mountain area on different days. Furthermore, the moderate profit expectation contributes to the profitability of this business model (here the sufficiency strategy of moderation in profit (see section 5.2.5) is applied).

5.2.3 Sufficiency by limiting company size regarding the number of employees

(Capacity limitation with indirect effect – sufficiency through the limitation of resources)
Business case: Ruprecht Möbeldesign GmbH, Wengi, CH

The company Ruprecht Möbeldesign offers high-quality carpentry work for furniture, kitchens and interior design. The owner Martin Ruprecht, who founded the company in 1994, rejects mass-produced work and has created working conditions that clearly stand out from the industry average in terms of quality.

A) Martin Ruprecht limits the number of employees (nine people), most of whom work part-time, in order to meet the desired quality level. This sufficiency strategy, which is also mentioned by Beyeler/Jaeger-Erben (2022), corresponds to the level of self-limitation.

B) The manager strives to ensure that he and the employees enjoy their work and that the customers are more than satisfied. Together with his employees, he focuses on excellent work and customer service and attaches great importance to the corporate culture. The employees are given freedom to design and are involved, for example, in the conception of furnishings and furniture. Like their boss, the employees are entitled to seven weeks of holiday[44] and receive a higher salary than is customary in the industry. The employees' dedication has a positive effect on the quality of their work and customer satisfaction is high due to the above-average quality of customer service.

C) Due to the high quality of the products and services and the resulting high customer satisfaction, the company enjoys a high level of reputation and is often recommended to others. Customers are willing to pay higher prices for the high-quality products, as described by Bocken/Short (2016), which is why the company has been able to avoid participating in price-squeezing public tenders for many years.

4 In Switzerland, 4 to 5 weeks of holiday are common for the age group concerned.

5.2.4 Sufficiency by product range policy

(Capacity limitation with indirect effect – Sufficiency through the limitation of consumption – influencing consumption patterns – marketing measures)
Business case: Karl Siegel Vertriebs-GmbH & Co.KG, Brand Rymhart, Stade, GER

The family business Karl Siegel Vertriebs-GmbH & Co.KG was founded in 1948, is now run by the fourth generation and currently employs around 35 people. Until winter 2021/2022, the company produced knitwear under a different brand. The brand Rymhart was launched in 2011 following the idea to produce high-quality, weatherproof outdoor clothing in the form of knitwear.

A) The key characteristic of Rymhart is its extremely limited product range in the textile sector of highest quality (woollen jumpers, hats, T-shirts), combined with a classic and timeless design (an additional strategy: sufficiency through product design, as described, for example, by Freudenreich/Schaltegger 2022). The sufficiency strategy of limitation of the range of products and services, which in business management terms can be attributed to marketing, corresponds to the sufficiency level of reduction described above in this business case. Bocken/Short (2016) depict this sufficiency strategy as concentrating on products of the highest quality, while Schneidewind and Palzkill (2011) speak of streamlining a product range.

B) Karl-Frank Siegel, the managing director, strives to produce garments that people really need. The few things that are really necessary should be loved by the customers because of the quality. Accordingly, the company is not satisfied simply with an ecologically sustainable product and service design but also generates outstanding quality and product responsibility, which results in above-average customer satisfaction. It would be more economical not to aim for this high standard. The company produces on site and offers repairs, refurbishing and alterations to extend the life cycle of the textiles (here, further sufficiency strategies are used: limiting the radius of action with regard to production as well as offering repair services [Niessen/Bocken 2021]). This approach creates an intensive relationship between user and product (Beyeler/Jaeger-Erben 2022).

C) The company hardly invests in advertising (another sufficiency strategy with regard to marketing measures used [Gossen et al. 2019; Gossen/Kropfeld 2022]). The high level of customer satisfaction, which is confirmed by positive feedback on the company's website, means that, according to the managing director, 65 to 70 per cent of new customers can be attributed to recommendations. Product-related services such as repairs and refurbishing also contribute to the conspicuously high reputation.

5.2.5 Sufficiency through moderate profits

(Limitation of monetary claims with direct impact)
Business case: Premium, Hamburg, GER

Beyeler/Jaeger-Erben (2022) assert, "even though sufficiency practitioners are not primarily oriented toward profit maximization, it does not mean that sufficiency does not generate revenues" (16). Such practitioners implement their strategies by primarily committing to the corporate purpose and not putting profit orientation at the center of their actions (Beyeler/Jaeger-Erben 2022). The following business case implements this sufficiency strategy in a radical form. Uwe Lübbermann founded Premium in Hamburg in 2001. The company produces and distributes various beverages.

A) Together with the Premium Collective, Uwe Lübbermann pursues an unconventional form of business management. Among other things, the company explicitly aims to make no profit, which corresponds to the sufficiency strategy level of complete renunciation of any profit option. Lübbermann considers that the "Premium-Kollektiv", as the company now calls itself, must have made a mistake if a profit was made because someone then apparently had too much money taken out of their pocket. When calculating the bottle prices, an amount for reserves in times of crisis is included but no profit share. Nevertheless, a profit was made several times in the company's history. This repeatedly resulted in prices being lowered.

B) The main motive for founding and developing the company was to show that a company can be run fairly and "politically correctly" and still survive on the market. Uwe Lübbermann even claims that the actual product is the "operating system" of the Premium Collective. The drinks produced are only a means to an end; something completely different could also be produced (Lübbermann/Herberhold 2021). The company uses a whole range of other sufficiency strategies, which cannot all be mentioned here for lack of space.

C) For 22 years, the Premium Collective has shown that it is possible to break with all the usual rules of business management and still survive on the market. This possibility is promoted by the management of a solidary value network (Bocken et al. 2022), whose members directly negotiate those prices, and cost rates that guarantee the survival of all participating companies.

The network organizer creates flexible decision-making processes that allow the stakeholders to adapt to changing structures and framework conditions through new supply and price agreements and to cover costs. Since all stakeholders can have a say in key decisions, there is a network with many people and organizations ready to support in times of crisis.

5.2.6 Sufficiency through the limitation of entrepreneurial wages

(Limitation of monetary claims with direct impact)
Business case: Länggass Tee AG, Bern, CH

Just as a company's profits can be restrained, so, too, can salaries. In November 2013, a federal referendum for fair wages took place in Switzerland. The popular initiative "1:12 für gerechte Löhne" (1:12 for fair wages) advocated that the highest wage of a company should not be more than 12 times higher than the lowest wage paid by the company (Bundeskanzlei der Schweizerischen Eidgenossenschaft 2023). What is usually discussed in the context of fair wages (Bottino et al. 2016) can be classified as a corporate sufficiency strategy. Limiting wages can have an ecologically sustainable effect because some potential financial resources are not available for consumption. This lack leads to the avoidance of CO_2 emissions. The Premium Collective mentioned above uses this strategy, as does the family business Länggass-Tee AG in Bern. Katrin and Gerhard Lange founded the company in 1983, a specialist tea shop with about 40 employees today. The company is currently in the process of transferring management from the first to the second generation. The company orients itself towards maximum product and service quality.

A) The founders paid themselves the same wages as the employees for several decades. Currently, the pay gap in the company is in the range of 1 to 1.5, including the salaries of the members of the executive board, and is comparatively small. The sufficiency strategy in this case corresponds to the level of self-limitation.

B) The founders are convinced that human interaction between the management and the employees does not allow for high salary differences, among other things. Because of this starting position, the members of the executive board have at certain times in the past reflected on what motivates them for their work if it is not a special salary. This reflection has led to a range of innovative products and services of excellent quality being launched, which are a pleasure not only for the executives but also for the employees and the customers.

C) The chosen sufficiency strategy – in addition to other measures – has a positive effect on the working atmosphere. The company staff and management are closely knit and times of crisis are shared. In addition, the outstanding quality of the products and services contributes to high customer loyalty.

5.2.7 Sufficiency by limiting shareholders' profit expectations

(Limitation of monetary claims with direct impact)
Business case: EWS Elektrizitätswerke Schönau e.G., Schönau, GER

In 1994, Ursula and Michael Sladek and other electricity rebels from the citizens' initiative "Parents for a Nuclear-Free Future" founded Elektrizitätswerke Schönau GmbH (EWS), a 100 percent subsidiary of Netzkauf GbR. EWS currently has five subsidiaries. Since 1997, it has been generating and supplying green electricity to households and businesses. As a result of the liberalization of the electricity market in 1998, the company currently supplies 230,000 customers Germany-wide.

A) The associated registered cooperative, which was founded in 2009, employs about 80 people and has more than 11,000 members, who can purchase a minimum of five to a maximum of fifty shares, at 100 Euro each in 2022 (Elektrizitätswerke Schönau 2021). These shares do not earn interest and dividends are distributed depending on how business is going, a decision made by the general assembly. In this case, the strategy corresponds also to the level of self-limitation.

B) The management strives to run the company according to its own values and to be able to use entrepreneurial freedom independently of profit-oriented investors, as also described by Beyeler/Jaeger-Erben (2022).

C) Due to the eventful history of the company and the strong commitment to ecological energy supply, the company enjoys a high reputation. Strong customer loyalty and a sufficiently high number of shareholders ensure the company's viability.

6. Discussion

Based on a critical analysis of the current sufficiency debate and a systematic evaluation of instructive case studies, this article leads to five key insights.

a) Until now, the sufficiency discourse has focused almost exclusively on the demand or consumption side (Jungell-Michelsson/Heikkurinen 2022). This truncated view overlooks the fact that there are various starting points and options for sufficiency strategies in the corporate sector (Princen 2003; Scherhorn 2015; Maurer 2019).
b) Motivations to implement sufficiency-oriented measures or change ways of working are not limited to environmental or ecological imperatives, as is usually assumed. Questions on purpose-creation (Bocken et al. 2022) or resilience (Schneidewind/Palzkill 2011, Folkers/Paech 2020), all focusing on particular objectives or ensuring high quality (Bocken/Short 2016), or organizational culture (Bocken/Short 2016) have proven to be no less relevant in justifying the use of corporate sufficiency strategies (Maurer/Paech forthcoming).
c) Sufficiency strategies do not necessarily equate to "sacrificing" (Zeyen/Beckmann 2019) or losing something. The case studies examined suggest that certain forms of voluntary limitations can be associated with both organizational stability and long-term business success.

d) The opportunities of entrepreneurial sufficiency extend over a surprisingly broad spectrum, covering almost all fields in business management. Until now, these opportunities have barely been acknowledged in sustainability research.
e) The sufficiency strategies systematically presented here are not a theoretical construct, they exist in reality, i.e. they have been empirically proven. The taxonomy and analysis presented here are based on forms of entrepreneurial sufficiency activities for which at least one case could be identified.

7. Conclusion

The cases presented here cannot be considered empirically representative, but they do open up the "sense of possibility" (Pfriem 2017: 17) for a conceivable transformation towards (more) sufficiency in an exemplary way, regardless of whether it is crisis-related, consciously politically steered, or a gradual spread of entrepreneurial patterns of action that can currently only be observed as niche phenomena. This article is devoted to the latter and thus ties in with insights that Schumpeter (2006 [1912]) has developed, albeit with the opposite goal, by tracing the origin of economic change back to innovative, and thus to a certain extent non-conforming, entrepreneurial personalities. This voluntaristic approach serves to explain economic growth, not in the sense of 'more of the same' but rather through the creation of new solutions and procedures that differ from previous orientations. What this entails is therefore more than 'just' economic change. It is more a case of what Pfriem (2006) understands by corporate strategies as cultural offers to society.

The present field of investigation raises questions: Are there powerful and stubborn personalities, especially entrepreneurs, who contribute to the spread of new orientations from the niche but in the opposite direction of development compared to Schumpeter (2006 [1912]), namely as a turn towards the less? And if so, can their motives, which in one way or another lead to sufficiency, be described as a purpose that, despite all situational differences, reveals generalizable patterns?

If we take an overarching view of the examples analyzed and of the associated discourse, we could speak of factors that create meaning, factors that are not simply set apart from growth, globalization, or complex technology according to a negative definition but ones that counter the maximization of surplus with another perspective of entrepreneurial fulfilment. Two basic trends are striking. First, a consistent improvement or assurance of quality, which by no means only concerns the ecological or other attractiveness of the goods, and consequently competitiveness, but represents itself as an end for entrepreneurial creation: The work that is regarded as successful (quality for its own sake) obviously provides more satisfaction than the revenue generated by it. A quasi-craft or even artistic attitude in the sense of Sennett (2008) is recognizable. In some cases, the sense of purpose relates more to a processual quality, namely the corporate culture, employee satisfaction, or the direct, sometimes hierarchy-free, interaction with them. Another quality is the direct encounter with customers whose satisfaction is an indicator of the company's success.

The second trend is a change in value systems, which occurs in two ways: First, as a measurement of the entrepreneurial sense in terms of the social benefit that results from it (climate protection, justice, solving social problems, resilience, etc.) and, second, as new trade-offs arise between individual preferences with regard to one's own lifestyle and business requirements. Thus, some entrepreneurial decision-makers do not seem to be willing to subject their personal scope for development and values to the logic of the market and competition but are willing to forgo opportunities for expansion in exchange for, for example, more leisure time and reflection as well as adherence to principles – as long as this does not jeopardize the company's existence.

Finally, the following implications are relevant:

a) In research and practice, the view should be broadened for sufficiency in companies beyond ecological sustainability.
b) It is likely that corporate sufficiency in this broader sense is much more common than has been apparent so far. This broadness should be taken into account in management training as well as in classic business studies.
c) It seems reasonable to assume that corporate sufficiency does not necessarily go hand in hand with renunciation but can also be based on fulfilment, life satisfaction and the creation of meaning. This alternative can lead to corporate sufficiency undergoing a reframing in theory and practice and gaining in appeal.

References

Barby, Clara/Barker, Richard/Cohen, Ronald/Eccles, Robert/Heller, Christian/Mayer, Colin/Roche, Bruno/Serafeim, George/Stroehle, Judith/Younger, Rupert/Zochowski,Robert (2021): "Measuring Purpose – An Integrated Framework," 25.5.2023 (https://enactingpurpose.org/assets/measuring-purpose---an-integrated-framework.pdf).

Beyeler, Laura/Jaeger-Erben, Melanie (2022): "How to make more of less: Characteristics of sufficiency in business practices." In: Frontiers in Sustainability 3, pp. 1–25. https://doi.org/10.3389/frsus.2022.949710.

Bocken, Nancy M. P./Niessen, Laura/Short, Samuel William (2022): "The Sufficiency-Based Circular Economy – An Analysis of 150 Companies." In: Frontiers in Sustainability 3, 899289. https://doi.org/10.3389/frsus.2022.899289.

Bocken, Nancy M. P./Short, Samuel William (2016): "Towards a sufficiency-driven business model: Experiences and opportunities." In: Environmental Innovation and Societal Transitions 18, pp. 41–61. https://doi.org/10.1016/j.eist.2015.07.010.

Bottino, Eleonora/García-Muñoz, Teresa/Goddio, Cintia/Kujal, Praveen (2016): "What is a fair wage? Reference points, entitlements and gift exchange." In: Journal of Behavioral and Experimental Economics 63, pp. 125–135. https://doi.org/10.1016/j.socec.2016.06.002.

Braun, Virginia/Clarke, Victoria (2006): "Using thematic analysis in psychology." In: Qualitative Research in Psychology 3/2, pp. 77–101. https://doi.org/10.1191/1478088706qp063oa.

Braun, Virginia/Clarke, Victoria (2021): Thematic analysis: A practical guide. London: Sage.

Bruce, Annette/Jeromin, Christoph (2020): Corporate Purpose: Ein Erfolgskonzept der Zukunft, Wiesbaden: Springer Gabler.

Bundeskanzlei der Schweizerischen Eidgenossenschaft (2023): "Eidgenössische Volksinitiative 1:12 – Für gerechte Löhne," 19.8.2023 (https://www.bk.admin.ch/ch/d/pore/vi/vis375t.html).

Elektrizitätswerke Schönau (2021): "Integrierter Geschäftsbericht," 27.5.2023 (https://www.ews-schoenau.de/export/sites/ews/ews/genossenschaft/.files/ews-integrierter-geschaeftsbericht-2021.pdf).

Enacting Purpose Initiative (2021): "Purpose, strategy and performance," 2.6.2023 (https://enactingpurpose.org/).

Fink, Larry (2018): "A Sense of Purpose, Larry Fink's 2022 Letter to CEOs," 18.5.2023 (https://aips.online/wp-content/uploads/2018/04/Larry-Fink-letter-to-CEOs-2018-BlackRock.pdf).

Fitzthum, Gerhard (2020): "Im Skigebiet Schatzalp ist Kunstschnee verpönt," 25.4.2023 (https://www.welt.de/reise/nah/article205168007/Skigebiet-Schatzalp-in-der-Schweiz-Kunstschnee-ist-hier-verpoent.html).

Folkers, Manfred/Paech, Niko (2020): All you need is less: Eine Kultur des Genug aus ökonomischer und buddhistischer Sicht, München: Oekom.

Freudenreich, Birte/Schaltegger, Stefan (2020): "Developing sufficiency-oriented offerings for clothing users: Business approaches to support consumption reduction." In: Journal of Cleaner Production 247, 119589. https://doi.org/10.1016/j.jclepro.2019.119589.

Gossen, Maike/Ziesemer, Florence/Schrader, Ulf (2019): "Why and how commercial marketing should promote sufficient consumption: A systematic literature review." In: Journal of Marcomarketing 39/3, pp. 252–269. http://doi.org/10.1177/0276146719866238.

Gossen, Maike/Kropfeld, Maren Ingrid (2022): ""Choose nature. Buy less." Exploring sufficiency-oriented marketing and consumption practices in the outdoor industry." In: Sustainable Production and Consumption 30, pp. 720–736. https://doi.org/10.1016/j.spc.2022.01.005.

Gronemeyer, Marianne (2009 [2002]): Die Macht der Bedürfnisse, Reinbek bei Hamburg: Rowohlt.

Helfferich, Cornelia (2011): Die Qualität qualitativer Daten: Manual für die Durchführung qualitativer Interview, Wiesbaden: Verlag für Sozialwissenschaften, Springer Fachmedien.

Hirschi, Andreas (2012): "Callings and work engagement: Moderated mediation model of work meaningfulness, occupational identity, and occupational self-efficacy." In: Journal of Counseling Psychology 59/3, pp. 479–485. https://doi.org/10.1037/a0028949.

Jäger, André (2022): Suffizienz als Leitstrategie von Unternehmen: Potenziale, Chancen und Risiken am Beispiel der Gemeinwohlökonomie, München: Oekom.

Jungell-Michelsson, Jessica/Heikkurinen, Pasi (2022): "Sufficiency: A systematic literature review." In: Ecological Economics 195, 107380. https://doi.org/10.1016/j.ecolecon.2022.107380.

Lübbermann, Uwe/Herberhold, Lennart (2021): Wirtschaft hacken – Von einem ganz normalen Unternehmer, der fast alles anders macht, Marburg, Büchner.

Murray, Alan (2019): "America's CEOc seek a new purpose of the corporation," 25.5.2023 (https://fortune.com/longform/business-roundtable-ceos-corporations-purpose/).

Maurer, Christel (2017): Beseelte UnternehmerInnen: Plädoyer für einen Wandel in der Wirtschaft, Bern: Zytglogge.

Maurer, Christel (2019): "Unternehmerische Suffizienz, persönliches Glück & ökologische Verantwortung." In: Peter Buchenau, (eds.): Chefsache Zukunft: Was Führungskräfte von morgen brauchen, Wiesbaden: Springer Gabler, pp. 385–405.

Maurer, Christel/Paech, Niko (forthcoming): "Nachhaltigkeit durch sinnstiftendes und suffizientes Unternehmertum." In: Reinhard Paulesich, (eds.): Ethisch ökologische Unternehmenspolitik, Wiesbaden: Springer, Gabler.

Mosimann, Markus/Lettau, Marc (2012): Das Holzhaus der Zukunft: Ökologisch bauen mit menschlichem Mass, Zürich: Rotpunkt.

Niessen, Laura/Bocken, Nancy, M. P. (2021): "How can business drive sufficiency? The business for sufficiency framework." In: Sustainable Production & Consumption 28, pp. 109–1103. https://doi.org/10.1016/j.spc.2021.07.030.

Paech, Niko (2016): "Befreiung vom Überfluss: Grundlagen einer Wirtschaft ohne Wachstum." In: Fromm Forum 20, pp. 70–76.

Pfriem, Reinhard (2017): "Ökonomik als Möglichkeitswissenschaften." In: Ökologisches Wirtschaften 32, pp. 16–18. https://doi.org/10.14512/OEW320216.

Pfriem, Reinhard (2006): "Unternehmensstrategien sind kulturelle Angebote an die Gesellschaft." In: Forschungsgruppe Unternehmen und gesellschaftliche Organisation (FUGO) (eds.): Perspektiven einer kulturtheoretischen Perspektive der Unternehmung, Marburg: Metropolis.

Princen, Thomas (2003): "Principles for sustainability: From cooperation and efficiency to sufficiency." In: Global Environmental Politics 3/1, pp. 33–50. https://doi.org/10.1162/152638003763336374.

Reheis, Fritz (1998): Die Kreativität der Langsamkeit: Neuer Wohlstand durch Entschleunigung, Darmstadt: Primus.

Ryff, Carol D. (1989): "Happiness is everything, or is it? Explorations on the meaning of psychological well-being." In: Journal of Personality and Social Psychology 57/6, pp. 1069–1081. https://doi.org/10.1037/0022-3514.57.6.1069.

Sachs, Wolfgang (1993): "Die vier E's. Merkposten für einen massvollen Lebensstil." In: Politische Ökologie 11/33, pp. 69–72, 6.12.2023 (https://epub.wupperinst.org/frontdoor/deliver/index/docId/66/file/66_Sachs.pdf).

Schatzalp (2023): "Slow Mountain," 10.4.2023 (https://www.schatzalp.ch/slowmountain/).

Scherhorn, Gerhard (2015): Wachstum oder Nachhaltigkeit: Die Ökonomie am Scheideweg, Erkelenz: Altius.

Schneidewind, Uwe/Palzkill-Vorbeck, Alexandra (2011): "Suffizienz als Business Case: Nachhaltiges Ressourcenmanagement als Gegenstand einer tranzdisziplinären Betriebswirtschaftslehre." In: Wuppertal Institut für Klima, Umwelt, Energie GmbH, Impulse Zur WachstumsWende 2, pp. 4–20, 6.12.2023 (https://epub.wupperinst.org/frontdoor/deliver/index/docId/3955/file/ImpW2.pdf).

Schumpeter, Joseph (2006 [1912]): Theorie der wirtschaftlichen Entwicklung, Berlin: Duncker & Humblot.

Sennett, Richard (2008): Handwerk, Berlin: Berlin.

Stroehle, Judith/Soonawalla, Kazbi/Metzner, Marcel (2022): "Through the looking glass: tying performance and materiality to corporate purpose." In: Journal of the British Academy 10/5, pp. 87–123. https://doi.org/10.5871/jba/010s5.087.

Waterman, Alan S. (1981): "Individualism and Interdependence." In: American Psychologist 36/7, pp. 762–773. http://dx.doi.org/10.1037/0003-066X.36.7.762.

Willan, Becky (2020): "The evolution of purpose wash and how to avoid it." In: Ceo Today Magazine, 12.6.2023 (https://www.ceotodaymagazine.com/2020/12/the-evolution-of-purpose-wash-and-how-to-avoid-it/).

Zeyen, Anica/Beckmann, Markus (2019): Social entrepreneurship and business ethics: Understanding the contribution and normative ambivalence of purpose-driven venturing, New York: Routledge.

The Future of Organizations

Understanding Business Model Implications of Shifting from Profit to Purpose

Maren Ingrid Kropfeld and André Reichel

Abstract *This chapter explores the evolution of organizations towards sufficiency-oriented business models, encompassing necessary shifts in governance, ownership, financing, and the implications for the business model when transitioning from a profit-focused organization to a purpose-driven one.*

1. Introduction

Respecting social, ecological and economic boundaries demands not just technological advances but also behavioral shifts and a democratic discourse on societal well-being independent of economic growth (IPCC 2022). To implement sufficiency as a sustainability strategy, openness to transcending growth and considering the implications of a degrowth society and economy is crucial. This new reality beyond growth necessitates novel forms of organizations and organizing, prompting an examination of the concepts of profit and purpose for firms.

The predominant focus in research literature and business practice on profit, rather than purpose, poses a central challenge (Kelly 2012). Furthermore, the entire structure of a business, its business model, is fundamentally oriented towards profit rather than sufficiency (Beyeler/Jaeger-Erben 2022). However, by reframing the business perspective towards purpose – the raison d'être of a company – and establishing sufficiency as the company's purpose, a myriad of implications for both business model and organizational structure unfolds. In the subsequent discussion, we explore the interplay between business model and organizational structure and the transformations they must undergo to align with sufficiency principles (see Figure 1). Governance, as a structural element of an organization, and value proposition, as the initial part of any business model, are conjoined here to underscore the normative aspects inherent in both organizational structure and business model. Both are intimately linked to the purpose of conducting business: why are we doing what we do and for whom? Ownership and value creation intertwine, as stakeholders, serving dual roles as owners and contributors to value creation, take center stage. Without stakeholders, there is neither an organization nor its product. Financing and value capture are inherently connected and constitute the bridge to profit, construed as the net positive value of a company's assets. This conceptual model allows for the fusion of purpose and profit, commencing with purpose and allowing profit aspects to emerge organically through the pairings of organizational structure and business model.

Adopting sufficiency as the central tenet of business mandates a fundamental reconsideration of traditional business practices, necessitating innovative approaches that prioritize resource efficiency, social responsibility and long-term sustainability over the relentless pursuit of profit. Drawing on Kelly's (2012) recommendations for a more generative organizational design and Bocken et al.'s (2022) work based on DEAL's (2021) proposal for a transition to a new economy, we contend that the organizational structure for sufficiency-oriented businesses should be reimagined to serve the organization's purpose, embrace stakeholder engagement, introduce new financing models to allow for alternative financing, ownership and governance models, and ultimately foster collaboration across the organization's boundaries to build and engage in collaborative communities of sufficiency practices.

These redesigns will impact and be impacted by the organization's business model, encompassing its value proposition, value creation and value capture. This chapter explores the paradigm shift necessary for businesses to transition from a profit-driven mindset to one that is genuinely sufficiency-oriented, spotlighting the potential benefits and challenges in realizing this transformative journey towards a more sustainable and responsible business model.

Figure 1: Interplay between Organizational Structure and the Business Model.

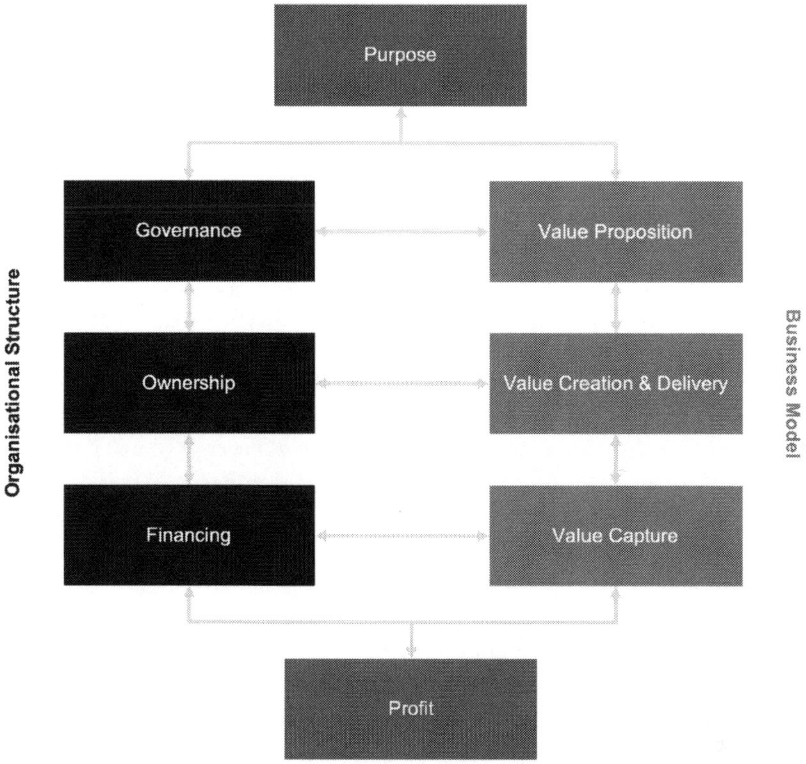

2. Organizational shift from profit to purpose

2.1 Purpose

Purpose assumes a pivotal role for businesses, not only as an overarching framework but also as a catalyst for exploring the role of business within society (Hollensbe et al. 2014). This perspective recognizes businesses as integral parts of society, not separate entities. Accordingly, they should adopt acceptable societal standards, fostering alignment rather than opposition between societal and business values. Our perspective is teleological, involving an inquiry into the rationale or purpose behind phenomena. This includes addressing fundamental questions about the purpose of a business, the intended purpose of a product, the beneficiaries and the justification underlying these elements. Alongside the epistemological understanding of meaning, purpose holds significance in the organizational context. The synthesis of purpose and meaning is imperative for the coherent construction of sense within organizations (Weick 1995).

Embracing a focus on purpose invites exploration into how corporate purpose and its driving values can be effectively harnessed to serve the common good. By directly coupling purpose with societal success – the telos of business being a positive contribution to society – profits are derived from delivering products and services in a model that inherently has a positive impact on society. Sufficiency-oriented business models are conceptualized as delivering such value to both society and the environment (Reichel 2013; Bocken/Short 2016; Profijt 2018).

Central to this is the need to embed sufficiency principles in the core purpose, leading businesses to conscientiously assess and measure their impact on people, values, resources and the environment, taking responsibility for their actions (Bocken et al. 2022). Following Kelly (2012), we understand an organization's purpose to be based on its values and institutionalized within the organization and its organizational set-up. According to Kelly (2012), however, this "living purpose" might not be enough to ensure an organization's positive impact. It is also dependent on other design issues such as the organizational structure and the business model.

Businesses can support sufficiency-oriented consumption practices by adapting their business models (Bocken/Short 2016). For that, they will have to redirect their whole value chain to relate to sufficiency-related meanings, produce and market products that support sufficiency-oriented consumption practices and provide possibilities for skills development (Bocken/Short 2016; Niessen/Bocken 2021; Gossen/Kropfeld 2022). This includes a multilateral negotiation of the value proposition of new practices (e.g., product longevity) between the business and its stakeholders, a reciprocal learning and change process of shared practices between the business and consumers in the value creation (e.g., consumer education) and finally new payment models, profit sufficiency and non-monetary value capture (e.g., pay-per-use models; Bocken/Short 2016). Bocken et al. (2022) demonstrated that not all sufficiency strategies are inherently grounded in sustainability or sufficiency-oriented purpose. Nevertheless, these strategies adhere to sufficiency principles, emphasizing factors such as the provision of high-quality products or the enhancement of experiences, diverging from a singular focus on profit maximization.

By engaging with purpose-driven models that align with sufficiency principles, businesses have the potential to become agents of positive change, contributing to a sustainable and flourishing society. In the following, we will elaborate on the individual elements of sufficiency-driven business models and their implications for the organizational structure followed by an evaluation of their relation to a profit- vs. purpose-orientation.

2.2 Value proposition

The value proposition comprises ideas, meanings and understandings of the value created by a business and who the beneficiaries of that value are, namely the customers (Osterwalder/Pigneur 2010). Value is a normative judgement about the benefits of something for someone. Classically, a value in the business context is perceived in economic terms, expressed in money. The notion of value in sufficiency-oriented business models, however, extends beyond mere economic considerations and utility functions, encompassing social and ecological aspects. In general, the value proposition in a business model is a promise by the business that it will offer products and services that enhance its customers' practices, and in our perspective, their ecological and social well-being (Korkman et al. 2010). The value proposition is thus intimately connected to the purpose of the business. The recipients of value include not only those who purchase the product or service but also those who are affected by its externalities, encompassing all stakeholders who experience positive or negative outcomes resulting from the value proposition.

2.3 Governance

A stakeholder-oriented, purpose-based value proposition impacts the governance structure of an organization and can at the same time be enabled or hindered by it. For a sufficiency-orientation, the understanding of governance in business organizations must undergo a profound transformation, moving from a profit-focused approach to one that encompasses the interests of all stakeholders (Aguilera et al. 2021; Naciti et al. 2022; Zaman et al. 2022). This shift in governance is also closely linked to the changing perspective on purpose, which plays a pivotal role in shaping governance structures (Levillain et al. 2019).

Purpose serves as a guiding force for both the value proposition as well as the governance structure of a business. "Mission-controlled governance" is an essential structural element of purpose-driven organizations towards achieving meaningful outcomes beyond profit (Kelly 2012). Aligning the governance structure with purpose fosters a culture of shared values and responsible decision-making. Purpose-driven governance ensures that the organization's strategies and actions are structurally anchored, in line with broader societal needs and not dependent upon the inclinations of individuals (Cardona et al. 2019; Kelly 2012; Levillain/Segrestin 2019; George et al. 2022).

Traditionally, governance in business organizations has revolved around the principle of maximizing shareholder value, placing significant emphasis on the responsibility of directors and executives to act in the best interests of shareholders (Kelly 2012; Ntim 2017). This narrow perspective has primarily centered decision-making on financial metrics and short-term shareholder returns. However, the emergence of social and environmental challenges has prompted a broader understanding of governance that recognizes the importance of considering the interests of all stakeholders (Karpoff 2021).

The shift towards stakeholder-centric governance acknowledges that businesses operate within a broader ecosystem. It emphasizes the inclusion of stakeholders such as employees, customers, communities and the environment, recognizing their significance to organizational success. This evolution has been driven by the realization that sustainable long-term growth necessitates a more holistic approach to governance, one that considers the diverse needs and perspectives of all stakeholders (Mason/Simmons 2014).

Stakeholder inclusion in governance entails providing avenues for their participation and representation in decision-making processes. By engaging stakeholders through mechanisms such as advisory boards, stakeholder forums and collaborative decision-making, organizations foster transparency, trust and accountability. This inclusive approach ensures that the perspectives and interests of all stakeholders are considered alongside financial considerations, leading to more balanced and sustainable outcomes (Fahad/Rahman 2020; Hamad et al. 2020). Such involvement of external stakeholders in governance processes is a key factor for sufficiency-oriented businesses to better understand social and environmental impacts of their operations to work towards mutually beneficial solutions (Karpoff 2021).

Sufficiency-oriented governance also necessitates a re-evaluation of leadership and accountability structures within organizations. Traditional governance models often focus on hierarchical structures and top-down decision-making, which may not align with sufficiency-oriented principles. In sufficiency-oriented businesses, leadership becomes more decentralized and collaborative, fostering shared decision-making and empowering employees at all levels. This inclusive approach ensures that diverse perspectives are considered, leading to more innovative and sustainable solutions (Holmberg/Larsson 2018; Bocken et al. 2022).

Additionally, sufficiency-oriented governance requires a shift in performance metrics and incentive structures. Instead of solely focusing on financial metrics, organizations need to adopt a balanced set of indicators that capture social, environmental and economic dimensions. Key performance indicators should align with the organization's purpose and sustainability goals, providing a holistic view of its impact. Incentive systems can be redesigned to reward behaviors that support sufficiency-oriented values, such as resource efficiency, innovation and stakeholder engagement (Gossen/Kropfeld 2022).

In conclusion, sufficiency-oriented governance represents a paradigm shift in the way organizations approach decision-making, stakeholder engagement and accountability. By moving beyond a shareholder-centric focus and embracing stakeholder inclusion, sufficiency-oriented businesses can align their governance structures with their purpose and values. This transition involves decentralizing leadership, fostering collaboration and re-evaluating performance metrics and incentives.

2.4 Value creation & delivery

As stakeholders become integrated into an organization's governance structure, the fundamental value creation process of sufficiency-oriented business models is closely tied to cultivating a relationship with and educating consumers. Value emerges as businesses and consumers engage in practices and work to enhance them (Korkman et al. 2010). This aligns with Kelly's (2012) concept of redefining the social boundaries of organizations, encompassing not only value creation but also the ownership structure (cf. 2.5) and extending to the establishment of "ethical networks". Building upon the idea of networks, we will further explore the concept of communities engaged in sufficiency practices, elucidating how businesses delineate their boundaries through this form of boundary work.

Customers play an active role in sufficiency-oriented business models. Both customers and business representatives participate in shared practices that negotiate and develop behavior change towards sufficiency (Kropfeld/Reichel 2021). The integration of customers as prosumers, their shift away from mere consumers and the establishment of shared practices blur traditional business boundaries. Consistent with Velter et al.'s (2020) framework for sustainable business model innovation, mutual boundary changes are crucial for achieving sustainable value creation through multi-stakeholder engagement and alignment. Choice editing requires a shared understanding between both parties regarding the envisioned improvements in practices and the respective roles each side plays. An open business model approach promotes value co-creation within shared practices, enabling organizations to effectively address customers' needs and desires and facilitate a transition towards sufficiency-oriented behavior change (Coombes/Nicholson 2013).

It is imperative to educate consumers and involve them in the value creation process. Collaborative innovation, skills transfer to support new and enhanced sufficiency practices and the generation of economic, social and environmental value are essential characteristics of the "Business Model of Enough" (Kropfeld/Reichel 2021). These collaborative principles should be mirrored in the organization's governance structure and manifested in sufficiency-promoting business models, such as consumer education and joint negotiation and awareness-raising of how much consumption is enough, supporting self-sufficiency, life extension or repair services, no-ownership models, or second-hand sales (Niessen/Bocken 2021; Bocken et al. 2022).

2.5 Ownership

Ownership in business organizations is conventionally perceived through a legalistic lens, with a primary focus on shareholders as the proprietors. However, a materialist perspective challenges this narrow conception by acknowledging that all individuals contributing to value creation are "owners", irrespective of their shareholder status (Thomsen/Rose 2004; Baars/Spicer 2017). This implies that collaborative value creation models (cf. 2.4) and stakeholder-oriented governance structures (cf. 2.3) would naturally lean towards placing the ownership of an organization in the hands of the stakeholders, thereby reshaping the "social boundaries" of the organization (Kelly 2012). This would address the "remoteness between ownership and operation", described by Keynes (1933) as the "evil in the relations among men" (ibid: 756).

The legalistic standpoint perceives ownership as a contractual relationship between shareholders and the corporate entity, primarily concerned with financial rights and interests. Shareholders are often regarded as the principal owners, holding decision-making power and entitlement to profits. In contrast, we align with Veldman and Willmott (2017) in differentiating a materialist perspective of the organization from the classical legalist understanding. The materialist perspective acknowledges that ownership extends beyond legal constructs, considering all contributors to value creation – including employees, customers, suppliers and communities – as "owners". This expanded understanding challenges the shareholder-centric notion and emphasizes the need for inclusive ownership structures that recognize the diverse roles and contributions of individuals within the organization (Veldman/Willmott 2017). It also challenges the hierarchical power dynamics traditionally associated with ownership and promotes a more collaborative and participatory approach to decision-making (Biggemann et al. 2014; Javeed/Lefen 2019).

Consequently, ownership is no longer solely rooted in financial investment but also in the active involvement and commitment to the organization's purpose and values by the organization's stakeholders. This shift demands a reassessment of ownership structures and mechanisms that surpass traditional legal contracts. Collaborative ownership models, such as co-operatives, employee ownership, or community ownership, can be explored to empower stakeholders and distribute decision-making power more equitably (Cheney et al. 2014; Kelly 2012). Beyeler and Jaeger-Erben (2022) validate this notion in their study of sufficiency-oriented businesses, where they found that these businesses prefer legal structures such as limited liability companies, family-owned businesses, or non-profit associations, all enabling independence to pursue their purpose rather than shareholder profit.

In conclusion, sufficiency-oriented businesses challenge the traditional understanding of ownership by recognizing the contributions of all stakeholders involved in value creation. This expanded view of ownership calls for inclusive ownership structures and collaborative decision-making processes.

2.6 Value capture

The query of ownership is conventionally tied to its finances and thus value capture models. Value captured refers to the benefit delivered to the organization and, in the case of sustainable organizations, its stakeholders (Yang et al. 2017). Regarding financial ownership, financial statements connect to financial markets, where the feedback loop encourages increasing profits to maintain the organization's value and/or stock price ascent (Kelly 2012). If shareholder profit is not the primary financial goal, and investments are tied to purpose-oriented outcome expectations, alternative value capturing and measuring principles must be applied (Beyeler/Jaeger-Erben 2022). Sustainable organizations will capture not only monetary value but also the value created for the environment and society (Yang et al. 2017).

Sufficiency-oriented business models also capture economic and non-economic value beyond traditional monetary terms or even consciously forgo additional profit resulting from higher market shares, prices, or sales volumes (Bocken/Short 2016). While economic returns are generated, the true benefits of social and ecological value-added often transcend precise monetary measurements. Non-monetary value can be captured through frameworks such as triple-bottom-line accounting, enabling organizations to showcase their holistic impact (Elkington 1998). However, challenges persist in accurately quantifying and valuing non-monetary value (Nesterova 2020). This necessitates a transformation of accounting practices, involving expanding cost accounting beyond financial considerations to encompass social and ecological impact and redefining profit accounting to include the broader value generated by sufficiency-oriented businesses (Dienes et al. 2016; Joshi/Li 2016). While capturing the positive impact, i.e. value created for the environment and society, organizations should also consider accounting for their potential negative impact, possible mitigation strategies and their role within the wider sustainability transition (Bocken et al. 2022).

Despite sales generation and ongoing economic growth appearing to be vital strategies for businesses to survive in the current growth-oriented economy (Khmara/Kronenberg 2018), this creates tensions and potential contradictions for sufficiency-oriented businesses. These businesses attempt to justify such tensions by arguing that their offerings will replace less sustainable ones and help moderate consumption while experimenting with alternative value capture and payment models such as pay-per-use or contracting models (Bocken et al. 2020; Nesterova 2020; Gossen/Heinrich 2021; Gossen/Kropfeld 2022).

2.7 Financing

Closely linked to the allocation of captured value is the financing model of the organization. Financing is a crucial aspect of business operations, influencing the ability to pursue sufficiency-oriented goals. Traditionally, financing options have been limited to internal positive net cash flow, equity financing, or debt financing, which also has implications for the ownership structure of the organization. In sufficiency-oriented businesses with diffused ownership and a focus on making do with less, the conventional financing landscape needs to evolve (Gillan et al. 2021; Kim/Li 2021). Sufficiency-oriented financing aligns with the principles of sufficiency, extended ownership and stakeholder inclusion, embracing alternative sources of financing beyond traditional monetary capital (Breton-Miller/Miller 2016; Salvioni/Gennari 2016).

Sufficiency-oriented businesses prioritize social and ecological value creation and capture, extending beyond the narrow focus on monetary returns. Consequently, the sources of financing for these businesses need to align with sufficiency principles and their broader purpose rather than focusing on monetary profit maximization for investors. In addition to traditional equity and debt financing, sufficiency-oriented businesses can explore alternative sources of financing that support their mission, such as impact investing, crowdfunding, grants and collaborative partnerships (Beyeler/Jaeger-Erben 2022). Involving stakeholders as financiers keeps the control of the organization in the hands of those close to it and is thus directly related to the ownership structure of an organization (Kelly 2012).

Alternative sources of financing can provide not only monetary capital but also expertise, networks and support from like-minded stakeholders who share the organization's values and goals. Impact investors, for instance, are attracted to businesses that generate positive social and environmental impacts alongside financial returns. Crowdfunding platforms offer opportunities for sufficiency-oriented businesses to engage with a community of supporters who resonate with their purpose and are willing to contribute financially (Beyeler/Jaeger-Erben 2022; Laasch 2018).

Sufficiency-oriented businesses must strike a balance between financial viability and their commitment to social and ecological well-being. By aligning financing sources with sufficiency principles and reimagining accounting practices to capture non-monetary value, sufficiency-oriented businesses can effectively account for their business case. This enables them to communicate their impact, attract like-minded investors and supporters and contribute to a more sustainable and inclusive economy.

3. Beyond profit

The ultimate unresolved dilemma facing sufficiency-oriented business models revolves around the extent and way profit can or should be pursued. Strictly interpreted, sufficiency implies relinquishing additional economic profit and renouncing perpetual growth (Khmara/Kronenberg 2018), thereby placing sufficiency-oriented businesses within the postgrowth and degrowth discourse (Nesterova 2020). Thus far, this perspective has not been widely embraced by most businesses, even those inclined towards sufficiency (Bocken et al. 2022). Instead of advocating for consumers to completely abandon consumption, these businesses tend to offer alternative, less resource-intensive options to an expanding customer base (Bocken/Short 2016; Nesterova 2020; Gossen/Kropfeld 2022). Schaltegger et al. support this approach by asserting that "[g]rowth of a sustainable company at the cost of unsustainable companies in a consolidated market (i.e., no market growth) leads to a structural change of the market towards sustainability" (2016: 276). Kelly (2012) distinguishes between a profit-making and profit-maximization orientation, which can be interpreted as a form of profit sufficiency – making just enough profit to sustain a business over the long run. It is evident that for profit sufficiency, a company must comprehend its own cost structure and value capture, forming a feedback loop back to the beginning towards purpose. Sufficiency-oriented businesses may still be profit-making, but, firstly, financial profit is not the sole value captured; secondly, increasing these profits is not the organization's purpose; and thirdly, this profit is often bound to a specific purpose (e.g., in foundation-owned or benefit organizations) or in the hands of its stakeholders (e.g., in cooperatives) rather than narrowly defined shareholders.

Ultimately, businesses aiming to promote sufficiency must embrace the notion of independence from economic growth, adopting an a-growth perspective (Khmara/Kronenberg 2018; Nesterova, 2020; Banerjee et al. 2021). Gebauer (2018) argues that successful non-growing companies distinguish between quantitative growth (material accumulation and expansion) and qualitative growth (adding ecological and social value through their solutions). The qualitative growth dimension could be measured in terms of impact scales and sufficiency-based metrics such as the lifespan of products, waste avoided, repair rates, etc. (Bocken et al. 2022). To date, businesses have primarily implemented efficiency or consistency strategies and metrics without questioning the increasing quantity of production (Heikkurinen et al. 2019). However, such a decrease in production and consumption is necessary to reach a sustainable level that, in the spirit of a steady-state economy (Daly 1991), can be maintained in the long run (Khmara/Kronenberg 2018). It implies a de-emphasis on profit maximization and a focus on benefiting the community and community ownership (Johanisova et al. 2013).

Figure 2: From Profit to Purpose for Sufficiency-based Organizations.

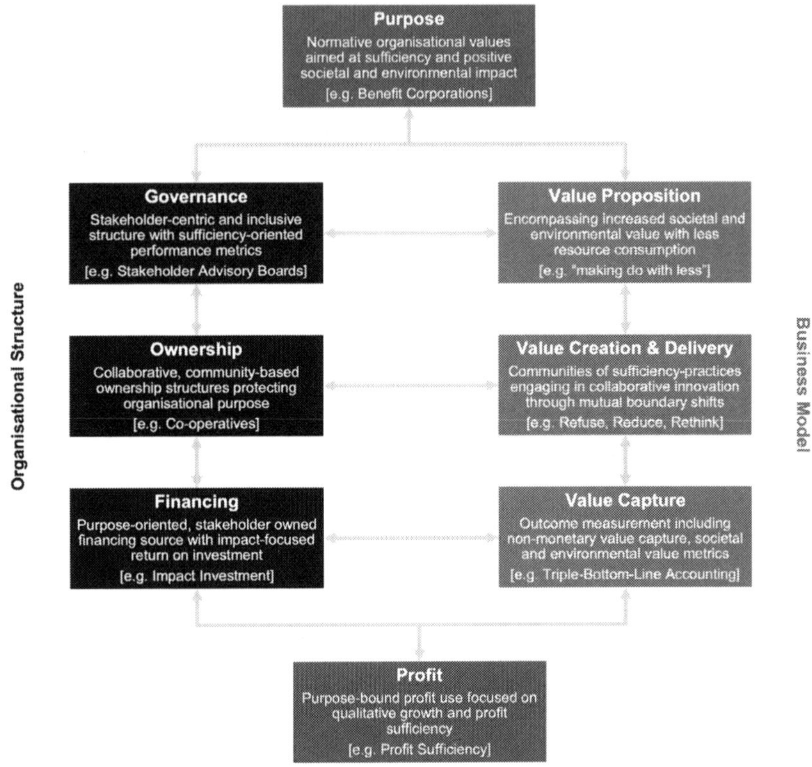

4. Conclusion

The consequences of adopting a sufficiency orientation for an organization's structure and business model, as discussed earlier, suggest that the future of sufficiency-oriented organizations lies in purpose-driven strategies prioritizing sustainability, stakeholder inclusion and responsible resource management (see Figure 2). By incorporating sufficiency-oriented principles into governance, ownership, financing and accounting, organizations can navigate the complexities of the modern world while contributing to societal well-being and ecological balance. Effective sufficiency strategies, such as "refuse" strategies (Bocken et al. 2022), hinge on the entire business model and organizational structure aligning with this purpose. Illustrative examples of such organizations include eco-communities, cooperatives, non-profit organizations, or benefit corporations (Banerjee et al. 2021; Khmara/Kronenberg 2018; Kelly 2012; Nesterova 2020; Trainer 2020; Veleva 2021). These approaches are consistent with Kelly's (2012) concept of "Ethical Networks", characterized as communities of sufficiency practices (Kropfeld/Reichel 2021). This concept underscores boundary-spanning activities and stakeholder integration in all aspects of an organization, including business collaborations, supplier relations, customer collaborations, or research collaborations (Bocken et al. 2022).

The transition towards strongly sufficiency-oriented organizations requires a commitment to continuous learning, collaboration and the pursuit of shared values by organizations. They must establish networks and foster active collaboration across their organization's boundaries, enhancing stakeholder integration and broadening the scope of value capture principles. This commitment should also be evident in the education and roles of entrepreneurs, as well as in sustainability reporting mechanisms, to enhance transparency about the organization's activities. From a policy perspective, alternative legal structures for organizations, such as benefit corporations or companies with tied assets (Stiftung Verantwortungseigentum e.V. [SEV] 2023), are necessary to embed the idea of purpose-led organizations in a legal framework.

However, it is crucial to understand that sufficiency is not merely an additional sustainability strategy but rather constitutes a normative core around which purpose can be built, providing the organization with direction and a clear mission. Only then can our perspective on the relationship between the business model and organizational structure evolve, and only then can we shift our perceptions of profit from maximization or even profit-making towards the natural conclusion of achieving the purpose of a sufficiency-driven business: making do with less.

References

Aguilera, Ruth V./Aragón-Correa, J. Alberto/Marano, Valentina/Tashman, Peter A. (2021): "The Corporate Governance of Environmental Sustainability: A Review and Proposal for More Integrated Research." In: Journal of Management 47/6, pp. 1468–1497. https://doi.org/10.1177/0149206321991212.

Baars, Grietje/Spicer, Andre (eds.). (2017): The corporation: A critical, multi-disciplinary handbook, Cambridge: Cambridge University Press.

Banerjee, Subhabrata Bobby/Jermier, John M./Peredo, Ana Maria/Perey, Robert/Reichel, André (2021): "Theoretical perspectives on organizations and organizing in a post-growth era." In: Organization 28/3, pp. 337–357. https://doi.org/10.1177/1350508420973629.

Beyeler, Laura/Jaeger-Erben, Melanie (2022): "How to make more of less: Characteristics of sufficiency in business practices." In: Frontiers in Sustainability 3. https://doi.org/10.3389/frsus.2022.949710.

Biggemann, S., Williams, M., & Kro, G. (2014). Building in sustainability, social responsibility and value co-creation. Journal of Business & Industrial Marketing, 29(4), 304–312. https://www.emerald.com/insight/content/doi/10.1108/JBIM-08-2013-0161/full/html.

Bocken, Nancy M. P./Morales, Lisa Smeke/Lehner, Matthias (2020): "Sufficiency Business Strategies in the Food Industry – The Case of Oatly." In: Sustainability 12/3, 824. https://doi.org/10.3390/su12030824.

Bocken, Nancy. M. P./Niessen, Laura/Short, Samuel William (2022): "The Sufficiency-based Circular Economy – An Analysis of 150 Companies." In: Frontiers in Sustainability 3, 899289. https://doi.org/10.3389/frsus.2022.899289.

Bocken, Nancy M. P./Short, Samuel William (2016): "Towards a sufficiency-driven business model: Experiences and opportunities." In: Environmental Innovation and Societal Transitions 18/3, pp. 41–61. https://doi.org/10.1016/j.eist.2015.07.010.

Cardona, Pablo/Rey, Carlos/Craig, Nick (2019): "Purpose-driven Leadership." In Carlos Rey, Miquel Bastons/Phil Sotok (eds.), Purpose-driven Organizations, Cham: Palgrave Macmillan, pp. 57–71. https://doi.org/10.1007/978-3-030-17674-7_5.

Cheney, George/Santa Cruz, Iñaki/Peredo, Ana Maria/Nazareno, Elías (2014): "Worker cooperatives as an organizational alternative: Challenges, achievements and promise in business governance and ownership." In: Organization 21/5, pp. 591–603. https://doi.org/10.1177/1350508414539784.

Coombes, Philip H./Nicholson, John D. (2013): "Business models and their relationship with marketing: A systematic literature review." In: Industrial Marketing Management 42/5, pp. 656–664. https://doi.org/10.1016/j.indmarman.2013.05.005.

Dienes, Dominik/Sassen, Remmer/Fischer, Jasmin (2016): "What are the drivers of sustainability reporting? A systematic review." In: Sustainability Accounting, Management and Policy Journal 7/2, pp. 154–189. https://doi.org/10.1108/SAMPJ-08-2014-0050.

Elkington, John (1998): "Accounting for the Triple Bottom line." In: Measuring Business Excellence 2/3, pp. 18–22. https://doi.org/10.1108/eb025539.

Fahad, P./Rahman, P. Mubarak (2020): "Impact of corporate governance on CSR disclosure." In: International Journal of Disclosure and Governance 17/2–3, pp. 155–167. https://doi.org/10.1057/s41310-020-00082-1.

George, Gerard/Haas, Martine/Joshi, Havovi/McGahan, Anita/Tracey, Paul (2022): Handbook on the Business of Sustainability: The Organization, Implementation, and Practice of Sustainable Growth. London: Edward Elgar. http://dx.doi.org/10.4337/9781839105340.

Gillan, Stuart. L./Koch, Andrew/Starks, Laura T. (2021): "Firms and social responsibility: A review of ESG and CSR research in corporate finance." In: Journal of Corporate Finance 66, 101889. https://doi.org/10.1016/j.jcorpfin.2021.101889.

Gossen, Maike/Kropfeld, Maren Ingrid (2022): "“Choose Nature. Buy Less.” Exploring Sufficiency-oriented Marketing and Consumption Practices in the Outdoor Industry." In: Sustainable Production and Consumption 30, pp. 720–736. https://doi.org/10.1016/j.spc.2022.01.005.

Gossen, Maike/Schrader, Ulf (2018): "Welche Potenziale die Digitalisierung für ein suffizienzförderndes Marketing bringt." In: Ökologisches Wirtschaften 1/33, pp. 8–9. https://doi.org/10.14512/oew330108.

Hamad, Salaheldin/Draz, Muhammad Umar/Lai, Fong-Woon (2020): The Impact of Corporate Governance and Sustainability Reporting on Integrated Reporting: A Conceptual Framework. In: SAGE Open 10/2, 215824402092743. https://doi.org/10.1177/2158244020927431.

Heikkurinen, Pasi/Young, C. William/Morgan, Elizabeth (2019): "Business for sustainable change: Extending eco-efficiency and eco-sufficiency strategies to consumers." In: Journal of Cleaner Production 218, pp. 656–664. https://doi.org/10.1016/j.jclepro.2019.02.053

Hollensbe, Elaine/Wookey, Charles/Hickey, Loughlin/George, Gerard/Nichols, Cardinal Vincent (2014): "Organizations with Purpose." In: Academy of Management Journal 57/5, pp. 1227–1234. https://doi.org/10.5465/amj.2014.4005.

Holmberg, John/Larsson, Johan (2018): "A Sustainability Lighthouse – Supporting Transition Leadership and Conversations on Desirable Futures." In: Sustainability 10/11, 3842. https://doi.org/10.3390/su10113842.

IPCC [Hans-Otto Pörtner, Debra C. Roberts, Melinda Tignor, Elvira Poloczanska, Katja Mintenbeck, Andrés Alegría, Marlies Craig, Stefanie Langsdorf, Sina Löschke, Vincent Möller, Andrew Okem, Bardhyl Rama (eds.)] (2022): "Climate Change 2022: Impacts, Adaptation and Vulnerability. Contribution of Working Group II to the Sixth Assessment Report of the Intergovernmental Panel on Climate Change," Cambridge, New York: Cambridge University Press, 3056. https://doi.org/10.1017/9781009325844.

Javeed, Sohail Ahmad/Lefen, Lin (2019): "An Analysis of Corporate Social Responsibility and Firm Performance with Moderating Effects of CEO Power and Ownership Structure: A Case Study of the Manufacturing Sector of Pakistan." In: Sustainability 11/1, 248. https://doi.org/10.3390/su11010248.

Johanisova, Nadia/Crabtree, Tim/Fraňková, Eva (2013): "Social enterprises and non-market capitals: a path to degrowth?" In: Journal of Cleaner Production 38, pp. 7–16. https://doi.org/10.1016/j.jclepro.2012.01.004.

Joshi, Satish/Li, Yue (2016): "What Is Corporate Sustainability and How Do Firms Practice It? A Management Accounting Research Perspective." In: Journal of Management Accounting Research, 28/2, pp. 1–11. https://doi.org/10.2308/jmar-10496.

Karpoff, Jonathan M. (2021): "On a stakeholder model of corporate governance." In: Financial Management, 50/2, pp. 321–343. https://doi.org/10.1111/fima.12344.

Kelly, Marjorie (2012): Owning Our Future. The Emerging Ownership Revolution, San Francisco: Berrett-Koehler Publishers.

Keynes, John Maynard (1933): "National Self-Sufficiency." In: The Yale Review 22/4, pp. 755–69, 6.12.2023 (http://gesd.free.fr/knat33.pdf).

Khmara, Yaryna/Kronenberg, Jakub (2018): "Degrowth in business: An oxymoron or a viable business model for sustainability?" In: Journal of Cleaner Production 177, pp. 721–731. https://doi.org/10.1016/j.jclepro.2017.12.182.

Kim, Sang/Li, Zhichuan Frank (2021): "Understanding the Impact of ESG Practices in Corporate Finance." In: Sustainability 13/7, 3746. https://doi.org/10.3390/su13073746.

Korkman, Oskar/Storbacka, Kaj/Harald, Bo (2010): "Practices as markets: Value co-creation in e-invoicing." In: Australasian Marketing Journal 18/4, pp. 236–247. https://doi.org/10.1016/j.ausmj.2010.07.006.

Kropfeld, Maren Ingrid/Reichel, André (2021): "Das Geschäftsmodell des Genug. In: Ökologisches Wirtschaften – Fachzeitschrift 36/3, pp. 30–34. https://doi.org/10.14512/OEW360330.

Kropfeld, Maren Ingrid/Reichel, André (2021): "The Business Model of Enough: Value Creation for Sufficiency-Oriented Businesses." In: Annabeth Aagaard/Florian Lüdeke-Freund/Peter Wells (eds.), Business Models for Sustainability Transitions, Cham: Palgrave Macmillan, pp. 163–189. https://doi.org/10.1007/978-3-030-77580-3_6.

Laasch, Oliver (2018): "Beyond the purely commercial business model: Organizational value logics and the heterogeneity of sustainability business models." In: Long Range Planning 51/1, pp. 158–183. https://doi.org/10.1016/j.lrp.2017.09.002.

Levillain, Kevin/Brakman Reiser, Dana/Segrestin, Blanche/Stahl, Günter K./Voegtlin, Christian (2019): "The Purpose Driven Corporate Forms: Tackling Grand Societal Challenges with Innovations in Governance and Corporate Responsibility." In: Valuation Studies 6/1, pp. 87–93.

Levillain, Kevin/Segrestin, Blanche (2019): "From primacy to purpose commitment: How emerging profit-with-purpose corporations open new corporate governance avenues." In: European Management Journal 37/5, pp. 637–647. https://doi.org/10.1016/j.emj.2019.07.002.

Mason, Chris/Simmons, John (2014): "Embedding Corporate Social Responsibility in Corporate Governance: A Stakegolder Systems Approach." In: Journal of Business Ethics 119, pp. 77–8. https://doi.org/10.1007/s10551-012-1615-9.

Naciti, Valeria/Cesaroni, Fabrizio/Pulejo, Luisa (2022): "Corporate governance and sustainability: a review of the existing literature." In: Journal of Management and Governance 26/1, pp. 55–74. https://doi.org/10.1007/s10997-020-09554-6.

Nesterova, Iana (2020): "Degrowth business framework: Implications for sustainable development." In: Journal of Cleaner Production 262, 121382. https://doi.org/10.1016/j.jclepro.2020.121382.

Ntim, Collins. G./Soobaroyen, Teerooven/Broad, Martin J. (2017): "Governance structures, voluntary disclosures and public accountability." In: Accounting, Auditing & Accountability Journal 30/1, pp. 65–118. https://doi.org/10.1108/AAAJ-10-2014-1842.

Osterwalder, Alexander/Pigneur, Yves (2010): Business model generation: A handbook for visionaries, game changers, and challengers, Hoboken: John Wiley & Sons.

Profijt, Markus (2018): "Mobilitätssuffizienz als Lösungsbeitrag zur Treibhausgasreduktion." In: Ökologisches Wirtschaften 3/3, pp. 35–39. https://doi.org/10.14512/OEW330335

Reichel, André (2013): "Das Geschäftsmodell des Weniger." In: Politische Ökologie 135, pp. 92–98.

Salvioni, Daniela/Gennari, Francesca (2016): "Corporate governance, ownership and sustainability." In: Corporate Ownership & Control 13/2, pp. 606–614. https://ssrn.com/abstract=2754493.

Schaltegger, Stefan/Lüdeke-Freund, Floria/Hansen, Erik G. (2016): "Business Models for Sustainability: A Co-Evolutionary Analysis of Sustainable Entrepreneurship, Innovation, and Transformation." In: Organization & Environment 29/3, pp. 264–289. https://doi.org/10.1177/1086026616633272.

Stiftung Verantwortungseigentum e.V. [SEV] (2023): "Verantwortungseigentum," 20.11.2023 (https://stiftung-verantwortungseigentum.de/verantwortungseigentum).

Thomsen, Steen/Rose, Caspar (2004): "Foundation Ownership and Financial Performance: Do Companies Need Owners?" In: European Journal of Law and Economics 18, pp. 343–364.

Trainer, Ted (2020): "De-growth: Some suggestions from the Simpler Way perspective." In: Ecological Economics 167, 106436. https://doi.org/10.1016/j.ecolecon.2019.106436.

Veldman, Jeroen/Willmott, Hugh (2017): "Social ontology and the modern corporation." Cambridge Journal of Economics 41/5, pp. 1489–1504. https://doi.org/10.1093/cje/bex043.

Veleva, Vesela (2021): "The role of entrepreneurs in advancing sustainable lifestyles: Challenges, impacts, and future opportunities." In: Journal of Cleaner Production 283, 124658. https://doi.org/10.1016/j.jclepro.2020.124658.

Velter, Myrthe G. E./Bitzer, Verena/Bocken, Nancy M. P./Kemp, Rene (2020): "Sustainable business model innovation: The role of boundary work for multi-stakeholder alignment." In: Journal of Cleaner Production 247, 119497. https://doi.org/10.1016/j.jclepro.2019.119497.

Weick, Karl E. (1995): Sensemaking in Organizations, Thousand Oaks: Sage Publications.

Wieland, Josef (2017): "Relationale Führung und intersektorale Governance." In: Maren Lehmann/Marcel Tyrell (eds.), Komplexe Freiheit, Wiesbaden: Springer Fachmedien, pp. 237–257. https://doi.org/10.1007/978-3-658-14969-7_11.

Yang, Miying/Vladimirova, Doroteya/Evans, Steve (2017): "Creating and Capturing Value Through Sustainability." In: Research-Technology Management 60/3, pp. 30–39, https://doi.org/10.1080/08956308.2017.1301001.

Zaman, Rashid/Jain, Tanusree/Samara, Georges/Jamali, Dima (2022): "Corporate Governance Meets Corporate Social Responsibility: Mapping the Interface." In: Business & Society 61/3, pp. 690–752. https://doi.org/10.1177/0007650320973415.

Depths of Sufficiency in Business

Diving Through the Planes of Social Being

Iana Nesterova and Hubert Buch-Hansen

Abstract *This chapter uses Roy Bhaskar's four planes of social being to contemplate what sufficiency in business should entail on each of them for transformations to be serious and holistic. Implementing sufficiency needs to be deep and processual. It is a function not only of business but of society in general.*

1. Introduction

Bringing about a genuinely sustainable society necessitates societal transformations. Contemplating and addressing such transformations seriously requires a holistic approach. A holistic approach would at once capture various domains of social reality, from our societies' material and energy exchanges with nature to the intimate level of our inner being through which we relate with the human and non-human world around us. Focusing on aspects solely in one domain does not suffice. On their own, small-scale individual actions, personal transformations, or policies directed at selected phenomena in society (e.g., education or production) will not result in a genuine sustainable change. Fortunately, one does not have to choose between various domains. It is possible to take into consideration all of them at the same time. One way in which different levels of social reality can be identified and seen together holistically is through the lens of Roy Bhaskar's social ontology (theory of social being). Elsewhere, we have argued for this social ontology to be useful for understanding transformations towards a genuinely sustainable society (Buch-Hansen et al. 2024; Buch-Hansen/Nesterova 2021; Buch-Hansen/Nesterova 2023).

Roy Bhaskar, the founder of critical realist philosophy of science, was deeply concerned with human emancipation (Bhaskar 2009), as well as with ecological degradation (Bhaskar et al. 2010). According to Bhaskar, social being simultaneously exists and unfolds on four interconnected planes. These planes are (1) material transactions with nature, (2) social interactions between people, (3) social structure, and (4) intrasubjectivity or simply inner being (Bhaskar 2008). This ontology implies that social being is complex, relational and multi-layered. The four planes encompass both the material and the immaterial or spiritual aspects of being, incorporating everything from the depths of individual human's psyche to humans' material interactions with nature. Thus, we can think of this social ontology as deep. Social transformations towards a genuinely sustainable society, which take into considerations this depth, can be called deep transformations (Buch-Hansen et al. 2024).

This conception of social being is useful for reflecting on, and proposing change in, various domains of social existence. It encourages one to remember that when zooming in on any phenomenon, event, or social entity, it is essential not to lose sight of how this phenomenon, event or social entity exists on, unfolds on, affects and is influenced by different levels of social being.

In this chapter, we zoom in on a particular social entity, a business, and view it through the lens of Bhaskar's social ontology. Rather than describing how business in general exists and changes on each of the planes of social being as a social entity, we will focus on the sufficiency aspect of business. Doing so allows us to honor and dive deeper into sufficiency through the four planes of social being. Multiple recent works have called for a careful consideration of sufficiency in relation to business and its practices (Bocken/Short 2016; Nesterova 2020a; Niessen/Bocken 2021; Jungell-Michelsson/Heikkurinen 2022; Beyeler/Jaeger-Erben 2022; Nesterova/Jungell-Michelsson 2023). Sufficiency is argued to be at the core of genuine sustainability and an essential part of the constellation of sustainable business practices (Nesterova 2020a; Robra et al. 2020). As a principle, it proposes a constructive alternative both to harsh and depriving asceticism and unrestrained materialistic growth. In relation to sustainability, sufficiency is understood as "'enoughness' of human doings in relation to ecosystems – an end in itself and a means for sustainable consumption and production" (Jungell-Michelsson/Heikkurinen 2022: 6). Sufficiency has a positive connotation. It creates a space for exploration of non-materialistic pursuits and growth in situations where materialistic growth is unsustainable and undesirable (Buch-Hansen/Nesterova 2023). We contribute to the recent efforts of sufficiency scholars by bringing critical realist philosophy of science and ontological considerations into the conversation. Importantly, we deviate from assuming that a business can be either sufficient or not sufficient (Jungell-Michelsson/Nesterova, this volume; Nesterova et al. 2023). Rather, sufficiency manifests itself in businesses in different parts of their operations, and its manifestation may not be consistent over time (Nesterova/Jungell-Michelsson 2023).

2. Depth ontology and sufficiency in business

2.1 Material transactions with nature

The plane of material transactions with nature concerns humanity's exchanges with nature in terms of both matter and energy. It concerns, for instance, the resources humans use to sustain life and their economic activities, the waste resulting from these activities, which goes back into nature, and carbon emissions. For a genuinely sustainable society to come about, humanity's material transactions with nature need to improve drastically on the global scale. In this context, sufficiency needs to manifest in the form of producing mostly for genuine human needs rather than wants (Buch-Hansen et al. 2024). This is challenging to translate directly into individual business practice, not least since the boundary between needs and wants is often blurred. For instance, a business can produce food (in principle, a human need), which satisfies a desire (e.g., game meat or chocolate, see Nesterova/Jungell-Michelsson 2023), or is an important part of culture, tradition, or a ritual. Outlining precisely what constitutes genuine human needs and then tightly controlling production for genuine needs would require bureaucratic if not authoritarian overseeing. Such an approach is not one we advocate. However, businesspersons can still contemplate production for genuine and diverse needs, first and foremost by choosing to operate in the sectors of the economy that aim at satisfaction of needs (food, shelter, energy, education, transport, medicine) rather than hedonic wants.

A business can implement sufficiency not only by operating within a sector that aims to satisfy human needs but also by limiting the variety of products it produces. This allows it to focus on quality, durability and knowledge of the individual product and its components, the aftercare and receiving feedback from consumers, allowing the business to improve its product.

Sufficiency can also be manifested in considerations of the local nature and its resources, i.e., seeing the location as sufficient and developing responsibility towards the place which houses the business. Sufficiency of location (Nesterova/Jungell-Michelsson 2023) relates closely to the call for localization within the sustainability discourse (Trainer 2012) and the call for an increased sensitivity towards local nature and places (Nesterova 2022a, 2022b, 2023). In this context, it is important to acknowledge that in many (if not all) instances, localization still entails long supply chains.

Sufficiency manifests in production processes and in handling of materials and energy by producers and service providers. In the situation of unfolding ecological degradation, such processes are something businesses are often expected to engage in, in a more ecological manner so as to play their role in sustainability transformations. However, it may be that a more sustainable implementation of sufficiency practices results from deeper, underlying principles. That is, for businesses to implement sufficiency practices in terms of their material transactions with nature some guiding principles beyond sufficiency itself may be necessary. Elsewhere, we propose that gentleness and care may constitute such principles (Buch-Hansen 2021; Buch-Hansen/Nesterova 2023). These principles can become part of reflection and a constellation of principles and values which shape a gentler way of being in the world, including the practices we manifest in business. Other principles and values in such a constellation may include human scale and simplicity (Schumacher 1973), non-violence (Naess 1989), awe (Schneider 2015), wildness (Leopold 1949) and perhaps especially the unity between an individual human being (and thus their actions) and the rest of the world (Steiner 2011).

2.2 Social interactions between people

It is a condition of human existence that humans are in the world with other humans (Heidegger 2001; Steiner 2011) and thus engage in social interactions. Considerations such as what to produce and how, how to use resources sufficiently and how to take the location into account require collaboration. A business is a community of humans who may choose to implement sufficiency into business operations, naturally within the constraints imposed by the social structures within which the business is embedded. Essentially, it is via social interactions that sufficiency gets a chance to manifest itself in business. Apart from ongoing dialogues on implementation of sufficiency in business operations concerning material transactions with nature, the principle of sufficiency can be applied to social interactions within the internal social dynamic of the business. For instance, our own interactions, as researchers, with businesses in Sweden reveal that some businesspersons apply the sufficiency principle to the number of meetings, aiming for it to be lagom ("just right" in Swedish) rather than too many or too few. Too many meetings could indicate micromanaging and a lack of freedom, while too few create a sense of loneliness and indifference. The same principle of "just right" applies to the duration of meetings. Contemplating what is just right allows businesses to create an organizational culture where sufficiency is explored.

Interactions between people also occur outside the internal world of businesses. They occur between businesses and their customers, local communities, municipalities, universities and activists. Sufficiency will not become a genuine and sustainable feature of societies if only one group of humans is willing to engage with it. Participation of civil society, businesspersons and humans working for state apparatuses is necessary (Buch-Hansen et al. 2024). It is necessary to create spaces where different groups of people can come together and explore opportunities to implement sufficiency as a principle in their own organizations. Importantly, in such spaces imperfection of the practice of sufficiency needs to be celebrated rather than seen as a failure. A meaningful benchmark for sufficiency (e.g., what sufficient production may be, what is the right number of employees or the perfect company size) hardly exists in practice. That is, while it is possible to theorize such benchmarks, the practice of business itself is always imperfect and processual. Critical realism emphasizes the need to bring together theory and practice (Hartwig 2007). Further to this, any theory of limits should be put in (empathetic) dialogue with the unfolding of the lives of real businesses.

Communicating with customers to figure out what is sufficient is necessary. Above we noted that production for needs is important to take good care of nature's resources and to honor nature's limits. What constitutes needs can be understood via a dialogue between businesses and customers. Naturally, for sufficiency in business to be a sustainable practice, customers should likewise have embarked on sustainability journeys, and businesses can help customers embark on such journeys. Working with activists (e.g., climate activists, zero waste and voluntary simplicity practitioners) who already find themselves on sustainability journeys can help sufficiency-orientated businesspersons understand more sustainable modes of being and patterns of consumption, and what products can support sufficiency efforts of consumers. Working with activists entails inter-personal interactions. Small-scale, local businesses are perhaps best positioned to engage in such interactions. Moreover, conversations about sufficiency may start at various events organized by local municipalities and universities.

2.3 Social structures

On the plane of social structures, businesses as organizations can work together with other organizations to collectively transform the current system of 'the more, the better' towards one where sufficiency becomes desirable and a value in itself. One group of actors with whom businesses can work together, for instance, are higher education institutions. The system of education plays an important role in challenging the dominant (capitalist and unsustainable) logics and creating spaces for new imaginaries (Kaufmann et al. 2019). In business schools, it is often the case that growth in business, rather than sufficiency, is highlighted as a crucial goal. This is done without bringing into focus the severe downsides which come with the pursuit of growth, such as the involvement of investors (venture capitalists, angel investors, banks, see Parker 2018) who may and do impose their own desires and pursuits for profit onto the businesspersons, thus alienating them from their initial idea, conception, or plan of how to develop their business. In other words, the business is no longer theirs. At the same time, businesses that have sufficiency at the heart of their operations are overlooked or may even be seen or presented as unsuccessful and compared in an unfavorable manner to businesses which pursue growth. However, for genuine sustainability, a new approach to the study of business is needed (Nesterova 2021). This implies a different definition of success and acknowledgement of diverse ways of doing business. In the practice of education, learning about businesses to which sufficiency is central may imply including post-growth business literature in curricula, facilitating exchange between sufficiency businesses, students and educators, listening to the stories of relevant start-ups and providing opportunities for students to do their internships in businesses orientated towards sufficiency.

2.4 Inner being

We pay particular attention to the plane of humans' inner being since this is a plane which has often been overlooked in the business sustainability discourse (Buch-Hansen/Nesterova 2023). For sufficiency to be desirable and possible, a significant shift in humans' worldviews, modes of being and ways of relating with the world is necessary. And while implementing sufficiency in business cannot be reduced to any one plane of social being, the plane of inner being has a causal effect on the unfolding of sufficiency-orientated pursuits on the other planes of being. This is so because it is human beings who practice: only humans can act (Danermark et al. 2002).

To suggest that humans have a desire and potential to transform their businesses towards genuinely sustainable models necessitates a certain (positive) view of human nature. Further to this, we rely on the humanistic tradition, which highlights humanity, humanness and the potential of our species (Moss 2015). This tradition focuses on human qualities and abilities, such as creativity, love, fellow-feeling, freedom, growth, concern, care, kindness, awe, consciousness, awareness, self-transcendence and self-actualization. And while it is impossible to claim that human nature is indeed inherently good (it is easy to find examples of the contrary), the humanistic tradition points out that presenting humans in either a pathological or a mechanistic manner, as done respectively by psychoanalysis and behaviorism, entails "the risk of harming humans by inviting them to lower their expectations of what is humanly possible" (Moss 2015: 4). This view also finds resonance in the field of moral philosophy: while humans are indeed animals with instincts and bodily needs, we also have natural capacities for gentleness, care, solidarity, compassion and love, and these attitudes and feelings affect our decision-making and our being in the world in general (Midgeley 2003; Sayer 2011). Moreover, the "way in which we think of ourselves – the picture we form of our essential nature – directly affects the way we live" (Midgley 2003: xvi). Here, we assume that businesspersons themselves are essentially human and thus good (but not perfect) and have a potential to develop their human qualities even further, which opposes Perlman's assumption that businesspersons are beings "whose living humanity has been thoroughly excavated" (Perlman 1983: 31). We also suggest that humanness and growth therein is likewise manifested in society at large. This is significant inasmuch as sufficiency requires participation of society in general, not only of businesspersons.

First and foremost, stepping on the path of sufficiency requires assigning a positive value to it, rather than seeing it as a sacrifice. This means stepping away from materialistic pursuits and instead valuing, anticipating and pursuing growth in creativity, love, fellow-feeling, empathy and other human qualities. Elsewhere (Buch-Hansen et al. 2024), we adopt Erich Fromm's (2013) terminology to highlight the distinction between materialistic and non-materialistic pursuits. Fromm (2013) distinguishes between two modes: of having and of being. The mode of having signifies attachment to material goods and status, possessiveness and ownership of goods and humans. The mode of being signifies the opposite: non-attachment to the material and exploration of one's own humanity. Critical realism, which provides philosophical grounds for our work, sees the mode of being as essentially human, i.e., in line with our nature. For instance, Hartwig (2001: 140–141), relying on Roy Bhaskar's theorizing of humans, notes that humans are "both essentially one or united as a species and with the rest of the pluriverse; essentially creative; oriented to being, not having or 'attachment'; enlightened, not ignorant; disposed to engage in 'spontaneous right action'; and, above all, free." Essentially, the mode of being needs to prevail for sufficiency to become an important part of humans' set of values and a desirable practice. It is often the case that the businesspersons who implement sufficiency practices into their business models also incorporate sufficiency, one way or another, in their personal lives via practicing, e.g., mindfulness, spirituality, a minimalist lifestyle and voluntary simplicity (cf. Elgin 2013; Elgin/Mitchell 1977; Schmid/Nesterova 2023). Such personal practices can, and in practice appear to, spill over into the way business as an entity relates with the world/acts therein. In our own conversations with businesspersons, we often notice how the implementation of sufficiency by businesspersons is a result of their own willingness to do so rather than an imposition from the world around them. Indeed, the (capitalist) system typically incentivizes growth rather than sufficiency. Values adopted freely by businesspersons may be the most sustainable or life-long ones, finding their way into businesses and their operations.

Hence, sufficiency needs to become an inherent and valued part of a worldview and morality of individuals, arrived at via their personal development journeys and implemented, in the words of Steiner (2011: 138), "out of love" rather than out of a sense of duty or even worse, fear of authorities. Yet, various social systems can support (as well as discourage or constrain) such journeys of personal development and self-transformation, and this is what we turn to next.

3. Systemic constraints and policies

It would have been a welcomed unfolding in the social reality if implementing sufficiency in business was simply a matter of knowledge about various practices of sufficiency and having one's heart in the right place. However, in reality, implementing sufficiency on each of the four planes is immensely challenging. This is so because implementation is always constrained by the conditions of the capitalist system, to which sufficiency is alien and detestable, and the fact of humans' thrownness into the world with its existing and sustained structures and systems (Heidegger 2001). That is to say that the capitalist system pre-exists businesspersons and their businesses rather than being something of their own choosing and creation. Due to its pre-existing the businesspersons, they are forced to face the ways the system operates while often having little say (but not no say) in how the system works.

Running a business to which sufficiency is central may sound like a good idea not only to sustainability scholars but also to businesspersons. However, despite its appeal, many may find themselves in situations where the pursuit of growth is imposed due to the way financing works. Self-funding or financing a business with the help of friends and family (though not without its own challenges) is a privileged situation, which is not accessible to many. For those who cannot self-fund or acquire the necessary funding via friends and family, or where the business idea necessitates large amounts of funding, looking for other options becomes necessary (Nesterova 2020b). Other options include, for instance, banks, venture capitalists and angel investors (Parker 2018). Yet, as indicated above, such financing means giving up a share of the business and its profits as well as alienation of the businesspersons from their business due to the involvement of other actors. These actors may not share the same ideas about sufficiency and sustainability, thus imposing their own logics of, e.g., growth and profit seeking. Such constraints to sufficiency are thus structural rather than individual. Borrowing and external financing may be seen as a compromise by a businessperson: they get an opportunity to pursue their business idea while giving up a share and opening up their project to external influences. Thus, it is not necessarily so that the businessperson her/himself is a greedy and egocentric profit-maximiser as neoclassical economics suggests. Rather, they are constrained by the system in multiple ways: this concerns financing as well as fear of stepping on a path different to the norm.

To help businesses engage more seriously with sufficiency as a principleacross all the four planes, it is necessary to create spaces and conditions in which such engagements can thrive. We propose a range of policies to actualize sufficiency in business on all the four planes. Though we relate various policies to each of the four planes, it is important to note that each policy is likely to have effects beyond any one plane and that creating space for sufficiency requires implementation of multiple policies (Buch-Hansen et al. 2024). On the plane of material transactions with nature, governments can create better legislation for instituting exchange of waste between businesses. What constitutes waste for one business is a resource for another. Missing out on the opportunity to use waste as a resource may force businesses to extract more from nature than would otherwise have been necessary. Some businesses note a lack of clarity in terms of dealing with waste infrastructure and a lack of organization of exchange events (Nesterova 2020b). On the plane of social interactions, working time reduction (Spencer 2022) can free up time for businesspersons to engage with other humans such as activists, local communities and researchers – engagements that can result in contemplations of ways in which sufficiency has been and can be implemented. Many policies can and should target the plane of social structure since the change towards sustainability undoubtedly needs to be structural. Here, instituting increased participation is important, so as to ensure that businesspersonshave an opportunity to have a say on the matters which can assist them in practicing sufficiency in business – such as financing, law-making and infrastructure. Universal basic income (UBI) can remove some of the financial worries which businesspersons have in terms of providing for themselves and their families. This can create space for operating business more mindfully via contemplating the principles and philosophy of business (including sufficiency). Moreover, businesses to which sufficiency in its different forms is central are often manifestations of creative efforts by the businesspersons (Nesterova 2020b). Oftentimes, such businesses grow out of a hobby or a passion, a concern about the world or a particular group of people, non-humans, or nature. Starting such a business is a challenging enterprise, both mentally and financially. Free time is needed for humans to contemplate whether starting such a business is a good idea, and if so, how this idea can materialize. A UBI can assist in taking a break from normal commitments to allow space for contemplation. For existing businesses, avoiding venture capitalists, angel investors and banks can help them step on the path of sufficiency rather than growth and profit maximization. Low or no-interest financing can be instituted by governments.

On the plane of inner being, education is important. An education reform would include reconsideration of how microeconomics is taught and what is meant by success. Wider inclusion of sufficiency in business should no longer be a personal choice of individual lecturers but a compulsory part of university curricula. Microeconomics is often taught in combination with other fields of knowledge such as marketing and finance, which serve the interests of capital and contribute to a destructive mode of being. For striving towards sufficiency to replace striving towards (material) growth in society, microeconomics could be taught in combination with, for instance, deep ecology and eco-philosophy.

4. Conclusion

In this chapter, we turned to Roy Bhaskar's philosophy of critical realism to contemplate social being on the planes of humanity's material transactions with nature, social interactions, social structures and inner being. We discussed sufficiency in relation to each of these planes, noting that for it to become a genuine and truly sustainable part of business practice, as well as part of businesspersons' worldviews, it needs to unfold and be supported on all the four planes. We theorize the implementation of sufficiency as deep and processual. It needs to unfold everywhere, from becoming a value for individual humans to becoming a principle in humanity's use of resources on different scales. However, this unfolding is a process, hence our call for avoiding labelling businesses as sufficient or not.

While sufficiency may evoke thoughts related to foregoing and sufficing, it does not have to be related to these terms. Sufficiency in fact may be part of growth, something that we advocate fully even for a post-growth economy (Buch-Hansen/Nesterova 2023). Sufficiency can be part of a growth process for both business but perhaps even more so for businesspersons. It is part of a growth process since it requires shedding the norm of growthism and materialism and developing a completely different way of relating with the world which entails deep respect for nature, fellow humans and non-humans.

References

Beyeler, Laura/Jaeger-Erben, Melanie (2022): "How to make more of less: Characteristics of sufficiency in business practices." In: Frontiers in Sustainability 3, pp. 1–25. https://doi.org/10.3389/frsus.2022.949710.

Bhaskar, Roy (2008): Dialectic: The Pulse of Freedom, London: Routledge.

Bhaskar, Roy (2009): Scientific Realism and Human Emancipation, London: Routledge.

Bhaskar, Roy/Frank, Cheryl/Høyer, Karl Georg/Naess, Petter/Parker, Jenneth (2010): Interdisciplinarity and Climate Change: Transforming Knowledge and Practice for Our Global Future, London: Routledge.

Bocken, Nancy M. P./Short, Samuel W. (2016): "Towards a sufficiency-driven business Model: Experiences and opportunities." In: Environmental Innovation and Societal Transitions 18, pp. 41–61. https://doi.org/10.1016/j.eist.2015.07.010.

Buch-Hansen, Hubert (2021): "Modvækst som paradigme, politisk projekt og bevægelse." In: Nyt fokus: Fra økonomisk vækst til bæredygtig udvikling 17, pp. 6–9. http://www.nytfokus.nu/nummer-17/modvaekst-som-paradigme-politisk-projekt-og-bevaegelse/.

Buch-Hansen, Hubert/Koch, Max/Nesterova, Iana (2024): Deep Transformations: A Theory of Degrowth, Manchester: Manchester University Press.
Buch-Hansen, Hubert/Nesterova, Iana (2021): "Towards a Science of Deep Transformations: Initiating a Dialogue between Degrowth and Critical Realism." In: Ecological Economics 190, 107188. https://doi.org/10.1016/j.ecolecon.2021.107188.
Buch-Hansen, Hubert/Nesterova, Iana (2023): "Less and More: Conceptualising Degrowth Transformations." In: Ecological Economics 205, 107731. https://doi.org/10.1016/j.ecolecon.2022.107731.
Danermark, Berth/Ekström, Mats/Jakobsen, Liselotte/Karlsson, Jan Ch. (2002): Explaining Society: Critical Realism in the Social Sciences, London: Routledge.
Elgin, Duane (2013): "Voluntary Simplicity – a Path to Sustainable Prosperity." In: Social Change Review 11/1, pp. 69–84. https://doi.org/10.2478/scr-2013-0006.
Elgin, Duane/Mitchell, Arnold (1977): "Voluntary Simplicity – Life-style of the Future." In: The Futurist 11/4, pp. 200–261. http://dx.doi.org/10.1108/eb053820.
Fromm, Erich (2013 [1976]): To Have or to Be?, London: Bloomsbury.
Hartwig, Mervyn (2001): "New Left, New Age, New Paradigm? Roy Bhaskar's From East to West." In: Journal for the Theory of Social Behaviour 31/2, pp. 139–165. http://dx.doi.org/10.1111/1468-5914.00152.
Hartwig, Mervyn (2007): Dictionary of Critical Realism, London: Routledge.
Heidegger, Martin (2001 [1927]): Being and Time, Oxford: Blackwell.
Jungell-Michelsson, Jessica/Heikkurinen, Pasi (2022): "Sufficiency: A Systematic Literature Review." In: Ecological Economics 195, 107380. https://doi.org/10.1016/J.ECOLECON.2022.107380.
Kaufmann, Nadine/Sanders, Christoph/Wortmann, Julian (2019): "Building New Foundations: The Future of Education from a Degrowth Perspective." In: Sustainability Science 14, pp. 931–941. https://doi.org/10.1007/s11625-019-00699-4.
Leopold, Aldo (1949): A Sand County Almanac: And Sketches Here and There, Oxford: Oxford University Press.
Midgley, Mary (2003): Heart and Mind, London: Routledge.
Moss, Donald (2015): "The Roots and Genealogy of Humanistic Psychology." In: Kirk J. Schneider/J. Fraser Pierson/James F. T. Bugental (eds.), The Handbook of Humanistic Psychology: Theory, Research, and Practice, London: Sage, pp. 3–18.
Naess, Arne (1989): Ecology, Community and Lifestyle, Cambridge: Cambridge University Press.
Nesterova, Iana (2020a): "Degrowth Business Framework: Implications for Sustainable Development." In: Journal of Cleaner Production 262, 121382. https://doi.org/10.1016/j.jclepro.2020.121382.
Nesterova, Iana (2020b): Small Business Transition towards Degrowth, Derby: University of Derby.
Nesterova, Iana (2021): "Small Firms as Agents of Sustainable Change." In: Futures 127, 102705.

Nesterova, Iana (2022a): "Business of Deep Transformations: How Can Geography Contribute to Understanding Degrowth Business?" In: Geography and Sustainability 3/2, pp. 105–113. https://doi.org/10.1016/j.geosus.2022.03.004.

Nesterova, Iana (2022b): "Being in the World Locally: Degrowth Business, Critical Realism, and Humanistic Geography." In: Frontiers in Sustainability 3, 829848. https://doi.org/10.3389/frsus.2022.829848.

Nesterova, Iana (2023): "Responsibilities towards Places in a Degrowth Society: How Firms Can Become More Responsible via Embracing Deep Ecology." In: Society Register 7/1, pp. 53–74. https://doi.org/10.14746/sr.2023.7.1.03.

Nesterova, Iana/Jungell-Michelsson, Jessica (forthcoming): "A Business of Deep Transformations Is a Business of Sufficiency." In: David Skrbina/Toni Ruuska/Tina Nyfors (eds.) Sufficiency in Nature, Leiden: Brill.

Nesterova, Iana/Beyeler, Laura/Niessen, Laura (2023): "Business of deep transformations: A non-binary approach." In: Bits & Bäume Journal 2, pp. 82–86. https://doi.org/https://doi.org/10.14279/depositonce-17526.

Niessen, Laura/Bocken, Nancy M. P. (2021): "How Can Businesses Drive Sufficiency? The Business for Sufficiency Framework." In: Sustainable Production and Consumption 28, pp. 1090–1103. https://doi.org/10.1016/j.spc.2021.07.030.

Parker, Simon (2018): The Economics of Entrepreneurship, Cambridge: Cambridge University Press.

Perlman, Fredy (1983): Against His-Story, against Leviathan, Detroit: Black & Red.

Robra, Ben/Heikkurinen, Pasi/Nesterova, Iana (2020): "Commons-based peer production for degrowth? – The case for eco-sufficiency in economic organisations." In: Sustainable Futures 2, 100035. https://doi.org/10.1016/j.sftr.2020.100035.

Sayer, Andrew (2011): Why Things Matter to People: Social Science, Values and Ethical Life, Cambridge: Cambridge University Press.

Schmid, Benedikt/Nesterova, Iana (2023): "Unearthing Intentionality: Building Transformative Capacity by Reclaiming Consciousness." In: Environmental Values, in print.

Schneider, Kirk J. (2015): "Rediscovering Awe: A New Front in Humanistic Psychology, Psychotherapy, and Society." In: Kirk J. Schneider/J. Fraser Pierson/James F. T. Bugental (eds.), The Handbook of Humanistic Psychology: Theory, Research, and Practice, London: Sage, pp. 73–81.

Schumacher, Ernst Friedrich (1973): Small is Beautiful: A Study of Economics as if People Mattered, London: Blond & Briggs.

Spencer, David (2022): Making Light Work: An End to Toil in the Twenty-first Century, Cambridge: Polity.

Steiner, Rudolf (2011): The Philosophy of Freedom: The Basis for a Modern World Conception, Forest Row: Rudolf Steiner Press.

Trainer, Ted (2012): "De-growth: Do You Realise What It Means?" In: Futures 44, pp. 590–599.

Sufficiency and the Logic of Care
Transforming the Relationships, Practices and Temporalities of Businesses

Laura Beyeler

Abstract *Sufficiency in business represents a shift from a logic of profit towards a logic of care. The purpose of sufficiency-oriented businesses is to serve the fulfilment of needs. A logic of care transforms the relationships, practices and temporalities of businesses and represents leverage to enable sufficiency in praxis.*

1. Introduction

A growing number of studies and research fields are interested in ethics of care and its relevance for a just and ecological transformation of the economy and the society, for example, in sustainability sciences (Dengler et al. 2022; Gottschlich/Bellina 2017), in feminist care economics, or care geographies (Gibson-Graham et al. 2019). The connection between an ethic of care and the practical application of sufficiency is also gaining recognition in sufficiency research. A review by Jungell-Michelsson and Heikkurinen (2022) highlights altruism as a key foundation of sufficiency, indicating that individuals adopt sufficiency practices out of concern for the well-being of others and the environment. Caring for people and the planet has also been empirically identified as a characteristic of sufficiency in business practices (Beyeler/Jaeger-Erben 2022).

To examine the ethics of care in the context of sufficiency and business, it is important to understand the concept of care work. The capitalist economy separates productive and reproductive work, the latter being called unproductive (Dowling 2021; Eisler 2012). Within this hierarchical division of work, care work is only associated with social reproduction, which consists of the reproduction of labor power and life-sustaining activities (Dowling 2021). Feminist care economists call for an extension of care work to the productive sector while condemning the narrative that categorizes care work as unproductive. Knobloch (2019) pictures an economy of provision, in which all productive work is oriented towards the fulfilment of needs.

Thus, productive activity becomes care work the same as reproductive activity is. Care scholars advocate for the integration of an ethic of care into the productive sector and the entire economic activity. This signifies a transition from capitalist and growth-oriented means of production to a care and needs-centered economy (Knobloch 2019; Eisler 2012).

Since sufficiency differentiates between the production of goods and services that satisfy basic human needs and the ones that animate superfluous consumer wants (Gorge et al. 2014; Spengler 2018), it appears that sufficiency advocates for the same transition towards a needs-centered economy. From a sufficiency perspective, this transition represents a reduction in production and consumption volumes. From a care perspective, the transition can only occur with the integration of ethics of care in the production sectors. It becomes evident that following a logic of care in economic activity is an essential leverage point to enable sufficiency. This chapter argues that sufficiency can only be achieved if businesses embrace a logic of care. It claims that sufficiency-oriented businesses are inherently doing care work if they align their practices with the fulfilment of human and more-than-human needs.

To support this argumentation and illustrate the link between sufficiency and care in business practices, the author reviewed relevant care literature to identify and describe essential aspects of care. Based on the characteristics of care observed in care literature, empirical data from pioneering sufficiency-oriented businesses was analyzed with the goal of exploring which aspects of care sufficiency-oriented businesses are implementing and how a logic of care is shaping the business practices.

The following section gives a short review of the care literature and the essential characteristics of care. After describing the methodology of this research, the results present aspects of care that exist and emerge in sufficiency-oriented business practices. The discussion part discusses the implications of the empirical results for businesses and gives recommendations to further improve the logic of care in business practices.

2. Literature review on care

A look at the extensive literature on care reveals that the core of care lies in understanding and describing what human beings are (Tronto 1993; Lynch et al. 2021; Mol 2008). Humans are vulnerable and needy beings (Tronto 1993). They depend on others and on the social and ecological systems of which they are a part to meet their needs (O'Hara 1998). Care is thus a relational concept, namely that the well-being of humans depends on their ability to engage and care for the relationships with others around them (Hofmeister et al. 2019). Additionally, it is existential for vulnerable beings, such as humans, to receive care from others. The vulnerability of humans is more accentuated in some phases of their lifetime, for example, as new-borns or elderly people (Keller/Kittay 2017). In these phases, human beings require more attention and care than in other more autonomous phases. However, even in times of higher autonomy, humans are never emancipated from interdependent care relationships (Madörin 2007). When not as care receivers, humans give care to others in need, re-initiating a form of dependency and mutuality with other beings (Knobloch 2013). The fact that humans are relational and vulnerable beings counters the ideal of a solely autonomous, independent and rational homo economicus (Petit 2014). Instead, the ethics of care assert the diverse spectrum of human experiences, from vulnerability and mutual dependencies to periods of autonomy and insist on the manifold and diverse interdependencies present throughout human life (Keller/Kittay 2017).

However, human beings are not the only beings with needs and vulnerabilities and care relationships are not exclusive to them. Depending on the research fields and their focus, care theories differ in the question of agency in care relationships. Feminist economists, by redesigning economic mechanisms and norms, focus on humans as the primary recipients and providers of care (Aulenbacher et al. 2018; Plonz 2011; Madörin 2007; Ruby/Scholz 2018). In this case, humans are the main subjects of care relationships and own the agency to create, influence, or end caring relationships. Ecofeminism extends care agency to the relationships between humans and nature (Hofmeister et al. 2019; Dengler 2022; Bauhardt 2012). While the human body is an essential concern of care, embodying the vulnerability and limited nature of human beings, ecological feminists and science and technology studies pinpoint that all, human and non-human, bodies are part of nature and require care (Bauhardt 2017). A new relationship between the human and the more-than-human world, which overcomes the hierarchy and the opposition between nature and culture, is proposed by Haraway's concept of naturecultures (Haraway 2007). Naturecultures is a way of conceptualizing the interdependencies of all species, technologies, sciences, emotions or spiritualities that co-exist and co-produce nature and culture (Bauhardt 2019). In her book Matters of Care, Puig de la Bellacasa (2017) yields agency of care to all humans and other species as well as other-than-human entities that are interconnected in a web of life, leaving behind the anthropocentric relations between humans and nature (Bauhardt/Harcourt 2019). As Puig de La Bellacasa describes in her book chapter about the practice of permaculture, the matter of care in more-than-human worlds is "an attempt to decenter human ethical subjectivity by not considering humans as masters or even as protectors of but as participants in the web of Earth's living" (2017: 129).

As humans, animals, other living organisms, natural resources and non-living entities, such as objects and technologies created by humans, depend on care relationships to strive and exist in the world (Puig de la Bellacasa 2017), it becomes clear that care is unavoidable, permanent and always on-going (Puig de la Bellacasa 2017;

Dombroski 2020). Care necessitates constant work to fulfil the needs of the individuals living in the world. Besides being a relational concept, care is thus best understood as practice: a bundle of actions and thoughts oriented towards the fulfilment of human and more-than-human needs (Tronto 1993).

Care as a practice consists of all the activities performed every day by agents to sustain life. For care activities to take place, the presence of specific competencies, norms, values and materials is required. For example, attentiveness to one's own needs and to the needs of others is an essential competence in care practices (Sevenhuijsen 2018). Dependent relationships rely on attentiveness to receive care, to the extent that the absence of attentiveness can be considered a moral failure to give care (Tronto 1993). According to Sevenhuijsen (2018), attentiveness in care practices emerges from a series of skills and activities such as being present, seeing, listening, thoughtful speaking or being reliable. Additionally, care practices rely on scientific knowledge, specific technologies, or financial resources as their presence in the practices can enhance and support the fulfilment of needs (Mol 2008). The lack of financial resources available in care sectors, such as health care or the education system, is regularly denounced by feminist economic researchers as one major factor of deficient care systems (Himmelweit 2007; Schmitt et al. 2018; Gubitzer/Mader 2011). Finally, care as a practice is not individualist. It is an act of collaboration that builds upon a culture of solidarity where every member takes responsibility for the interdependent relationships (O'Hara 1998; Conradi 2015). Solidarity and collaboration are thus important values and norms that enable and support care practices.

Describing care as practice further shows that good care is not reliant on a set of moral principles, as modern ethics would advocate (Mol 2008). Rather, good care depends on the situation and the context and will always emerge from the care practice itself (ibid.). Everyone receiving care has different needs and might react differently to the care interventions. Thus, good care relies on the capability to respond to individual needs, the specific context of the situation and the acceptance that vulnerable beings, things and life are unpredictable (Mol 2008). For Tronto (1993), good care can also be described as a process that requires attentiveness, responsibility, competencies of care-giving and responsiveness.

However, a good care process is not simple, as mentioned by Tronto: "Care involves conflict; to resolve this conflict will require more than an injunction to be attentive, responsible, competent, and responsive" (1993: 150). The care process is ambivalent, and many conflicts will arise while doing care. Dilemmas and trade-offs between the needs of different groups of people, different species or living organisms and the material or natural resources are inherent to care (Cook/Trundle 2020). It is usual that, within care practices, contradictory elements exist and sit together in tension, for example, competitiveness and solidarity; hope and disappointment; suffering and release (Nguyen et al. 2017; Puig de la Bellacasa 2017; Mol 2008). With the emergence of conflicts, ambivalence, risks and insecurities, it reveals that doing care is not always attractive or easy. It entails difficult decision-making or complications.

Additionally, time plays an important role in the care process because care work is time-intensive. Productivity gains and time efficiency of care activities are often not possible without a deterioration of the quality of the care work (Aulenbacher/Dammayr 2014; Himmelweit 2007). Moreover, the care process necessitates time for experimentation of new paths, adaptation to the unpredictable and learning from experiences (Kohlen 2018; Mol 2008). Care temporalities challenge dominant narratives of constant progress, productivity gain and efficiency optimisation (Kohlen 2018; Mol 2008). Care requires making time for the "in-efficient" and "un-productive" but existential work of sustaining life (Puig de la Bellacasa 2015).

3. Method

This chapter observes and analyses how care manifests and materializes in sufficiency-oriented businesses. Interviews and podcasts with representatives or founders from 14 sufficiency-oriented businesses have been analyzed through the lens of care. The sufficiency-oriented businesses have been selected from different online databases and websites from associations of businesses for the common good, B corporations, or regional circular economy associations. Additionally, several Google searches with keywords related to sufficiency were conducted. To be selected in the sample, the businesses had to correspond to the following criteria:

- The business must operate with at least one and preferably several of the lessen strategies according to Schneidewind and Palzkill-Vorbeck (2011): *Decluttering, decelerating, disentangling and decommercialization*.
- The business must actively and publicly identify with a sufficiency-oriented purpose, explicitly quoting a reduction of material and resource use or of consumption or production volumes in their mission statement.
- The business is part of the fashion and electronic sector. These two sectors have been selected because both sectors showed interest in and experimented with sufficiency strategies. Moreover, similar and comparable sufficiency strategies, such as long-lasting product designs, repair or reuse offerings or support for consumption reduction, were identified in both sectors.
- To ensure comparability, the selection of businesses was limited to the European context. The selected businesses had primary data (interviews) and secondary data (e.g., websites, blogs, advertising, social media) available in German, French and English.

The collected data (interviews or podcasts with the founders of the businesses and secondary data such as websites, blog posts, videos and newsletters) were analyzed through the lens of care with the help of characteristics of care identified in the care literature. A literature review in several research fields applying care theories, such as care economics, ecofeminism, ethics of care, geographies of care or science and technology studies, has been conducted to understand what care is and which core aspects define it. Four relevant aspects of care served as categories and orientation to deductively analyze the empirical data:

- *Care as a relational concept*: which care relationships exist in sufficiency-oriented businesses?;
- *Care as a practice*: which competencies, norms, values, technologies or resources relevant to care practices are observable in sufficiency-oriented businesses?;
- *Care as an ongoing and unattractive process*: which ambivalences, conflicts or learning aspects are present in sufficiency-oriented businesses?;
- *Temporalities of care*: which temporalities exist and are experienced in sufficiency-oriented businesses?

By analyzing the interactions and the emergence of the elements of care in the practices of sufficiency-oriented businesses, this chapter tries to explore the formation of a logic of care in businesses. A logic that could be useful to apply to other conventional businesses when a transition towards sufficiency is aimed for. Integrating sufficiency in business practices could be facilitated by concentrating not only on specific sufficiency strategies but also by implementing an entirely different logic, from a logic of capital to a logic of care. The results of this inductive-deductive research process are presented in the next section.

4. Care in sufficiency-oriented businesses

4.1 Care as a relational concept

The sufficiency-oriented businesses from the study see their organization as an entity connected to other actors. They often acknowledge their own vulnerability and their dependency on the well-being of other actors. In consequence, the business's internal and external relationships shift from a logic of exploitation, competition and growth towards a logic of care for each other, for nature and for the material world.

First, the relationship of sufficiency-oriented businesses with other economic and societal actors shifts from competition to collaboration and solidarity. Sufficiency practitioners repeatedly mention the importance of personally knowing their stakeholders, in the sense that they often develop personal and close relationships with other like-minded organizations. They work together to exchange knowledge and competencies, to receive feedback and improve their practices, or to join forces for lobby activities. For example, a French sufficiency-oriented fashion brand gathered 400 sustainable fashion brands to lobby for legislation that would encourage a reduction of production volumes, support reuse and enable the decarbonization of production processes (En Mode Climat 2022). An economy in the logic of competition assumes that the individualistic homo economicus is unable to collaborate and that individuals thrive when competing with others (Knobloch 2019). For care scholars, it is apparent that vulnerable and dependent beings rely on collaboration to fulfil their needs and act for the common good (Knobloch 2013). The attention sufficiency-oriented businesses pay to the actors surrounding them and the collaboration for the common good are both an expression of a logic of care. This attention for the needs of others is not exclusive to proximate actors. While most of the businesses in the study highlight the efforts to foster the local relationships with producers, they also pay heed to the needs of others in other regions that are also connected to the businesses through their activities. For example, to increase fairness in the sourcing and mining of mineral resources, Fairphone builds alliances in the market to improve working conditions and set better standards for resource extraction and social justice (Fair Cobalt Alliance 2023).

Second, a business itself is a subject of care with its own specific needs that have to be met. A care relationship within and with the business itself is thus observable in praxis. Sufficiency practitioners reflect on the essence of being a business. For them, being a business means serving the common good and delivering goods and services that fulfil human or more-than-human needs. Purposes for the common good and for social and environmental justice that the sufficiency practitioners describe include reducing the amount of new goods produced, setting fair and just working conditions for all as default in their industry or producing without or with minimal environmental impacts: "It is not just a marketing talk. Hopaal's entire business is organized and continues to be organized around the purpose of answering to human needs, instead of creating desires" (Hopaal, publicly available podcast, December 2020, author's translation).

Sufficiency-oriented businesses understand and acknowledge their own limitations and vulnerabilities. No business in the sample envisions endless growth of their organization and production. Loom, a French clothing brand, for example, shared its effort to remain a small team with a limited number of employees. This results from a desire to keep the activities and the organization of the business at a human scale and in consequence be able to stay attentive to the needs within or outside of the business (Plonz 2011). Additionally, sufficiency practitioners recognize the impossibility of endless economic growth on a planet with limited resources. Thus, sufficiency practitioners envision an end to their own organizational and material growth. Like every living being, sufficiency-oriented businesses from the study experience a phase of growth until they reach a mature size in the market. Once they reach a legitimate size, which allows the business to influence other actors or set specific standards for their industry, sufficiency practitioners continue to grow but by different means. Sufficiency practitioners qualitatively grow by transferring knowledge and ideas, improving the quality of products and supply chains, creating synergies with other actors, or investing in the growth of their economic ecosystem.

In addition to the boundaries and essence of the business itself, the internal relationships among employees, investors and decision-making individuals of the business are worthwhile consideration. Sufficiency practitioners in the data reflect on their relationships with capital owners, decision makers, people with strategic responsibility, as well as employees. The ownership and responsibility for the business are often distributed among like-minded individuals and groups or remain in the hands of the founders who retain control over the sufficiency-oriented practices. Following a logic of care, sufficiency practitioners make an effort to avoid powerful dependencies between the people involved in the financing, management and labor of the company. Democratic decision-making processes or capital involvement of the employees are possible internal relationship forms that emerge from a logic of care.

Finally, sufficiency practitioners redefine their relation towards consumption. Instead of consumption driven by consumer wants and desires, sufficiency-oriented businesses in the study acknowledged that products and services should exist to serve human needs, such as shelter, clothing, education or health care and assistance (Gough 2015; Jonas et al. 2023). Thus, sufficiency practitioners only offer goods and services that aim at fulfilling basic human needs. Sufficiency practitioners ask which goods and services are necessary to fulfil human and more-than-human needs and how much of these goods and services must be delivered. The production of new products can, for example, be avoided if unused and functional second-hand products are made available for reuse or with repair services that increase the use of existing products. The pursuit of insatiable consumption preferences with the animation of individual desires and wants is thus irrelevant in sufficiency-oriented business practices.

4.2 Care as a practice

Care as a practice is the understanding that care is not limited to a value or an emotion that individual people have. Care consists of actions and thoughts oriented toward the fulfilment of needs (Tronto 1993). As described in the literature review, care practices require specific competencies, values or materials to perform the activities and enable good care. In the data, elements that are essential for care practices and influence the sufficiency practices have been identified.

Care practices require an awareness of unmet needs and a responsibility to fulfil them. Both attentiveness and a sense of responsibility are present and play an important role in sufficiency-oriented practices. All sufficiency practitioners identified growth imperative and affluence as the main drivers of current environmental and social crises. They are attentive to social justice or unfair production practices in global supply chains and to a call from civil society to develop alternative production and consumption practices. They describe a need for reduction of material dependency and production volume if life on this planet is to be sustained. In other words, the sufficiency practitioners are attentive to the unmet needs of different agents of care, namely nature and its ecosystems, workers in supply chains, consumers or citizens that have little to no choice of affordable sufficiency-oriented consumption practices. Then, by shifting towards sufficiency, they take responsibility and actively develop business practices that allow them to meet these unmet needs.

Further competencies that support the development of these sufficiency-oriented practices are transparent and constant communication between the businesses and their stakeholders, creativity and resilience. For example, sufficiency-oriented businesses use their platform to educate and share knowledge about the shortcomings and problems of current economic practices. They critically reflect on them and communicate how they try to overcome them. Their solution-oriented doings require creativity to find new paths and resilience to oppose capitalist norms while ensuring the viability of the business.

In redefining the business' relationship with others, values such as solidarity and collaboration become dominant in sufficiency-oriented practices: "It is very important for us to appreciate others. We do not speak about competition; we do not see others as competitors. We are co-change makers [...]. It is important for us to create good relationships" (TEIL, personal interview, August 2021, author's translation). Collaboration and solidarity are observable in the alliances they form to do lobby activities, in the financial and ideal support companies and organizations give to each other or in the networks they are building to spread their practices. Appreciation for the relationships, for the products or for the natural and material resources used or preserved in their activities is also an important aspect of sufficiency-oriented businesses that relate to a logic of care.

On the material dimension, one similarity between care and sufficiency-oriented practices is that financial means are essential for a successful process. However, both sufficiency practices and care practices often lack financial resources because they are not economically profitable and sometimes produce more costs than revenues. Sufficiency practitioners engage in sufficiency practices despite low revenues. Fortunately, sufficiency practitioners manage to find financial investments. They receive financial resources outside of a growth-oriented shareholder system. Sufficiency-oriented businesses are funded often by personal investments, by foundations, the community of consumers or investments from other profitable sufficiency-oriented projects. These investments are often less bound to expected returns on investment demanded by shareholders. They give the sufficiency practitioners time and space to experiment with new forms of doing business with low monetary pressure.

4.3 Care as an ongoing and unattractive process

As described in the care literature, care is not always attractive. It is an ongoing effort shaped by ambivalences and conflicts, which requires time and learning competencies. These care characteristics are mirrored in the sufficiency-oriented business practices.

In the dominant capitalist system, profit maximization, returns on investments, or rapid growth are the norms and standards of doing business (Donaldson/Walsh 2015). It is difficult and inconvenient for sufficiency-oriented businesses to resist and go against these norms. Some of the sufficiency strategies of the businesses in this study, such as a reduction of working hours for employee well-being, lifelong repair or reuse services, or the creation of a trustful and close relationship with sustainable suppliers, all necessitate time, money and endurance. Even if sufficiency-oriented practices seem inconvenient, the logic to care for the people and the planet is attractive and motivating enough to resist capitalist norms. The inconvenience of sufficiency becomes bearable and even desirable when the business practices switch from a logic of environmental and social destruction to the logic of care (Mol 2008).

Additionally, the experience of sufficiency-oriented businesses reveals ambivalences in their practices. Similarly to a care treatment, in which a care team must respond to unpredictable turns, problems or complications (Mol 2008), sufficiency practitioners stumble and face contradictions between their intentions and the outcomes of their activities. One prominent strategy used by sufficiency practitioners is the early involvement of consumers in the design and production phases of the supply chain (Niessen/Bocken 2021). For example, consumers pre-order the products before the production process begins, with the aim of only producing products that are needed and ensuring a long-lasting use of the products (Stumpf/Varela 2022). When products are customized to consumers' needs, the probability of long use of the products increases (Kropfeld/Reichel 2019; Reichel 2013). While involving consumers before production is an effective method to limit the production of new goods, rebound effects are possible. The early involvement of consumers can still animate unnecessary consumption desires (Beyeler/Jaeger-Erben 2022). The ambivalence lies in the difficulty for both consumers and producers to differentiate between consumption wants and needs (Gough 2015). Consumers might unconsciously pre-order products that they do not necessarily need because they are embedded in an economic system that prioritizes wants over needs. The contradiction between the reduction intentions of the strategies and the potential increase in consumption necessitates an awareness of the difference between needs and desires. Such an awareness is not always observable in the data of this study. A participatory process involving different stakeholders and defining needs collaboratively might be a useful addition to the pre-order strategies of sufficiency-oriented businesses (Guillen-Royo 2020). Ambivalences are not negative or unsuccessful. Practitioners can learn from them and adapt their practices. It is likely that ambivalent circumstances co-exist until new paths, solutions, or structures unfold.

4.4 Temporalities of care

Beyond the dominant narrative of productivism and time efficiency, Puig de la Bellacasa (2015: 4) highlights that different social and ecological temporalities exist side by side:

> Looking at temporality from the perspective of everyday experience shows that time is not an abstract category, nor just an atmosphere, but a lived, embodied, historically and socially situated experience. Time is not a given, it is not that we have or do not have time, but that we make it through practices (ibid).

The sufficiency practitioners from the study similarly experience and produce different temporalities within their daily practices. The practitioners describe an attempt to slow down the production and consumption rhythm. They want to take time to produce at their pace specially to ensure high product quality and longevity. Moreover, repair services, lifelong product guarantees, reuse possibilities and secondary markets are all efforts to reduce the frequency of material consumption. The experience of slowing down also emerges from the time-intensive work the sufficiency practitioners are doing. Controlling and ensuring social standards, collaborating with like-minded partners or sustaining careful relationships with them are time-intensive activities that automatically slow down the daily processes of businesses.

The sufficiency-oriented practices are additionally influenced by long-term planning and visioning. Many costly actions taken in the present day might only have effects and benefits in the long-term, for example, for future generations. However, sufficiency practitioners also report a feeling of urgency that influences their actions. Although their activities require time and the planning is oriented toward long-term achievements, the environmental and social crises drive the practitioners to act now and diffuse their practices fast enough to rapidly tackle challenges such as climate change.

5. Discussion

Looking at sufficiency-oriented business practices from a lens of care revealed that sufficiency and care have many interferences. To orient the business practices towards the fulfilment of needs is leading businesses into a logic of care. The logic of care that sufficiency-oriented businesses in this study tend to adhere to shapes many elements in their practices. One main result of this study is that sufficiency-oriented businesses recognize the vulnerable, interconnected and dependent nature of human beings. Interdependent and vulnerable beings require relationships with other beings to fulfil their needs. Sufficiency-oriented businesses see their stakeholder relationships as care relationships. They are aware of their own needs and the needs of other actors in their environment, and they recognize that the fulfilment of these needs can only be reached in collaboration and solidarity with others.

Many feminist scholars denounce the inability of capitalist and neoliberal institutions to meet the fundamental needs of humans and more-than-humans (Winker 2015). Only needs that warrant purchasing power are selected and offered on the free market (ibid). Fundamental needs, such as health care, education or childcare, are undervalued and barely fulfilled for everyone in the world (Plonz 2011; Knobloch/Kleinert 2022; Winker 2015). Additionally, the social and environmental costs in the supply chain, which are externalized and ignored by many conventional businesses, represent further unmet needs that a company in a capitalist logic does not account for (Bauhardt 2014). With their efforts to reduce production and consumption volumes as a means of environmental protection and social justice, sufficiency-oriented businesses take a responsibility to fulfil fundamental needs that neoliberal and capitalist systems often neglect. Sufficiency orientation in businesses is a matter of care, essential to counteract the continuous neglect of care that neoliberalism is perpetuating.

Sufficiency-oriented business practices have developed essential care competencies, such as attentiveness, responsibility, transparent communication, creativity and resilience. The values of solidarity and the appreciation of the value of humans and more-than-humans are also essential care elements observed in sufficiency-oriented business practices. Lacking financial means can however jeopardize the sufficiency-oriented practices, which is a common and recurrent problem of care work and activities in the reproductive sector (Dowling 2021). As care scholars have highlighted, care requires time and is often inefficient in generating capital accumulation (Razavi 2012; Gubitzer/Mader 2016; Raghuram et al. 2009). Sufficiency in business practices makes time for care activities. A logic of care requires accepting the diversity of temporalities that exist in different contexts or periods and for different care subjects (Puig de la Bellacasa 2015; Raghuram et al. 2009).

Moreover, the integration of sufficiency in business practices is filled with contradictions and ambivalences, as it shifts business relations and references on many scales (Nesterova/Buch-Hansen 2023). In this non-binary and non-linear process, capitalist elements and sufficiency strategies can temporarily co-exist (Nesterova et al. 2023). Learning loops, solidarity, patience, creativity or the ability to adapt to the unpredictable are a few examples of competencies that sufficiency practitioners develop to persevere and continue to care. From a care perspective, contradictions and ambivalences are inherently part of the practices (Mol 2008). Thus, the integration of sufficiency in business practices can be approached with empathy and kindness, instead of fearing a transformation due to inconsistencies (Nesterova et al. 2023).

Despite the many elements of care identified in sufficiency-oriented businesses, it is interesting to highlight the aspects of care that are still missing in the data to further improve a logic of care in the context of businesses. One relationship of the businesses that is not redefined by the business in the study is the relationship to nature and the more-than-human world. In a logic of care, the relationship between nature and the more-than-human world is not solely centred around the interests and needs of humans. Rather, the interconnectivity and interdependency with the more-than-human world are emphasised and every species and organism of nature becomes part of ethics and culture (Bauhardt/Harcourt 2019). It is worthy to observe the approach permaculture has when it comes to the role and responsibility of humans in a non-anthropocentric system. Puig de la Bellacasa describes humans' role as a member of nature as follows:

> In spite of this nonhuman-centred stance, of the affirmation that humans are not separated from natural worlds, permaculture ethics cultivate specific ethical obligations for humans. Collective-personal actions are also moved by ethical commitment and an exigency to respond in this world. Possibly, this ethically decentred form of obligation conveys a tension but not, I believe, a contradiction (2017: 129).

Sufficiency-oriented businesses similarly might assume ethical obligations not only to protect nature but also to actively care for nature's needs. For example, more-than-human beings could be involved as actors in the production process, as consumers are as well. Even though sufficiency practitioners acknowledge the vulnerability of nature and engage in practices that minimize or suppress negative environmental impacts, human needs and ethics are still at the center of their businesses. A relationship shift from anthropocentrism to human beings embedded in a web of interdependent animals, plants, microorganisms or natural resources was not observed in the empirical data and has yet to be put into practice.

When sufficiency-oriented businesses acknowledge their own limitations of the businesses, they envision an end to their organizational and material growth. When reflecting upon the limitations of humans or other beings, care theories include the consideration and act of ending specific care relationships. Care is not only about creating connections to meet needs but also about a conscious disconnection of care relationships if they do not serve the purpose anymore or if they are causing more harm than good to the goal (Pitt 2018; Puig de la Bellacasa 2017). In the logic of care, sufficiency-oriented businesses could reflect upon and consider their own end. To imagine what happens when the purpose of a sufficiency-oriented business is accomplished could be an active practice of sufficiency in business. Because needs are satiable or changing with time, technological improvement or societal structure, some (unsustainable) business practices can become obsolete for the well-being of society and nature (Heyen et al. 2017). Thus, in a matter of care, sufficiency-oriented businesses ought to consider ending their activities or switching to deliver other prevailing needs as soon as their practices are not caring anymore. To consider ending some parts of the business or taking unsustainable products from the market might especially be relevant for conventional businesses which would be willing to start a sufficiency-oriented transformation process.

Due to the vulnerabilities and dependencies, care relationships are always asymmetric and thus exposed to power relations and abuse (Jochimsen 2019; Martin et al. 2015). By rendering care invisible, neoliberal institutions systematically discriminate against some social groups, for example, by preventing access to good care for people according to their bodily or mental abilities, their race, their class, their gender or their sexual orientation (Tronto 1993). Studies in the UK or in the United States depict the higher exposure to illness or early death of Black, Asian and other minority ethnic groups due to systemic and discriminating factors such as economic insecurity or lack of access to medical insurance (Platt/Warwick 2020; Raifman/Raifman 2020). At the same time, the people with the least access to care services are the ones who carry out most of the care work (Tronto 1993). Privileged people can pass the devalued care work to others. This shift of unwanted care work to others is a recurrent exercise of power in Western history as described by Aulenbacher et al.:

> From a historical viewpoint the transnationalization of care work is by no means new: under colonialism, the people snatched from African countries included not insignificant numbers of women and girls, who had to 'serve' as domestic slaves in their owners' households.[…] In the 21st century, the employment of care workers in middle- and upper-class households of high-income countries has developed into the most important labor market for female migrants worldwide (2018: 4, author's translation).

Care relationships have always been vulnerable to power and discrimination, especially in capitalist, patriarchal and colonial contexts. Introducing a logic of care does not magically dissolve power inequalities and injustice. Thus, even with a logic of care, sufficiency-oriented businesses must be responsive to inequalities and possible power abuse and be constantly aware of the vulnerability of care relationships. A logic of care only goes hand in hand with a concept of justice (Tronto 1993) and is a de-colonial intersectional and queer feminist project according to many care scholars (Bauhardt 2012; Dengler 2022; Raghuram 2016). Some of the producing sufficiency-oriented businesses in this study are yet to follow such a decolonial path as their concept of fairness or solidarity is often still connected to extractivist patterns when resources are extracted in the Global South solely for consumption in the Global North (Riofrancos 2020).

Finally, in the capitalist context, in which all the companies in this study are embedded, narratives of care might be utilized for commercial purposes. As Puig de La Bellacasa (2017: 9) describes: "Calls for caring are everywhere, from the marketing of green products, by which companies compete to show how much they care, to the purchase of recycled items, by which consumers show that we care". However, a logic of care in businesses does not manipulate care values for marketing purposes and discourses. Thus, scholars and practitioners ought to be attentive to narratives manipulating care without deviation from the logic of profit and growth. A logic of care goes beyond marketing. It radically transforms business doings in an anticapitalist manner and reorients production and consumption practices towards the fulfilment of human and more-than-human needs.

References

Aulenbacher, Brigitte/Dammayr, Maria (2014): "Krisen des Sorgens – Zur herrschaftsförmigen und widerständigen Rationalisierung und Neuverteilung von Sorgearbeit." In: Brigitte Aulenbacher/Maria Dammayr (eds.), Für sich und andere sorgen – Krise und Zukunft von Care in der modernen Gesellschaft, Weinheim, Basel: Beltz/Juventa Verlag, pp. 65–76, 7.12.2023 (http://www.worldcat.org/oclc/865739432).

Aulenbacher, Brigitte/Dammayr, Maria/Riegraf, Brigit (2018): "Care und Care Work." In: Fritz Böhle/G. Günter Voß/Günther Wachtler (eds.), Handbuch Arbeitssoziologie, Wiesbaden: Springer VS, pp. 747–66. https://doi.org/10.1007/978-3-658-21704-4_22.

Bauhardt, Christine (2012): "Feministische Ökonomie, Ökofeminismus und Queer Ecologies – Feministisch-materialistische Perspektiven auf gesellschaftliche Naturverhältnisse." In: Gender... Politik... Online 4/1, 7.12.2023 (https://www.fu-berlin.de/sites/gpo/pol_theorie/Zeitgenoessische_ansaetze/Bauhardtfemoekonomie/Bauhardt.pdf).

Bauhardt, Christine (2014): "Solutions to the crisis? The Green NewDeal, Degrowth, and the Solidarity Economy: Alternatives to the capitalist growth economy from an ecofeminist economics perspective." In: Ecological Economics 102, pp. 60–68. https://doi.org/10.1016/j.ecolecon.2014.03.015.

Bauhardt, Christine (2017): "Living in a Material World. Entwurf Einer Queer-Feministischen Ökonomie." In: GENDER 1, pp. 99–114. https://doi.org/10.3224/gender.v9i1.07.
Bauhardt, Christine (2019): "Nature, Care and Gender: Feminist Dilemmas" In: Christine Bauhardt/Wendy Harcourt (eds.), Feminist Political Ecology and the Economics of Care: In Search of Economic Alternatives, Abingdon, New York: Routledge, pp. 16–35.
Beyeler, Laura/Jaeger-Erben, Melanie (2022): "How to Make More of Less: Characteristics of Sufficiency in Business Practices." In: Frontiers for Sustainability 3, 949710. https://doi.org/10.3389/frsus.2022.949710.
Conradi, Elisabeth (2015): "Redoing Care: Societal Transformation through Critical Practice." In: Ethics and Social Welfare 9/2, pp. 113–29. https://doi.org/10.1080/17496535.2015.1005553.
Cook, Joanna/Trundle, Catherine (2020): "Unsettled Care: Temporality, Subjectivity, and the Uneasy Ethics of Care." In: Anthropology and Humanism 45/2, pp. 178–83. https://doi.org/10.1111/anhu.12308.
Dengler, Corinna (2022): "Critical Realism, Feminisms, and Degrowth: A Plea for Metatheory-Informed Pluralism in Feminist Ecological Economics." In: International Journal of Pluralism and Economics Education 13/1, pp. 23–42. https://doi.org/10.1504/IJPEE.2022.124571.
Dengler, Corinna/Lang, Miriam/Seebacher, Lisa Mo (2022): "Care: An Overview of Strategies for Social-Ecological Transformation in the Field of Care." In: Nathan Barlow/Livia Regen/Noémie Cadiou/Ekaterina Chertkovskay/Max Hollweg/Christina Plank/Merle Schulken/Verena Wolf (eds.), Degrowth & Strategy. How to Bring about Social-Ecological Transformation, Mayfly Books, pp. 219–234, 7.12.2023 (https://www.degrowthstrategy.org/wp-content/uploads/2023/09/Degrowth-n-Strategy-2022.pdf).
Dombroski, Kelly (2020): "Caring Labour: Redistributing Care Work." In: J K Gibson-Graham/Kelly Dombroski (eds.), The Handbook of Diverse Economies, Cheltenham, UK: Edgar Elgar, pp. 154–62.
Donaldson, Thomas/James P. Walsh (2015): "Toward a Theory of Business." In: Research in Organizational Behavior 35, pp. 181–207. https://doi.org/10.1016/j.riob.2015.10.002.
Dowling, Emma (2021): "Caring in Times of a Global Pandemic: Introduction." In: Historical Social Research 46/4, pp. 7–30. https://doi.org/10.12759/hsr.46.2021.4.7-30.
Eisler, Riane (2012): "Economics as If Caring Matters." In: Challenge 55/2, pp. 58–86. https://doi.org/10.2753/0577-5132550203.
En Mode Climat (2022): "En Mode Climat: Mouvement d'acteurs Du Textile Contre Le Réchauffement Climatique." June 26, 2023 (https://www.enmodeclimat.fr/).

Fair Cobalt Alliance (2023): "Fair Cobalt Alliance – Our Purpose." October 9, 2023 (https://www.faircobaltalliance.org/).
Gibson-Graham, J. K./Cameron, Jenny/Healy, Stephen/McNeill, Joanne (2019): "Roepke Lecture in Economic Geography – Economic Geography, Manufacturing, and Ethical Action in the Anthropocene." In: Economic Geography 95/1, pp. 1–21. https://doi.org/10.1080/00130095.2018.1538697.
Gorge, Hélène/Herbert, Maud/Robert, Isabelle (2014): "What Do We Really Need? Questioning Consumption Through Sufficiency." In: Journal of Macromarketing 35/1, pp. 1–12. https://doi.org/10.1177/0276146714553935.
Gottschlich, Daniela/Bellina, Leonie (2017): "Environmental Justice and Care: Critical Emancipatory Contributions to Sustainability Discourse." In: Agriculture and Human Values 34/4, pp. 941–53. https://doi.org/10.1007/s10460-016-9761-9.
Gough, Ian, (2015), "Climate Change and Sustainable Welfare: The Centrality of Human Needs." In: Cambridge Journal of Economics 39/5, pp. 1191–1214. https://doi.org/10.1093/cje/bev039.
Gubitzer, Luise/Mader, Katharina, (2011), "Care-Ökonomie. Ihre theoretische Verortung und Weiterentwicklung." In: Kurswechsel 4, pp. 7–21, 7.12.2023 (http://epub.wu.ac.at/).
Guillen-Royo, Mònica (2020): "Applying the Fundamental Human Needs Approach to Sustainable Consumption Corridors: Participatory Workshops Involving Information and Communication Technologies." In: Sustainability: Science, Practice, and Policy 16/1, pp. 114–27. https://doi.org/10.1080/15487733.2020.1787311.
Haraway, Donna (2007): When Species Meet. University of Minesota Press.
Heyen, Dirk Arne/Hermwille, Lukas/Wehnert, Timon (2017): "Out of the Comfort Zone – Governing the Exnovation of Unsustainable Technologies and Practices." In: GAIA 26/4, pp. 326–31. https://doi.org/https://doi.org/10.14512/gaia.26.4.9.
Himmelweit, Susan (2007): "The Prospects for Caring: Economic Theory and Policy Analysis." In: Cambridge Journal of Economics 31/4, pp. 581–99. https://doi.org/10.1093/cje/bem011.
Hofmeister, Sabine/Mölders, Tanja/Deininger, Michaela/Kapitza, Katharina (2019): "Für welche ‚Natur/En' sorgen wir? Kritisch feministische Perspektiven auf aktuelle Care-Debatten im sozial-ökologischen Kontext." In: GENDER 11/1, pp.125–39. https://doi.org/10.3224/gender.v11i1.09.
Jochimsen, Maren (2019): "Die Gestaltungskraft des Asymmetrischen – Asymmetrie und Abhängigkeit als Ausgangspunkt ökonomischen Denkens und Handelns." In: Ulrike Knobloch (eds.), Ökonomie des Versorgens – Feministisch-kritische Wirtschaftstheorien im deutschsprachigen Raum, Weinheim, Basel: Beltz/Juventa Verlag, pp. 68–88.
Jonas, Michael/Novy, Andreas/Bärnthaler, Richard/Karabaczek, Veronica/Plank, Leonard/Schinko, Thomas (2023): "Theorien des Wandels und der Gestaltung von Strukturen: Bereitstellungsperspektive." In: Christoph Görg/Verena Mad-

ner/Andreas Muhar/Andreas Novy/Alfred Posch/Karl W. Steininger/Ernst Aigner, APCC Special Report: Strukturen für ein klimafreundliches Leben, Berlin, Heidelberg: Springer Spektrum, pp.1–25.

Jungell-Michelsson, Jessica/Heikkurinen, Pasi (2022): "Sufficiency: A Systematic Literature Review." In: Ecological Economics 195, 107380. https://doi.org/10.1016/J.ECOLECON.2022.107380.

Keller, Jean/Kittay, Eva Feder (2017): "Feminist Ethics of Care." In: Ann Garry/Serene J. Khader/Alison Stone (eds.), The Routledge Companion to Feminist Philosophy, New York, Abingdon: Routledge, pp. 540–55.

Knobloch, Ulrike (2013): "Sorgeökonomie als kritische Wirtschaftstheorie des Sorgens." In: Hans Baumann/Iris Bischel/Michael Gemperle/Ulrike Knobloch/Beat Ringger/Holger Schatz (eds.), Care statt Cash, Zürich: Denknetz, pp. 9–23.

Knobloch, Ulrike (2019): Ökonomie des Versorgens – Feministisch-kritische Wirtschaftstheorien im deutschsprachigen Raum. Weinhem, Basel: Beltz/Juventa Verlag.

Knobloch, Ulrike/Kleinert, Ann-Christin (2022): "Sorge-Glossar" In: Ulrike Knobloch/Hildegard Theobald/Corinna Dengler/Ann-Christin Kleinert/Christopher Gnadt/Heidi Lehner (eds.), Caring Societies – Sorgende Gesellschaften. Neue Abhängigkeiten oder mehr Gerechtigkeit?, Weinheim, Basel: Beltz/Juventa Verlag, pp. 294–328.

Kohlen, Helen (2018): "Geschlechtergerechte Sorgearbeit im Horizont der Care-Ethik." In: Ulrich M. Gassner/Julia von Hayek/Alexandra Manzei/Florian Steger (eds.), Geschlecht und Gesundheit, Baden-Baden: Nomos, pp. 245–75. https://doi.org/10.5771/9783845293875-253.

Kropfeld, Maren Ingrid/Reichel, André (2019): "The Value of 'Enough' Sufficiency-Based Consumer Practices and Value Creation in Business Models." In: Proceedings of the 4th International Conference on New Business Models: New Business Models for Sustainable Entrepreneurship, Innovation, and Transformation, pp. 1–18.

Lynch, Kathleen/Kalaitzake, Manolis/Crean, Margaret (2021): "Care and Affective Relations: Social Justice and Sociology." In: Sociological Review 69/1, pp. 53–71. https://doi.org/10.1177/0038026120952744.

Madörin, Mascha (2007): "Neoliberalismus und die Reorganisation der Care." In: Hans Baumann/Beat Ringger/Holger Schatz/Walter Schöni/Bernhard Walpen (eds.), Denknetz-Jahrbuch 2007, Zürich: Denknetz, pp. 141–62.

Martin, Aryn/Myers, Natasha/Viseu, Ana (2015): "The Politics of Care in Technoscience." In: Social Studies of Science 45/5, pp. 625–41. https://doi.org/10.1177/0306312715602073.

Mol, Annemarie (2008): The Logic of Care. London and New York: Routdledge Taylor and Francis Group. https://doi.org/10.4324/9780203927076.

Nesterova, Iana/Beyeler, Laura/Niessen, Laura (2023): "Business of Deep Transformations – A Non-Binary Approach." In: Patricia Jankowski/Anja Höfner/Marja Lena Hoffmann/Friederike Rohde/Johanna Graf (eds.), Shaping Digital Transformation for a Sustainable Society – Contributions from Bits & Bäume, Berlin: Technische Universität Berlin, pp. 82–86. https://doi.org/https://doi.org/10.14279/depositonce-17526.

Nesterova, Iana/Buch-Hansen, Hubert (2023): "Degrowth and the Circular Economy: Reflecting on the Depth of Business Circularity." In: Journal of Cleaner Production 414, 137639. https://doi.org/10.1016/j.jclepro.2023.137639.

Nguyen, Minh T. N./Zavoretti, Roberta/Tronto, Joan C. (2017): "Ethics and Social Welfare Beyond the Global Care Chain: Boundaries, Institutions and Ethics of Care." In: Institutions and Ethics of Care, Ethics and Social Welfare 11/3, pp. 199–212. https://doi.org/10.1080/17496535.2017.1300308.

Niessen, Laura/Bocken, Nancy M. P. (2021): "How can Businesses drive Sufficiency? The Business for Sufficiency Framework." In: Sustainable Production and Consumption, 28, pp. 1090–1103. https://doi.org/10.1016/j.spc.2021.07.030

O'Hara, Sabine U. (1998): "Internalizing Economics: Sustainability between Matter and Meaning." In: International Journal of Social Economics 25/2/3/4, pp. 175–95. https://doi.org/10.1108/03068299810193380.

Petit, Emmanuel (2014): "The Ethics of Care and Pro-Environmental Behavior." In: Revue d'Economie Politique 124/2, pp. 243–67. https://doi.org/10.3917/redp.242.0243.

Pitt, Hannah (2018): "Questioning care cultivated through connecting with more-than-human communities." In: Social and Cultural Geography 19/2, pp. 253–74. https://doi.org/10.1080/14649365.2016.1275753.Platt, Ross/Warwick, Lucinda (2020): "Are Some Ethnic Groups More Vulnerable to COVID-19 than Others?" London: The Institute of Fiscal Studies,

Plonz, Sabine (2011): "Mehrwert und Menschliches Maß – Zur ethischen Bedeutung der feministisch-ökonomischen Care Debatte." In: Das Argument 292, pp. 365–80, 7.12.2023 (http://www.sabine-plonz.de/fileadmin/media/downloads/aufsaetze/DA292_Care.pdf).

Puig de la Bellacasa, Maria (2015): "Making Time for Soil: Technoscientific Futurity and the Pace of Care." In: Social Studies of Science 45/5, pp. 691–716. https://doi.org/10.1177/0306312715599851.

Puig de la Bellacasa, Maria (2017): Matters of Care – Speculative Ethics in More Than Human Worlds. Minneapolis: University of Minesota Press.

Raghuram, Parvati (2016): "Locating Care Ethics beyond the Global North." In: Acme: An International Journal for Critical Geographies 15/3, pp. 511–13.

Raghuram, Parvati/Madge, Clare/Noxolo, Pat (2009): "Rethinking Responsibility and Care for a Postcolonial World." In: Geoforum 40, pp. 5–13. https://doi.org/10.1016/J.GEOFORUM.2008.07.007.

Raifman, Matthew A./Raifman, Julia R. (2020): "Disparities in the Population at Risk of Severe Illness From COVID-19 by Race/Ethnicity and Income." In: American Journal of Preventive Medicine, 40/1, pp. 137–39. https://doi.org/10.1016/j.amepre.2020.04.003.

Razavi, Shahra (2012): "Rethinking Care in a Development Context: An Introduction." In: Development and Change 42/4, pp. 873–03. https://doi.org/10.1002/9781118297261.ch1.

Reichel, André (2013): "Das Geschäftsmodell des Weniger." In: Politische Ökologie (eds.), Vom Rechten Maß: Suffizienz als Schlüssel zu mehr Lebensglück und Umweltschutz, Munich: Oekom, pp. 92–98.

Riofrancos, Thea (2020): "Extractivism and Extractivismo." In: Global South Studies: A Collective Publication with The Global South, 13.10.2023 (https://globalsouthstudies.as.virginia.edu/key-concepts/extractivism-and-extractivismo).

Ruby, Sophie/Scholz, Sylka (2018): "Care, Care Work and the Struggle for a Careful World from the Perspective of the Sociology of Masculinities." In: Österreich Z Soziol 43, pp. 73–83. https://doi.org/10.1007/s11614-018-0284-z.

Schmitt, Sabrina/Mutz, Gerd/Erbe, Birgit (2018): "Care-Ökonomien – Feministische Beiträge Zu Care in Den Wirtschaftswissenschaften." In: Österreichische Zeitschrift für Soziologie 43/1, pp. 7–18. https://doi.org/10.1007/s11614-018-0282-1.

Schneidewind, Uwe/Palzkill-Vorbeck, Alexandra (2011): "Suffizienz als Business Case: Nachhaltiges Ressourcenmanagement als Gegenstand einer transdisziplinären Betriebswirtschaftslehre." In: Wupperthal Institut für Klima und Energie (eds.), Impulse zur WachstumsWende 2, 30.10.2023 (http://nbn-resolving.de/urn:nbn:de:bsz:wup4-opus-39553www.econstor.eu).

Sevenhuijsen, Selma (2018): "Care and Attention." In: South African Journal of Higher Education 32/6, pp. 30–31. https://doi.org/10.20853/32-6-2711.

Spengler, Laura (2018): Sufficiency as Policy – Necessity, Possibilities and Limitations. Baden-Baden: Nomos.

Stumpf, Lukas/Varela, Guillermo (2022): "Mythos: Pre-Order gegen Überproduktion." In: Alexa Böckel/Jan Quaing/Ilka Weissbrod/Julia Böhm, Mythen der Circular Economy, pp. 99–105. https://doi.org/10.25368/2022.163.

Tronto, Joan C. (1993): Moral Boundaries – A Political Argument for an Ethic of Care. New York: Routledge.

Winker, Gabriele (2015): Care Revolution: Schritte in eine solidarische Gesellschaft, Bielefeld: transcript.

Part B –
Experiences of Sufficiency in Business

Sufficiency as a Core Building Block of Community-Supported Business Models

Introducing an Innovative Business Model Type for Sufficiency

Jana-Michaela Timm and Michaela Hausdorf

Abstract *This chapter introduces a novel phenomenon that is spreading in practice into the scholarly debate on sufficiency in business: community-supported business models (CSBMs). We argue that sufficiency is a core building block of CSBMs, discuss three sufficiency-related principles and provide practical examples of CSBMs in varying business fields.*

1. Introduction

In line with the sustainable development goals (SDGs), the idea of a so-called sufficiency economy is regarded as one of the most valuable strategies for meeting human needs within the planetary boundaries (Alexander 2015; Niessen/Bocken 2021). This strategy advocates moderating production and consumption to reduce environmental deterioration while guaranteeing a beneficial, healthy life for all beings (Niessen/Bocken 2021). Scholars are increasingly exploring how businesses can apply sufficiency thinking and foster sustainable production and consumption (Bocken et al. 2022; Bocken/Short 2016; Gossen/Kropfeld 2022; Jungell-Michelsson/Heikkurinen 2022; Niessen/Bocken 2021). Our study aims to contribute to this discourse by directing scholarly attention to a novel phenomenon that is growing in practice: community-supported business models (CSBMs). We argue that sufficiency is a core building block of CSBMs (Bloemmen et al. 2015; Debucquet et al. 2020), meaning it is worth exploring CSBMs as new forms of business that contribute to broader sustainability transformations (Aagaard et al. 2021; Bocken et al. 2014; Geissdoerfer et al. 2018; Lüdeke-Freund/Dembek 2017; Stubbs/Cocklin 2008).

In this chapter, we first elaborate on the background and roots of CSBMs. Second, we show how these businesses contribute to the sufficiency economy by following the three sufficiency-related core principles of *direct instead of indirect relationships*, *needs orientation instead of growth orientatio*, and *solidarity-based contribution in-*

stead of fixed prices. Third, we provide practical examples of CSBMs that have implemented these principles in a variety of business fields, i.e. renewable energy, agriculture and sustainable mobility. With our study, we contribute to research on sufficiency in business by introducing CSBMs as innovative business models that provide a novel perspective on sufficiency-oriented ways of thinking and doing business, discuss limitations and deliver valuable ideas for future research.

2. Sufficiency business models

Scholars have identified three strategies for achieving the UN climate summit goal of slowing global warming and reducing anthropogenic climate-damaging emissions: efficiency, consistency and sufficiency (Brinken et al. 2022; Huber 2000; Speck et al. 2022). Efficiency usually refers to technical innovations that increase performance with less effort, such as LED lamps, cars with electric or hybrid engines or micro-memory storage chips. Consistency refers to imitating natural flows in production, for instance by producing with renewable materials or energy and closing loops. However, both efficiency and consistency strategies can still fall into the trap of causing increased resource depletion due to so-called *rebound effects* when total production is not eased (Beyeler/Jaeger-Erben 2022; Kropfeld/Reichel 2021). These strategies furthermore do not question the habits and patterns of the system itself.

Hence, the third strategy of sufficiency advocates limited consumption. To address limited natural resources, climate change and the threat of biodiversity loss, sufficiency strategies strive to save energy and resources in absolute terms (Bocken et al. 2022; Gossen/Kropfeld 2022; Niessen/Bocken 2021). Sufficiency in past decades has mainly been a matter of individual behavior and lifestyle, advocating that people solely consume what is necessary for a good life, hence promoting a minimalist lifestyle (Kropfeld 2023). Today, it is increasingly recognized as a necessary building block for sustainable societal development that not only protects natural resources but also asks the question of what is actually needed for a good life (Gossen/Kropfeld 2022; Jungell-Michelsson/Heikkurinen 2022). Sufficiency has simultaneously found its way into business research and practice (Beyeler/Jaeger-Erben 2022).

Sufficiency business models, also referred to as "business models of enough" (Kropfeld/Reichel 2021: 164) describe how businesses can propose, create and capture value for a broad range of stakeholders beyond organizational boundaries (Niessen/Bocken 2021; Schaltegger et al. 2016) while moderating production and avoiding rebound effects (Kropfeld/Reichel 2021). Similar to other sustainable business models, value proposition defines what type of value is created for which stakeholders; value creation refers to how this value is created and with which stakeholders; while value capture explains how value is captured and dispersed (Schaltegger et al. 2016).

Concrete sufficiency strategies on the business model level range from the three well-known approaches of reducing, avoiding and reusing (Price/Joseph 2000; Bocken/Short 2016) to more granular strategies like regionalization, decluttering, slowing down and de-commercialization (Sachs 2015; Schneidewind/Palzkill-Vorbeck 2011). Bocken and Short (2016) empirically examined six sufficiency-based business model innovations: sharing/no ownership, demand reduction services, moderating sales and promotion, extending product life, direct reuse and full life cycle sufficiency. Bocken, Morales and Lehner (2020) explored sufficiency business models in the food industry, presenting a framework encompassing twelve business strategies for sufficiency. Kropfeld and Reichel (2021) synthesized insights from previous studies as they developed a generic framework for sufficiency-oriented business models that builds on a social practice theoretical perspective encompassing the following three dimensions: (1) materials (tools, machines, physical infrastructure), (2) competences (personal skills for carrying out a practice) and (3) meanings (ideas, meanings and understandings) as core social practice dimensions (Shove et al. 2015). Finally, Niessen and Bocken (2021) developed a comprehensive framework for sufficiency in business, drawing on an extensive literature review, a practice search, as well as 13 semi-structured interviews. They presented 16 business-for-sufficiency strategies within a matrix encompassing rethink, reduce and refuse; as well as less clutter, less speed, less distance and less market. The 16 strategies include green alternatives, design strategies, awareness-raising, life-extension services and many more. Consolidating these insights, we conclude that the current scholarly debate on sufficiency business models presents a broad range of valuable business strategies and frameworks that contribute to a sufficiency economy.

We argue that these strategies mainly operate in a market-based mode and generate volatile revenues. This means that the ventures sometimes create more profit than they actually need to cover the costs of running their business and for reinvestment, while sometimes revenues fall short. On the one hand, generating profits that exceed the needs of running the business and fulfilling shareholder payments tends to strongly contribute to (over)exploiting social and ecological resources (Büscher et al. 2012; Stubbs/Cocklin 2008). In our current market-based system, profits are often achieved thanks to not factoring in the externalized costs of (non-) human nature and well-being (Upward/Jones 2016; Wells/Bristow 2007). On the other hand, falling short of covering the costs of businesses leads to precarious living conditions for the entrepreneurs (Berglund 2017; Conen/Schippers 2019).

Accumulating the revenues of all of these individual businesses reminds us of "Doughnut Economics" (Raworth 2017). We suggest that exceeding financial and social needs on the business level may result in economies that overshoot the ceiling of natural and social foundations, while falling short of financial and social needs brings about economies that fall below the social foundation of the doughnut. Hence, volatile revenues can be problematic both on the business model as well as on broader economic levels. This is where CSBMs can come into play, as they support entrepreneurs in precisely generating the revenues needed to run their business within the natural and social boundaries in an environmentally, socially and economically sufficient manner.

3. Community-supported business models

Community-supported businesses represent a "holistic approach [...] based upon trust, cooperation and ecologically responsible behaviours" (Bloemmen et al. 2015: 110). Their business models directly link producers and consumers while enabling a close relationship between both parties (Debucquet et al. 2020). Community-supported businesses are founded and run by a single person or team that provides access to products and services for (and to some extent with) a *community* of consumers. The community of consumers provides the material and immaterial resources[1] needed and, in turn, receives the product or service (often on a regular basis) (Hausdorf/Timm under review: 5; see Figure 1).

Figure 1: General overview of the relationship between providers and consumers in community-supported businesses. (Adapted from Hausdorf/Timm under review)

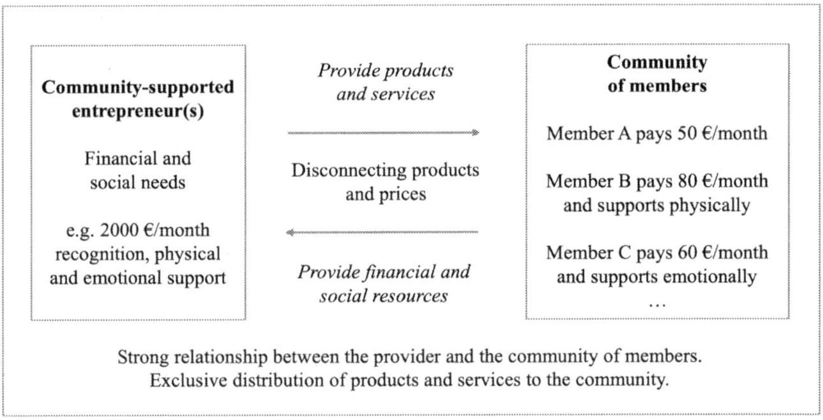

1 Material resources refer, for example, to money and items that help the producer(s)/provider(s) set up and run their businesses. Immaterial resources refer, for example, to (wo)manpower at the production site, knowledge transfer, the social network and social and emotional support for the entrepreneur.

The concept of CSBMs stems from agriculture. More than eighty years ago, Japanese farmers started to build close relationships with consumers to sell their regional, healthy products directly to them (Medici et al. 2021). Meanwhile, these close relationships between producers and consumers dispersed internationally and became known as *community-supported agriculture* (CSA). Recent decades saw community-supported businesses primarily set up in response to major societal challenges such as demographic shifts and environmental degradation (Elmes 2018; O'Hara/Stagl 2001). These were of a politically inspired nature.

Recently, the concept of community-supported agriculture has been increasingly applied to other business sectors around the world (Rommel 2017; Szuster et al. 2021; Zhao/Jia 2020). For example, there are community-supported fisheries in Southeast Asia, community-supported retail stores in the United Kingdom and community-supported restaurants in the USA (Szuster et al. 2021; Zhao/Jia 2020).

It is important to distinguish community-*supported* businesses from community-*based* businesses. In community-based businesses, a community of people jointly starts a business that is usually fruitful for their specific region (Peredo/Chrisman 2006; Peredo/McLean 2013; Sinnicks 2020). In contrast, solo entrepreneurs or teams set up community-*supported* businesses for (and partly with) a community of people. Moreover, we can distinguish community-supported businesses from cooperatives. While a cooperative's members jointly own and manage their venture, members of community-supported businesses usually do not own the organization but receive the products and services from the producer (Bacq et al. 2020; Davila/Molina 2017). Nevertheless, cooperatives are often suitable as legal forms for CSBMs.

Community-supported businesses are attracting increasing scholarly attention as environmentally, socially and economically sustainable ventures (Bloemmen et al. 2015; Rommel 2017). They contribute to a healthy environment by providing environmentally friendly products and services (Cristiano 2021; Tang et al. 2019), enhancing entrepreneurs' working conditions (Cristiano 2021; Elmes 2018) and ensuring economic stability and resilience (Brinson et al. 2011; Cristiano 2021). Previous research has shown that, in practice, different types of CSBMs exist (Bloemmen et al. 2015; Cameron 2015; Woods et al. 2017). Transactional CSBMs use their community in a mechanical way, perceiving it as a means to achieve a specific goal. In contrast, relational CSBMs understand the community as an end in itself, create value via the strong participation of their community members and capture value with a solidarity-based proportional pricing model. Hybrid CSBMs combine elements of both transactional and relational types of CSBMs (Hausdorf/Timm under review). In the following, we refer to the *relational* type when elaborating on CSBMs. This type is known for building particularly close relationships between producers and consumers, which enables it to function more environmentally, socially and economically sustainably than transactional and hybrid CSBMs.

We argue that relational CSBMs have even more to offer than 'just' being particularly sustainable: They represent an ideal type of a concrete and already-existing sufficiency business model that enables ventures to operate within the safe space between the social foundation and the ecological ceiling (Bloemmen et al. 2015; Raworth 2017). In the following, we discuss how sufficiency forms the core building block of CSBMs.

4. Sufficiency as the core building block of CSBMs

We argue that sufficiency forms the core building block of CSBMs, as these ventures (1) have direct instead of indirect relationships with stakeholders, (2) are characterized by a needs instead of a growth orientation and (3) use solidarity-based contributions instead of fixed prices.

Direct instead of indirect relationships. According to Freudenreich and Schaltegger (2020), avoiding overproduction is a core building block of sustainable production in a sufficiency-oriented business. Although one way to prevent overproduction is via made-to-order production (Niessen/Bocken 2021), CSBMs provide another way to reach this goal: their direct and personal relationships between producers and consumers (Debucquet et al. 2020; Woods et al. 2017). This closeness enables both parties to negotiate production quantity, quality, as well as wages, and helps eliminate the need for the producer to sell more products during good times in order to prepare for hard times (Bloemmen et al. 2015). In contrast, it is possible for the producer to constantly offer as many products or services as needed at a fair wage while sharing the entrepreneurial risk with all parties involved (Parot 2015). Hence, direct relationships between producers and consumers contribute to sufficiency as they work to prevent overproduction. Second, direct relationships between producers and consumers lead to high levels of communication, which fosters members' appreciation for the product or service (Debucquet et al. 2020). For example, surveys show that members highly value the fruits and vegetables they receive from a community-supported farm (Bloemmen et al. 2015; Debucquet et al. 2020; Rommel 2017), as they learn how much time and effort it takes to grow the harvest. Ultimately, this can foster sufficiency by raising awareness and reducing food waste. According to Niessen and Bocken (2021), education and communication are effective and valuable sufficiency-oriented businesses strategies for changing consumption patterns. Usually, newsletters, podcasts, blog posts and social media content are used as communication media (Niessen/Bocken 2021), whereas CSBMs concentrate on personal communication. Third, direct and trustful relationships build the foundation for a 'sufficiency mindset' that is indispensable for the following two principles.

Needs orientation instead of growth orientation. There is an ongoing scholarly debate about whether sufficiency-oriented businesses should generate profit and grow or not. On the one hand, some researchers argue that sufficiency strategies can unlock novel sources of profit (Bocken 2017; Boons/Lüdeke-Freund 2013), that (economic) growth has the potential to move customers away from unsustainable products and services (Niessen/Bocken 2021), and that profit is necessary for business survival (Khmara/Kronenberg 2018). On the other hand, as discussed above, generating profits that exceed the costs of running a business tends to contribute to (over)exploiting social and ecological resources (Büscher et al. 2012; Stubbs/Cocklin 2008), as they are often based on not factoring in the externalized costs of (non-)human nature and well-being (Upward/Jones 2016; Wells/Bristow 2007). CSBMs can offer a solution to this problem: Focusing on needs orientation instead of profit orientation, CSBMs aim to satisfy producers' and consumers' needs instead of maximizing profits (Bloemmen et al. 2015). The producer offers a limited number of products or services while avoiding overproduction (ibid.). At the beginning of each economic year, community-supported producers openly, faithfully and transparently communicate the material and immaterial resources needed to offer the sustainable product or service in a so-called bidding round (Loebbering 2018; Rommel 2017). Financial resources cover the costs of the endeavor (instead of generating profits) and guarantee constant revenue for the entrepreneur for a fixed timeframe, usually one year (Bloemmen et al. 2015; Brinson et al. 2011; Cristiano 2021). Community-supported entrepreneurs describe needs orientation in the context of their antagonistic attitude towards profit orientation: They strive to cover costs, enabling them to offer sustainable products or services instead of maximizing their profits (Hausdorf/Timm under review). Needs orientation enables CSBMs to meet the requirements of members and entrepreneurs, thus promoting sufficiency while counteracting economic growth. Ultimately, needs orientation is a practical means of helping entrepreneurs generate the precise revenue required to operate their business on proper environmental, social and economic terms.

Solidarity-based contributions instead of fixed prices. Entrepreneurs face a challenge when selling sustainable products and services, as they attempt to internalize as many external factors as possible to offer their products and services at prices that are fair and environmentally, socially and economically sustainable (Upward/Jones 2016; Wells/Bristow 2007). However, this often leads to expensive products and services that bear the risk of becoming exclusive and affordable only to high-income customers (D'Souza et al. 2006). This is why recent research recommends that businesses implement a broader range of sufficiency strategies, such as resale services to extend product lifetimes or no-ownership strategies like rental, leasing and sharing (Niessen/Bocken 2021). CSBMs can enrich this debate by bringing in solidarity-based contribution structures as novel mechanisms that simultaneously enable fair *and* inclusive prices. Solidarity-based contribution structures are a core element of CSBMs and are put into practice through bidding rounds (Diekmann 2020; Loebbering 2018; Rommel 2019). When preparing for a bidding round, entrepreneurs determine the material and immaterial resources they need for their work (Bloemmen et al. 2015). Then, they communicate these needs among their members and commence the bidding round (Diekmann/Theuvsen 2019). According to their income, members have the opportunity to offer individual contributions that can differ substantially between them. Thus, individuals with highly divergent financial budgets are able to participate (Loebbering 2018; Rommel et al. 2022). Contributions can be understood as proportions of income for paying for a service or product, instead of a fixed price that is the same for everybody, independent of their income. For example, for the same amount and the same quality of products or services, a member with a monthly net income of €1,400 would contribute €42 per month, whereas a member with a monthly net income of €3,500 would pay €105 per month, i.e. the same three-percent portion of their respective income (see Figure 1). In other words, both members pay a price that is proportional to their income (Cristiano 2021; Tang et al. 2019; Zhen et al. 2020). This logic is very socially inclusive, as high-income groups enable low-income groups to participate when each member provides a financial contribution that is proportional to her/his budget. Products and prices are detached from each other, and the members instead provide the material and immaterial resources necessary for the business to operate (Diekmann/Theuvsen 2019; Rommel et al. 2022). Bidding rounds permit entrepreneurs to receive the financial amount needed to operate the business and cover their personal, financial and social-emotional costs/needs as they run the business – no more, no less.

5. Examples of CSBMs in practice

To provide some practical examples of CSBMs, we screened the websites of two larger networks for community-supported businesses in Germany: one of them is the MYZELIUM educational center for community-supported initiatives (MYZELIUM 2023). The other one is CSX Netzwerk, an association of people who work, research or consult in the field of community-supported businesses (CSX Netzwerk 2023). Both websites provide rich lists of CSBs of which we present three cases in the following. We selected initiatives providing comparably detailed information on their websites and that stem from a variety of sectors.

Community-supported energy provider. SoLocal Energy aims to contribute to the global bottom-up sustainability transformation by empowering local communities. To reach this goal, the business offers, among other things, professional self-help communities for installing renewable energy systems. SoLocal Energy applies all of the three sufficiency principles presented above: the entrepreneurs directly cooperate with their community of consumers who would like to acquire a renewable energy unit. The group also takes responsibility for each other as they apply the solidarity-based proportional pricing model, rendering this approach very socially inclusive. Moreover, they act in a needs-oriented manner by calculating the financial costs of the material, scaffold and staff (SoLocal Energy 2023). It could nevertheless be criticized that SoLocal Energy, although promoting self-sufficiency, does not achieve a reduction in overall energy consumption. This is in fact true for their self-help communities that install renewable energy units, although they do regularly set up other communities such as neighborhood climate transition groups that contribute their climate protection and renewable energy experience.

Community-supported winery. Due to vast amounts of pesticides, high competition levels, questionable working conditions and sometimes even high levels of overproduction, conventional winemaking belongs in the category of less-than-sustainable businesses (Christ/Burritt 2013). Switching to organic farming only partially solves this problem, as the winemaker still takes on the entire risk of crop failure or sales problems, in these cases adjusting prices that make wine less affordable to lower-income groups (ibid.). The community-supported winemaker Jan-Philipp Bleeke walks a different path: Independent of the wine market and market price pressures, he shares costs and the harvest with his winery members (JPB Winemaking 2023). Bleeke has built up a community of members with which he maintains a close dialogue, mutual learning and an exchange of ideas. Members become co-winemakers while sharing responsibility and risk, paying a monthly contribution that they establish as part of a bidding round at the beginning of the growing season. This secures the operating costs for the winemaker for one year (including his wages). In return, the members receive the entire harvest – which is highly dependent on weather conditions and may as a result be abundant or lacking. With his community-supported winery, Bleeke contributes to the sufficiency economy in how he produces his wine in a sustainable, sufficient manner. His members guarantee they will take their agreed-upon portion of the wine – Bleeke will face neither sales problems nor overproduction as a result. Nevertheless, wine is a luxury item that consumes extensive amounts of water in its production. Hence, when seriously wanting to contribute to a sufficiency economy, consumers should question what and how much wine they actually need.

Community-supported car sharing. Conventional car sharing is usually offered in large cities (Zhou/Park 2020). For people in smaller towns or rural areas, there is often no alternative to owning a vehicle, in part because car-sharing is simply not a viable option. Moreover, there is a paradox in the incentive system of car sharing. On the one hand, a provider would welcome a shared car for economic reasons (partially for environmental reasons as well, assuming customers replace their own vehicle). On the other hand, walking or cycling is even more preferable for environmental reasons; here, infrequent shared car use would be similarly preferable (Hausdorf/Timm under review). Hence, it becomes difficult to find a suitable incentive structure that covers the costs for the car sharing provider but at the same time does not make driving more attractive than walking or cycling. The car sharing provider Vianova.coop founded a community-supported way of enabling neighborhoods in rural areas to create a car sharing opportunity and no longer have to own their cars (Vianova.coop 2023). Six to eight users share the fixed costs of the vehicle in solidarity through bidding rounds while the variable costs are borne individually. Here, the providers try to solve the incentive problem while the community meets the business' demands in a needs-oriented manner. One of the most salient critiques of car sharing is that people who have never owned a car but instead cycle or take public transport become car sharers and start driving. This might certainly be the case in some instances at Vianova.coop, even though the provider tries to solve this problem via open, honest communication, as well as raising awareness, enabled by the direct relationships between the provider and the members (ibid.).

6. Discussion

To date, scholars have identified a broad range of sufficiency business strategies (Bocken/Morales/Lehner 2020; Bocken/Short 2016; Kropfeld/Reichel 2021; Niessen/Bocken 2021; Schneidewind/Palzkill-Vorbeck 2011). However, we argue that these strategies mainly follow conventional business paradigms by operating within market-based structures while generating volatile revenues. In this article, we outlined that, in the market-based paradigm, there is a tendency towards creating financial profits that exceed the costs of running the business and meeting the needs of the entrepreneur(s) and interests of their shareholders, while profit generation is often connected to social or ecological exploitation (Büscher et al. 2012; Stubbs/Cocklin 2008). In contrast, falling short of the financial goals required to cover the costs of a business endeavor may lead to precarious living conditions of the producers or environmental degradation, and external costs that as a result need to be absorbed by society at a later stage (Berglund 2017; Conen/Schippers 2019). We argue that this market-based operating mode is incompatible with a sufficiency economy, which strives for a sustainable economy within the prevailing social foundation and ecological ceiling (Raworth 2017; Stubbs/Cocklin 2008). Here, we introduce CSBMs as business models that build on sufficiency principles not yet considered in research. With direct relationships between producers and consumers and a needs-oriented, solidarity-based financing structure, CSBMs manage the balancing act of precisely generating the revenue that is necessary to run a business while fulfilling the needs of the entrepreneur(s) and stakeholders.

CSBMs can be better understood by contrasting them to market-based corporations that establish sufficiency strategies. For example, Patagonia generates profits and reinvests these in sustainable projects that help combat the climate crisis and protect the environment. The sufficiency-oriented business VAUDE also generates profits but distributes 60 percent of the surplus to shareholders, while investing 40 percent in a sustainable corporate strategy via its reserves (VAUDE 2023). In contrast to these two examples, CSBMs generate exactly the financial and social resources needed to run their business – no more, no less. They figuratively neither fall below the social foundation, nor overshoot the ecological ceiling but instead attempt to operate within a safe space for humanity (Raworth 2017). These businesses seem perfectly equipped to contribute to a sufficiency economy – one of "Having enough for a healthy meaningful life, but without excess" (Bocken/Short 2020: 2).

However, there are some limitations to the potential of CSBMs when it comes to promoting a sufficiency economy. First, there is the issue of providers and members mutually agreeing on what products and services constitute the basic needs necessary for a good life. For example, some people might decide that a cruise holiday is an absolute necessity or that they want to eat fresh caviar from the Caspian Sea every day. Indeed, it is difficult to agree on what a sufficient standard of living exactly means, and it is certainly possible to take advantage of CSBMs to fulfil unsustainable wants rather than sufficiency-oriented needs. Nevertheless, so far, all CSBMs known to the authors offer sustainable products and services. A reason for this could be the collective nature of these businesses, enabling them to start processes of "reflective practice and collective meaning-making" (Le Ber/Branzei 2010: 190) and being well-equipped to negotiate which wants and needs are necessary while contributing to a sufficiency economy.

The second concern addresses the inclusive impact of CSBMs. With their solidarity-oriented pricing structure, these business models aim to let people from all financial backgrounds participate (Cristiano 2021; Tang et al. 2019; Zhen et al. 2020). However, some scholars question whether CSBMs are as inclusive as they intend to be (e.g. Loebbering 2018; Werling 2022) because sustainable products and services often only reach middle- and high-income groups. To date, empirical research is missing that shows whether CSBMs tend to be elitist; chances are, however, that this currently still proves to be the case. This raises the question of whether other sufficiency-oriented strategies are better suited towards inclusively taking the entire society along on the journey towards a sufficiency economy.

This thought brings us to the final limitation: The direct partnerships between producers and members, needs orientation and the solidarity-based financing structure are strategies containing vast potential for promoting a sufficiency economy. However, they should not be understood as exclusive strategies; they can effectively unfold their potential when combined with other sufficiency-oriented strategies such as sharing, short-distance promotion or questioning consumption (Bocken/Short 2016; Kropfeld/Reichel 2021; Niessen/Bocken 2021).

7. Conclusion

This chapter contributes to the current scholarly debate on sufficiency in business by introducing CSBMs as innovative models that provide a novel perspective on sufficiency-oriented businesses. Close partnerships between producers and consumers and a needs-oriented, solidarity-based financing structure enable these ventures to precisely generate the revenue needed for running their businesses in an environmentally, socially and economically sufficient way.

We have presented three examples of CSBMs from the energy, agricultural and mobility fields, discussing the extent to which these businesses promote a sufficiency economy. The discussion has shown that CSBMs indeed contribute to sufficient production and consumption within a socially just space in which humanity can thrive (Raworth 2017) while also facing crucial challenges. Hence, while the three core principles discussed in this chapter enrich the scholarly debate on sufficiency strategies, they should not be understood as stand-alone principles. Rather, CSBMs can combine these core principles with other sufficiency-oriented business strategies identified in previous research, such as local production, sharing or dematerialization strategies (Bocken/Short 2016; Kropfeld/Reichel 2021; Niessen/Bocken 2021).

Based on our own observations in literature and practice, this chapter provides a first glimpse at how CSBMs promote a sufficiency economy. Future research could explore the intersection between CSBMs and sufficiency more empirically and in greater detail, for example, by analyzing a larger number of practical examples through in-depth interviews. Grounded theory could be a support here, constructing an explanatory theory that sheds light on how exactly CSBMs can foster sufficiency. Moreover, it would be fruitful to explore CSBMs' potential to contribute to a sufficiency economy on a broader scale, i.e. when numerous CSBMs settle in one area and cooperate. Such transformation paths could be explored in a real-life environment within a living lab, accompanied by in-depth interviews, group discussions and ethnographic research. Eifel Myzel constitutes this kind of exciting environment in which a large number of CSBMs are currently emerging (Eifel Myzel 2023).

References

Aagaard, Annabeth/Lüdeke-Freund, Florian/Wells, Peter (2021): Business Models for Sustainability Transitions, Basel: Springer International. https://doi.org/10.1007/978-3-030-77580-3.

Alexander, Samuel (2015): Sufficiency Economy, Melbourne: Simplicity Institute.

Bacq, Sophie Catherine/Hertel, Christina Julia/Lumpkin, G. Tom (2020): "Societal impact at the nexus of entrepreneurship and community – Taking stock and looking ahead" In: Academy of Management Annual Meeting Proceedings 20/1. https://doi.org/10.5465/AMBPP.2020.288.

Berglund, Karin (2017): "Social entrepreneurs: Precious and precarious." In: Caroline Essers/Pascal Dey/Deirdre Tedmanson/Karen Verduyn (eds.), Critical Perspectives on Entrepreneurship. Challenging Dominant Discourses, New York: Routledge, pp. 17–35.

Beyeler, Laura/Jaeger-Erben, Melanie (2022): "How to make more of less: Characteristics of sufficiency in business practices." In: Frontiers in Sustainability 3/2022, 131. https://doi.org/10.3389/frsus.2022.949710.

Bloemmen, Marjolijn/Bobulescu, Roxana/Le, Nhu Tuyen/Vitari, Claudio (2015): "Microeconomic degrowth: The case of community supported agriculture." In: Ecological Economics 112, pp. 110–115. https://doi.org/10.1016/j.ecolecon.2015.02.013.

Bocken, Nancy M. P. (2017): "Business-led sustainable consumption initiatives: impacts and lessons learned." In: Journal of Management Development 36/1, pp. 81–96. https://doi.org/10.1108/JMD-10-2014-0136.

Bocken, Nancy M. P./Allwood, Julian (2012): "Strategies to reduce the carbon footprint of consumer goods by influencing stakeholders." In: Journal of Cleaner Production 35, pp. 118–129. https://doi.org/10.1016/j.jclepro.2012.05.031.

Bocken, Nancy M. P./Short, Samuel William (2016): "Towards a sufficiency-driven business model: Experiences and opportunities." In: Environmental innovation and societal transitions 18, pp. 41–61. https://doi.org/10.1016/j.eist.2015.07.010.

Bocken, Nancy M. P./Morales, Lisa Smeke/Lehner, Matthias (2020): "Sufficiency business strategies in the food industry – The case of Oatly." In: Sustainability 12/3, 824. https://doi.org/10.3390/su12030824.

Bocken, Nancy M. P./Niessen, Laura/Short, Samuel William (2022): "The Sufficiency-Based Circular Economy – An Analysis of 150 Companies." In: Frontiers in Sustainability 3, 899289. https://doi.org/10.3389/frsus.2022.899289.

Bocken, Nancy M. P./Short, Samuel William/Rana, Padmakshi/Evans, Steve (2014): "A literature and practice review to develop sustainable business model archetypes." In: Journal of cleaner production 65, pp. 42–56. https://doi.org/10.1016/j.jclepro.2013.11.039.

Boons, Frank/Lüdeke-Freund, Florian (2013): "Business models for sustainable innovation: state-of-the-art and steps towards a research agenda." In: Journal of Cleaner Production 45, pp. 9–19. doi: 10.1016/j.jclepro.2012.07.007.

Brinken, Julius/Trojahn, Sebastian/Behrendt, Fabian (2022): "Sufficiency, consistency, and efficiency as a base for systemizing sustainability measures in food supply chains." In: Sustainability 14/11, 6742. https://doi.org/10.3390/su141 16742.

Brinson, Ayeisha/Lee, Min-Yang/Rountree, Barbara (2011): "Direct marketing strategies: the rise of community supported fishery programs." In: Marine Policy 35/4, pp. 542–548. https://doi.org/10.1016/j.marpol.2011.01.014.

Büscher, Bram/Sullivan, Sian/Neves, Katja/Igoe, Jim/Brockington, Dan (2012): "Towards a synthesized critique of neoliberal biodiversity conservation." In: Capitalism nature socialism 23/2, pp. 4–30. https://doi.org/10.1080/10455752.2012.6 74149.

Cameron, Jenny (2015): "Enterprise innovation and economic diversity in community-supported agriculture: sustaining the agricultural commons." In: Gibson-Graham, Julie Katherine/Roelvink, Gerda/St Martin, Kevin (eds.), Making other worlds possible: Performing diverse economies, Minnesota: Minnesota Press, pp. 53–71.

Christ, Katherine/Burritt, Roger (2013): "Critical environmental concerns in wine production: an integrative review" In: Journal of Cleaner Production 53, pp. 232–242. https://doi.org/10.1016/j.jclepro.2013.04.007.

Conen, Wieteke/Schippers, Joop (2019): Self-employment as precarious work: A European perspective, Cheltenham: Edward Elgar.

Cristiano, Silvio (2021): "Organic vegetables from community-supported agriculture in Italy: Emergy assessment and potential for sustainable, just, and resilient urban-rural local food production." In: Journal of Cleaner Production 292, 126015. https://doi.org/10.1016/j.jclepro.2021.126015.

"CSX Netzwerk," 25.7.2023 (https://www.gemeinschaftsgetragen.de/).

Davila, Anabella/Molina, Christiane (2017): "From silent to salient stakeholders: A study of a coffee cooperative and the dynamic of social relationships." In: Business & Society 56/8, pp. 1195–1224. https://doi.org/10.1177/0007650315619626.

Debucquet, Gervaise/Guillotreau, Patrice/Lazuech, Gilles/Salladarré, Frédéric/ Troiville, Julien (2020): "Sense of belonging and commitment to a community-supported fishery. The case of Yeu Island, France." In: Review of Agricultural, Food and Environmental Studies 101/4, pp. 439–459. https://doi.org/10.1007/s4 1130-020-00101-3.

Diekmann, Marie (2020): „Community Supported Agriculture-Innovative Nischenstrategie für landwirtschaftliche Betriebe?" In: Berichte über Landwirtschaft-Zeitschrift für Agrarpolitik und Landwirtschaft 98/1, pp.1–21. https://doi.org/10 .12767/buel.v98i1.278.

Diekmann, Marie/Theuvsen, Ludwig (2019): „Soziale Nachhaltigkeit durch Community Supported Agriculture: Hält das Konzept, was es verspricht?“ In: Soziologie und Nachhaltigkeit 5/1, pp. 91–110. https://doi.org/10.17879/sun-2019-2473.

D'Souza, Clare/Taghian, Mehdi/Lamb, Peter/Peretiatkos, Roman (2006): “Green products and corporate strategy: an empirical investigation.” In: Society and business review 1/2, pp. 144–157. https://doi.org/10.1108/17465680610669825.

“Eifel MYZEL,” 27.7.2023 (https://eifel-myzel.de).

Elmes, Michael (2018): “Economic inequality, food insecurity, and the erosion of equality of capabilities in the United States.” In: Business & Society 57/6, pp. 1045–1074.

Freudenreich, Birte/Schaltegger, Stefan (2020): “Developing sufficiency-oriented offerings for clothing users: Business approaches to support consumption reduction.” In: Journal of Cleaner Production 247, 119589. https://doi.org/10.1016/j.jclepro.2019.119589.

Geissdoerfer, Martin/Vladimirova, Doroteya/Evans, Steve (2018): “Sustainable business model innovation: A review.” In: Journal of cleaner production 198, pp. 401–416. https://doi.org/10.1016/j.jclepro.2018.06.240.

Gossen, Maike/Kropfeld, Maren Ingrid (2022): ““Choose nature. Buy less.” Exploring sufficiency-oriented marketing and consumption practices in the outdoor industry.” In: Sustainable Production and Consumption 30, pp. 720–736. https://doi.org/10.1016/j.spc.2022.01.005.

Hausdorf, Michaela/Timm, Jana-Michaela (under review): “Innovative business models for societal transitions: Towards a definition and typology of community-supported business models.”

Huber, Joseph (2000): Industrielle Ökologie: Konsistenz, Effizienz und Suffizienz in zyklusanalytischer Betrachtung. Baden-Baden: Open Access Repository.

„JPB Winemaking,“ 25.7.2023 (https://jpbwinemaking.com/ and https://gemeinschaftsgetragen.de/wein-solawi-an-der-mosel/).

Jungell-Michelsson, Jessica/Heikkurinen, Pasi (2022): “Sufficiency: A systematic literature review.” In: Ecological Economics 195, 107380. https://doi.org/10.1016/j.ecolecon.2022.107380.

Khmara, Yaryna/Kronenberg, Jakub (2018): “Degrowth in business: an oxymoron or a viable business model for sustainability?” In: Journal of Cleaner Production 177, pp. 721–731. https://doi.org/10.1016/j. jclepro.2017.12.182.

Kropfeld, Maren (2023): “Lifestyles of enough exploring sufficiency-oriented consumption behavior from a social practice theory perspective.” In: Journal of Consumer Culture 23/2, pp. 369–390. https://doi.org/10.1177/14695405221095008.

Kropfeld, Maren Ingrid/Reichel, André (2021): “The Business Model of Enough: Value Creation for Sufficiency-Oriented Businesses.” In: Annabeth Aagaard/Florian Lüdeke-Freund/Peter Wells (eds.), Business Models for Sustainability Transitions, Cham: Palgrave Macmillan, pp. 163–189. https://doi.org/10.1007/978-3-030-77580-3_6.

Le Ber, Marlene/Branzei, Oana (2010): "(Re) forming strategic cross-sector partnerships: Relational processes of social innovation." In: Business & Society 49/1, pp. 140–172. https://doi.org/10.1177/0007650309345457.

Loebbering, Sophie (2018): Zukunftsfähige Wirtschaftsgemeinschaften – Übertragung des Community Supported Agriculture-Ansatzes (CSA) auf das Bäckerhandwerk (CSB). Münster, University of Applied Sciences.

Lüdeke-Freund, Florian/Dembek, Krzysztof (2017): "Sustainable business model research and practice: Emerging field or passing fancy?" In: Journal of Cleaner Production 168, pp. 1668–1678. https://doi.org/10.1016/j.jclepro.2017.08.093.

Medici, Marco/Canavari, Maurizio/Castellini, Alessandra (2021): "Exploring the economic, social, and environmental dimensions of community-supported agriculture in Italy." In: Journal of Cleaner Production 316, 128233. https://doi.org/10.1016/j.jclepro.2021.128233

"MYZELIUM," 25.7.2023 (https://myzelium.com/).

Niessen, Laura/Bocken, Nancy M. P. (2021): "How can businesses drive sufficiency? The business for sufficiency framework." In: Sustainable Production and Consumption 28, pp. 1090–1103. https://doi.org/10.1016/j.spc.2021.07.030.

O'Hara, Sabine/Stagl, Sigrid (2001): "Global food markets and their local alternatives: A socio-ecological economic perspective." In: Population and environment 22/6, pp. 533–554. https://doi.org/10.1023/A:1010795305097.

Parot, Jocelyn (2015): AMAP, the French CSA model: Business as usual or social movement (Working Paper No. 2), Aubagne: Urgenci International Network Working Paper Series.

"Patagonia," 25.7.2023 (https://eu.patagonia.com/de/de/ownership/ and https://www.zeit.de/2023/15/patagonia-umweltschutz-wachstum-oekologischer-kapitalismus).

Peredo, Anna Maria/Chrisman, James (2006): "Toward a theory of community-based enterprise." In: Academy of management Review 31/2, pp. 309–328. https://doi.org/10.5465/amr.2006.20208683.

Peredo, Anna Maria/McLean, Murdith (2013): "Indigenous development and the cultural captivity of entrepreneurship." In: Business & Society 52/4, pp. 592–620. https://doi.org/10.1177/0007650309356201.

Price, Jane/Joseph, Jeremy (2000): "Demand management – A basis for waste policy: A critical review of the applicability of the waste hierarchy in terms of achieving sustainable waste management." In: Sustainable Development 8/2, pp. 96–105. https://doi.org/10.1002/(SICI)1099-1719(200005)8:2<96::AID-SD133>3.0.CO;2-J.

Raworth, Kate (2017): Doughnut Economics: seven ways to think like a 21st-century economist, Vermont: Chelsea Green.

Rommel, Marius (2017): Zukunftsfähige Wirtschaftsgemeinschaften (CSX) – Übertragung der CSA-Logik auf andere Versorgungsfelder. Oldenburg: Carl von Ossietzky Universität Oldenburg.

Rommel, Marius (2019): Developing a Concept of the International Community Supported Agriculture in order to foster Sustainability in Global Food Systems. Lüneburg: Leuphana Universität Lüneburg.

Rommel, Marius/Posse, Dirk/Wittkamp, Moritz/Paech, Nico (2022): "Cooperate to transform? Regional cooperation in community supported agriculture as a driver of resilient local food systems." In: Walter Leal Filho/Marina Kovaleva/Elena Popkova (eds.), Sustainable Agriculture and Food Security, Cham: Springer International, pp. 381–399.

Sachs, Wolfgang (2015): "Suffizienz. Umrisse Einer Ökonomie Des Genug." In: Uwf UmweltWirtschaftsForum 23/1–2, pp. 3–9. https://doi.org/10.1007/s00550-015-0350-y.

Schaltegger, Stefan/Hansen, Erik G./Lüdeke-Freund, Florian (2016): "Business models for sustainability: Origins, present research, and future avenues." In: Organization and Environment 29/1, pp. 3–10. https://doi.org/10.1177/1086026615599806.

Schneidewind, Uwe/Palzkill-Vorbeck, Alexandra (2011): "Suffizienz Als Business Case: Nachhaltiges Ressourcenmanagement als Gegenstand einer transdisziplinären Betriebswirtschaftslehre." In: Wuppertal Institut für Klima, Umwelt, Energie GmbH, Impulse Zur WachstumsWende 2, pp. 4–20, 30.10.202 (https://epub.wupperinst.org/frontdoor/deliver/index/docId/3955/file/ImpW2.pdf).

Sinnicks, Matthew (2020): "The just world fallacy as a challenge to the business-as-community thesis." In: Business & Society 59/6, pp. 1269–1292. https://doi.org/10.1177/0007650318759486.

"SoLocal Energy," 25.7.2023 (https://www.solocal-energy.de/ and https://waswirtunkoennen.jetzt/2022/09/01/gemeinschaftsgetragenes-wirtschaften-csx/).

Speck, Olga/Möller, Martin/Grießhammer, Rainer/Speck, Thomas (2022): "Biological concepts as a source of inspiration for efficiency, consistency, and sufficiency." In: Sustainability 14/14, 8892. https://doi.org/10.3390/su14148892

Stubbs, Wendy/Cocklin, Chris (2008): "Conceptualizing a "sustainability business model" In: Organization and environment 21/2, pp. 103–127. https://doi.org/10.1177/1086026608318042.

Szuster, Brian/Bernstein, Jennifer/Kuldilok, Kulapa/Cecil, William (2021): "Small-scale shrimp farming and community supported fisheries in Southeast Asia." In: Journal of Southeast Asian Studies 52/3, pp. 539–553. https://doi.org/10.1017/S0022463421000588.

Tang, Haiying/Liu, Ying/Huang, Guoqin (2019): "Current status and development strategy for community-supported agriculture (CSA) in China." In: Sustainability 11/11, 3008. https://doi.org/10.3390/su11113008.

Upward, Antony/Jones, Peter H. (2016): "An ontology for strongly sustainable business models: Defining an enterprise framework compatible with natural and social science." In: Organization & Environment 29/1, pp. 97–123. https://doi.org/10.1177/1086026615592933.

"VAUDE," 27.7.2023 (https://nachhaltigkeitsbericht.vaude.com/gri/vaude/nachhaltiges-wirtschaften.php#:~:text=Der%20Gro%C3%9Fteil%20der%20Gewinne%20wird,%2DFamilie%20von%20Dewitz%2C%20ausgesch%C3%BCttet)

"Vianova Coop," 27.7.2023 (https://gemeinsam-mobil.net/erfolgsgeschichten/gemeinschaftsbasiertes-e-carsharing/)

Wells, Peter/Bristow, Gillian (2007): "Embedding eco-industrialism into local economies: the search for sustainable business and policy paradigms." In: Progress in Industrial Ecology, an International Journal 4/3–4, pp. 205–218. https://doi.org/10.1504/PIE.2007.015187.

Werling, Mara (2022): Von der Marktlogik in eine gemeinschaftsbasierte Wirtschaft – Potenziale und Hemmnisse bei der Diffusion von CSX. Siegen: Universität Siegen.

Woods, Timothy/Ernst, Matthew/Tropp, Debra (2017): Community supported agriculture: New models for changing markets. Washington, D.C.: U.S. Department of Agriculture. 10.22004/ag.econ.316239.

Zhao, Xin/Jia, Peihong (2020): "Towards sustainable small-scale fisheries in China: a case study of Hainan." In: Marine Policy 121, 103935. https://doi.org/10.1016/j.marpol.2020.103935.

Zhen, Huayang/Gao, Wenzeng/Jia, Li/Qiao, Yuhui/Ju, Xuehai (2020): "Environmental and economic life cycle assessment of alternative greenhouse vegetable production farms in peri-urban Beijing, China." In: Journal of Cleaner Production 269, 122380. https://doi.org/10.1016/j.jclepro.2020.122380.

Zhou, Yan/Park, Sangmoon (2020): "The regional determinants of the new venture formation in China's car-sharing economy." In: Sustainability 13/1, 74. https://doi.org/10.3390/su13010074.

Digging for Roots of Sufficiency in the Food Industry

Exploring How Ecological Embeddedness Supports Sufficiency in Business

Jessica Jungell-Michelsson and Iana Nesterova

Abstract *This chapter explores sufficiency in the food industry. We suggest that sufficiency is a process that can be enhanced through ecological embedding in food organisations. By looking at two empirical examples from Finland, we analyse the degrees and qualities of ecological embeddedness as an element of "sufficiencing" in the food business.*

1. Introduction

Sufficiency is increasingly acknowledged as an important element of strongly sustainable consumption and production. Within sustainability science, strong sustainability is often contrasted with weaker forms of sustainability based on whether the approach focuses on either qualitative (eco-efficiency) or quantitative (sufficiency) changes. Strong sustainability emphasizes the need to reduce overall resource use (quantity) to avoid transgressing planetary boundaries and calls for system-level transformations (e.g., degrowth or a steady-state economy), while weak sustainability follows dominant economic logics and incremental (qualitative) solutions within current systems (e.g., greener technology or process efficiency) (Neumayer 2003; Landrum/Ohsowski 2018). Given the magnitude at which multiple social and ecological crises are currently occurring (Ceballos et al. 2015; Foster et al. 2010), scholars have argued that weak sustainability measures must be complemented to a greater extent with efforts based on the premise of strong sustainability (Lehtonen/Heikkurinen 2022). Sufficiency may serve as an alternative organising principle for doing so (Princen 2003).

Sufficiency is based on the idea that human activity can and should be organised in such a way that it does not exceed the carrying capacity of the planet and allows other, i.e. beyond human, forms of life to thrive. Sufficiency is, moreover, characterised by an ethic of solidarity, since it pursues modes of living that are accessible to everyone instead of being premised on some enjoying a materially intensive lifestyle while the basic needs of others are not satisfied (Naess 1995). Thus, sufficiency has been conceptualised as both a means to strongly sustainable production and consumption as well as an end in itself (Jungell-Michelsson/Heikkurinen 2022). It is a state of "enoughness" both philosophically and materially; a human mindset that is oriented towards needs rather than wants and quality of life instead of ever-increasing consumption. Sufficiency goes hand in hand with a non-utilitarian approach to nature, humans and non-humans, and it rests on the assumption that humans have the ability for reflection, self-transformation and care for others and nature (Buch-Hansen/Nesterova 2023). On an individual level, sufficiency can manifest as intuitive common sense, e.g., knowing when you have had enough chocolate before beginning to feel sick or avoiding food waste, or as more active choices to reduce consumption in general, e.g., minimalism or voluntary simplicity (Elgin 2013; Elgin/Mitchell 1977). However, sufficiency is about more than just consumption limits and individual lifestyle choices. Thinking in terms of sufficiency creates space for new ways of theorising about sustainable economic activity. It means thinking differently about familiar economic categories, such as production, consumption and exchange (Heikkurinen/Bonnedahl 2019). Sufficiency cannot be left to consumers alone to implement but also requires transformative actions by those who produce what we consume, i.e. industry actors and businesses.

The operationalisation of sufficiency in business depends on the type of industry in question. In a genuinely sustainable society, some industries would cease to exist altogether (Buch-Hansen et al. 2024), e.g., fast fashion or the fossil fuel industry, while others will remain essential. The latter include industries that satisfy basic human needs, such as those involved in providing housing and food. While the question of what constitutes human needs remains unresolved, the need for food is beyond dispute. It is almost impossible to imagine human life without food in its different forms and appearances, as it serves our energy needs and is a key element of many cultures, rituals and traditions. At the same time, the environmental pressure put on nature due to various food processes is enormous (Campbell et al. 2017) and the social double burden (hunger in some parts of the world and obesity in others) keeps growing (Popkin at al. 2020). The modern food industry and agricultural system has become ever more efficient and productive, but it has been insensitive to the impacts on the health of nature and people (McGreevy et al. 2022). Efficiency has outcompeted quality and sufficiency and global market gains have outcompeted regional sensitivity and adaptation to local environments. Consequently, food production and consumption have a central position in the transformation of societies towards strong sustainability (see, e.g. Jungell-Michelsson/Autio 2022; Nelson/Edwards 2021; Nesterova 2022). Yet, the meaning of sufficiency in terms of food production and its operationalisation in the food business remain a rather untouched area of research.

This chapter contributes to efforts at understanding how sufficiency in the food industry could come into being. We "dig for the roots" of sufficiency in the food industry by exploring the concept of ecological embeddedness and analysing empirical examples from two different food businesses.

2. Sufficiency in food production and business

Navigating sufficiency in food production is not straightforward, as food not only satisfies the nutritional needs of humans but also their social and cultural needs (Rozin 1996). Food is related to culture, tradition and rituals and is a central component of our everyday lives. Food is a space where social and biological needs meet and become intertwined. For instance, the Swedish tradition of fika does not merely entail consuming coffee and sweet snacks, but is a space where people meet in a less formal atmosphere that facilitates well-being and bonding. Moreover, food production is characterised by diversity. It can take different forms, from foraging (gathering) and hunting, which throughout human history were the main forms of food production (Gowdy 1998), to the production of food by large businesses. While foraging for one's own use is perhaps the most sustainable and sufficiency-orientated mode of food production (see, e.g. Gowdy 2020), in modern societies most food production occurs in other spaces, such as small farms or large corporations. Here, we focus on those spaces rather than food production for the purpose of self-sufficiency.

In general, sufficiency in production implies reflecting on the direct and indirect business implications of striving for enough rather than more (Jungell-Michelsson/Heikkurinen 2022). In this sense, sufficiency is not opposed to other pursuits, principles and theoretical considerations (such as efficiency and circularity). Indeed, it is part of a constellation of principles that will hopefully bring genuinely sustainable production into existence (Nesterova 2020). Elsewhere, we have noted that sufficiency in business needs to concern the following domains: nature at large, location, humans, non-humans and the self (Nesterova/Jungell-Michelsson forthcoming). That is to say, for sufficiency to become an essential part of business, decision-makers need to consider treading lightly on the earth, be attentive to local nature and non-humans in concrete locations and develop worldviews that are compatible with strong sustainability. This creates a holistic framework for sufficiency, but it may still be perceived as an abstract ideal: something to strive for rather than a perfect end-state. In reality, businesses' relationships to sufficiency are more akin to journeys that involve navigating complex and diverse socio-economic landscapes rather than a one-off adoption of ideal practices (Nesterova 2023). In this case, we suggest referring to this journey not as the adoption of sufficiency or becoming perfectly sufficient but rather as "*sufficiencing*".

Sufficiencing in the food industry necessitates fundamentally different worldviews than those currently prevalent in most growth-oriented Western markets. In their discussion of sustainable food systems in a post-growth world, McGreevy et al. (2022: 1012) suggest that human food consumption patterns will need to be reshaped according to a new set of values and principles that prioritise regeneration over extraction, distribution over accumulation, commons over private ownership, care over control and sufficiency over efficiency. In such a system, food would be produced at rhythms that correspond more with nature, showing sensitivity towards the ecological carrying capacity and concern for local human and non-human communities. Hence, sufficiency in food production systems "engages social-ecological limits that are linked to community health and well-being, to field-level agroecologies and to their 'nested' positions within wider ecologies" (ibid: 1012). In practice, this would require adopting business models and strategies that treat nature as a key stakeholder and primary constraining factor for production while placing emphasis on value flows that extend beyond just financial ones (Brozovic 2020). Such business models aim at longer-term value creation not only in economic terms but also in ecological and social terms, by prioritising regenerative practices that show care for, not control of, natural cycles. Sufficiency in food production would allow for adequate nutrition as well as cultural expression for all groups of people while preserving local land- and seascapes (McGreevy et al. 2022).

For a business operating in the food industry, sufficiency can also be implemented as business models that support consumers in moderating their food consumption. Food production and consumption are inherently intertwined, and food sustainability is often socio-materially mediated through, e.g., product packages or marketing (Jungell-Michelsson/Autio 2022). By rethinking sales tactics and marketing practices, food businesses can inspire or nudge consumers towards greater sufficiency in food consumption, such as shifting to plant-based diets or reducing food waste (Heikkurinen at al. 2019; Sandberg 2021). In comparison to other consumables, food is challenging to 'design' or produce for reuse, repair or extended life-time use (without technical or chemical moderation); practices which otherwise have been identified as effective ways for businesses to promote sufficient consumption (Niessen/Bocken 2021). Instead, food businesses can focus on avoiding over-selling and urge consumers to, e.g., buy only what is needed. This has been done, for instance, by the German organic food retailer Bio Company, which in 2019 successfully launched the "Buy Less" (*Kauf Weniger*) campaign in an effort to make their customers more conscious of their food purchasing behaviour and food waste (Bio Company 2020).[1] Bocken et al. (2020) advise food businesses to

1 Similar efforts can be found in other countries, too; e.g., in Sweden the food retailer ICA encourages consumers to plan their food shopping in a way that avoids unnecessary purchases and uses food leftovers as much as possible (ICA 2023).

base their sufficiency strategies on the three top tiers of the waste hierarchy, concentrating on business activities that support consumers in reusing (e.g., providing refillable packaging or repurposing food), reducing (e.g., developing products that last or changing consumer perceptions about "ugly" vegetables) and avoiding (e.g., shortening ingredient lists or choice editing towards eco-friendly diets). Here, sufficiency can manifest in food business through a producer's or retailer's efforts to curb demand, and consequently, overall resource use (Bocken/Short 2016).

Yet, sufficiencing not only takes place in the socio-economic spheres of the food industry between producers and consumers. Food production is essentially a natural process, connected to the local ecologies and places from which the food originates. Indeed, food production has historically been rooted quite literally in the natural environment and specific places. As Goodman/Sage (2016: 1) state: "there is almost nothing more geographical than food in the ways that it intimately interlinks production and consumption, nature and society, bodies and landscapes, the global and the local, and indeed, spaces, places and everywhere between." Modern food production has, however, altered such links in many respects and "food from nowhere" is the rule now rather than the exception in most highly industrialised societies. Due to the present possibilities to utilise long supply chains and high technology, food production can be rooted in one place, yet continue somewhere else, e.g., fruits and vegetables shipped to far-away destinations for processing. Moreover, new technologies, such as vertical hydroponic agriculture, have allowed humans to grow food that is not seasonal or native and without reliance on the soil and the sun (see, e.g., Nesterova 2022). Yet, if the food business is to become more aligned with principles of strong sustainability and sufficiency, it must reconnect with natural processes and start following strategies that are more sensitive to local ecological systems (Landrum/Ohsowski 2018). We therefore turn to exploring the idea of ecological embeddedness as an important part of sufficiencing in the food industry.

3. Ecological embedding in the food business

The idea of embeddedness was originally introduced to describe the ties and values created between social networks and economic activities and has often been applied to alternative food networks (AFNs)[2] (Granovetter 1985; Sonnino/Marsden 2006). For food system sustainability, however, it is crucial to acknowledge that socio-economic relations are also embedded within ecological relations, i.e. ecologi-

2 *Alternative food networks* is a term used for food provision systems that fall outside the conventional model of food production and consumption, with the aim of re-socialising and re-spatialising food, such as farmers' markets, community-supported agriculture or garden selling (cp. Sonnino/Marsden 2006).

cally embedded. That is to say, the economic activity of a business is embedded in the broader natural systems, and nature is not only a source of economic resources but inherently entangled with all economic processes. Since the idea of ecological embeddedness can be characterised as "intrinsically ambivalent, contingent, and dynamic" (Goodman 2003: 2), we chose to synthesise insights from agri-food as well as management and organisation studies to create a framework for analysing the link between ecological embeddedness and sufficiency in the food business. Based on the existing literature, we understand ecological embeddedness as three-dimensional sensitivity, as outlined below.[3]

The spatial dimension: sensitivity towards place. Ecological embeddedness implies a sense of place, particularly towards the biophysical environment and ecological material conditions. From a managerial standpoint, Whiteman/Cooper suggest that this means "the degree to which a manager is rooted in the land – that is, the extent to which the manager is on the land and learns from the land in an experiential way" (2000: 1267), i.e. having deep knowledge about the dynamics of the local natural environment. However, such a definition runs the risk of over-romanticising indigenous practices and rural, alternative modes of food production (Banerjee/Linstead 2004; Morris/Kirwan 2011). The spatial dimension of ecological embeddedness should instead be understood as something more holistic, which could best be described through the notion of topophilia (Tuan 1974; Shrivastava/Kennely 2013). Topophilia implies deep understanding, affection and care for certain places. In other words, "place rootedness" consists of the emotional energy directed towards a certain place (which can be both biophysical and human-constructed) in a mental process that does not necessarily require continuous physical presence in the natural landscape. For a food business, this translates into what Shrivastava/Kennely call place-based organising: "place-based economic activities are complex and rich, culturally and naturally rooted, positively inimitable, and, most important, conducted with deep respect for the soil and habitus that provide the generative force" (2013: 92). In other words, the spatial dimension of ecological embeddedness implies a connection to biophysical places but can involve different degrees of proximity to the land.

The moral dimension: sensitivity towards other beings. Based on the notion of topophilia, ecological embeddedness presumably also encompasses a moral dimension. To be ecologically embedded means having an ecological conscience and extending human morality to the non-human world. For businesses, this means shifting towards more eco-centric organising (Heikkurinen et al. 2016), i.e. treating nature, including its various beings (human and non-human), as a key stakeholder

3 While we recognise that social embeddedness (cp. Granovetter 1985) and the systematic study of it has great relevance in this context, too, we focus here on the ecological aspects of embeddedness, which so far have been less studied in relation to food production.

in all socio-economic activity. This necessitates a transformation in individual moral agency since companies, despite facing increasing pressure for corporate responsibility, do not have a conscience of their own; it is the individuals in the company that do. Thus, ecological embeddedness encompasses more than simply recognising the influence of nature on economic activity. It involves knowledge and beliefs about ecosystem functioning (Whiteman/Cooper 2000) and, perhaps even more importantly, an ethos based on respect for and reciprocity towards the land. By "the land" we do not mean just soil but also the whole energy cycle that constitutes and is constituted by all soils, waters, plants and animals (Leopold 1949). These animals include humans, who also inhabit "the land" and satisfying the basic food needs of all human groups should likewise be a central moral focus in food production. In an ecologically embedded organisation, managers and other organisational members need to take responsibility for the biotic community in the same way that they take responsibility for the social and economic ones. Hence, the moral dimension of ecological embeddedness emphasises individual moral agency in keeping the social metabolism within the carrying capacity of the planet.

The temporal dimension: sensitivity towards natural rhythms. Ecological embeddedness also has a temporal dimension to it in two respects. First, rather than merely asking whether individuals and organisations are statically embedded or not, it is more important to focus on the process of becoming more or less embedded. Ecological embeddedness can be understood as a continuum across which an organisation can move, a process of *embedding*, and food businesses can engage in various activities that allow them to either deepen their relationship to the land or disconnect from it (Murdoch et al. 2000; Winter 2003; Penker 2006). Thus, the degree and quality of ecological embeddedness varies over time. Second, Murdoch et al. propose that, particularly in the context of food, ecological embeddedness involves "re-establishing biological, as opposed to industrial, processes within food chains" (2000: 116). To be ecologically embedded means to be sensitive to temporal changes in nature. In food production, this manifests in the form of seasons and varying production phases, as ecological conditions dictate when and at what pace food can be produced. Industrialisation and globalisation have disconnected the conventional food industry from this natural rhythm, and many foods are produced irrespective of natural seasons. Consequently, AFNs are often presented as being more sensitive towards natural rhythms (Winter 2003; Morris/Kirwan 2011), but ecological embeddedness does not exclude market logic and cannot automatically be equated with alternativeness (Winter 2003; Penker 2006). Hence, we suggest that the temporal dimension of ecological embeddedness implies a sensitivity towards the natural rhythms of change and can exist in varying types of organisations and contexts.

Overall, for ecological embeddedness to make analytical sense, the focus should not be on whether an organisation is embedded or not but rather where and how it is embedded (Penker 2006) and to what degree and at what level of quality (Murdoch et al. 2000; Winter 2003). Ecological embeddedness is not static, nor is it pre-assigned only to specific types of businesses, organisations or individuals. It is a process characterised by different modes of embeddedness at different points in time. Manifested as sensitivity towards spatial and temporal aspects in the natural environment, as well as an ethic directed towards the land, ecological embeddedness may serve as a foundation for more sufficiency-oriented businesses and sustainable food systems.

4. Exploring different food businesses

To explore the nature of ecological embeddedness in the food business, we rely on a qualitative study from the Finnish food industry. Finland offers an interesting empirical context in terms of food sustainability due the northern location of the country and its limited farming season. The study is based on semi-structured interviews with 20 Finnish food companies of different sizes and types, ranging from small-scale agri-food businesses to large global food corporations. During 2021–2022, the first author interviewed the companies' sustainability managers and CEOs[4] to examine how sustainability is understood within the organisation, what the organisation does when faced with sustainability issues and how sustainability has become visible in organisational practices. A total of 23 interviews,[5] each lasting between 55 and 90 minutes, together with the companies' written sustainability material (web pages and sustainability reports), formed the basis for a content analysis of how the organisations make sense of sustainability (see also Jungell-Michelsson/Autio 2022) and whether elements of ecological embeddedness can be identified in the activities of the said business.

To best capture the varying qualities and degrees of ecological embedding and sufficiencing, we tell the story of two significantly different food businesses in the form of vignettes.[6] Based on the collected data, we chose to narrate and analyse 'The Local Farm' (a small-scale local farming business, operating through AFNs) and 'The

4 The interviewees were selected based on how actively they are involved in their organisation's sustainability matters. Hence, the position of the interviewee varied depending on the company. Typically, the CEO was the most informed person in smaller companies. In larger companies, sustainability was often managed by a specific sustainability (and/or communications) manager.

5 In three of the 20 companies included in the study, additional interviews were conducted due to a need for more information or if the company itself recommended that the researchers interview more than one sustainability manager.

6 To respect the anonymity of the respondents, no real names are provided in the vignettes. All references to places and products have been pseudonymised.

Food Corp' (a large food corporation with global supply chains, operating in the conventional food business market) because they contrast so strongly with each other, and hence, represent the diversity of experiences in food production sustainability and "digging for roots" of sufficiency in the food industry.

4.1 Vignette 1: The Local Farm

> But we know how to do it. Humans as a society know how to do it. You just buy the stuff that is growing at the time of the year from someone you know who doesn't live too far away. – Chris, The Local Farm

Chris and Emma took a leap of faith when they left their "normal" 9-to-5 office jobs to become small-scale farmers. Except for allotment gardening, they had no professional experience with farming but felt a need to downscale their hectic life and focus on something that brings them joy: good food and growing vegetables. The motivation for this lifestyle change was not purely environmental, and the main aim was not to become self-sufficient but rather to create a way of earning a living from a more down-to-earth and self-managed job. After some lucky coincidences, they came across a small farm in southern Finland, including a house and some land and started their vegetable farming business. The Local Farm now grows around 50 varieties of vegetables and herbs, which they sell to selected supermarkets, through REKO rings[7] and to higher-end restaurants in the area. The main business, however, comes from selling ready-packed weekly 'veggie bags' to local customers who place their orders through a Facebook group. The 50–100 regular customers who pick up their bags come to the farm because they value the localness and perceived high quality of the vegetables. The customers enjoy the event of visiting the farm, where they sometimes even get to pick their kale and pumpkins themselves directly from the growing beds. While this creates a positive bond between the customers and the farm, Chris is concerned that he can only serve a limited group of people instead of providing "everyone's veggies".

Everything from sowing seeds to sales takes place at the 1.5-hectare big farm and within a radius of 15 km (which includes rural as well as more urban areas); even the fertilisers are provided by neighbours who have a horse farm. The Local Farm grows vegetables organically and through regenerative farming practices. The sales follow the harvesting season in Finland, starting from rhubarb in the spring to root vegetables, pumpkins and cabbage in the autumn. The rhythm of the work follows the natural seasons: during spring and summer, Chris and Emma work long hours

7 REKO is a retail and distribution model that offers customers a way to order products directly from the producer, without the need for middlepersons. REKO stands for Rejäl Konsumtion, which is Swedish for fair consumption.

almost every day of the week, while in the winter there might be farming-related work only for one day, leaving room for other tasks and free time. In the winters, Emma continues to do some of her previous consultancy work, to balance the family's financial situation, as they do not yet make enough from the farming business for both of them to live on. Starting the farm has required financial investments and the sales are always insecure, depending on the weather, climate, animals and customers. The aim is to also keep The Local Farm at a small-scale level in the future, but Chris and Emma still hope that they can reach a stage where the farm is a self-sustaining business.

One ecological challenge for The Local Farm has been improving the soil. Chris and Emma manage the farm with a great respect for nature, but it takes time to learn and understand the dynamics and conditions of the local environment. They have tried different growing methods (e.g., "no-dig" beds) and are thinking about raising some animals so that they can produce their own fertilisers and keep everything in cycle at the farm. Chris and Emma started The Local Farm almost from scratch and had to learn many things along the way. However, according to Chris, most challenges of this kind can be solved quite easily by just looking at the plants and the ground: "You look at your plants and it becomes pretty obvious if something is wrong. And you see when you do things right that the ground improves, you just see the life, it smells better and takes some more water." Therefore, all vegetables at the Local Farm are grown from seeds instead of ready plants, which would be quicker and easier. It enables Chris and Emma to be more in control of the growing process and to monitor how the soil and the plants are developing. According to Chris and Emma, it is the best way to produce tasty, high-quality vegetables and food.

4.2 Vignette 2: The Food Corp.

> Nature – it's where our food essentially comes from. We are dependent on nature. So maybe we should then get nature to steer our business a bit more and not the other way around. – Anna, The Food Corp.

When Anna chose to accept the position of sustainability manager at The Food Corp., it was because she knew that this was a company that was serious about its sustainability work. For Anna, who loves spending time in nature and growing stuff in her garden, it was important to work for a food company that values nature and understands its impact on nature. The Food Corp. can be called a multinational food corporation within FMCG (fast-moving consumer goods). With raw material sourced from nearly 50 countries, its own production sites in seven countries and products sold in 40 countries, The Food Corp. truly is an international business. The company owns many well-known food brands with products in several categories, such as sweets, snacks, frozen meals and dried foods. The assortment covers products that require sourcing raw material from countries on the other side of the globe, including everything from small-scale farmers in local villages to larger cooperatives and big-scale farms. The raw material is processed, packed and branded at The Food Corp.'s own factories across Europe, and the ready products are sold through conventional food retail outlets, i.e. food stores and supermarkets. The company has always been recognised for its high-quality products and responsible business governance, but as knowledge about (un)sustainability in the food industry has increased, The Food Corp. has decided to step-up its efforts in sustainable food production.

The Food Corp. wants to be a sustainability forerunner in the industry. In practice, this has meant engaging in systematic sustainability work during the last few years, including adopting a specific sustainability strategy, enacting several sustainability-related programmes and hiring sustainability experts to carry out the implementation of different actions. At first, many of the actions focused on minimising CO_2 emissions at the company's own production sites, but The Food Corp. has recognised that most emissions are created at the agricultural stage and is now focusing more on improving primary production processes on the fields and farms where the raw materials for the company's products are cultivated. The company is aware that most negative and positive environmental and social impacts are created at the beginning of the supply chains, and The Food Corp. is therefore trying to engage more actively on a local scale through supply chain certification schemes as well as direct actions. Examples include a climate project where The Food Corp. has worked together with local farmers to improve nutrient management and deploy regenerative agricultural practices, a project to enhance biodiversity on farms throughout Europe and a project where a percentage of the sales of a product goes to developing better water systems on farms in ecologically vulnerable areas. Such projects have required regular visits to the fields and farming locations in question to collaborate with the primary producers and better understand both the social and environmental dynamics of the specific places. As Anna emphasises: "It is all about local conditions and local variations."

According to Anna, one of the biggest challenges in working with sustainability in the food industry has to do with combining the different rhythms of people, business and nature. When The Food Corp. engages in developing more environmentally friendly agricultural practices, the changes and possible improvements to the soil and in harvests can be seen at the earliest during the next harvesting season or even later. Such engagements are thus done without any short-term benefits for The Food Corp.'s business or any tangible changes in the products for the consumers. It is done for the sake of nature, which, according to Anna, sometimes can be challenging to pitch (internally and externally) in FMCG businesses. Another struggle for The Food Corp. is handling the multitude of sustainability issues that arise in its global operations. The company cannot "fix" everything at once and has to prioritise efforts. So far, the most pressing issues from an environmental standpoint have been to find ways to decrease CO_2 emissions throughout the products' supply chains and to enhance biodiversity (e.g., through regenerative farming). These efforts are still a work in progress, but Anna already has some ideas about what she personally hopes will be "the next big thing" in The Food Corp.'s sustainability work: To implement the idea of planetary boundaries and for the business to start following the seasons and natural cycles. This will, however, require "a change in mindset and thinking", as Anna puts it.

5. Discussion

The Local Farm and The Food Corp. disclose two significantly different stories of moving towards more sustainable food production and consumption. One is about downscaling, re-localising to the countryside and aiming for small-scale agriculture with closer relationships to nature and consumers. The other one is about creating corporate sustainability strategies, investing in supply chain projects to minimise environmental impact and balancing consumer business logics. From the perspective of ecological embedding, the empirical examples highlight the challenges of bringing together "land ethics" (Leopold 1949) and food production practices in large, multinational companies due to the nature of business operations. In a smaller, local company, where the business, the land and the owners are deeply intertwined, ecological embedding can manifest directly in the business operations. In a large global company, the business is detached from the actual places and natural processes that provide the foundation for the business, making it difficult to develop deep connections between the business and the land(s). However, the vignettes illustrate that elements of ecological embedding are not limited only to small-scale, local agrifood businesses. Rather, ecological embedding both looks different and manifests differently in various types of businesses. While The Food Corp. cannot be as sensitive towards specific places, natural rhythms and seasons as The Local Farm can, it is not impossible for the company to make nature a key stakeholder in the business (Brozovic 2020). Embarking on a journey of ecological embedding in food production is in essence a mental process of turning one's attention to local, natural circumstances and taking responsibility for the non-human world, "the land". Land is something immediate but also part of something bigger: the Earth at large, towards which people exhibit concern and with which they experience unity (Yaden et al. 2017). Such individual moral agency can be identified in both stories presented above. Despite differences, the core of the stories is similar: a journey aimed at becoming more embedded in nature, which often involves trade-offs, conflicts and doubt. We now reflect on these journeys in relation to the three dimensions of ecological embeddedness.

The spatial dimension. Place rootedness is apparent in the story of The Local Farm. Chris and Emma live directly on and off the land that provides the products for their small business. Through their constant presence on the land and the daily time spent with the soil and the plants, they learn and develop together with their immediate biophysical environment. The Food Corp., in contrast, has operations in several countries and sources agricultural products from across the globe, including places with varying characteristics (e.g., urban factory areas, small-scale tea farms and large grain fields). This makes it impossible to be physically present on all the land(s) involved in the company's food production. The Food Corp. has, indeed, acknowledged the importance of engaging at the local agricultural level, and managers have increasingly visited the areas of primary production to develop better knowledge of the specific places where the company has connections. Yet, the multitude of places and natural environments involved in the business limits the possibilities for company managers to "learn from the land in an experimental way" (Whiteman/Cooper 2000: 1267). This is, however, not to say that other modes of food business do not also face trade-offs in the same manner. While the owners of The Local Farm are highly sensitive to the place where they live, they still rely on other places in the world. For instance, REKO rings and marketing of the farm and its products necessitate reliance on high technology (social media), which is not place-based.

The moral dimension. Sensitivity towards the non-human and human involves moral struggles that can be distinguished in both vignettes. The Local Farm's careful farming methods (regenerative, keeping everything in cycle at the farm) and provision of organic, nutritious food directly to customers shows respect towards and responsibility for both people and the land. Yet, it should be noted that the business was not founded purely based on altruistic aims but also on more selfish grounds, such as doing what feels fun (growing vegetables) and working without a boss. Despite downscaling and going "back to the land", Chris and Emma are still concerned about pricing, marketing and the sales of their products, indicating that deep ecological connections do not rule out a business mindset. Moreover, as Chris has acknowledged, there is a risk that The Local Farm's food becomes part of an elitist food trend instead of being "everyone's veggies", as the products might not be accessible to all due to price as well as physical location. In comparison to The Local Farm, The Food Corp. provides products to the main food retail market and the "ordinary consumer". The company's products are available and accessible to a large group of people and are an important part of the everyday food intake of many. Additionally, the business is important for supporting many people's livelihoods. The Food Corp., however, struggles to continue serving a broad range of consumers with good and affordable food while at the same time changing the modes of food production and consumption towards sustainability. Radical changes, e.g., suddenly deciding not to produce certain products or quitting the business altogether, could lead to negative consequences in terms of farmers losing their livelihoods and consumers losing some of their everyday food options. The decision of just what communities (biotic and human) to take responsibility for becomes challenging in a globally spread-out business, as the moral issues also become more diverse.

The temporal dimension. Ecological embedding in a food production context means being sensitive towards natural rhythms of change and the seasons. The Local Farm is based on providing only those vegetables that can be naturally grown during certain times of the year. The fact that the business is small and local makes it easier for the owners to adapt to ecological changes since they are not spread out over a geographically vast area encompassing different seasons. The downside of this practice, however, is that The Local Farm does not provide a steady income throughout the whole year, and Chris and Emma have to return to "regular" work during some months of the year. Hence, they have to dis-embed and re-embed (Murdoch et al. 2000) themselves to some extent as the seasons change to and from winter. In contrast, The Food Corp. maintains steady operations throughout the year. Yet, due to the company's constant presence in several places and various ecological surroundings, it becomes almost impossible to adapt the business to the natural seasons, as the scope of its operations may encompass many different seasons simultaneously. The Food Corp. has indeed made efforts to prioritise the rhythms of farming instead of business, e.g., through its engagements in agroecological development projects, which do not materialise directly in new consumer products or business gains. This illustrates an attempt to adapt to temporal elements of ecological embedding, but aligning the business with ecological and social rhythms is still seemingly a challenge, as Anna highlighted. The process of embedding is restrained by the scale and the logic of the business, making it questionable whether a multinational FMCG company ever really can align itself with the natural seasons.

In summary, it would be overly simplistic to say that The Local Farm is ecologically embedded and that The Food Corp. is not. Both businesses face their own struggles within each of the three dimensions, and sometimes the business is successful in one dimension at the expense of another. For instance, The Local Farm is sensitive towards place and the rhythms of change, but this comes at the cost of providing their products only for a certain group of customers. The Food Corp., on the other hand, can make their products accessible to more people, but this comes at the cost of being less sensitive towards places and the rhythms of natural change. Our empirical examples illustrate that the scale of the food business limits the degree to which an organisation can be ecologically embedded. Yet, food businesses of different kinds and sizes can place themselves upon and move along the continuum of ecological embedding, and thus, the potential of larger companies to pursue sufficiency should not be ruled out.

6. Conclusions

In this chapter, we contributed to a deeper understanding of sufficiency in the food industry. Since sufficiency generally presupposes a shift of focus from (unlimited) wants to vital needs, it may seem that the study of food production should be easy: food is a basic need and there needs to be enough of it for everyone. However, food production satisfies not only the nutritional needs of humans but also cultural and social ones. Moreover, food production is carried out by a great variety of organisations, ranging from small-scale farms and cooperatives to multinational corporations. Hence, we have suggested that sufficiency in the food industry should not be defined as an ideal state of production or business but rather as a process, which we have called "sufficiencing". While this process can take various forms, the underlying driver is an aspiration to organise production and consumption in a way that does not exceed the carrying capacity of the planet. It is essentially about a change in the human mindset towards engaging in more ecologically sensitive actions. Therefore, we proposed that ecological embeddedness – here defined as sensitivity towards place, other beings and natural rhythms – may enhance sufficiencing in food organisations. Acknowledging sufficiencing as well as ecological embedding as part of a process allows us to account for a wide range of food business rather than proposing that it is only alternative, small-scale, highly localised producers who can be sustainable. Such thinking also takes into account the opportunities for larger businesses, which many humans rely on to satisfy their needs for food, to step onto the pathways of strong sustainability.

The empirical examples we have explored are (intentionally) contrasting, which brings forth the diversity of challenges that various businesses face. In our exploration, we have deliberately moved away from providing calculations and attempting to quantify sufficiency. Rather, our interest lies in exploring nuances and imperfections, in understanding the stories and journeys of businesses. Digging for roots of sufficiency in food production brings to the surface trade-offs and doubts, which are a part of reality for all kinds of food-producing organisations. Our aim has not been to excuse the practices of large-scale, multinational corporations but to empathise with all kinds of struggles involved in stepping onto alternative pathways. It is only in theory that corporations can suddenly become local or cease to exist, and it would be reductionist to say that only those who live directly on and off the land can understand and appreciate nature and ecosystems. As our empirical examples show, stronger moral agency towards nature, humans and non-humans can develop among owners and managers of various kinds of businesses. As Leopold stated in his classic work, *The Land Ethic*: "no important change in ethics was ever accomplished without an internal change in our intellectual emphasis, loyalties, affections, and convictions" (1949: 113). Such individual transformations are unique depending on the people and businesses in question. Yet, showing the kind of sensitivity towards the land that we have argued for here is more easily done if "the land" is close and visibly comprehensible, so that one can see the consequences and reciprocities of one's actions on nature (Nesterova 2023). Hence, there is a limit to how large a food organisation can be in an ideal case in order to still be deeply ecologically embedded.

Overall, it is not challenging to theorise about strongly sustainable food production through, e.g., seasonal, small-scale, organic food or using only native species of plants. The issue is rather how to step onto alternative pathways, such as sufficiencing, considering that food production is diverse and complex and connected to multiple other systems in society. For instance, most consumers in highly industrialised countries today do not live according to the seasons but rather follow standardised season-less diets. For food producers to be able to embed themselves ecologically, consumer-side adjustments are needed as well, such as (re)learning how to preserve food or adapting meals to the seasons. Viewing sufficiency as a process rather than an ideal benchmark allows us to perceive it not as something obstructive, associated only with imposed limits, or as something unachievable for the vast majority of organisations in the food industry but as a welcoming activity of contemplation and exploration, which can be approached with curiosity and empathy. We propose that ecological embedding supports such activity. Every food business, regardless of the modes of production, can support stronger moral agency towards the land and create room for digging for the roots of strongly sustainable food production and consumption.

References

Banerjee, Subhabrata Bobby/Linstead, Stephen (2004): "Masking subversion: Neocolonial embeddedness in anthropological accounts of indigenous management." In: Human Relations 57/2, pp. 221–247. https://doi.org/10.1177/0018726 7040429.

Bio Company (2020): "BIO COMPANY treibt öko voran," 6.12.2023 (https://www.bi ocompany.de/downloads/pm/pressemitteilung-bio-company-jahresabschluss meldung-2020.pdf).

Bocken, Nancy M. P./Morales, Lisa Smeke/Lehner, Matthias (2020): "Sufficiency business strategies in the food industry – The case of Oatly." In: Sustainability 12/3, 824. https://doi.org/10.3390/su12030824.

Bocken, Nancy M. P./Short, Samuel William (2016): "Towards a sufficiency-driven business model: Experiences and opportunities." In: Environmental Innovation and Societal Transitions 18, pp. 41–61. https://doi.org/10.1016/j.eist.2015.07. 010.

Brozovic, Danilo (2020): "Business model based on strong sustainability: Insights from an empirical study." In: Business Strategy and the Environment 29/2, pp. 763–778. https://doi.org/10.1002/bse.2440.

Buch-Hansen, Hubert/Koch, Max/Nesterova, Iana (2024): Deep transformations: A theory of degrowth, Manchester: Manchester University Press.

Buch-Hansen, Hubert/Nesterova, Iana (2023): "Less and more: Conceptualising degrowth transformations." In: Ecological Economics 205, 107731. https://doi.org/10.1016/j.ecolecon.2022.107731.

Campbell, Bruce M./Beare, Douglas J./Bennett, Elena M./Hall-Spencer, Jason M./Ingram, John S.I./Jaramillo, Fernando/Ramankutty, Navin/Sayer, Jeffrey A./Shindell, Drew (2017): "Agriculture production as a major driver of the Earth system exceeding planetary boundaries." In: Ecology and Society 22/4, 8. https://doi.org/10.5751/ES-09595-220408.

Ceballos, Gerardo/Ehrlich, Paul R./Barnosky, Anthony D./García, Andrés/Pringle, Robert M./Palmer, Todd M. (2015): "Accelerated modern human–induced species losses: Entering the sixth mass extinction." In: Science Advances 1/5, 1400253. https://doi.org/10.1126/sciadv.1400253.

Elgin, Duane (2013): "Voluntary simplicity – a path to sustainable prosperity." In: Social Change Review 11/1, pp. 69–84. https://doi.org/10.2478/scr-2013-0006.

Elgin, Duane/Mitchell, Arnold (1977): "Voluntary simplicity – life-style of the future." In: The Futurist 11/4, pp. 200–261. http://dx.doi.org/10.1108/eb053820.

Foster, John Bellamy/Clark, Brett/York, Richard (2010): The ecological rift: Capitalism's war on the Earth, New York: Monthly Review Press.

Goodman, David (2003): "The quality 'turn' and alternative food practices: reflections and agenda." In: Journal of Rural Studies 19/1, pp. 1–7. https://doi.org/10.1016/S0743-0167(02)00043-8.

Goodman, Michael K./Sage, Colin (2016): Food transgressions: Making sense of contemporary food politics, Abingdon: Routledge.

Gowdy, John M. (1998): Limited wants, unlimited means: A reader on hunter-gatherer economics and the environment, Washington: Island Press.

Gowdy, John M. (2020): "Our hunter-gatherer future: Climate change, agriculture and uncivilization." In: Futures 115, 102488. https://doi.org/10.1016/j.futures.2019.102488.

Granovetter, Mark (1985): "Economic action and social structure: The problem of embeddedness." In: American Journal of Sociology 91/3, pp. 481–510. https://www.jstor.org/stable/2780199.

Heikkurinen, Pasi/Rinkinen, Jenny/Järvensivu, Timo/Wilén, Kristoffer/Ruuska, Toni (2016): "Organising in the Anthropocene: An ontological outline for ecocentric theorising." In: Journal of Cleaner Production 113, pp. 705–714. https://doi.org/10.1016/j.jclepro.2015.12.016.

Heikkurinen, Pasi/Bonnedahl, Karl Johan (2019): "Dead ends and liveable futures: A framework for sustainable change." In: Karl Johan Bonnedahl/Pasi Heikkurinen (eds.), Strongly sustainable societies: Organising human activities on a hot and full Earth. Routledge: Abingdon, pp. 289–301.

Heikkurinen, Pasi/Young, C. William/Morgan, Elizabeth (2019): "Business for sustainable change: Extending eco-efficiency and eco-sufficiency strategies to consumers." In: Journal of Cleaner Production 218, pp. 656–664. https://doi.org/10.1016/j.jclepro.2019.02.053.

ICA (2023): "Så minskar du ditt matsvinn," 30.8.2023 (https://www.ica.se/artikel/minska-matsvinnet-sa-gor-du/).

Jungell-Michelsson, Jessica/Autio, Minna (2022): "Transforming Foodways: Sustainability Sensemaking Processes Among Finnish Food Companies." In: Ethnologia Fennica 49/2, pp. 36–65. https://doi.org/10.23991/ef.v49i2.113006.

Jungell-Michelsson, Jessica/Heikkurinen, Pasi (2022): "Sufficiency: A systematic literature review." In: Ecological Economics 195, 107380. https://doi.org/10.1016/j.ecolecon.2022.107380.

Landrum, Nancy E./Ohsowski, Brian (2018): "Identifying worldviews on corporate sustainability: A content analysis of corporate sustainability reports." In: Business Strategy and the Environment 27/1, pp. 128–151. https://doi.org/10.1002/bse.1989.

Lehtonen, Tommi/Heikkurinen, Pasi (2022): "Sufficiency and Sustainability: Conceptual Analysis and Ethical Considerations for Sustainable Organisation." In: Environmental Values 31/5, pp. 599–618. https://doi.org/10.3197/096327121X16328186623878.

Leopold, Aldo (1989 [1949]): A Sand County Almanac, and Sketches Here and There, Oxford: Oxford University Press.

McGreevy, Steven R./Rupprecht, Christoph D.D./Niles, Daniel/Wiek, Arnim/Carolan, Michael/Kallis, Giorgos/Kantamaturapoj, Kanang/Mangnus, Astrid/Jehlička, Petr/ Taherzadeh, Oliver/Sahakian, Marlyne/Chabay, Ilan/Colby, Ashley/Vivero-Pol, Jose-Luis/Chaudhuri, Rajat/ Spiegelberg, Maximilian/Kobayashi, Mai/Balázs, Bálint/Tsuchiya, Kazuaki/Nicholls, Clara/ Tanaka, Keiko/Vervoort, Joost/Akitsu, Motoki/Mallee, Hein/Ota, Kazuhiko/Shinkai, Rika/ Khadse, Ashlesha/Tamura, Norie/Abe, Kenichi/Altieri, Miguel/Sato, Yo-Ichiro/Tachikawa, Masashi (2022): "Sustainable agrifood systems for a post-growth world." In: Nature Sustainability 5/12, pp. 1011–1017. https://doi.org/10.1038/s41893-022-00933-5

Morris, Carol/Kirwan, James (2011): "Ecological embeddedness: An interrogation and refinement of the concept within the context of alternative food networks in the UK." In: Journal of Rural Studies 27/3, pp. 322–330. https://doi.org/10.1016/j.jrurstud.2011.03.004.

Murdoch, Jonathan/Marsden, Terry/Banks, Jo (2000): "Quality, nature, and embeddedness: Some theoretical considerations in the context of the food sector." In: Economic Geography 76/2, pp. 107–125. https://doi.org/10.2307/144549.

Naess, Arne (1995): "Deep ecology and lifestyle." In: Stephan Bodian/George Sessions (eds.), Deep ecology for the 21st century: Readings on the philosophy and practice of the new environmentalism. London: Shambhala, pp. 259–261.

Nelson, Anitra/Edwards, Ferne (2021): Food for degrowth: Perspectives and practices, London: Routledge.

Nesterova, Iana (2020): "Degrowth business framework: Implications for sustainable development." In: Journal of Cleaner Production 262, 121382. https://doi.org/10.1016/j.jclepro.2020.121382.

Nesterova, Iana (2022): "Being in the world locally: Degrowth business, critical realism, and humanistic geography." In: Frontiers in Sustainability 3, 829848. https://doi.org/10.3389/frsus.2022.829848.

Nesterova, Iana (2023): "Responsibilities towards places in a degrowth society: How firms can become more responsible via embracing deep ecology." In: Society Register 7/1, pp. 53–74. https://doi.org/10.14746/sr.2023.7.1.03.

Nesterova, Iana/Jungell-Michelsson, Jessica (forthcoming): "A business of deep transformations is a business of sufficiency." In: David Skrbina/Toni Ruuska/Tina Nyfors (eds.) Sufficiency in nature, Leiden: Brill.

Neumayer, Eric (2003): Weak versus strong sustainability: exploring the limits of two opposing paradigms, Celtenham: Edward Elgar Publishing.

Niessen, Laura/Bocken, Nancy M. P. (2021): "How can businesses drive sufficiency? The business for sufficiency framework." In: Sustainable Production and Consumption 28, pp. 1090–1103. https://doi.org/10.1016/j.spc.2021.07.030.

Penker, Marianne (2006): "Mapping and measuring the ecological embeddedness of food supply chains." In: Geoforum 37/3, pp. 368–379. https://doi.org/10.1016/j.geoforum.2005.09.001.

Popkin, Barry M./Corvalan, Camila/Grummer-Strawn, Laurence M. (2020): "Dynamics of the double burden of malnutrition and the changing nutrition reality." In: The Lancet 395/10217, pp. 65–74. https://doi.org/10.1016/S0140-6736(19)32497-3.

Princen, Thomas (2003): "Principles for sustainability: from cooperation and efficiency to sufficiency." In: Global Environmental Politics 3/1, pp. 33–50. https://doi.org/10.1162/152638003763336374.

Rozin, Paul (1996): "The socio-cultural context of eating and food choice." In: Herbet L. Meiselman/Halliday J. H. MacFie (eds.), Food choice, acceptance and consumption, Boston: Springer, pp. 83–104.

Sandberg, Maria (2021): "Sufficiency transitions: A review of consumption changes for environmental sustainability." In: Journal of Cleaner Production 293, 126097. https://doi.org/10.1016/j.jclepro.2021.126097.

Shrivastava, Paul/Kennelly, James J. (2013): "Sustainability and place-based enterprise." In: Organization & Environment 26/1, pp. 83–101. https://doi.org/10.1177/1086026612475O.

Sonnino, Roberta/Marsden, Terry (2006): "Beyond the divide: rethinking relationships between alternative and conventional food networks in Europe." In: Journal of Economic Geography 6/2, pp. 181–199. https://doi.org/10.1093/jeg/lbi006.

Tuan, Yi-Fu (1974): Topophilia: A study of environmental perception, attitudes, and values, Englewood Cliffs: Prentice-Hall.

Whiteman, Gail/Cooper, William H. (2000): "Ecological embeddedness." In: Academy of Management Journal 43/6, pp. 1265–1282. https://doi.org/10.2307/1556349.

Winter, Michael (2003): "Embeddedness, the new food economy and defensive localism." In: Journal of Rural Studies 19/1, pp. 23–32. https://doi.org/10.1016/S0743-0167(02)00053-0.

Yaden, David Bryce/Haidt, Jonathan/Hood Jr., Ralph W./Vago, David R./Newberg, Andrew B. (2017): "The Varieties of Self-Transcendent Experience." In: Review of General Psychology 21/2, pp. 143–160. https://doi.org/10.1037/gpr0000102.

Cultures of Sufficiency in Food Businesses

Proposing a Processual Systems Approach to Understand Cultures of Sufficiency

Joshua Hurtado Hurtado, Heini Salonen, Tina Nyfors, Pasi Heikkurinen and Kristoffer Wilén

Abstract *This chapter proposes a processual systems approach to examine organizational cultures of companies that practice sufficiency. We illustrate our approach by examining a food system and business network ecosystem in Finland: Agroecological Symbiosis. We show that maintaining a culture of sufficiency in companies is a continuous and evolving process.*

1. Introduction

Business organizations as powerful economic enactors have a significant role in defining, adopting and realizing sustainability practices. Currently, most businesses operate from a growth-oriented and competitive standpoint often at odds with environmental and social well-being (Heikkurinen/Bonnedahl 2013; Nesterova 2021). Such businesses tend to also emphasize efficiency and profitability in their goals and actions (Heikkurinen et al. 2019), as reflected in their organizational cultures. A culture of expansion, affluence and excess combined with effective organization can be seen as one of the root causes of the ongoing sustainability crisis (Smircich 1983). These cultures also disregard the role and agency of non-human actors. They differ markedly from cultures based on sufficiency which emphasize community, sharing, and the well-being of people and nature (Princen 2005; Jungell-Michelsson/Heikkurinen 2022). Business research traditionally portrays organizational culture as an instrument to be controlled and molded for managerial purposes, like superior economic performance (Chatman/O'Reilly 2016). The functionalist approach to studying organizational culture remains popular, as most studies use the instrumental view to examine the relationship between organizational culture and organizational performance (ibid). This view of culture is claimed to fail to provide a deep and rich understanding of organizational culture (Alvesson 2002).

Our approach to organizational cultures builds on the notions of *process* and *systems*, where the organization is conceptualized both as a process embedded in a cultural fabric, comprising an interplay between artefacts, values and basic assumptions (Whitehead 1978; Schein 1990), and as "a spatio-temporal concentration of energetic flows from the human and non-human worlds, where it is empirically impossible to pinpoint the boundaries between the registers of mind and matter" (Heikkurinen/Ruuska et al. 2021: 23). Inspired by Gregory Bateson (2000) and Kenneth Boulding (1956), we understand the organization as a systemic entity amongst other (more or less) ordered systems. On culture, our study draws on Pettigrew (1979) who also described creating organizational cultures in terms of processes and systems of becoming. He defined culture as a system, consisting of meanings given to tasks and people's actions at a time. In addition to an organization's culture being a system in itself, it is embedded in other systems, be they subsystems or oversystems of the organization, and interacts with them. For earthbound phenomena, like human doings and sayings, the planet operates as a focal system of survival and meaning.

In this study, we further assume that changing organizational culture may enable businesses to effectively adopt sustainable practices (Harris/Crane 2002; Baumgartner 2009). By espousing a set of beliefs, values and behaviors aligned with sufficiency, businesses could reduce their negative environmental and social impacts. However, addressing culture at the superficial artefact level is unlikely to lead to profound and sustained change in business culture. An examination of the underlying, taken-for-granted premises is needed, as noted by Harris and Crane (2002).

The purpose of this chapter is to understand the possibilities and the role of cultural processes in organizing business activities in line with the notion of sufficiency and outline a processual systems approach for the study of cultures. We find that such an approach to culture can lead to a more profound understanding of the principles underpinning business activities and what business actors consider effective, rational, or even possible in doing business. Identifying and understanding cultural elements that, on the one hand, prevent businesses from breaking free from old patterns of behavior and, on the other hand, enable adopting new practices in line with the logic of sufficiency (Princen 2005), is crucial to changing current business cultures to minimize human environmental impact. We claim that a mere technical focus on impacts is inadequate for reaching the ambitious targets of sustainability, manifested in the discourses and rhetoric of climate neutrality, net positive emissions and dematerialization. In other words, cultures of sufficiency go beyond calculations and measuring. Complementing the strategy of efficiency with one of sufficiency requires a closer examination of cultural aspects. In this chapter, we develop a frame that consists of three culturally embedded elements: enactors, enablers and enactments. We theoretically elaborate a processual systems approach to study sufficiency in business, illustrating the approach using a case from a local, sustainable food system based on Agroecological Symbiosis developed in Palopuro, Finland.

We consider the system of Agroecological Symbiosis created in Palopuro to exemplify a case of sufficiency in business because it illustrates how businesses, as key enactors, have gone beyond a focus on profits, striving to meet human needs, like nutrition, community and collaboration. The businesses at Palopuro practice agroecological food production and generate renewable energy. Together they form the food system of Agroecological Symbiosis, in which they engage in reciprocal and mutually beneficial interactions with a wide range of other enactors. The businesses operating within Agroecological Symbiosis are concerned with remaining within the ecosystems' ecological boundaries and localizing production. Paying attention to elements of organizational culture, which we claim are processual, can sustain the sufficiency practices of businesses like those taking part in the system of Agroecological Symbiosis in Palopuro.

2. Organizational culture embedded in the ecosystem

2.1 Three generic cultural elements: enactors, enablers, enactments

We focus on three generic elements to understanding cultures of sufficiency, namely enactors, enablers and enactments. These three elements often feature prominently – yet separately – in the sustainability transitions and organizational sustainability literature (Sabella/Eid 2016; Heikkurinen et al. 2021; Wadham et al. 2023). In our view, they offer a useful base for building a conceptual frame to approach sufficiency in business.

We understand enactors as the principal (human and non-human) agents in each cultural setting, which reproduce or change the situation, be they dominant norms and practices or hegemonic institutions. When discussing agency in the context of sustainability transitions, the focus has been predominantly on human enactors, from individuals to corporate and political organizations (Fischer/Newig 2016). This anthropocentric perspective manifests in business cultures through the dominant understandings of sustainability: the triple bottom-line or linking together the economic, social and environmental domains of sustainability (Bonnedahl/Heikkurinen 2019). Even in accounts that address the need to consider non-human life forms, they are seen as external concerns rather than internal to sustainability practices (Nicholson/Kurucz 2019).

In contrast, recent research on sustainable business argues that the preference for human activity has been institutionalized at the expense of the non-human world and is complicit in increasing human environmental impact (Heikkurinen et al. 2016). The strong sustainability perspective overcomes this anthropocentric focus to integrate the concerns of other species and socio-ecological systems, aiming to respect the integrity of individuals and species (Bonnedahl/Heikkurinen 2019). Recent discussions on sustainability practices for organizations highlight the relational nature of the agents that respect planetary boundaries. For example, Heikkurinen et al. note that "a key means of respecting nonhumans is to blur the boundaries between earthbound actors. Different forms of life unfold in a complex conjoint genesis with humans" (2021: 278).

Both human enactors (individuals, producer and consumer groups, organizations) and non-human enactors (plants, animals, fungi, microorganisms and ecosystemic elements like bodies of water) comprise sufficiency cultures. Individual human enactors can design a business model that adopts sufficiency as a central premise. The business itself, in its organizational charter, can embody sufficiency by describing its ethos and practice (Bocken/Short 2016; Kropfeld/Reichel 2021; Niessen/Bocken 2021). But non-human elements can also guide the practice and ethos of sufficiency in business. As Ortiz-Przychodzka et al. (2023) suggest, non-human entities negotiate with humans in performing economic activities. The authors give the example of bees, animals which make valuable honey in trees. This prompts humans who would otherwise cut down the trees to leave them alone so that they can later obtain honey from the bees' natural activities. Some bees defend themselves against wood producers and might sting them if threatened. These interactions suggest that the non-human world possesses more agency than often acknowledged from an anthropocentric viewpoint and can influence the activities of human beings towards sufficiency.

The second element of our frame, enablers, are the cultural elements that combine with biophysical elements and steer the enactors towards sustainability and specifically towards cultures of sufficiency in business. Culture does not only include artefacts, such as the products a business creates or the logotypes it uses, or restrict itself with an instrumental practice, such as establishing codes of conduct inside an organization to improve organizational performance. Culture, for us, operates akin to a constitutive worldview that underlies the values and basic assumptions that push the enactors towards sufficiency (or away from it) (Schein 1990). This culture becomes visible in organizational settings, which establish the parameters for the enactors. The enactors themselves contribute to the creation of culture through interactions that are informed or steered by their specific set of values and assumptions.

Enablers contributing to cultures of sufficiency in business go beyond general sustainability enablers in organizational culture. At the broadest scale, the constitutive worldview of cultures of sufficiency in business is premised on "enoughness" (Jungell-Michelsson/Heikkurinen 2022). This worldview manifests as an enabler through visions, values, business models, strategies and communication. According to Kantabutra (2020), sustainability-based organizational visions should provide clarity and stability, be future-oriented and satisfy stakeholders. Organizational values that favor sustainability in corporations include perseverance against challenging conditions, responsibility towards society and the environment, innovation, generosity and integrity (Assortagoon/Kantabutra 2023). Business models that embrace sufficiency encourage sharing, extend product life, facilitate the reuse of existing products and offer immaterial services focused on enhancing social well-being and personal abilities (Bocken/Short 2016; Gossen et al. 2019). Niessen and Bocken (2021) propose that business sufficiency strategies could be structured according to four dimensions: consuming fewer items and resources (*less clutter*), designing products to last and be used for longer (*less speed*), producing and consuming locally and disentangling value chains (*less distance*) and encouraging consumers to be self-sufficient and collaborate (*less market*) (see also Sachs 1993). In other words, business strategies should aim at increasing the quality of production. Decreasing the amount of production and influencing customers to consume better and consume less are desirable (Heikkurinen et al. 2019). Influencing consumers so that they share the values of sufficiency requires effective communication. Gossen and Heinrich (2021) show how digitalisation allows companies to promote sufficiency communication through multiple channels and forms of content and suggest that inspiring customers to reduce consumption and change social norms may influence lifestyle changes, which in turn could benefit sufficiency-oriented companies.

The third element of our frame, enactments, focuses on the actions of, and interactions among, the human enactors, as well as on the dynamics between humans and non-humans. Enactments create and reveal culture: acting reflects underlying values and assumptions about the world and normative commitments and may contribute to changing organizational settings and cultural norms, as well as stabilizing them over time. At the scale of sustainable production, sufficiency enactments can manifest as a paradigm shift in business logic, where businesses *change priorities* by moving towards non-consumerism and escaping the imperative of maximizing profits (Jungell-Michelsson/Heikkurinen 2022). In the clothing industry, Freudenreich and Schaltegger (2020) suggest actions such as creating physically durable items of clothing, reusing high-quality clothing items and designing modular clothing with detachable parts as enactments of sufficiency. Niessen and Bocken (2021) similarly identify offering repair and refurbishing services, producing and consuming local products, organizing workshops to help others build their own furniture and grow their own food and buying and selling in second-hand shops as enactments of sufficiency.

Sufficiency enactments also refer to the relationships between the enactors themselves and the meaning they assign to the enactments. Beyeler and Jaeger-Erben (2022) highlight the social meanings of sufficiency in business, where enactments should manifest care, patience, local embeddedness, happiness and joy, among other features. Moreover, the authors note, developing competencies is necessary for sufficiency business practice. Sufficiency enactments therefore include acquiring repairing skills, receiving feedback and continuously learning, building communities, collaborating with others and involving other stakeholders.

2.2 Processual system approach on enactors, enablers and enactments

We propose that the enactors, enablers and enactments constitute a frame that should be considered through a *processual systems* approach. Organizational cultures consist of multiple, interrelated processes that span a limited period of time and achieve partial stability, which we recognize when we encounter a particular culture. If we were to examine a food organization, which engages in food self-provisioning practices, we might find a process where two enactors – the self-provisioning farmer and the crop – are engaged in a mutually-nurturing relationship. In this simplified example, we disregard processes that would in reality be included, such as decision-making processes over work responsibilities or the kind of crops to be cultivated. The biophysical enabler in this case would be a fertile plot of land that allows the crop to grow in the regional climate. The enactments at this scale of analysis could consist of providing nutrients and watering the plants over many days and months. The crop is thus sustained by the farmer, and the crop gives the farmer their means of sustenance. This cycle repeats itself for this relationship and is replicated by other farmers in the organization.

We identify processuality in how the different elements of our frame constitute one another. In our example, the self-provisioning farmer and the crop are responsible for the continued sustenance of each other. The enabler of the fertile plot of land also creates the possibility for this relationship to flourish: it provides nutrients to the crops and gives the self-provisioning farmer a territory which allows them to identify and act as a farmer. The enabler, in this sense, is one condition of possibility for the enactors to exist. The same principle applies for the enactments: the enactment of watering the plants, done by the farmer towards the crops, reflects the action that sustains the mutually-nurturing relationship between the farmer and the crop. Without this enactment, the crop would perish, while the farmer would not obtain the food they need.

Moreover, we identify processuality in our frame because the enactors, enablers and enactments can themselves be transformed into each other, depending on the perspective of analysis and the temporality of the phenomenon under scrutiny. In the example of the food self-provisioning farmer, the fertile plot of land could be considered a more prominent enactor if looked at from a non-human perspective, which gives to the other enactor, the crops, the necessary nutrients to survive. Enablers for this relationship to flourish would be sunlight and humidity in the soil. The enactments between these two enactors would consist of growing fruits and vegetables, which provide food for the self-provisioning farmer but also the means by which the plants reproduce themselves. If we shift the scope of the analysis to the organizational level, we could consider membership statutes as enablers of decision-making – an instance of enactments – that the self-provisioning farmer – an instance of enactor – has to make to maintain continuity and meet their responsibilities within the organization.

Figure 1: The Enactors, Enablers, Enactments frame through a processual systems approach. (Commissioned by the authors)

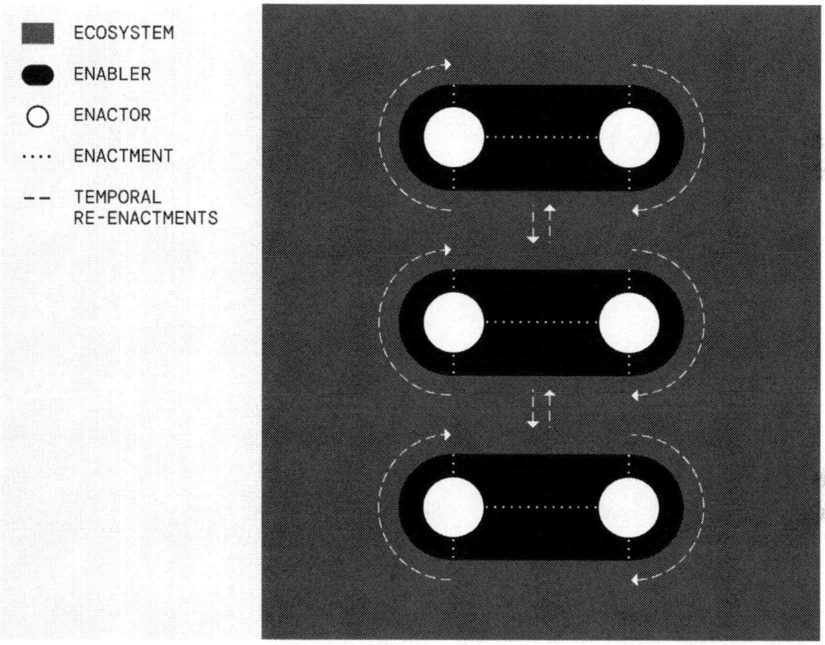

Figure 1 illustrates how we conceptualize the processual systems approach with the three elements of our frame. The enactors relate to one another in the form of enactments, and this is facilitated by the temporal, biophysical and cultural enablers. This relationship between each of these elements is re-enacted throughout time, giving it partial stability as a form of organizational culture. We propose this processual systems approach to the analysis of sufficiency cultures in business because it provides a starting point for identifying where elements that run counter to sufficiency and sustainability emerge and where sufficiency-oriented action should be implemented.

3. Case Agroecological Symbiosis: a food system that focuses on sufficiency

Agroecological Symbiosis (AES) is a sustainable food system model developed in Finland to reach sustainability at the system-level. The first of its kind was developed at Knehtilä farm, in Palopuro village, in southern Finland. More specifically, AES is:

> a form of food production and processing in which the farms, the food processors, and the energy producers function in an integrated and local manner. The operations are running in spatial proximity to each other allowing efficient material and energy integration (Helenius et al. 2020: 3).

Our analysis of AES is based on information obtained from three sources: 1) published academic research, 2) videos and websites that document processes in the AES food system, and 3) from ongoing research by some of this chapter's authors. The published academic research used ethnographic and participatory methods (Helenius et al. 2020; Mazac et al. 2021), which we considered valuable to present a textured depiction of the on-site dynamics at the Palopuro AES. The videos and websites offer an entry point to examining the enactments occurring at the Palopuro AES between different enactors from a systemic perspective (Healthy Future Project 2016; Eerikäinen 2019; Stenger 2022). Our own ongoing research involves interviewing the designers and participants of AES, including the leaders of two businesses that operate in the Knehtilä farm, where farming and food production takes place, and in Palopuro village. While this chapter offers more of a theoretical contribution, we ground our analysis of the culture at AES with information obtained from these sources.

The AES food system at Palopuro consists of a network of businesses, farmers and local inhabitants. Local entrepreneurs manage chicken coops and henhouses, vegetable farms and local biogas and food processing plants. The Global Network of Lighthouse Farms (2020) describes the Knehtilä farm as having an area of 380 hectares, where farmers cultivate cereals and buckwheat for both human food and chicken feed. The cereals undergo processing into organic snacks, granola and flakes, which are meant for human consumption. AES in the Knehtilä farm is also a net producer of renewable energy in the form of biogas. The biogas is then purified into biomethane in the on-site dry-anaerobic digesting biogas plant. The biomethane is used for farming activities in the AES and the surplus is sold to car drivers.

AES itself was designed as an alternative food system model that would reconfigure how food is produced in agriculture, processed for consumption and delivered to its consumers, although business activity is conducted within AES and is part of its central dynamics. In the Palopuro AES, several companies conduct business in partnership with the farmers and processors. For example, an energy company invested in a biogas plant in the village as part of the AES, anticipating that the energy system in Finland will be more distributed in the future and wishing to partner with customers who have farms. Another company also works as part of the Palopuro AES and manages the supply chain, sales and agricultural production. Similarly, adopting a systemic perspective, farmers and processors earn their income through their business activities in the AES and interact with the final consumers of the agricultural produce in local and regional farmers' markets (Helenius et al. 2018).

The Palopuro AES in the Knehtilä farm is unique in Finland for three reasons. First, the biogas plant is the first in Finland built inside a crop farm, as biogas plants were previously built farther away from food-production sites. Second, the presence of multiple business organizations and human enactors (i.e. the farmers, processors and other local entrepreneurs) has been characterized as a multi-enterprise network with complementary business models that symbiotically support one another (Global Network of Lighthouse Farms 2020). Finally, the location of the Palopuro AES in the Knehtilä farm benefits from its history as a site of local cultural activity. The farm consequently invested in the construction of a meeting facility, small local restaurants and facilities for local artists and acting companies. For these reasons, while AES was originally developed as an agroecological food system, it can also be understood as a business ecosystem for food and renewable energy.

3.1 Enactors in the Agroecological Symbiosis of Palopuro

The sufficiency enactors in the Palopuro AES in the Knehtilä farm comprise both human and non-human enactors. The on-the-ground, human enactors are farmers and processors, who tend to the non-human enactors in the Palopuro AES and maintain the machinery and facilities. Other human enactors influence the AES' design, business model and organizational culture, like company administrators and analysts, academics, public officials and company CEOs. Finally, we find human enactors who do not have a continuous presence in the Palopuro AES but who support its existence, business activities and organizational culture by gathering there for convivial activities like drinking coffee, having meals, talking and enjoying the landscape. These consumers mostly live nearby in the Palopuro village, but some also come from other Finnish towns and cities. In addition to consumers, artists, musicians and acting companies occasionally provide entertainment and sustain the cultural traditions of Palopuro and the Knehtilä farm.

The human enactors are the most visible enactors to human observers and an ethnographic vignette beautifully captures the centrality of the human enactors to maintain the Palopuro AES as a sufficiency-based food system and renewable energy business ecosystem:

> People gather down both sides of the long tables, with exuberant conversations and easy smiles – this is a joyful space. Folks mingle about the vendor tables, kids run through the crowd, sellers stand behind collections of hand-crafted goods and wares for sale. The air is warm and heavy with the smell of coffee and cake. The room buzzes and hums with layers of sound (Mazac et al. 2021: 196).

This vignette displays the variety of human enactors that – at ephemeral moments – give the Palopuro AES a vibrant and dynamic social life.

The farmers' markets and café vendors of the Knehtilä farm are businesses that promote sufficiency by focusing on consumer needs instead of wants (Bocken/Short 2016). They form long-term relationships with their customers to bring them back to experience the farm's dynamic social life, but they also emphasize to their customers that by consuming products from the farm, they contribute to a sustainable agriculture business. Additionally, the food and energy businesses in the farm educate their customers on sufficiency by allowing them to see behind-the-scenes of food and energy production processes and the closed loops of the Palopuro AES. In doing so, they foster a reconsideration of sustainable production and consumption in consumers (Bocken et al. 2020).

The non-human enactors in the Palopuro AES are the various plants and crops cultivated on the farmland. These crops consist mainly of rapeseed, oats, barley, buckwheat, wheat, rye and oil hemp (Stenger 2022). Additionally, various animal species reside on the Knehtilä farm. Chickens are part of the poultry raised for human consumption, but other domesticated animals that inhabit the farmland include horses, sheep, goats and rabbits. Numerous other species also inhabit the place as part of the natural wildlife, including insects, wild birds and frogs.

AES is designed to make the relationships between the main enactors complementary rather than competitive, which favors sufficiency. Not all relationships, however, persist without conflict. A civil servant involved in AES' design emphasized that building an AES requires people with matching skills to willingly organise to make it successful: "You have to find the right collaborators, you have to agree, and you have to find the right economic bases for everybody" (Interviewee 1). The relationships between the human and non-human enactors are also negotiated: insects and birds might find the crops tasty and feed on them, reducing their value for the human enactors. The domesticated farm animals also need to be cared for and live as stress-free as possible, in order to produce quality food and manure.

3.2 Enablers of Agroecological Symbiosis at Palopuro

The enablers of sufficiency at the Palopuro AES can be divided into two categories: biophysical and socio-cultural enablers. The biophysical enablers refer to those combinations of natural and human-made elements that provide the material foundations for the AES to be operational and successful as a business ecosystem based on sufficiency. These enablers include spatial proximity between elements – farming location, biorefineries, chicken coops, the bakery and the mills, manures, feedstock, etc. – that enables optimal resource efficiency through symbiotic design and adaptiveness of the agroecosystem to its geographical location. Together, the enablers contribute to sufficiency by orienting the farmers' and processors' attention to the agroecosystem's productive capacity and ensuring that the AES only produces what its own internal inputs allow, without external biomass and nitrogen inputs, and that the soil retains fertility over time (Helenius et al. 2020)

The socio-cultural enablers refer to the values and behavior of the human beings working within, supporting or connected to the Palopuro AES. Values and assumptions manifest as behavior that enables adopting a culture of relationships and reciprocity towards human beings and ecosystem services. The human enactors realize that an "ecosystem has multiple functions in the mosaic that comprises the biosphere; while it is still used by humans to extract products and value, humans are obliged to return these services" (Helenius et al. 2020: 5). Without this socio-cultural enabler, the human enactors would behave in an extractive way as aligned with the dominant industrial food system (Mazac et al. 2021).

Two additional socio-cultural enablers reinforce the relational and reciprocal behavior and highlight the importance of linking oneself affectively with the food system. The first is the development of a sense of food and food citizenship that psychologically and socio-culturally connects people to the food system they are part of and benefit from (Helenius et al. 2020). AES does this by openly and transparently explaining its food and energy production system and how the AES operates to be self-sufficient and discussing the relevance of this mode of production in the recurring cultural events hosted at Knehtilä farm. While this sense of food and food citizenship remains under development, the fact that the local population enjoys convening and consuming the fresh products of the Palopuro AES in the café at Knehtilä farm suggests that they recognize the value of this form of food production.

The second socio-cultural enabler is the sense of community. One of the human enactors of the Palopuro AES describes this enabler in the following terms: "[a] mutual understanding, how they [people] feel and how they live. And an overall compassion can be cultivated by being there, to understand that you are also part of the system" (Interviewee 5). This enactor noted that a significant challenge in cultivating this sense of community is that human enactors struggle to ascribe to AES the fact that the spaces in the Knehtilä farm were created to facilitate their gatherings and socio-cultural events and that eating fresh organic products is enabled because of their proximity to their place of production. Fostering connections at the cognitive and affective level is meant to strengthen the operations of the Palopuro AES and nudge the enactors towards sufficiency.

Importantly, we highlight that the biophysical enablers work as enablers because of their interaction with the socio-cultural ones. That is, biophysical enablers such as spatial proximity and biological diversity adopt an enabling function because AES designs them to operate the way they do in producing food and energy. Without interacting with the socio-cultural enablers, the biophysical enablers would still exist, but there is no guarantee that they would constitute enablers for the business ecosystem.

Policy also plays a crucial role in creating an enabling environment for initiatives such as AES. This includes improving the financial viability for sufficiency-oriented production (Niessen/Bocken 2021; Beyeler et al. 2022). Relevant policies could systematically support desired features and types of food businesses while discouraging unsustainable ones as well as remove subsidies on the former (Nyfors et al. 2020).

3.3 Enactments of Agroecological Symbiosis at Palopuro

In this chapter, we limit ourselves to describing the most prominent enactments that contribute to the sufficiency culture of AES. The first set of enactments involves those which we call *sufficient production enactments*, which focus on the ecological aspects of food and energy production in the AES. These enactments include rotating the crops to optimize the fertility of the soil, feeding the chickens and other livestock, collecting manure, processing the manure for the production of biogas, drying the grains, fertilizing the crops with the digestate (i.e. the residue of the biogas production process) and recycling phosphorus and other mineral plant nutrients (Koppelmäki et al. 2019; Helenius et al. 2020; Stenger 2022). These enactments represent sufficient production because the production of food and energy based on AES constrains itself by respecting the biophysical limits of the agroecosystem, thus abiding by the AES principle of "what is enough must not exceed what is too much for the ecosystems that the human shares with other species, both presently and in the future" (Helenius et al. 2020: 8).

A second set of enactments, the *socio-cultural behavior* enactments, capture all the human activities in the AES that contribute to sufficiency. These activities start at the production stage and continue until the moment of consumption and the performance of convivial activities. The enactments include designing the green manure leys, protecting biodiversity, self-processing of primary organic products, cooking food for local consumption, planning musical and cultural events for the local population and, perhaps most importantly, boosting the food literacy of the consumers through informative talks and events (Mazac et al. 2021). Numerous socio-cultural enactments result from cocreation facilitated by academics and policymakers, but the main enactors remain the local farmers, a bakery owner, the food processing businesses and the biogas energy company. Together, they developed the AES model and modified it to suit their individual needs but also the economic and socio-cultural needs of Palopuro village (Helenius et al. 2020). The socio-cultural enactments, important for businesses in AES, continuously combine with the sufficient production enactments to orient the businesses as organizations and the individual human members towards sufficiency.

The final set of enactments constitute *non-human* enactments. Because we, the authors of this chapter, are human beings, we cannot properly characterize the significance of these enactments, but we can identify them by relying on second-hand accounts and observation. Some of the non-human enactments we identify include pollination, eating, excreting, reproducing, defending one's offspring, grazing, swimming and communicating with other enactors with body language. Important for the sufficiency culture of AES as a business ecosystem is that the enactments of the non-humans provide parameters for humans to understand whether they are engaging in behaviors that go against sufficiency premises. For example, disrupted reproduction patterns among wildlife would cause concern since they might indicate something in the ecosystem limits the different enactors' ability to continue with their eco-sufficient enactments.

3.4 Agroecological Symbiosis as a culture of sufficiency through the processual lens

AES embodies a culture of sufficiency in business because the enactors, enablers and enactments are oriented to produce enough or just what is needed, while ensuring staying within biophysical capacities of the agroecosystem without exceeding them. AES also represents sufficiency in business because the members of the business ecosystem – farmers, processors, local entrepreneurs and the local population in their role as consumers – do not seek to maximize their profits and extract resources at the expense of humans and non-humans. The way the enactors relate to one another via their enactments and facilitated by the enablers in the Palopuro AES reveals a careful consideration of the needs of the other enactors and of the whole agroecosystem. The business culture of sufficiency embodied by AES allows each enactor to benefit from the operations on the farm's premises when operating successfully.

We exemplify the processual character of the AES culture of sufficiency by describing how AES operates at a system level in Palopuro. We limit our description because of space constraints but outline the main processes at the system level and characterize them according to their temporal perspective and the co-constitution of elements. Figure 2 displays these processes.

Figure 2: The Palopuro AES as a series of interconnected processes at the system level. (Commissioned by the authors)

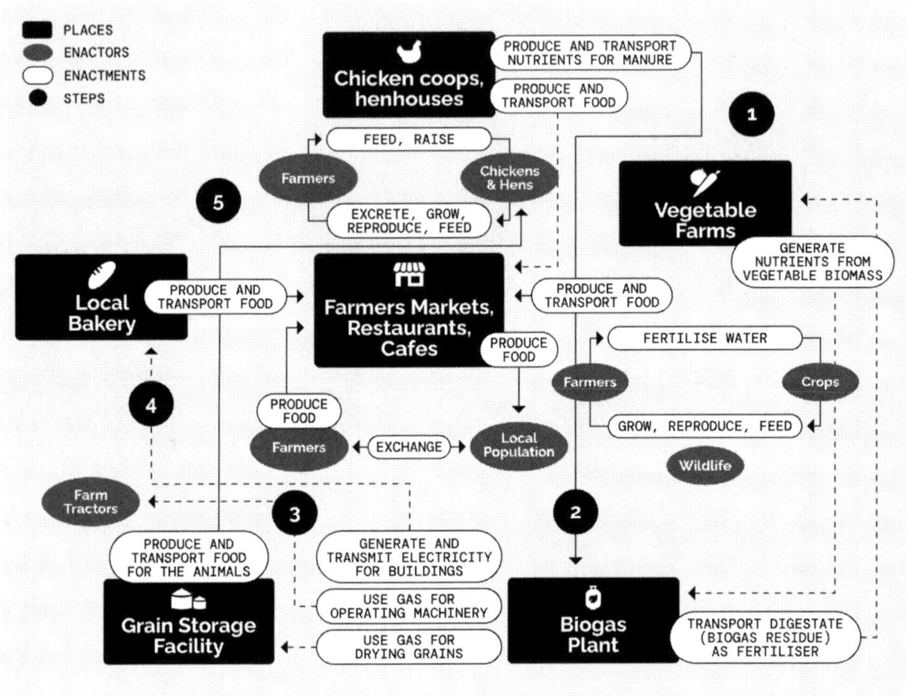

The first process is the food production in the chicken coops and henhouses and in the vegetable farms. The enactors involve the farmers, the chickens and hens and the crops. The farmers feed and raise the chickens and hens, while the hens excrete, grow, reproduce and feed themselves, in the process giving the farmers what they need in the form of manure, eggs and eventually chicken meat. The farmers fertilize and water the crops, among other actions, while the crops grow, reproduce and eventually feed the farmers. Wildlife also becomes an enactor in the vegetable farms because the farmers respect it with minimal intervention. These enactments are performed throughout time and may evolve according to the enactors' needs, creating patterns of enactments that do not devolve into extractive forms seen in the industrial food systems.

The second process displayed is the collection of manure from the chicken coops and the henhouse and the biomass obtained from some crops in the vegetable farms. The farmers, taking the role of enactors, collect these elements and transport them to the biogas plant. This is where the third process occurs: dry anaerobic digestion transforms the manure and the biomass into biogas. This biogas is then used to dry grain, drive the tractors and power up other mobile machinery and to provide electricity for the organic bakery. At the same time, the digestate is returned in the form of fertilizer to the vegetable farms. The fourth process involves the farmers obtaining grain to feed the animals, represented by the chickens and hens in our example. Both the crops in the vegetable farms and the chickens and hens reciprocate what the farmers do by replicating their enactments in the first process. Together, processes one to four depict the *symbiotic* processes in the Palopuro AES, which encourage sufficiency.

The final process involves the farmers and processors adding value to their food products so that they can sell them on-site at the farmers' markets, the restaurants and the cafés. In our example, the main human enactors are the farmers and the local population. These two enactors perform the enactment of exchange, where the local population act as consumers for the farmers' organic products, giving them money in return. Importantly, the enactments between farmers and the local population do not end in the enactment of exchange. Instead, they persist over time, as the local population gradually cultivates a sense of connection towards the Palopuro AES and (from what we have seen and been told) wishes to return periodically. In periodically returning to the Palopuro AES, the customers evolve from mere consumers to food citizens.

Specific to the culture of sufficiency at the Palopuro AES, food and energy production is intentionally displayed (whenever possible) to the local population. The local population gradually recognizes that the AES system works because of its closed loops of matter and energy flows but also because it respects the agroecosystem's biophysical limits and the farmers remain attentive to the needs of the farm animals and wildlife. This is done to limit consumption of the customers when participating in economic exchanges at the farmers' markets, restaurants and cafés, allowing the farmers and processors to practice eco-sufficient production. This remains an ongoing process because instilling sufficiency ideas presents similar challenges to creating a community, like creating stable, affective bonds, mutual understanding and compassion for others.

4. Discussion

Our processual systems approach exemplifies how businesses could be oriented towards sufficiency by identifying the enactors, their enablers of sufficiency and how their enactments further or constrain sufficiency. The business enactors in AES – individual farmers and the farmer's markets, cafés, food processing and energy production companies – illustrate several business sufficiency strategies as explained by Bocken et al. (2020) and by Beyeler and Jaeger-Erben (2022). They enact conscious sales and marketing techniques by focusing on needs and aiming for long-term relationships with customers. They encourage their customers to rethink their relationship to consumption and their relationship to others –that is, they cultivate sociocultural enablers of sufficiency – by showing them the behind-the-scenes production processes and the other enactors involved. These experiences elicit the formation of an emotional bond with the Palopuro AES system, which works to affect and change the underlying assumptions of the customer enactors. This interrelationship between the various enactors acts as a process where engaging consumers and the building of community become the enablers that allow consequent enactments of a sufficiency culture. Over time, this cyclical process creates, maintains and reproduces a culture that espouses sufficiency principles. The various businesses also collaborate with local stakeholders (including non-human enactors, like wildlife and the farm animals), limit the production space through localized production and limit the consumption space by making products available mostly in nearby regions.

Furthermore, the businesses in AES embody the cross-cutting characteristics discussed by Beyeler and Jaeger-Erben (2022) of care, openness to learning, and patience. Care for the well-being of the employees and the environment underpins the operation of the AES system and manifests along the entire supply chain (from the farms to the service points like restaurants and cafés). The Palopuro AES system, being the first of its kind, involves continuous learning from all enactors involved, as the businesses continuously reorient themselves to ensure remaining within the ecosystems' boundaries. Patience is manifested, for example, in the discussions among different businesses, who collaboratively decide on what to farm and serve at the local restaurants and cafés, depending on the season and the needs of the agroecosystems.

Our processual systems approach suggests that for the practice of sufficiency in business, it is important to cultivate the socio-cultural enablers that allow sufficiency to be sustained, or even enhanced, over time. For example, a relational and reciprocal culture should be fostered as an enabler to incentivize producers and consumers to respect the boundaries of ecosystems, in this case the agroecosystems AES relies on. This is done at Palopuro by showing the local population the production processes and explaining their relevance, thereby creating a sense of connection and reciprocal care between the ecosystems, the producers and the consumers. Similarly, as depicted in Figure 2, the interconnected processes require the continuous performance of sufficiency enactments so that the businesses maintain stability in their sufficiency practices. The performance of the enactments should be distributed: it is not enough for only producers or only consumers to perform them, but all members in a business ecosystem (firms, the local population, policy designers) should aim to enact sufficiency as a core feature of their business practice, thereby also creating a shared culture of sufficiency.

The case of AES also highlights the need to move from anthropocentric to a more nuanced ecocentric thinking when trying to conceive a sustainable business. Or as

Korten (2021) argues: to move from "ego-nomics" towards "eco-nomics" – a system based on community that acknowledges the limits of a living earth but produces enough for material sufficiency and understands that the precondition for any business is a healthy and complex web of life. Specific business policies for achieving these goals could fall under the *nudging* and *cooperation* categories discussed by Nyfors et al. (2020). AES shows how nudging policies for sufficiency in business could include making the customer enactors aware of the whole life cycle of a product and creating spaces that facilitate reciprocal relations between enactors, while AES illustrates cooperation policies by having different businesses in a food system making decisions together and complementing the others' business models.

5. Conclusion

In addition to developing a processual systems approach to the study of sufficiency in business and particularly focusing on culturally sensitive elements of enactors, enablers and enactments, we make two main contributions. First, we show how an approach to studying business cultures of sufficiency can benefit from moving beyond an anthropocentric understanding of organizations, businesses and stakeholders. In the enactors, enablers and enactments frame, we position the non-human enactors as equally relevant to the sufficiency processes of businesses as the human enactors and hereby take a more inclusive approach to phenomena. This responds to the call for non-anthropocentric research designs and allows us to see that an organizational business culture that promotes sufficiency needs to understand the multiple enactments performed by the enactors within it as matter-energy flows that connect the human to the non-human world (Heikkurinen/Ruuska et al. 2021).

Our second main contribution is about highlighting how practicing and sustaining a culture of sufficiency in business is *a continuous and evolving process*. Sufficiency practices are not one-and-done singular enactments but a web of enactments that should be stable over time to work. This is important to keep in mind when trying to integrate sufficiency ideas into a non-sufficient business. It is not enough to organize specific events that promote sufficiency or to perform singular enactments aligned to sufficiency ideas. Instead, multiple interconnected processes should be reorganized in line with sufficiency. This reorganization towards sufficiency takes time. As we see in the case of AES, significant challenges remain, like orienting the human enactors to recognize themselves as a community and instilling ideas about sufficiency in consumers, which is necessary to reduce tensions between the organizational aims and the external operational environment. For this reason, once enactments of sufficiency are performed, they *need to continue being performed* so that sufficiency becomes a focal new norm for the business and for the wider socio-cultural ecosystem.

Funding

Joshua Hurtado's work was supported by the Maj and Tor Nessling Foundation, grant agreement 202200237. Tina Nyfors' work was supported by the Tiina and Antti Herlin Foundation. This work was also supported by the Research Council of Finland grant number 343277 – Skills of self-provisioning in rural communities (SOS) Research Project.

References

Alvesson, Mats (2002): Understanding Organizational Culture, London: Sage.

Assoratgoon, Waewkanee/Kantabutra, Sooksan (2023): "Toward a Sustainability Organizational Culture Model." In: Journal of Cleaner Production 400, 136666. https://doi.org/10.1016/j.jclepro.2023.136666.

Bateson, Gregory (2000): Steps to an Ecology of Mind: Collected Essays in Anthropology, Psychiatry, Evolution, and Epistemology, Chicago: University of Chicago Press.

Baumgartner, Rupert J. (2009): "Organizational Culture and Leadership: Preconditions for the Development of a Sustainable Corporation." In: Sustainable Development 17/2, pp. 102–113. https://doi.org/10.1002/sd.405.

Beyeler, Laura/Jaeger-Erben, Melanie (2022): "How to Make More of Less: Characteristics of Sufficiency in Business Practices." In: Frontiers in Sustainability 3, 949710. https://doi.org/10.3389/frsus.2022.949710.

Bocken, Nancy/Smeke Morales, Lisa/Lehner, Matthias (2020): "Sufficiency Business Strategies in the Food Industry – The Case of Oatly." In: Sustainability 12/3, 824. https://doi.org/10.3390/su12030824.

Bocken, Nancy/Short, Samuel William (2016): "Towards a Sufficiency-Driven Business Model: Experiences and Opportunities." In: Environmental Innovation and Societal Transitions 18, pp. 41–61. https://doi.org/10.1016/j.eist.2015.07.010.

Bonnedahl, Karl Johan/Heikkurinen, Pasi (2019): "The Case for Strong Sustainability." In: Karl Johan Bonnedahl/Pasi Heikkurinen (eds.), Strongly Sustainable Societies: Organising Human Activities on a Hot and Full Earth, Abingdon: Routledge, pp. 1–20.

Boulding, Kenneth (1956): "General Systems Theory: The Skeleton of Science." In: Management Science 2/3, pp. 197–208. https://www.jstor.org/stable/2627132.

Chatman, Jennifer A./O'Reilly, Charles A. (2016): "Paradigm Lost: Reinvigorating the Study of Organizational Culture." In: Research in Organizational Behavior 36, pp. 199–224. https://doi.org/10.1016/j.riob.2016.11.004.

Eerikäinen, Tapio (2019): "Solving It Together" (Policy Presentation). Helsinki, LUKE: Natural Resources Institute Finland.

Fischer, Lisa-Britt/Newig, Jens (2016): "Importance of Actors and Agency in Sustainability Transitions: A Systematic Exploration of the Literature." In: Sustainability 8/5, 476. https://doi.org/10.3390/su8050476.

Freudenreich, Birte/Schaltegger, Stefan (2020): "Developing Sufficiency-Oriented Offerings for Clothing Users: Business Approaches to Support Consumption Reduction." In: Journal of Cleaner Production 247, 119589. https://doi.org/10.1016/j.jclepro.2019.119589.

Global Network of Lighthouse Farms (2020): "Palopuro Agroecological Symbiosis: Finland." In: Community, Energy Production & Biogas (blog), Global Network of Lighthouse Farms 2020, 6.12.2023 (https://www.lighthousefarmnetwork.com/lighthouse-farms/palopuro-agroecological-symbiosis).

Gossen, Maike/Heinrich, Anneli (2021): "Encouraging Consumption Reduction: Findings of a Qualitative Study with Clothing Companies on Sufficiency-Promoting Communication." In: Cleaner and Responsible Consumption 3, 100028. https://doi.org/10.1016/j.clrc.2021.100028.

Gossen, Maike/Ziesemer, Florence/Schrader, Ulf (2019): "Why and How Commercial Marketing Should Promote Sufficient Consumption: A Systematic Literature Review." In: Journal of Macromarketing 39/3, pp. 252–69. https://doi.org/10.1177/0276146719866238.

Harris, Lloyd C./Crane, Andrew (2002): "The Greening of Organizational Culture: Management Views on the Depth, Degree and Diffusion of Change." In: Journal of Organizational Change Management 15/3, pp. 214–34. https://doi.org/10.1108/09534810210429273.

Healthy Future Project (2016): "Knehtila Tila – Menu Introduction – Minna Sakki-Eerola and Paula." [Video]. Palopuro, 6.12.2023 (https://www.youtube.com/watch?v=wToR4TRRHzs).

Heikkurinen, Pasi/Bonnedahl, Karl Johan (2013): "Corporate responsibility for sustainable development: a review and conceptual comparison of market- and stakeholder-oriented strategies." In: Journal of Cleaner Production 43, pp. 191–198. https://doi.org/10.1016/j.jclepro.2012.12.021.

Heikkurinen, Pasi/Clegg, Stewart/Pinnington, Ashly H./Nicolopoulou, Katerina/Alcaraz, Jose M. (2021): "Managing the Anthropocene: Relational Agency and Power to Respect Planetary Boundaries." In: Organization & Environment 34/2, pp. 267–86. https://doi.org/10.1177/1086026619881145.

Heikkurinen, Pasi/Rinkinen, Jenny/Järvensivu, Timo/Wilén, Kristoffer/Ruuska, Toni (2016): "Organising in the Anthropocene: An Ontological Outline for Ecocentric Theorising." In: Journal of Cleaner Production 113, pp. 705–14. https://doi.org/10.1016/j.jclepro.2015.12.016.

Heikkurinen, Pasi/Ruuska, Toni/Kuokkanen, Anna/Russell, Sally (2021): "Leaving Productivism behind: Towards a Holistic and Processual Philosophy of Ecological Management." In: Philosophy of Management 20, pp. 21–36. https://doi.org/10.1007/s40926-019-00109-w.

Heikkurinen, Pasi/Young, C. William/Morgan, Elizabeth (2019): "Business for Sustainable Change: Extending Eco-Efficiency and Eco-Sufficiency Strategies to Consumers." In: Journal of Cleaner Production 218, pp. 656–64. https://doi.org/10.1016/j.jclepro.2019.02.053.

Helenius, Juha/Hagolani-Albov, Sophia E./Koppelmäki, Kari (2020): "Co-Creating Agroecological Symbioses (AES) for Sustainable Food System Networks." In: Frontiers in Sustainable Food Systems 4, pp. 1–16. https://doi.org/10.3389/fsufs.2020.588715.

Helenius, Juha/Koppelmäki, Kari/Sophia E., Hagolani-Albov (2018): "Agroecological Symbiosis." In: Scaling-up Agroecology to Achieve the Sustainable Development Goals: 2nd International Symposium on Agroecology. Helsinki: University of Helsinki/FAO, 6.12.2023 (http://www.fao.org/agroecology/database/detail/es/c/1144155/).

Jungell-Michelsson, Jessica/Heikkurinen, Pasi (2022): "Sufficiency: A Systematic Literature Review." In: Ecological Economics 195, 107380. https://doi.org/10.1016/j.ecolecon.2022.107380.

Kantabutra, Sooksan (2020): "Toward an Organizational Theory of Sustainability Vision." In: Sustainability 12/3, 1125. https://doi.org/10.3390/su12031125.

Koppelmäki, Kari/Parviainen, Tuure/Virkkunen, Elina/Winquist, Erika/Schulte, Rogier P. O./Helenius, Juha (2019): "Ecological Intensification by Integrating Biogas Production into Nutrient Cycling: Modeling the Case of Agroecological Symbiosis." In: Agricultural Systems 170, pp. 39–48. https://doi.org/10.1016/j.agsy.2018.12.007.

Korten, David (2021): "Ecological Civilization: From Emergency to Emergence," 6.12.2023 (https://davidkorten.org/wp-content/uploads/2021/11/Korten-EcoCiv-11032021.pdf).

Kropfeld, Maren Ingrid/Reichel André (2021b): "The Business Model of Enough: Value Creation for Sufficiency-Oriented Businesses." In: Annabeth Aagaard/Florian Lüdeke-Freund/Peter Wells (eds.), Business Models for Sustainability Transitions, Cham: Springer, pp. 163–189. https://doi.org/10.1007/978-3-030-77580-3_6.

Mazac, Rachel/Hagolani-Albov, Sophia E./Tuomisto, Hanna L. (2021): "Agroecological Symbiosis." In: C. Parker Krieg/Reetta Toivanen (eds.), Situating Sustainability: A Handbook of Contexts and Concepts, Helsinki: Helsinki University Press, pp. 195–210.

Nesterova, Iana (2021): "Small Firms as Agents of Sustainable Change." In: Futures 127, 102705. https://doi.org/10.1016/j.futures.2021.102705.
Nicholson, Jessica/Kurucz, Elizabeth (2019): "Relational Leadership for Sustainability: Building an Ethical Framework from the Moral Theory of "Ethics of Care." In: Journal of Business Ethics 156/1, pp. 25–43. https://doi.org/10.1007/s10551-017-3593-4.
Niessen, Laura/Bocken, Nancy M. P. (2021): "How Can Businesses Drive Sufficiency? The Business for Sufficiency Framework." In: Sustainable Production and Consumption 28, pp. 1090–1103. https://doi.org/10.1016/j.spc.2021.07.030.
Nyfors, Tina/Linnanen, Lassi/Nissinen, Ari/Seppälä, Jyri/Saarinen, Merja/Regina, Kristiina/Heinonen, Tero/Viri, Riku/Liimatainen, Heikki (2020): "Ecological Sufficiency in Climate Policy: Towards Policies for Recomposing Consumption." In: Futura 3.
Ortiz-Przychodzka, Stefan/Benavides-Frías, Camila/Raymond, Christopher M./Díaz-Reviriego, Isabel/Hanspach, Jan (2023): "Rethinking Economic Practices and Values As Assemblages of More-Than-Human Relations." In: Ecological Economics 211, 107866. https://doi.org/10.1016/j.ecolecon.2023.107866.
Pettigrew, Andrew M. (1979): "On Studying Organizational Cultures." In: Administrative Science Quarterly 24/4, pp. 570–81. https://doi.org/10.2307/2392363.
Princen, Thomas (2005): The logic of sufficiency, Cambridge: MIT Press.
Sabella, Anton R./Eid, Niveen L. (2016): "A Strategic Perspective of Social Enterprise Sustainability." In: Journal of General Management 41/4, pp. 71–89. https://doi.org/10.1177/030630701604100405.
Sachs, Wolfgang (1993): "Die vier E's. Merkposten für einen massvollen Lebensstil." In: Politische Ökologie 11/33, pp. 69–72, 6.12.2023 (https://epub.wupperinst.org/frontdoor/deliver/index/docId/66/file/66_Sachs.pdf).
Schein, Edgar H. (1990): "Organizational Culture." In: American Psychologist 45/2, pp. 109–119. https://psycnet.apa.org/doi/10.1037/0003-066X.45.2.109.
Smircich, Linda (1983): "Concepts of Culture and Organizational Analysis." In: Administrative Science Quarterly 28/3, pp. 339–358. https://doi.org/10.2307/2392246.
Stenger, Wif (2022): "Self-Sufficient Organic Finnish Farm Grows Its Own Fuel and a Greener Future." This Is Finland (blog), 7.12.2023 (https://finland.fi/life-society/self-sufficient-organic-finnish-farm-grows-its-own-fuel-and-a-greener-future/).
Wadham, Helen/Wallace, Carrianne/Furtado, Tamzin (2023): "Agents of Sustainability: How Horses and People Co-create, Enact and Embed the Good Life in Rural Places." In: Sociologia Ruralis 63/3, pp. 390–414. https://doi.org/10.1111/soru.12387.
Whitehead, Alfred North (1978): Process and Reality, New York: Simon and Schuster.

Social Media Communication for Sufficiency in Fashion

Investigating the Case of Houdini Sportswear on Instagram

Beatriz Garcia-Ortega, Javier Galan-Cubillo, F. Javier Llorens-Montes and Blanca de-Miguel-Molina

Abstract *This chapter examines the Instagram of Houdini Sportswear, a sustainability-focused fashion retailer, to reveal certain strategies promoting sufficiency-oriented consumption. Potential rebound effects and inconsistencies exist on Instagram, while it ignores other strategies identified in the literature. We contribute to understanding how fashion companies can utilize social media to foster sufficiency.*

1. Introduction

The prevailing growth- and profit-oriented economic and business model, far from promoting sustainable lifestyles, has been driven by relentless consumerism with ever-increasing demand and consumption (Jackson 2009; Gasper et al. 2019). This approach pays little heed to the increasingly evident planetary boundaries (Worrell/Carreon 2017) and is supported by the lack of internalization of the social and environmental costs of products and services (Kallis 2017). Materialism, a driving force behind this consumerism, continues to resist under the umbrella of "sustainable growth" supported by the 2030 Agenda (Gasper et al. 2019).

The fashion industry is known for its resource-intensive and polluting practices with serious large-scale negative environmental and social impacts (Niinimäki et al. 2020) and serves as a mirror of consumerism and materialism in our society. This has been reinforced by phenomena such as fast fashion and the limitless possibilities offered by the internet and social media that have revolutionized the way companies stay connected and interact with consumers (Buzzo/Abreu 2019; Reilly/Hynan 2014) and ultimately influence consumer behavior (Strähle/Gräff 2017).

Shifting away from overconsumption is a pressing sustainability challenge (Armstrong et al. 2015), and embracing more responsible and sustainable consumption patterns not only contributes to the mitigation of negative impacts but also promises a series of benefits for consumers and opens doors to new business opportunities (Garcia-Ortega et al. 2023). However, while many fashion companies have made substantial progress toward a circular economy and are reducing their impact per product throughout their value chain, the issue of (over)consumption of their products has remained largely unaddressed (Niinimäki et al. 2020).

In response to this problem, movements like slow fashion (Fletcher 2010) and sufficiency-driven business models (Bocken/Short 2016) advocate for a transition towards more mindful and conscious consumer behavior in purchasing, using, disposing and managing products. Companies may play an active and crucial role in this shift due to their influence on consumer motivations and behaviors (Gossen et al. 2019). However, achieving this transformation is in conflict with the prevailing economic and business model, necessitating extensive changes to overcome various economic, institutional, cultural, social and practical barriers (Veleva 2021; Niinimäki et al. 2020).

In this context, it is particularly interesting to examine how a fashion company with a pronounced focus on sustainable consumption leverages communication to promote sufficiency-oriented consumption, investigating the embracing of business strategies to reach this goal and assessing potential areas of improvement as a benchmark for other companies aiming to follow this approach. In this regard, this chapter expands upon the research conducted by Gossen and Kropfeld (2022), by adopting a recently proposed fashion-specific framework by Garcia-Ortega et al. (2023), which focuses on the promotion of sufficient consumption of fashion products. Thus, it takes the case study of Houdini Sportswear, a fashion retailer recognized for its strong orientation towards sustainability and its ambition for more sustainable consumption patterns (Holtström et al. 2019), and utilizes the mentioned framework to analyze the company's communication on the social media platform Instagram over a 12-month period from October 1, 2022 to September 30, 2023. This framework includes a set of strategies organized into three pillars for fashion companies to promote sufficient consumption: design for durability, alternative product/service systems and fair promotion and information (Garcia-Ortega et al. 2023).

As a result, the following research questions are established, organized in two blocks:

- Is Houdini Sportswear promoting sufficient consumption through its official Instagram account? If so, through which strategies?
- Are there areas for improvement? What lessons can managers of this and other companies in the fashion industry draw from this?

After this introduction, the literature review addresses the issue of overconsumption in fashion, the sufficiency-driven approach and the role of fashion companies in promoting sufficient consumption, with the strategies at their disposal. Subsequently, the case study and method are presented, followed by the presentation and discussion of results, and finally, conclusions are provided.

2. Literature review

Even though many fashion items such as clothing may be considered a basic need, consumption motives at different stages of fashion consumption have been dominated by emotional and social reasons governed by materialistic values (Pepper et al. 2009) rather than by rational or practical considerations (Cao et al. 2014). In addition to fulfilling basic needs and personal preferences, consumers may seek self-realization, express values or an image, construct an identity, secure social status or recognition, align with a particular group, follow or set trends, find attractive bargains, alleviate anxiety, mask personal issues or simply derive entertainment and enjoyment from the act of shopping (Gabriel 2021; Tarnanidis et al. 2015; Blazquez 2014; Fletcher 2013).

The sufficiency movement challenges the dominant consumer culture based on materialistic values and encourages the reconsideration of existing consumption levels and patterns to realize more responsible and sustainable consumption while pursuing well-being (Niessen et al. 2023; Bocken et al. 2022). This entails a focus on essential and relevant needs while discarding artificial needs, eliminating the superfluous or dispensable. Green demarketing initiatives of companies that encourage consumers to buy less and only what is truly needed for the sake of sustainability (Hesse/Rünz 2022; Armstrong Soule/Reich 2015) align with the promotion of sufficient consumption.

Consumers are purportedly the decision-makers when it comes to consumption. However, their individual or personal choices are highly influenced by the environment (Sheth 2020), conditioned not only by the embedded values in our society but also by the way companies shape their offering, value proposition, competitive strategy and marketing (Stål/Jansson, 2017; Bocken et al. 2014; Gossen et al. 2019).

Fashion businesses may find several motivations to promote sufficient consumption. They are becoming increasingly aware of the social and environmental impacts stemming from their products and services (Zhang et al. 2018). Some companies may be driven by altruistic or ethical motives, fostering a sufficiency-based approach due to self-conviction (Gossen et al. 2019). Furthermore, these businesses face mounting pressure and scrutiny from society and institutions, urging them to adopt more responsible practices (Bocken/Short 2016; Bocken 2017). They may aim to enhance their image, reputation and trustworthiness (Hwang et al. 2016; Bocken/Short 2016; Hajli 2014), ultimately seeking to build and maintain customer loyalty (Ndubisi 2007). Companies may also glimpse the symptoms of exhaustion of the dominant consumption-led growth model and look for new business opportunities

(Bocken/Short 2016; Jung/Jin 2016; Hwang et al. 2016), reducing their dependence on high sale volumes (Garcia-Ortega et al. 2023).

However, the adoption of a sufficiency-based approach poses a significant challenge for fashion companies. They operate in a highly competitive environment, where the prevailing norm is to continuously offer and sell more to sustain their business and maximize growth and profits while trying to decouple their growth from their negative impacts (Bocken/Short 2016; Hwang et al. 2016), sometimes overly focused on delivering short-term value to shareholders (Bocken/Short, 2016). Fashion companies in different segments have been criticized for their traditional aggressive sales, the use of fashion change agents to influence fashion followers or the 'fear of missing out' technique to encourage novelty-seeking and impulse buying among consumers (Blazquez et al. 2020). Fast fashion is a clear example against sufficient consumption, due to its formula to promote overconsumption consisting of big rotation and constant novelty, with easy access to the latest trend inexpensive products, often inspired by designs worn by celebrities (Niinimäki et al. 2020; Ozdamar Ertekin/Atik 2015; Cline 2013).

Overall, fighting overconsumption by encouraging sufficient consumption in fashion runs against the business logic mainstream (Garcia-Ortega et al. 2023) and requires bold and innovative business strategies (Freudenreich/Schaltegger 2020). Several studies have proposed models, frameworks or comprehensive lists of general or cross-sectoral business sufficiency strategies (i.e. Niessen/Bocken 2021; Gossen et al. 2019; Bocken/Short 2016). In turn, other researchers have taken a sector-specific approach, focusing on industries like food (Bocken et al. 2020) or fashion (Garcia-Ortega et al. 2023; Gossen/Heinrich 2021; Freudenreich/Schaltegger 2020). In particular, Garcia-Ortega et al. (2023) introduced a framework for fashion companies to foster a more sufficient consumption with three pillars or dimensions: design for durability, alternative product and service systems and fair promotion and information, with subsequent business strategies as shown in Table 1:

Table 1: Framework of business strategies to promote sufficient consumption (Garcia-Ortega et al. 2023)

Business strategies to promote sufficient consumption in fashion		
1. Design for durability *Design eco-efficient products to strengthen their lifespan and usability by fighting all kinds of obsolescence (physical, emotional or social)*	**2. Alternative product/service systems** *Adopt alternative product/service systems to keep products in use instead of product disposal; moderate acquisition of new items*	**3. Fair promotion & information** *Contribute to better-informed consumer decisions and practices. Influence and facilitate consumer attitudes, education and behaviour against physical, social and emotional obsolescence*
1.1 Design durable, reliable products that keep their physical and functional attributes over time	2.1 Offer repair, refurbishment or customization services	3.1 Moderate sales and promotion of new items – Avoid aggressive marketing campaigns based on successive collections and trends and/or low prices. – Avoid fostering the pleasure of shopping just for fun or to show status
1.2 Design easy-to-maintain, repair or refurbish products to keep their physical and functional attributes over time	2.2 Offer consultancy services on how to continue wearing or using products	3.2 Promote convenience and enjoyment of consuming and using responsibly through more sufficient lifestyle; promote needs against desire through logic of eco-efficient use to maximize resources involved in the product; nurture perception of products as durables and not as consumables
1.3 Design seasonless products, with durable emotional bond or emotionally upgradable to changing tastes, to keep their appeal or attractiveness over time	2.3 Facilitate collection of discarded products to give them second life (second-hand sale and/or donation)	3.3 Promote product's value (value proposition), convenience of extending its use by logic of maximizing return on investment and savings by avoiding new purchases. Possibility of higher selling price
1.4 Involve users in design to facilitate 1.3	2.4 Adopt access-based service models, via collaborative consumption, as part of sharing economy, with formulas such as rental, leasing, pay-per-use, wardrobe-sharing or swapping	3.4 Provide information on product impact (e.g., Higg Index tool), durability, use and care and reparability through labeling, information campaigns, etc.

3. Case study

The methodology employed is a qualitative single-case study, which facilitates a comprehensive examination of a specific case within a defined context (Eisenhardt/Graebner 2007). The approach followed is exploratory and illustrative (Gustafsson 2017) and serves to carry out a critical evaluation and provide recommendations.

The selected company is Houdini Sportswear, a Swedish privately owned fashion company, established in 1993, that designs and manufactures outdoor clothing and gear. It operates primarily in the business-to-consumer model, selling its products through its online store and its own physical retail locations, as well as through other partner retailers. Houdini Sportswear can be classified as an SME. As per its LinkedIn profile (Houdini Sportswear 2023a), as of October 2023, Houdini Sportswear employed more than 70 individuals, the majority of whom were located in Sweden. The company experienced a consistent double-digit turnover growth in recent years, with the exception of a temporary interruption caused by the COVID-19 pandemic. In 2022, its annual turnover amounted to approximately 20 million Euros (PFR 2023). Its main markets are Sweden and Norway, but it is also present in other countries such as Germany, Austria, Japan, China, the USA and Canada (Holtsröm et al. 2019).

As per the information provided on its website (Houdini Sportswear 2023b), its Swedish origins significantly influence the way the company perceives nature, society and human interaction. The company stands out for its strong sustainability orientation and its specific focus on pursuing a more sustainable consumption of its products. Some extracts of the 'Houdini Manifesto' issued by the company in November 2017 clearly illustrate the above as follows (Houdini Sportswear 2023b):

"The current system, where products are produced, used and discarded at an ever increasing pace, is not working. Our mission is to transform into a circular system in harmony with our world."
"We will fight overconsumption."
"We will keep working to maximize our negative footprint, move beyond zero, and leave an entirely positive impact on the world."

Although the concepts of sufficiency or sufficient consumption are not explicitly mentioned, they underlie its value proposition. As an example, the company refers to *"fight overconsumption"* or *"do more with less"* on its website, aligned with the principles of the sufficiency-driven approach (Bocken/Short 2016). On its website (Houdini Sportswear 2023b), it promotes physically and emotionally durable products and addresses different ways to extend the lifespan of its products. It has an initiative called "Houdini Reuse" since 2011 and provides a repair service in its stores (Houdini Sportswear 2023b). Additionally, the company has a dedicated section on its website for product care and reducing its negative impact. Furthermore, as an explorative alternative business initiative, in September 2023 the company opened its first "Houdini Circle", an experimental store that offers new products but also addresses circular business models such as renting, reusing and repairing (Houdini Sportswear 2023b). Thus, Houdini Sportswear can be considered as a referent in the fashion sustainability arena in order to analyze its communication through the social network Instagram from the lens of sufficient consumption.

Among the most popular social networks with written content utilized by Houdini, Instagram was chosen as the primary platform for analysis. The Instagram account was accessible through the following link: https://www.instagram.com/houdinisportswear/?hl=en. During the analysis period, spanning from October 1, 2022, to September 30, 2023, a total of 174 posts were published over regular intervals. These posts were individually examined by the first two authors to identify their purpose and associated codes related to sufficient consumption and other promotion strategies. In a subsequent step, the two authors collaborated to contrast and resolve any discrepancy in the assigned codes, thus reducing possible bias. The coding process combined a deductive approach, based on the established strategies in the adopted framework (Table 1, strategies 1.1 to 3.4 or opposite to them) and an inductive approach where the authors identified and grouped other emergent categories or themes throughout the posts. This additional inductive coding process for the remaining categories served to contextualize the promotion of strategies aimed at sufficient consumption and its relative weight and significance within the company's communication through this channel.

The next section presents and discusses the results and their implications in relation to the established research questions.

4. Results and discussion

As a result of the analysis carried out, Table 2 presents the classification of posts with illustrative examples of each code or theme identified.

Table 2: Classification of Houdini Sportswear Instagram posts between October 1, 2022, and September 30, 2023

Code	Quantity of posts	Example
Suffic. Strategy 1.1	4	*Durable performance at its finest: Mono Air marks a new generation of mid layers…* December 14, 2022.
Suffic. Strategies 1.1 & 3.2 combined	1	*Worn 100 times more than the average garment in the Western world, our Power Houdi has proven its worth to our users since 2003. Versatile, durable and oh so comfortable, this fleece is a gift that'll keep on giving.* December 8, 2022.
Suffic. Strategy 1.3	1	*. …The idea was to make a pair of pants with a robust, timeless model and all the benefits of modern performance fabrics.* July 31, 2023
Suffic. Strategy 2.1	1	*…Drawing inspiration from their past, HODAKOVA converts old garments and materials into luxury goods. For her FW23 show, she converted reclaimed Houdini garments into ready-to-wear pieces, giving them another life after they've been well-used on their adventures.* March 3, 2023.
Suffic. Strategy 2.4 (rental)	1	*Have you ever wondered which products are perfect for ski clothing rental? @cirkelsupply spoke to @houdinisportswear to understand their design principles, and the qualities that make for an awesome rental product!* April 12, 2023.
Suffic. Strategies 2.1 & 2.4 combined	1	*Have you tried Houdini Rental?* *Pick and choose your gear for each adventure and leave the hassle of washing, fixing or storing to us. Pop by our stores in Stockholm, Åre och Göteborg or click the link in bio to rent online! (Sweden only).* *Don't live in Sweden? Our partner @CirkelSupply delivers directly to your destination in the Swiss Alps.* February 2, 2023
Suffic. Strategies 2.1, 2.3 & 2.4 + Shop visiting/subscription promotion	7	*Houdini Circle is now open! Welcome to the world's first circular hub for outdoor apparel, where any garment you see can be bought new, rented or subscribed to.* *Rent, reuse, repair, buy, try or subscribe: The choice is yours. Welcome to the Circle* *Find Houdini Circle on Norrlandsgatan 12 in Stockholm.* September 28, 2023

Suffic. Strategy 3.2	23	*... Gustav has been serious about reducing his environmental impact for a few years – and that includes reducing his wardrobe. Taking on the #LiveLargeWithLess challenge last summer, Gustav stayed with it, landing in an overall wardrobe size of 15 garments which he's been using since summer last year.* August 8, 2023
Green marketing & Suffic. Strategy 1.1	1	*...The lanolin provides an all-natural DWR (durable water repellency), without adding any chemicals.* *The best part? Because the DWR is integrated in the yarn, rather than in a layer added on top of the fabric, it won't wash out. While it doesn't make for a fully waterproof fabric, Lana will protect you from showers and winter winds for a long period of time...* December 22, 2022
Total qty. of posts related to promoting sufficient consumption	**40**	
Green marketing	27	*Did you know that most waterproof clothing available today is a hazard to ourselves and the world around us? They're often treated with PFAS, a group of chemicals that don't break down naturally, are cancerous and have shown negative effects on both reproductive and immune systems for humans and animals.* *All Houdini outwear is made from circular performance fabrics and never treated with toxic PFAS. That's what we call the clean alternative.* November 18, 2022

Optimized design and production adjusted to demand (sufficiency on offering side)	3	*Back by popular demand: Less – made to order.* *With the launch of the Less project earlier this spring we took our very first steps in a long-term ambition to scale a made to order, micro factory program on a global level. That first batch was limited, and many of you have reached out asking for a second chance to get your hands on a Less Jacket or a pair of Less Pants.* *We are humbled and overwhelmed by the fantastic response and the fact that so many of you love Less as much as we do. Said and done, we have set it up with our friends at @a_industri_ who are now ready for another round of orders.* *This second batch of Less is open for orders from today until Friday 29 of June.* June 21, 2023
Total qty. of posts related to green product	**30**	
Environmental awareness/activism	6	*For the second year in a row, we're supporting our partners @naturskyddsforeningen for their special project to promote biodiversity: Operation Save the Bees...* June 9, 2023
Environmental activism & engaging promotion	3	*Our Ride Clean contest ends this month! Help stop PFAS and win a gift card worth 10 000 SEK. Join us in our mission towards a better outdoor industry. Help raise awareness on PFAS and win a gift card worth 10 000 SEK to spend on 100% PFAS-free Houdini gear.* February, 7, 2023
'Femvertising'	2	*Hailing from the USA and Norway, both Kjersti and Chanelle have a passion for combining their love for outdoor sports with a drive to support, encourage and empower women in the outdoor industry.* March 7, 2023
'Ethvertising'	1	*February 6th is Sámi National Day, commemorating the day Indigenous People of Sápmi in Northern Europe gathered for the first time in 1917 to unite behind their common cause: The fight for their rights...* February 6, 2023
'Disabletising'	1	*Meet Houdini Friends Albert and Beatrice, ski instructors at @viut_outdoor: A platform for deaf people and people with hearing loss to explore the outdoors.* December 5, 2022
Total qty. of posts related to social and environmental causes	**13**	

Conventional product promotion	51	*Our garments are designed to work together in a layering system. A smart combination of garments, fabrics and textures will enhance any outdoor experience, whether you're commuting in unpredictable weather or climbing big walls in the cold.* February 2, 2023
Product promotion opposite to Suffic. Strategy 3.1	2	*Last chance to order our first ever made on demand garments: Less Jackets & Pants...* June 29, 2023
Suffic. Strategy 2.3 & product promotion opposite to Suffic. Strategy 3.1 combined	1	*Psst: We've restocked our Reuse section on our website! Find your second-hand Houdini favorites online now before they're gone.* February 23, 2023
Total qty. of posts related to product promotion	**54**	
Company contribution	1	*...We might have come further than most, but I can humbly say that we don't have all the solutions. However, I can promise you this: Houdini will continue to play its part, without compromise, always with honesty and open source. I hope you will continue being our co-creators on this extraordinary ride...* December 29, 2022
Inspiring nature/adventure	13	*Meet our new friend Emma, bad ass skier and climber with an adventurous spirit!* *Originally from Skellefteå, Emma currently lives in Tromsö, Norway where she has access to world-class skiing and climbing. When she's not in the mountains, Emma works as a nurse in emergency care...* March 27, 2023
Customer engagement activity/event	19	*Giveaway Alert: Win two tickets to Banff Film Festival in Sweden!* *Adventure awaits! Tag a friend and win tickets for you and your pal to a cinematic adventure.* September 20, 2023
General customer engaging communication	4	*Friendly reminder to get outside!* June 19, 2023
Total qty. of posts	**174**	

The results show that the most recurrent posts are the ones related to conventional "product promotion" (n=54) focused on its features or functionality. Among these posts, three of them show a certain intention to stimulate demand. These posts, not to be considered as part of aggressive marketing campaigns, generate the "fear of missing out" (Blazquez et al. 2020), creating a sense of urgency that encourages consumers to take prompt action, which can be considered to go against the spirit of promoting sufficient consumption. While it is reasonable for any company to highlight the qualities of its products, regardless of its business approach, as explained later, these types of posts, although sporadic, do not align well with a sufficiency approach and raise doubts on the authenticity of the company's sustainable fashion marketing (Ritch 2023). Similar types of inconsistencies or contradictory promotion strategies were also found in the study of Niessen et al. (2023) when examining the historical print advertisements of fashion brand Levi's.

Another significant part of Houdini Sportswear's communication focuses on brand image associated with nature and adventure, with 13 posts, and customer engagement, primarily through various activities or events that promote interaction and brand connection, accounting for 19 posts. As a sign of its sustainability orientation, Houdini Sportswear dedicates a substantial part of its communication on Instagram to the environmentally sustainable nature of its products, with a total of 31 related posts, including 27 posts directly related to green marketing (Peattie/Charter 2012). The company positions itself as environmentally and socially responsible through 13 posts that advocate environmental awareness, gender equality causes ('femvertizing'), ethnic diversity causes ('ethvertizing'), and support for disabled individuals ('disabletizing').

In response to the first block of our research questions: *Is Houdini Sportswear promoting sufficient consumption through its Instagram official account? If so, through which strategies?*, the company's strong emphasis on sufficiency within its sustainability-oriented business approach is clearly reflected in the relatively high number of posts dedicated to it, specifically on the promotion of sufficient consumption, totaling 40 posts, 23 per cent of all posts. This is significant both in terms of quantity and as a percentage of the total, especially when compared to the research of Gossen and Kropfeld (2022), a study that focused on six outdoor industry companies engaging in sufficiency-oriented promotion initiatives. Nonetheless, this approach does not seem to be hindering its growth, as indicated by its business development and evolving figures.

Among the strategies adopted, strategy 3.2 from the reference framework stands out, consisting of promoting convenience and enjoyment of consuming and using responsibly through a more sufficient lifestyle. The company communicates in a recurrent, explicit and straightforward manner the need to rationalize the consumption of new products and provides examples of how to do this.

On the supply side, the company dedicates three posts to moderating and adjusting the quantity of production to meet demand and avoid surpluses. However, there is a potential rebound effect (Bocken et al. 2022) due to scarcity and collections running out, which could incentivize consumption.

Other identified strategies to encourage sufficient consumption through its posts with a relevant share include the product's physical and functional durability (strategy 1.1) and the promotion of alternative product or service systems that contribute to keeping products in use and moderating the acquisition of new products, such as repair or refurbishment (strategy 2.1), the sale of second-hand products (strategy 2.3) and the option to rent or share products (strategy 2.4), all offered in a store where the purchase of new products is just one of the alternatives. Even though these strategies primarily aim to promote more sufficient consumption, when considering all these offerings in the same store, it is reasonable to think about the company attracting customers to their shops and exposing them to new items, potentially generating a call-to-action effect that could lead to an increase in the purchase of new products (Garcia-Ortega et al. 2023).

Moreover, the company avoids aggressive marketing campaigns or fostering the pleasure of shopping solely for fun or to display status, in line with strategy 3.1. Nevertheless, the presence of posts that contradict this strategy, albeit few in number, might lead to thinking about anti-consumerist washing (Garcia-Ortega et al. 2023) and undermine the company's credibility in its sufficiency-focused approach.

The remaining strategies from the reference framework to promote sufficient consumption are barely addressed, even though some of them are specifically mentioned or have dedicated sections on the company's website. These include timeless product design for emotional durability (2.3) or product care tips to extend their lifespan (3.4). Additionally, there are no posts referring to designs that facilitate product repair or maintenance (1.2), the offering of consultancy services to help customers continue using products (2.2) or the promotion of a product's value and the convenience of extending its use by maximizing the return on investment (3.3). When recalling our second block of research questions: *Are there areas for improvement? What lessons can managers of this and other companies in the fashion industry draw from this?*, these are strategies that the company could naturally apply with minimal additional effort and that are currently underutilized or ignored. Implementing these strategies could reinforce the ones already in place, generating synergies with a multiplier effect on their effectiveness (Garcia-Ortega et al. 2023).

Comparing these results with those of Gossen and Kropfeld (2022), the most recurrent strategies to promote sufficient consumption present in this case study are consistent with those in the sample studied by those authors. In line with the adopted framework, the two studies also share the findings that these companies not only promote sufficiency in their communication but also integrate new business models as a part of their sufficiency approach, treating them as complementary concepts. Concerning the distinctions between the two studies, the absence of any mention of product design for repairability (strategy 1.2) is quite significant in the present case study, particularly given the availability and promotion of repair services (strategy 2.1). Similarly, the lack of product use and care advice (3.4) throughout the posts is remarkable. Additionally, in contrast to the findings of Gossen and Kropfeld (2022), Houdini Sportswear only features one post related to the timeless design of its products (strategy 1.3), which would help combat emotional obsolescence.

Thus, Houdini Sportswear can serve on the positive side as an illustrative example for managers in the industry for its clear commitment to sufficiency through the analysed social media platform and the recurrent embracement of certain strategies. Simultaneously, the study draws attention to the lack of consideration for various strategies in the adopted framework that could complement the existing ones, as well as the existence of questionable promotion techniques from the perspective of sufficient consumption, potentially casting doubt regarding the company's credibility and authenticity in its sustainability approach (Ritch 2023). Even firms with a remarkable sustainability orientation or clearly positioned in the sustainability arena may adopt a green (Peattie/Charter 2012) or a sufficiency-oriented marketing approach (Gossen et al. 2019) with the ultimate intention of fostering the consumption of their products by self-interest, not to mention falling into greenwashing (Ritch 2023; Gossen et al. 2019) or anti-consumerist washing practices (Garcia-Ortega et al., 2023).

5. Conclusions and implications

Following an extensive examination, categorization and analysis of the posts published by the fashion retailer Houdini Sportswear on the Instagram social network over the course of an entire year, and in response to the research questions, it can be concluded that Houdini Sportswear maintains a distinct sustainability focus marked by a pronounced sufficiency-driven approach in its posts. This approach is primarily underpinned by the promotion of the convenience and enjoyment of consuming and using the garments through a more sufficient lifestyle. This strategy falls within the ambit of the third pillar of strategies and is notably complemented by the overall avoidance of aggressive marketing campaigns that fuel consumerism, although with some occasional discrepancies.

From a theoretical perspective, this study contributes to the emerging literature that addresses the promotion of sufficient consumption through social media. It achieves this by applying Garcia-Ortega et al.'s (2023) framework of strategies in the context of social media communication and showing its relevance in exploring and assessing how fashion companies can utilize these platforms to promote sufficient consumption of their products, thereby influencing consumer motivations and behaviors. In this sense, this research extends the study by Gossen and Kropfeld (2022) by providing fresh empirical evidence based on a comprehensive and sector-focused framework on how sufficiency-oriented fashion companies can leverage social media and improve their communication in such endeavors.

In terms of managerial and practical implications, this study aims to raise awareness among management of the concept of sufficient consumption and serves as a benchmark for how a fashion company can promote sufficient consumption of their products through social media platforms by combining strategies from the three pillars or dimensions of the adopted framework. It also identifies aspects that may be addressed to enhance the effectiveness of these efforts, including a broader and more prolific adoption of strategies in their communication. Additionally, the study highlights the potential rebound effects of certain strategies and emphasizes the importance for companies to avoid contradictory messages in their communication and promotion which may bring doubts about potential anti-consumerist washing practices and affect their credibility. Furthermore, Houdini Sportswear serves as a prime example of how a commitment to sufficient consumption and the application of demarketing strategies do not hinder business growth.

Moreover, this study also holds implications for consumers and governmental bodies, both of which are key stakeholders alongside businesses on the path to a more sustainable economic and societal model. It contributes to raising consumer and societal awareness and provides criteria for assessing companies' sufficiency approaches and communication strategies. Additionally, it offers insights to institutions in shaping criteria and setting boundaries for corporate marketing policies.

Finally, this research has inherent limitations due to its single-case design and reliance solely on Instagram posts as the primary data source. Future investigations can build upon this work by incorporating other companies with similar or distinct sustainability orientations, thus allowing for comparative analysis. Furthermore, findings suggest a need for exploration into the true motives and authenticity of sustainable fashion marketing (Ritch 2023). This could be realized by conducting interviews with social media management teams or by assessing other marketing channels (Gossen/Kropfeld 2022). Additionally, extending the temporal scope of research (Niessen et al. 2023) can enable the analysis of how these strategies evolve over time, providing insights into historical and potential trends and the future trajectory of this field.

References

Armstrong, Cosette M./Niinimäki, Kirsi/Kujala, Sari/Karell, Essi/Lang, Chunmin (2015): "Sustainable product-service systems for clothing: exploring consumer perceptions of consumption alternatives in Finland." In: Journal of Cleaner Production 97, pp. 30–39. https://doi.org/10.1016/j.jclepro.2014.01.046.

Armstrong Soule, Catherine/Reich, Brandon (2015): "Less is more: is a green demarketing strategy sustainable?" In: Journal of Marketing Management 31/13–14, pp. 1403–1427. https://doi.org/10.1080/0267257X.2015.1059874.

Blazquez, Marta/Henninger, Claudia E./Alexander, Bethan/Franquesa, Carlota (2020): "Consumers' knowledge and intentions towards sustainability: A Spanish fashion perspective." In: Fashion Practice 12/1, pp. 34–54. https://doi.org/10.1080/17569370.2019.1669326.

Blazquez, Marta (2014): "Fashion shopping in multichannel retail: The role of technology in enhancing the customer experience." In: International Journal of Electronic Commerce 18/4, pp. 97–116. https://doi.org/10.1080/17569370.2019.1669326.

Bocken, Nancy M. P. (2017): "Business-led sustainable consumption initiatives: impacts and lessons learned." In: Journal of Management Development 36/1, pp. 81–96. https://doi.org/10.1108/JMD-10-2014-0136.

Bocken, Nancy M. P./Morales, Lisa Smeke/Lehner, Matthias (2020): "Sufficiency business strategies in the food industry – The case of Oatly." In: Sustainability 12/3, 824. https://doi.org/10.3390/su12030824.

Bocken, Nancy M. P./Niessen, Laura/Short, Samuel William (2022): "The Sufficiency-Based Circular Economy – An Analysis of 150 Companies." In: Frontiers in Sustainability 3, 899289. https://doi.org/10.3389/frsus.2022.899289.

Bocken, Nancy M. P./Short, Samuel William/Rana, Padmakshi/Evans, Steve (2014): "A literature and practice review to develop sustainable business model archetypes." In: Journal of Cleaner Production 65, pp. 42–56. https://doi.org/10.1016/j.jclepro.2013.11.039.

Bocken, Nancy M. P./Short, Samuel W. (2016): "Towards a sufficiency-driven business Model: Experiences and opportunities." In: Environmental Innovation and Societal Transitions 18, pp. 41–61. https://doi.org/10.1016/j.eist.2015.07.010.

Buzzo, Aline/Abreu Maria José (2019): "Fast Fashion, Fashion Brands & Sustainable Consumption." In: Subramanian Senthilkannan Muthu (eds.), Fast Fashion, Fashion Brands and Sustainable Consumption, pp. 1–17, Singapore: Springer. https://doi.org/10.1007/978-981-13-1268-7_1.

Cao, Huantian/Chang, Rita/Kallal, Jo/Manalo, Grace/McCord, Jennifer/Shaw, Jenna/Starner, Heather (2014): "Adaptable apparel: a sustainable design solution for excess apparel consumption problem." In: Journal of Fashion Marketing and Management 18/1, pp. 52–69. https://doi.org/10.1108/JFMM-08-2012-0046.

Cline, Elizabeth L. (2013): Overdressed: The shockingly high cost of cheap fashion, London: Penguin.

Eisenhardt, Kathleen M,/Graebner, Melissa E. (2007): "Theory building from cases: Opportunities and challenges." In: Academy of Management Journal 50/1, pp. 25–32. https://doi.org/10.5465/amj.2007.24160888.

Ellen-MacArthur-Foundation (2017): "A new textiles economy: Redesigning fashion's future," 7.12.2023 (https://www.ellenmacarthurfoundation.org/a-new-textiles-economy).

Fletcher, Kate (2010): "Slow fashion: An invitation for systems change." Fashion Practice 2/2, pp. 259–265. https://doi.org/10.2752/175693810X12774625387594.

Fletcher, Kate (2013): Sustainable Fashion and Textiles: Design Journeys, New York, Abingdon: Routledge.

Freudenreich, Birte/Schaltegger, Stefan (2020): "Developing sufficiency-oriented offerings for clothing users: Business approaches to support consumption reduction." In: Journal of Cleaner Production 247, 119589. https://doi.org/10.1016/j.jclepro.2019.119589.

Gabriel, Michelle Blair (2021): "Desire, power, and capitalism: A theoretical exploration of overconsumption in the global fashion industry." Breaking the system. Responsible Fashion Series Conference, University of Antwerp, 7.12.2023 (http://dx.doi.org/10.5281/zenodo.7988126).

Garcia-Ortega, Beatriz/Galan-Cubillo, Javier/Llorens-Montes, Francisco Javier/de-Miguel-Molina, Blanca (2023): "Sufficient consumption as a missing link toward sustainability: The case of fast fashion." In: Journal of Cleaner Production 399, 136678. https://doi.org/10.1016/j.jclepro.2023.136678.

Gasper, Des/Shah, Amod/Tankha, Sunil (2019): "The Framing of Sustainable Consumption and Production in SDG 12." In: Global Policy 10, pp. 83–95. https://doi.org/10.1111/1758-5899.12592.

Gossen, Maike/Heinrich, Anneli (2021): "Encouraging Consumption Reduction: Findings of a Qualitative Study with Clothing Companies on Sufficiency-Promoting Communication." In: Cleaner and Responsible Consumption 3, 100028. https://doi.org/10.1016/j.clrc.2021.100028.

Gossen, Maike/Kropfeld, Maren I. (2022). "'Choose nature. Buy less.' Exploring sufficiency-oriented marketing and consumption practices in the outdoor industry." In: Sustainable Production and Consumption 30, pp. 720–736. https://doi.org/10.1016/j.spc.2022.01.005

Gossen, Maike/Ziesemer, Florence/Schrader, Ulf (2019): "Why and How Commercial Marketing Should Promote Sufficient Consumption: A Systematic Literature Review." In: Journal of Macromarketing 39/3, pp. 252–269. https://doi.org/10.1177/0276146719866238.

Gustafsson, Johanna (2017): "Single case studies vs. multiple case studies: A comparative study. Academy of Business." Engineering and Science, Halmstad University, Sweden 12/1, pp. 1–15, 7.12.2023 (http://urn.kb.se/resolve?urn=urn:nbn:se:hh:diva-33017).

Hajli, M. Nick (2014): "A study of the impact of social media on consumers." In: International Journal of Market Research 56/3, pp. 387–404. https://doi.org/10.2501/IJMR-2014-025.

Hesse, Andreas/Rünz, Sofie (2022): "'Fly Responsibly': a case study on consumer perceptions of a green demarketing campaign." In: Journal of Marketing Communications 28/3, pp. 232–252. https://doi.org/10.1080/13527266.2020.1842483.

Holtström, Johan/Bjellerup, Charlotte/Eriksson, Johanna (2019): "Business model development for sustainable apparel consumption: The case of Houdini Sportswear." In: Journal of Strategy and Management 12/4, pp. 481–504. https://doi.org/10.1108/jsma-01-2019-0015.

Houdini Sportswear (2023a): 28.8.2023 (https://www.linkedin.com/company/houdini-sportswear/people).

Houdini Sporstwear (2023b): 3.10.2023 (https://houdinisportswear.com/en-eu).

Hwang, Chanmi/Lee, Youngji/Diddi, Sonali/Karpova, Elena (2016): ""Don't buy this jacket" Consumer reaction toward anti-consumption apparel advertisement." In: Journal of Fashion Marketing and Management: An International Journal 20/4, pp. 435–452. https://doi.org/10.1108/JFMM-12-2014-0087.

Jackson, Tim (2009): Prosperity without Growth: Economics for a Finite Planet, New York, Abingdon: Routledge.

Jung, Sojin/Jin, Byoungho (2016): "From quantity to quality: understanding slow fashion consumers for sustainability and consumer education." International Journal of Consumer Studies 40/4, pp. 410–421. https://doi.org/10.1111/ijcs.12276.

Kallis, Giorgos (2017): "Radical dematerialization and degrowth." In: Philosophical Transactions of the Royal Society – A Mathematical, Physical and Engineering Sciences 375/2095, 20160383. https://doi.org/10.1098/rsta.2016.0383.

Ndubisi, Nelson Oly (2007): "Relationship marketing and customer loyalty." In: Marketing Intelligence & Planning 25/1, pp. 98–106. https://doi.org/10.1108/02634500710722425.

Niessen, Laura/Bocken, Nancy M. P. (2021): "How Can Businesses Drive Sufficiency? The Business for Sufficiency Framework." In: Sustainable Production and Consumption 28, pp. 1090–1103. https://doi.org/10.1016/j.spc.2021.07.030.

Niessen, Laura/Bocken, Nancy M. P./Dijk, Marc (2023): "Sufficiency as Trend or Tradition? – Uncovering Business Pathways to Sufficiency through Historical Advertisements." In: Frontiers in Sustainability 4, 1165682. https://doi.org/10.3389/frsus.2023.1165682.

Niinimäki, Kirsi/Peters, Greg/Dahlbo, Helena/Perry, Patsy/Rissanen, Timo/Gwilt, Alison (2020): "The environmental price of fast fashion." In: Nature Reviews

Earth & Environment 1/4, pp. 189–200. https://doi.org/10.1038/s43017-020-0039-9.

Ozdamar Ertekin, Zeynep/Atik, Deniz (2015): "Sustainable markets: Motivating factors, barriers, and remedies for mobilization of slow fashion." In: Journal of Macromarketing 35/1, pp. 53–69. https://doi.org/10.1177/0276146714535932.

Peattie, Ken/Charter, Martin (2012): "Green marketing." In: Michael J. Baker (eds.), The Marketing Book, New York, Abingdon: Routledge, pp. 756–786.

Pepper, Miriam/Jackson, Tim/Uzzell, David (2009): "An examination of the values that motivate socially conscious and frugal consumer behaviours." In: International Journal of Consumer Studies 33/2, pp. 126–136. https://doi.org/10.1111/j.1470-6431.2009.00753.x.

PFR (2023): "Houdini Sportswear," 29.8.2023. https://poland.dealroom.co/companies/houdini_sportswear.

Reilly, Anne H./Hynan Katherine A. (2014): "Corporate communication, sustainability, and social media: It's not easy (really) being green." In: Business Horizons 57/6, pp. 747–758. https://doi.org/10.1016/j.bushor.2014.07.008.

Ritch, Elaine L. (2023): "Sustainable fashion marketing: green or greenwash?" In: Karin M. Ekström (eds.), Marketing Fashion: Critical Perspectives on the Power of Fashion in Contemporary Culture, New York, Abingdon: Routledge, pp. 187–205.

Sheth, Jagdish (2020): "Impact of Covid-19 on consumer behavior: Will the old habits return or die?" In: Journal of Business Research 117, pp. 280–283. https://doi.org/10.1016/j.jbusres.2020.05.059.

Strähle, Jochen/Gräff, Chantal (2017): "The role of social media for a sustainable consumption." In: Jochen Strähle (eds.), Green Fashion Retail, Singapore: Springer Nature, pp. 225–247. https://doi.org/10.1007/978-981-10-2440-5_12.

Stål, Herman I./Jansson, Johan (2017): "Sustainable consumption and value propositions: Exploring product–service system practices among Swedish fashion firms." In: Sustainable Development 25/6, pp. 546–558. https://doi.org/10.1002/sd.1677.

Tarnanidis, Theodore/Owusu-Frimpong, Nana/Nwankwo, Sonny/Omar, Maktoba (2015): "Why we buy? Modeling consumer selection of referents." In: Journal of Retailing and Consumer Services 22, pp. 24–36. https://doi.org/10.1016/j.jretconser.2014.09.004.

Veleva, Vesela (2021): "The role of entrepreneurs in advancing sustainable lifestyles: Challenges, impacts, and future opportunities." In: Journal of Cleaner Production 283, 124658. https://doi.org/10.1016/j.jclepro.2020.124658.

Worrell, Ernst/Carreon, Jesus Rosales (2017): "Energy demand for materials in an international context." Philosophical Transactions of the Royal Society – A Mathematical, Physical and Engineering Sciences 375/2095, 20160377. https://doi.org/10.1098/rsta.2016.0377.

Yakobovitch, Nadav/Grinstein, Amir (2016): "Materialism and the boomerang effect of descriptive norm demarketing: Extension and remedy in an environmental context." In: Journal of Public Policy & Marketing 35/1, pp. 91–107. https://doi.org/10.1509/jppm.14.064.

Zhang, Wujie/Guo, Jianfeng/Gu, Fu/Gu, Xinjian (2018): "Coupling life cycle assessment and life cycle costing as an evaluation tool for developing product service system of high energy-consuming equipment." In: Journal of Cleaner Production 183, pp. 1043–1053. https://doi.org/10.1016/j.jclepro.2018.02.146.

Towards Sustainable Fashion

Exploring Sufficiency-Oriented Business Models in French Fashion SMEs

Maëlle Soulis and Oksana Mont

Abstract *This study analyses seven sufficiency-oriented SMEs in the French fashion sector, categorizing their strategies into efficiency, shift and sufficiency. It reveals the tension in balancing sustainability with financial viability, highlighting the systemic challenges posed by consumer preference for fast fashion.*

1. Introduction

The fashion sector is a significant contributor to global environmental issues, responsible for roughly 10 per cent of global carbon emissions (Vesterinen/Syrjälä 2022: 1). It is the world's second-largest polluting industry, surpassed only by the oil sector (Pal 2017). The root of the problem lies in the fast fashion paradigm, which relies on short production and consumption cycles, low production costs, fleeting trends and inexpensive but low-quality materials. Fast fashion promotes a throwaway culture, exacerbating waste generation and escalating consumption levels (Diddi et al. 2019). In contrast, an emerging "slow fashion" movement challenges this unsustainable status quo, with sufficiency as its cornerstone principle (Fletcher/Grose 2012).

Research on the role of businesses in transitioning towards sufficiency-oriented business models, particularly in the fashion industry, remains nascent (Freudenreich/Schaltegger 2020). A limited number of studies have explored how fashion companies implement sufficiency in their business operations, such as Freudenreich and Schaltegger (2020), Garcia-Ortega et al. (2023) and Schauman et al. (2023). However, it remains ambiguous which of the strategies fashion companies employ are genuinely aligned with efficiency, shift or sufficiency approaches, as defined by Akenji et al. (2021).

Then, there is a noticeable gap in research concerning the financial ramifications of adopting sufficiency strategies in the fashion industry (Fletcher 2010; Gossen/

Kropfeld 2022). The prevailing economic system prioritizes strategies that maximize sales and profits, contrasting with the sufficiency model that seeks to curb consumption. This raises the question of whether businesses can realistically adopt a strategy that reduces consumption and at the same time is financially viable.

This chapter explores these research gaps by focusing on sufficiency-aspiring French small and medium-sized fashion businesses. Through interviews with seven companies that have already adopted some sufficiency-oriented strategies in their business models and an analysis of their online presence and company documentation, this chapter offers insights into how businesses can contribute to a sustainable society through sufficiency-oriented business models.

2. Literature review

2.1 From efficiency and shift to sufficiency in business strategies

The literature on sufficiency has a long pedigree (e.g., Princen 2003). Some scholars define it as changes in consumption patterns and a reduction in overall consumption levels (Sandberg 2021), while others suggest that sufficiency is about reducing absolute levels of consumption (Mont et al. 2022; Niessen/Bocken 2021). In consumption studies, sufficiency is defined as a self-imposed restriction on consumption (Figge et al. 2014). The role of business is seen as that of actively creating opportunities for consumers to reduce their consumption (Freudenreich/Schaltegger 2020). Yet, there is a degree of uncertainty concerning which strategies lead to an outright reduction in consumption volumes and which might indirectly influence consumption volumes by altering consumption patterns (Freudenreich/Schaltegger 2020).

Recent literature on sufficiency in the business context tends to amalgamate various business strategies – such as those focused on efficiency, shift and sufficiency (Akenji et al. 2021: 18–19) – under the broad umbrella of sufficiency. This approach risks diverting attention from the task of directly reducing overall consumption levels. It also complicates understanding of whether sufficiency-oriented initiatives are gaining traction in businesses and how sufficiency is being operationalized in practice.

For example, a recent study by Bocken et al. (2022) introduced the concept of a "sufficiency-based circular economy" and scrutinized one hundred and fifty companies using this lens. Twenty-two of these companies explicitly questioned the need to consume, and thirteen included sufficiency in their mission statements. A mere eight companies took steps to moderate sales by actively discouraging purchases or avoiding reduced pricing. The remaining companies had adopted well-established strategies. These included improvements in product design, which falls under efficiency strategies; and, to some extent, the use of circular and sharing business models as well as product-service systems, representing shift strategies. These strategies can potentially reduce consumption levels, but indirectly (Figge et al. 2014). This observation prompts questions regarding the level of ambition of these companies to directly engage in reducing overall consumption levels.

In a similar study, Garcia-Ortega et al. (2023) studied ten fast-fashion companies. The most commonly implemented strategies included efficiency-oriented and shift approaches such as offering take-back and resale services for discarded products, designing durable products and providing consumers with information about product durability, usage, care and environmental impact (see Table 1). These strategies were summarized as focusing on services, product design and communication about products. Meanwhile, strategies aimed at moderating consumption volumes or reducing the business models' dependence on selling new items were scarcely utilized.

Beyeler and Jaeger-Erben (2022) analyzed fourteen companies, focusing on dimensions of sufficiency in business practices; nine of these companies were from the fashion industry. Utilizing the framework by Schneidewind and Palzkill-Vorbeck (2011), the authors identified 19 business strategies classified into four categories: decluttering (less), decelerating (slower), disentangling (more local), and decommercialization (less market). The decluttering category encompassed strategies that targeted consumption levels more directly, including marketing aimed at reducing consumption, moderate sales and demand reduction services (sufficiency-oriented strategies). However, product service systems and sharing – i.e. shift strategies – were also included in this category. The remaining strategies were extending product life and shifting to reuse and repair (also shift strategies), focusing on local services and supply chains and encouraging prosumerism.

From the perspective of sustainability transformation, integrating efficiency-, shift- and sufficiency-oriented strategies offers the most promising pathway towards sustainability, as supported by various studies (Vita et al. 2019; Freudenreich/Schaltegger 2020; Akenji et al. 2021); companies should ideally engage in all three categories, as indicated by the abovementioned studies. Yet, it would be beneficial for scholarly inquiry to have a clear differentiation between these categories, rather than amalgamating them, when examining business models. We therefore advocate for a nuanced differentiation between sufficiency-oriented strategies, which target absolute reductions in consumption volumes by both consumers and businesses; shift-oriented strategies, which redirect consumption towards less environmentally impactful products and services through alternative business models; and efficiency-oriented strategies, which enhance the efficiency of products, services and operations, thereby potentially influencing consumption volumes indirectly through altered consumption patterns. Sufficiency-oriented strategies are generally categorized as strong sustainable consumption (Lorek/Fuchs 2019), whereas shift- and efficiency-oriented strategies are often classified as weak sustainable consumption (Dalhammar et al. 2022: 20).

Employing this differentiation shows that the companies investigated in previous research predominantly use shift- and efficiency-oriented strategies. Taking into account the rebound effects often associated with these approaches (Figge et al. 2014; Vita et al. 2019), as well as the broader criticism levelled against weak sustainable consumption strategies (Lorek/Fuchs 2019), it becomes evident that a transition is needed, both in practice and in research, from the current focus on shift- and efficiency-oriented strategies to a more profound adoption of sufficiency-oriented strategies (Figure 1).

Figure 1: Proliferation of efficiency, shift and sufficiency strategies in companies: the current vs. the desired state.

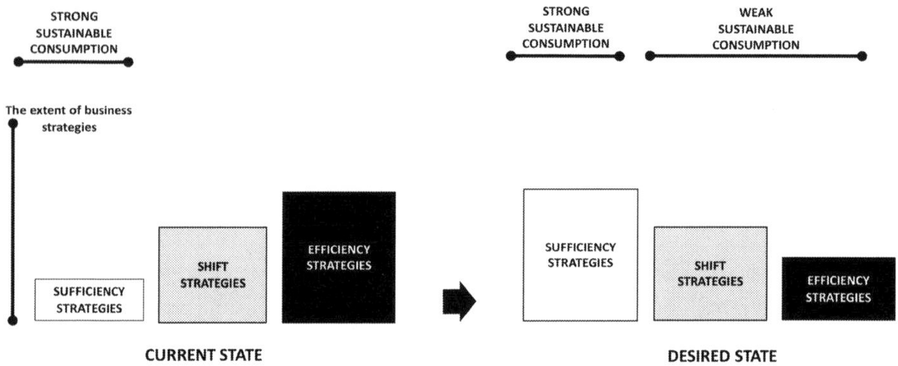

In the following section, we consolidate the numerous strategies employed by fashion companies aspiring towards sufficiency, as discussed in the academic literature. These strategies are then categorized according to the typology shown in Table 1.

2.2 Diversity of business strategies for efficiency, shift and sufficiency

In fashion, designing for sufficiency entails opting for environmentally preferable materials in production and high-quality materials that prolong the garment's lifespan; decelerate the production, use and disposal of garments; and reduce the need for producing new products over time (Fletcher/Grose 2012). Reducing the complexity of clothing designs and purposefully reducing the types of materials used helps produce clothes that are easier to reuse, repair and recycle. Designing for longevity offers an alternative to producing fast-fashion clothes. To achieve lasting appeal, sufficiency-driven fashion brands seek to create clothing with timeless designs (Bocken/Short 2016; Sandberg 2022). Examples include classic, simple and seasonless garments that do not follow fashion trends, do not carry a brand logo and/or can be adapted to various settings with accessories or by combining them with other garments. Thus, the timelessness of pieces goes beyond their physical attributes to encompass high-quality design and a long-lasting style that can be worn regardless of fashion trends or seasons.

Designing for extended product use further requires a shift in consumer behavior from acquiring garments to actively using them, which Fletcher refers to as moving from "owner-ship" to "user-ship" (2014: 235). Indeed, improving the physical durability of garments can only be effective if users make use of the functionality offered by durable products. This calls for changes in consumption patterns that can be accomplished by developing an emotional connection between the consumer and the product. Sufficiency-oriented clothing brands use various strategies to nurture emotional durability, such as customization, personalization and involvement of customers in the design and production process (Niessen/Bocken 2021). Another sufficiency strategy is adding services to support extended use, such as repair, upgrade or upcycling services, or teaching customers how to perform these practices through online DIY courses (Freudenreich/Schaltegger 2020; Gossen/Heinrich 2021).

Collaborative value creation is essential for practicing sustainability strategies and is pursued through open-ended design processes, experimentation, trial and error, and pre-ordering (Kozlowski et al. 2016). The relationship between sufficiency-oriented companies and customers extends beyond a single sales transaction, involving multiple interactions over the lifetime of the garments throughout the acquisition, use and post-use phases. By involving consumers in the design process, companies are able to produce clothes that closely match their needs, increasing the value of the garments to the users. This approach also supports conscious purchase decisions by encouraging consumers to reflect on the necessity of buying a particular product. Additionally, it enables companies to limit production to the number of ordered pieces, which minimizes waste (Beyeler/Jaeger-Erben 2022).

Sufficiency-oriented strategies often include marketing and communication efforts that actively discourage overconsumption (Gossen et al. 2019). More specific tactics might involve moderating sales and promotions by abstaining from consumer marketing campaigns or sales incentives like discounts, eliminating seasonal and limited fashion collections and operating without advertisements (Beyeler/Jaeger-Erben 2022). Companies aspiring to sufficiency often utilize social media to directly engage with consumers, solicit feedback, provide information about their operations and products and educate consumers about the environmental consequences of their consumption (Gossen/Kropfeld 2022).

Table 1: Sufficiency-oriented business strategies in the fashion industry

	Focus	**Examples of strategies**	**Sources**
Effi-ciency	Products	Clothes design for efficient material use; lower lifecycle impact; and customised and personalised design	Fletcher/Grose 2012; Bocken/Short 2016; Niessen/Bocken 2021; Bocken/Niessen/Short 2022; Beyeler/Jaeger-Erben 2022; Claxton/Kent 2020; Garcia-Ortega et al. 2023
	Services	Choice architecture: avoid selling high-polluting materials and clothes of poor quality on the market	Beyeler/Jaeger-Erben 2022
	Business model	Sell efficient products; increase sales; reduce per-unit price	Fletcher/Grose 2012; Buzzo/Abreu 2019
	Communication and marketing	Inform consumers about clothes' impact, use, care and refitting (e.g., through labelling and campaigns)	Bocken/Niessen/Short 2022; Garcia-Ortega et al. 2023
Shift	Products	Design durable clothes for physical, functional and emotional longevity; seasonless design; easy-to-maintain, mend, refurbish or upcycle	Fletcher/Grose 2012; Henninger et al. 2017; Bocken/Short 2016; Niessen/Bocken 2021; Bocken/Niessen/Short 2022; Beyeler/Jaeger-Erben 2022; Garcia-Ortega et al. 2023
	Services	Offer clothes extension services: (local) mending, refitting and tailoring services, take-back, upcycle, recycle	Freudenreich/Schaltegger 2020; Niessen/Bocken 2021; Bocken/Niessen/Short 2022; Coscieme et al. 2022
		Offer long warranty	Bocken/Niessen/Short 2022
		Support and offer reuse arrangements, e.g., organise collection of clothes for resale, donation and second-life	Fletcher/Grose 2012; Bocken/Short 2016; Niessen/Bocken 2021; Bocken/Niessen/Short 2022; Beyeler/Jaeger-Erben 2022; Coscieme et al. 2022; Garcia-Ortega et al. 2023

Shift	Business models	Product-service systems: no-ownership offers, pay-per-use offers; temporary access to products: renting, leasing, hiring	Stål/Jansson 2017; Coscieme et al. 2022; Bocken/Niessen/Short 2022; Beyeler/Jaeger-Erben 2022; Garcia-Ortega et al. 2023
		Sharing: offer an exchange platform for sharing and swapping clothes; clothes libraries and wardrobe-sharing; pay-per-use; membership fees	Pedersen/Netter 2015; Niessen/Bocken 2021; Bocken/Niessen/Short 2022; Beyeler/Jaeger-Erben 2022; Garcia-Ortega et al. 2023
		Circular business models that build on ideas of reuse, repair, recycle	Elf/Werner/Black 2022; Coscieme et al. 2022
	Communication and marketing	Communicate about product durability, how to wear and maintain clothes over a long period of time	Laitala/Boks/Klepp 2015; Garcia-Ortega et al. 2023
		Communicate about how and where to lease, rent or swap clothes	Stål/Jansson 2017; Garcia-Ortega et al. 2023
		Communicate about the benefits of reuse and second-hand clothes	Garcia-Ortega et al. 2023
Suffi-ciency	Products	Designing for slow fashion: customised, size-fit and durable clothes	Fletcher/Grose 2012; Laitala/Boks/Klepp 2015
		Produce products in local production facilities; short supply chains	Beyeler/Jaeger-Erben 2022
	Services	Support consumers in self-sufficiency and DIY, e.g., providing tools for sewing, mending or upcycling their clothes	Beyeler/Jaeger-Erben 2022; Freudenreich/Schaltegger 2020; Bocken/Niessen/Short 2022
	Business models	Premium pricing; long-term consumer management	Freudenreich/Schaltegger 2020; Beyeler/Jaeger-Erben 2022
		Produce clothes on demand	Buecher et al. 2018

Suffi-ciency	Communication and marketing	De-legitimise mass-produced and standardised clothes; question consumption levels/marketing for consumption reduction	Fletcher 2010; Gossen/Heinrich 2021; Bocken/Niessen/Short 2022; Beyeler/Jaeger-Erben 2022; Gossen/Kropfeld 2022
		Moderate sales; avoid discounts, seasonal sales	Bocken/Short 2016; Gossen/Heinrich 2021; Gossen/Kropfeld 2022; Beyeler/Jaeger-Erben 2022
		Moderate promotions and avoid advertising, e.g., aggressive marketing campaigns based on successive collections, trends and low prices	Bocken et al. 2014; Bocken/Short 2016; Gossen/Heinrich 2021; Gossen/Kropfeld 2022; Beyeler/Jaeger-Erben 2022
		Demand reduction strategies	Bocken/Short 2016; Niessen/Bocken 2021; Beyeler/Jaeger-Erben 2022; Gossen/Heinrich 2021; Gossen/Kropfeld 2022
		Promote convenience of extending product's use	Garcia-Ortega et al. 2023
		Promote needs over desires	Bocken/Short 2016; Garcia-Ortega et al. 2023

Table 1 demonstrates a detailed and classified account of strategies that fashion companies may employ to increase the efficiency of their products and operations, shift to alternative product categories and business models, and develop business models oriented towards sufficiency, as reported in the literature.

2.3 Rethinking purpose, profit and growth

Sufficiency-oriented businesses usually have a nuanced approach to profitability that diverges from the traditional focus on profit maximization. According to Wiefek and Heinitz (2018: 311), these businesses do not aim to maximize profits at any cost. Instead, they seek to achieve a level of profitability that allows them to cover operational expenses and pay salaries. This perspective aligns with Millstone's (2017: 174) distinction between profit seeking and profit maximization. While the latter prioritizes financial gains at the expense of environmental and social considerations, profit seeking aims for a balanced approach that mitigates the externalization of costs to stakeholders, including the environment and society.

Sustainable business models, including sufficiency-oriented businesses, aim to reduce negative environmental and social impacts while maintaining economic viability. These businesses focus on financial stability to sustain operations and fulfil broader social and environmental objectives (Bocken/Niessen/Short 2022). This approach is supported by research that examines profitability through the lens of financial viability rather than profit maximization (Katz/Page 2012).

In the fashion industry, sufficiency-oriented companies often adopt strategies that may appear counterintuitive in a market driven by high sales growth and market share (Bocken/Short 2016; Gossen/Heinrich 2021). To offset reduced production volumes, these companies employ premium pricing strategies (Gossen et al. 2019) that enable the producer to cover the total cost of making a product, including quality materials, durability, repair support, stakeholder well-being, and responsible supply chain and stakeholder practices.

The growth strategies of sufficiency-oriented businesses vary. Some aim for moderate or organic growth to maintain their values (Gebauer 2018), while others actively seek growth to expand their philosophy and market share of sustainable products and companies (Gossen/Heinrich 2021). These businesses often support ecosystem growth, which involves sharing knowledge and ideas within a community of like-minded companies and practitioners. This commitment often manifests through a focus on local embeddedness, fostering proximity and meaningful relationships with suppliers, consumers and other stakeholders (Beyeler/Jaeger-Erben 2022).

However, operating within a growth-oriented economy presents challenges, especially when public companies seek to deliver financial benefits for their shareholders above all other actors (Millstone 2017). In contrast, businesses aspiring to sustainability consider the benefits and costs to all stakeholders, including employees, customers, the environment and society (Reichel 2018). To maintain their independence and values, many sufficiency-oriented companies opt for limited liability or family-owned structures (Bocken et al. 2022). They also prefer mission-driven investors such as foundations, crowdfunding or personal investments (Beyeler/Jaeger-Erben 2022).

When these companies generate a profit, they strategically reinvest the funds to foster future development, improve internal business practices and cultivate long-term, high-quality relationships with their suppliers (Gebauer 2018). Additionally, they extend their support to other initiatives aligned with sufficiency-oriented goals, such as social movements and non-governmental organizations (Khmara/Kronenberg 2018). A subset of these sufficiency-oriented businesses choose to organize themselves as benefit corporations, thereby legally obligating themselves to pursue public benefits for a diverse range of stakeholders, in addition to fulfilling their duty to generate profits for shareholders (Hiller 2013).

3. Method

This study used qualitative research methods to conduct a multi-case investigation. The following set of criteria framed the sampling of the case companies:

- Sufficiency orientation: companies that publicly identify themselves with a sufficiency-oriented purpose and combine several sufficiency-oriented strategies.
- Business size: micro, small and medium-sized enterprises (SMEs).
- Fashion sector: B2C companies in the fashion industry.
- French region and language: companies located in France, with primary and secondary data available in French.

The sampling process resulted in the selection of seven companies. As a primary data source, seven semi-structured interviews were conducted between February and April 2023 with company representatives. The interview guide followed a list of questions about products, services and operations, business models, communication and marketing, and growth and profit. For every interview, questions and follow-up discussions were adapted to the specificities of each company. In a second phase, data triangulation was performed using secondary data collected from the companies' websites, blogs and Instagram accounts.

The data analysis was structured around four key categories: products, services, business models and communication and marketing, which offer insights about how sufficiency-oriented business models are being operationalized by the case companies (section 4). The categories of efficiency-, shift- and sufficiency-oriented fashion business strategies presented in Table 1 were used to classify strategies employed by the case companies (see Table 3). The interview material was also analyzed regarding the case companies' strategies and attitudes towards profits and growth (section 5).

Table 2: List of sufficiency-oriented companies

Company	Description	Interviewee's position in the organization	Collected secondary data
Company A	Size: 48 employees Founding year: 2016	Finance manager	Website (#1) Blog posts (#4) Instagram posts (#2)
Company B	Size: 3 employees Founding year: 2013	Director	Website (#1) Blog posts (#8)
Company C	Size: 2 employees Founding year: 2013	Co-founder	Website (#1) Instagram posts (#2)
Company D	Size: 3 employees Founding year: 2019	Co-founder	Website (#1) Blog posts (#4)
Company E	Size: 4 employees Founding year: 2021	Co-founder	Website (#1) Blog posts (#5)
Company F	Size: 1 employee Founding year: 2020	Director	Website (#1) Blog posts (#2)
Company G	Size: 2 employees Founding year: 2019	Co-founder	Website (#1) Blog posts (#7)

4. How do French fashion SMEs work with sufficiency?

This section presents the various ways in which the seven French SMEs operationalize the concept of sufficiency.

4.1 Products

The studied companies have divergent interpretations of what constitutes sustainability and sufficiency. Thus, they employ diverse clothing design strategies for producing durable and timeless products. The first group of companies we interviewed aligns closely with existing literature (Gossen/Heinrich 2021), offering classic, seasonless and neutral garments. These companies aim to create clothes that outlast seasonal fashion trends, encouraging consumers to use them for extended periods of time.

The second group takes a slightly different approach. They offer garments that are sufficiently original to attract customers but are designed with a level of moderation to ensure they do not become obsolete or go out of fashion quickly. This strategy aims to strike a balance between originality and longevity.

The third group of interviewed companies defines their offerings as timeless products based on authenticity. According to these companies, consumers' emotional connection with authentic garments encourages extended use. This perspective resonates with Chapman's (2009) theory on "emotionally durable design", which posits that emotional attachment to a product can extend its lifespan.

Across all these case companies, we observed a common thread: the integration of timelessness of design and durability of materials. This aligns with the literature on a "decelerating" approach to fashion (Freudenreich/Schaltegger 2020). These companies opt for robust materials that not only withstand wear and tear but also complement their design philosophies, enabling the garments to last longer in terms of both style and substance.

4.2 Services and operations

All companies adhere to the principle of producing less, aligning with their broader sustainable fashion goals. As one company representative said: "We have a sustainable fashion objective, which means producing less, rather than just making clothes out of organic or recycled cotton" (Company E). And they added, "Selling tons of clothes, even if produced sustainably, is nonsense". These statements encapsulate the essence of the sufficiency approach, advocating for a change in both the quantity and the manner of production, as described by Fuchs and Lorek (2005). Regarding actual production volumes, these companies assume what could be termed a stewardship role, as Bocken et al. (2014) suggest. They continuously engage with various stakeholders, including customers, suppliers and workers, to ensure their well-being. This engagement extends to the broader public whenever the financial situation permits.

Some of the case companies have implemented a co-creation strategy through pre-order and tailoring activities, where customers' contributions are pivotal in the design and manufacturing of clothing. For these companies, co-creation enhances the longevity of garments by ensuring they closely align with customers' expectations, thereby maximizing the likelihood that the clothes will be valued and worn for extended periods. These companies engage in co-creation by actively collaborating with customers throughout the design process and consistently gathering and incorporating feedback for improvement. One company, in particular, emphasizes the inclusion of women of various sizes and involves their customers in photoshoots as an integral part of their customization practices. While some strategies, like co-creation and pre-ordering, are well-documented in the literature (Fletcher 2014), others, such as customer model imagery, are less explored.

Furthermore, our interviewees emphasized the personal nature of the relationships that the companies establish with their customers, a sentiment that aligns with findings from Beyeler and Jaeger-Erben (2022) and Elf et al. (2022). This personal connection is especially pronounced in companies with smaller customer bases, where establishing such relationships is more feasible. These strategies cultivate a "learning relationship" with customers, facilitating continuous improvement (Spangenberg 2018).

Six of the case companies opt for distribution through retailers or pop-up stores as their primary distribution channels, with only one operating a physical store. The pop-up stores provide customers the opportunity to purchase existing items while also trying on prototypes for potential pre-orders. In this way, the companies seek to attract new customers who may be unfamiliar with the on-demand business model. Additionally, these pop-up stores serve as venues for selling second-hand items, hosting guest speakers and organizing workshops and events that foster a community of companies with similar values, as reported in Beyeler and Jaeger-Erben (2022).

Digital platforms are indispensable for all seven companies. Their websites serve not merely as online stores but also as platforms that provide extensive information on the company's history, mission, values, production processes and supplier networks. The companies utilize their blogs to establish their presence within a broader business network with similar sufficiency-oriented values. Their websites often feature repair guides and care instructions. Social media platforms like Facebook and Instagram are used to disseminate information, educate customers and gather customer feedback. These digital channels align well with strategies for raising awareness and consumer education, as discussed by Gossen and Kropfeld (2022).

All companies place great importance on supplier relationships. They maintain a manageable number of suppliers, all based in Europe. Most companies provide detailed information about their suppliers on their websites, including their names, functions, locations, contact persons, areas of expertise, initial collaboration dates and any certifications they may hold. One company described its suppliers as "more than manufacturers, but true partners" (Company C), emphasizing the years it took to find partners who share similar values, such as prioritizing quality over quantity. This concurs well with findings from previous research (Bocken et al. 2022).

4.3 Business models

The case companies predominantly offer clothing at mid-range and premium price points, which they and their customers deem justifiable for society and the environment. This aligns with existing literature on sufficiency-oriented business models

(Bocken et al. 2014; Gossen et al. 2019), where a premium pricing strategy is often employed. Unlike fast-fashion companies, which rely on high volumes and rapid turnovers, these companies maintain modest sales volumes and inventory levels. Through the use of pre-ordering strategies, several companies mitigate costs by avoiding producing items that are difficult to sell. Additionally, local design and manufacturing practices reduce costs by shortening supply chains and eliminating the need for distant intermediaries. However, it is worth noting that labor costs in local and Western European contexts are significantly higher than global production centers known for cheap labor and lower environmental and ethical standards (European Parliament 2020).

Operating primarily as e-commerce entities, the case companies derive most of their revenue from online sales and the rest from pop-up stores and traditional retail channels. Two distinct sales categories are in-stock sales from existing inventory and pre-order sales for items not immediately available. Unsold garments are collected from these outlets and are sold in subsequent seasons, a practice facilitated by the companies' focus on producing seasonless, trend-independent items.

Another way the companies generate profit is by offering free lifetime alterations and repairs on their products, services that are accessible in major French cities. One company has developed a take-back system, incorporating a deposit fee into the cost of its products. This enables customers to return garments they no longer use and receive a partial refund. The returned items are either integrated into a second-hand collection or recycled if their condition is beyond repair. Another company provides a personalized tailoring service alongside its ready-to-wear range. The companies that offer garment repair and tailoring often consider factors like proximity and cost to facilitate ease of repair (Millstone 2017). Additionally, one company is developing a business consultancy service, which will include customer guidance on repair services and a guide listing recommended brands for wardrobe upgrades.

According to the interviewed companies, their average profit margin ranges between 2.5 per cent and 4 per cent, falling below the conventional retail market margin of 6 to 11 per cent (McKinsey & Company 2023: 118). Traditional fashion retailers often start with higher margins that diminish as they discount unsold items. Sufficiency-oriented companies, however, set realistic and fair margins upfront and plan for the retrieval of unsold items at season's end. While achieving profitability remains a challenge in a market dominated by inexpensive, linear products, these companies find their business models to be both meaningful and fair. Nevertheless, two of the case companies have yet to reach profitability but are nearing the break-even point.

The companies in question are small in scale. They do not possess their own production facilities, machinery or equipment and thus rely on external suppliers for garment manufacturing. Given their limited resources, the founders often leverage their professional networks to source expertise, materials and services.

Regarding the initial capital for launching their businesses, all founders relied on personal funds, which were subsequently supplemented through crowdfunding, bank loans or fundraising efforts, as also mentioned by Bocken et al. (2022). Some of these companies also secured public subsidies, and two pursued grants specifically for research projects. These additional financial resources have been allocated to various activities, such as expanding the customer base, securing television and print media appearances, recapitalizing the business and strengthening equity.

4.4 Communication and marketing

While all companies strive to harmonise fashion with sufficiency, some opt not to explicitly employ the term "sufficiency", focusing instead on aesthetics and the joy and pleasure of garment selection. One company articulated sufficiency as "living well and ensuring that we utilize 100% of our wardrobe" with clothes that "bring us joy" (Company D). Conversely, others are direct about their philosophy on sufficiency, highlighting the relationship between well-being and quality through elegant, comfortable garments that instil confidence.

To align with a sufficiency-oriented approach, most companies cater to an environmentally and ethically conscious customer base who aspire to meaningful and healthy lifestyles. These customers view their clothing choices as an extension of their commitment to sustainability. One company explicitly targets professionals who frequently wear suits, possess significant purchasing power and are dedicated to "doing things right" (Company E). This customer group tends not to make impulsive purchases, aligning well with the company's pre-order business model.

The role of advertising and marketing is both crucial and contentious among the interviewed companies. One company admitted to engaging in "extremely little marketing" and avoiding advertising altogether (Company B). Other companies use digital advertising platforms like Google, Facebook and Instagram. Budget constraints led one company to focus solely on search engine optimization, while others allocate a specific budget for marketing activities, with search engine advertising taking up a significant portion. Two companies are exploring alternative avenues for visibility that better align with their sufficiency-oriented ethos: "We don't want to sacrifice our business model and our values on the altar of [customer] acquisition" (Company A). These companies cite referral programmes and word-of-mouth as better methods of gaining visibility. In line with existing literature, the companies adopt conscious sales and marketing strategies (Bocken/Short 2016) and engage in green demarketing by encouraging consumers to reduce their overall clothing consumption (Armstrong Soule/Reich 2015). They unanimously reject traditional discount-driven sales tactics, such as Black Friday and seasonal or limited collections.

Crucially, the case companies focus on fostering long-term customer relationships, as their business depends on customer loyalty and retention. Acquiring new customers through limited advertising proves to be a challenging task. Transparency is a cornerstone value and a strategic approach for these companies in nurturing enduring customer relationships. All companies, with one exception, adhere to complete transparency, detailing the materials used in their garments, their origins, certifications, environmental benefits and supplier information on their websites. Such transparency elicits positive feedback from their customer base.

According to the companies, the primary hurdle to implementing sufficiency-oriented business models is not the cost of their products but rather the challenge of raising awareness and altering consumer behavior. This aligns with the academic literature on sufficiency-oriented business models (Gossen/Kropfeld 2022). Some also contend that the core problem does not lie with financially constrained individuals who resort to fast fashion; instead, "it is the wealthiest parts of the population that pollute the most" (Company E). The real challenge lies in influencing those who have the financial capacity to make sustainable choices but who continue to opt for fast fashion. As one interviewee noted, "not everybody has the means to buy a shirt for €150 or €200", but the focus should be on customers who spend similar amounts on "poor-quality products" (Company D). Consumer education should aim to engage those who have the resources to effect change. Nevertheless, for many companies, "the ambition has always been to replace the [current] industry and consumption with a cleaner industry accessible to everyone" (Company A) and not merely to cater to the highest stratum of society.

Table 3 summarizes sufficiency-oriented business strategies in French fashion SMEs based on the information collected from interviews and secondary sources.

Table 3: Sufficiency-oriented business strategies in French fashion SMEs (Present ['+'], Absent ['-'], No available data ['o'])

Approach	Focus	Examples of strategies	French fashion SMEs						
			A	B	C	D	E	F	G
Efficiency	Products	Clothes design for efficient material use; lower lifecycle impact; customized and personalized design	+	+	+	+	+	+	+
	Services	Choice architecture: avoid selling high-polluting materials and clothes of poor quality on the market	+	+	+	+	+	+	+
	Business model	Sell efficient products; increase sales; reduce per-unit price	+	o	o	o	o	o	o
	Communication and marketing	Inform consumers about clothes' impact, use, care and refitting (e.g., through labelling and campaigns)	+	+	+	+	+	-	+
Shift	Products	Design durable clothes for physical, functional and emotional longevity; seasonless design; easy to maintain, mend, refurbish or upcycle	+	+	+	+	+	+	+
	Services	Offer clothes extension services: (local) mending, refitting and tailoring services, take-back, upcycle, recycle	-	+	-	+	+	-	-
		Offer long warranty	+	+	o	+	+	-	o
		Support and offer reuse arrangements, e.g., organize collection of clothes for resale, donation and second life	-	-	-	+	-	-	-

Shift	Business models	Product-service systems: no-ownership offers, pay-per-use offers; temporary access to products: renting, leasing, hiring	-	-	-	-	-	-	-
		Sharing – offer an exchange platform for sharing and swapping clothes; clothes libraries and wardrobe sharing; pay-per-use; membership fees	-	-	-	-	-	-	-
		Circular business models that build on ideas of reuse, repair, recycle	-	-	-	+	-	-	-
	Communication and marketing	Communicate about product durability, how to wear and maintain clothes over a long period of time	+	+	+	+	+	-	+
		Communicate about how and where to lease, rent or swap clothes	-	-	-	-	-	-	+
		Communicate about the benefits of reuse and second-hand clothes	-	-	-	-	-	+	+
Sufficiency	Products	Designing for slow fashion: customized, size-fit and durable clothes	+	+	+	+	+	+	+
		Produce products in local production facilities; short supply chains	+	+	+	+	+	+	+
	Services	Support consumers in self-sufficiency and DIY, e.g., providing tools for sewing, mending or upcycling own clothes	-	-	-	-	-	-	-
	Business models	Premium pricing; long-term consumer management	+	+	+	+	+	+	+
		Produce clothes on demand	+	-	+	+	-	-	-

Sufficiency	Communication and marketing	De-legitimize mass-produced and standardized clothes; question consumption levels/marketing for consumption reduction	+	+	+	+	+	+	+
		Moderating sales; avoiding discounts, seasonal sales	+	+	+	+	+	+	+
		Moderate promotions and avoiding advertising, especially aggressive marketing campaigns based on successive collections and trends and/or low prices	+	+	+	+	+	+	+
		Demand reduction strategies	+	+	+	+	+	+	+
		Promote convenience of extending product's use	+	+	+	+	+	+	+
		Promote needs over desires	+	-	+	-	+	-	+

5. How do French fashion SMEs reconcile sufficiency with profits and growth?

In line with existing literature, all companies maintain a critical stance towards the conventional economic growth model, offering alternative perspectives and practices. Company B adopts a non-growth strategy, limiting its annual turnover and the number of garments it produces and sells. This company contends that growth is not a natural occurrence but is intentionally pursued, often under external pressures that come at the expense of employees, suppliers, materials and environmental resources. Company A, which has seen significant growth since its inception, continually questions the implications of this growth, asking, "What do we do with this growth? Where does it take us?". This ongoing dialogue is crucial for the company as it seeks to uphold its original business model and values.

The remaining companies employ a blend of organic and external growth strategies for survival, although their desired levels of growth vary. Company F aims to boost its sales to ensure economic viability. Still, it has no aspirations to become a large enterprise, stating that "being sustainable is incompatible with being a huge company." Other companies are considering external investments and expansion, contingent on a certain level of customer interest and the emergence of potential partners and collaborative opportunities. However, they intend to grow in a manner that aligns with their values and philosophy of balanced growth. For instance, one company plans to redistribute its profits to causes that resonate with its ethos. Another asserts, "We have no excessive ambitions" and believes in balancing what they give and receive (Company G). Thus, although most companies do not consider abandoning material growth entirely (Beyeler/Jaeger-Erben 2022), they also recognize that moderate or organic growth is often inadequate for ensuring long-term financial sustainability. Consequently, they may turn to external growth strategies to secure their continued existence, as noted by Wiefek and Heinitz (2018). External growth can further their goal of expanding their market presence, thereby increasing the influence of sufficiency-oriented companies overall, as Gossen and Heinrich (2021) have noted.

Indeed, all the companies are united by a philosophy that focuses on the growth of sustainable fashion overall. The aim is to make sustainable options increasingly accessible to consumers while transforming an industry currently under the influence of fast fashion. In this landscape, sufficiency-oriented companies do not perceive each other as direct competitors. Instead, they see themselves as part of a network, commending each other as catalysts for sustainable consumption and occasionally collaborating. In an industry where sustainable fashion brands still represent a niche, these companies are committed to encouraging emerging fashion businesses to adopt sufficiency-oriented models. As articulated by one company, "there is room for all small brands on the market", and given that "our collective strength will always be dwarfed by the large fast fashion companies, the more of us there are striving to do things differently, the better" (Company D). These companies highly value knowledge sharing and are amenable to the idea of their business models being replicated by others, especially if it expands the reach of sustainable and sufficiency-oriented fashion.

6. Conclusions

Given the fashion industry's critical role in driving unsustainable consumption, there is a need to explore alternative business models prioritizing sustainability and sufficiency. The prevailing fast-fashion model perpetuates a throwaway culture, exacerbating environmental impacts. In contrast, emerging sufficiency-oriented fashion companies offer a compelling counter-narrative to this unsustainable model. This study sought to delve into the strategies employed by these companies and to differentiate them from other prevalent approaches, such as efficiency and shift (Akenji et al. 2021). Our findings are the following:

- In the category of efficiency, companies design customized and personalized products. They all avoid selling environmentally detrimental and low-quality garments. Their communication strategies predominantly focus on informing consumers about their products' ecological impact, proper use and maintenance.
- In the shift category, every company is committed to producing durable, seasonless and easy-to-maintain garments. While there are varied approaches to offering services like mending and refitting, none of the companies provides renting, leasing or sharing. Only one company uses a circular business model. Communication strategies in this category seek to inform consumers about the longevity and maintenance of the products.
- Finally, in the sufficiency category, all companies are united in their emphasis on slow fashion, focusing on customization, fit and durability. They also share a commitment to local production and short supply chains. Premium pricing and long-term customer engagement are the norm in their business models. Communication efforts are geared towards challenging the status quo of mass-produced fashion, moderating sales and promotions and fostering the benefits of product longevity.

The studied French fashion SMEs adopt a nuanced approach to profitability and growth. They do not aim for unchecked expansion or profit maximization. Instead, they focus on achieving profitability that sustains their operations and allows them to fulfil their broader social and environmental objectives. These companies often employ a combination of organic and external growth strategies and seek to always adhere to their core values. In contrast to most traditional companies, they do not view each other as competitors but as part of a collaborative network. They are open to the idea of their business models being replicated by others, particularly if it expands the reach of sustainable and sufficiency-oriented fashion. Our empirical data aligns well with the existing literature, while adding nuanced insights.

Future research should extend the investigation of sufficiency, shift and efficiency-oriented strategies in the fashion industry and potentially beyond. A particular focus is needed on the mechanisms enabling a meaningful transition from shift- and efficiency-oriented strategies to implementing sufficiency-oriented strategies. Both existing classifications of business strategies in the literature and the framework presented in this chapter warrant further refinement. These should be carefully tested through comparative case studies or large-scale quantitative analyses. While this study has initiated a discussion on the complex interplay between sufficiency and the traditional business goals of profit and growth, there is a need for additional research. Specifically, studies should examine the long-term financial viability of adopting sufficiency-oriented strategies. In this context, successful case studies could serve as valuable blueprints, encouraging more companies to embark on the journey towards sufficiency-oriented business models.

References

Akenji, Lewis/Bengtsson, Magnus/Toivio, Viivi/Lettenmeier, Michael/Fawcett, Tina/Parag, Yael/Saheb, Yamina et al. (2021): "1.5-Degree Lifestyles: Towards A Fair Consumption Space for All." Berlin: Hot or Cool Institute, 6.12.2023 (https://hotorcool.org/wp-content/uploads/2021/10/Hot_or_Cool_1_5_lifestyles_FULL_REPORT_AND_ANNEX_B.pdf).

Armstrong Soule, Catherine A./Reich, Brandon J. (2015): "Less Is More: Is a Green Demarketing Strategy Sustainable?" In: Journal of Marketing Management 31/13–14, pp. 1403–27. https://doi.org/10.1080/0267257X.2015.1059874.

Beyeler, Laura/Jaeger-Erben, Melanie (2022): "How to Make More of Less: Characteristics of Sufficiency in Business Practices." In: Frontiers in Sustainability, 131. https://doi.org/10.3389/frsus.2022.949710.

Bocken, Nancy M. P./Short, Samuel William/Rana, Padmakshi/Evans, Steve (2014): "A literature and practice review to develop sustainable business model archetypes." In: Journal of cleaner production 65, pp. 42–56. https://doi.org/10.1016/j.jclepro.2013.11.039.

Bocken, Nancy M. P./Niessen, Laura/Short, Samuel William (2022): "The Sufficiency-Based Circular Economy – An Analysis of 150 Companies." In: Frontiers in Sustainability 3, 899289. https://doi.org/10.3389/frsus.2022.899289.

Bocken, Nancy M. P./Short, Samuel W. (2016): "Towards a sufficiency-driven business Model: Experiences and opportunities." In: Environmental Innovation and Societal Transitions 18, pp. 41–61. https://doi.org/10.1016/j.eist.2015.07.010.

Buecher, Daniel/Gloy, Yves-Simon/Schmenk, Bernhard/Gries, Thomas (2018): "Individual On-Demand Produced Clothing: Ultrafast Fashion Production System." In: Stephan Hankammer/Kjeld Nielsen/Frank T. Piller/Günther Schuh/Ning Wang (eds.), Customization 4.0. Springer Proceedings in Business and Economics. Cham: Springer International Publishing, pp. 634–644. https://doi.org/10.1007/978-3-319-77556-2_40.

Buzzo, Aline/Abreu, Maria José (2019): "Fast Fashion, Fashion Brands & Sustainable Consumption." In: Subramanian Senthilkannan Muthu (eds.), Fast Fashion, Fashion Brands and Sustainable Consumption. Textile Science and Clothing Technology, Singapore: Springer, pp. 1–17. https://doi.org/10.1007/978-981-13-1268-7_1.

Chapman, Jonathan (2009): "Design for (Emotional) Durability." In: Design Issues 25/4, pp. 29–35. https://www.jstor.org/stable/20627827.

Claxton, Stella/Kent, Anthony (2020): "The Management of Sustainable Fashion Design Strategies: An Analysis of the Designer's Role." In: Journal of Cleaner Production 268, 122112. https://doi.org/10.1016/j.jclepro.2020.122112.

Coscieme, Luca/Manshoven, Saskia/Gillabel, Jeroen/Grossi, Francesca/Mortensen, Lars F. (2022): "A Framework of Circular Business Models for Fashion and Textiles: The Role of Business-Model, Technical, and Social Innovation." In: Sustainability: Science, Practice and Policy 18/1, pp. 451–462. https://doi.org/10.1080/15487733.2022.2083792.

Dalhammar, Carl/Mont, Oksana/Lehner, Matthias (2022): "Politik och styrning för hållbar konsumtion." Stockholm: Formas, 6.12.2023 (https://formas.se/analys-och-resultat/rapporter/2022-06-10-politik-och-styrning-for-hallbar-konsumtion.html).

Diddi, Sonali/Yan, Ruoh-Nan/Bloodhart, Brittany/Bajtelsmit, Vickie/McShane, Katie (2019): "Exploring Young Adult Consumers' Sustainable Clothing Consumption Intention-Behavior Gap: A Behavioral Reasoning Theory Perspective." In: Sustainable Production and Consumption 18, pp. 200–209. https://doi.org/10.1016/j.spc.2019.02.009.

Elf, Patrick/Werner, Andrea/Black, Sandy (2022): "Advancing the Circular Economy through Dynamic Capabilities and Extended Customer Engagement: Insights from Small Sustainable Fashion Enterprises in the UK." In: Business Strategy and the Environment 31/6, pp. 2682–2699. https://doi.org/10.1002/bse.2999.

European Parliament (2020): "Textile Workers in Developing Countries and the European Fashion Industry." Briefing, 8.

Figge, Frank/Young, William/Barkemeyer, Ralf (2014): "Sufficiency or Efficiency to Achieve Lower Resource Consumption and Emissions? The Role of the Rebound

Effect." In: Journal of Cleaner Production 69, pp. 216–224. https://doi.org/10.1016/j.jclepro.2014.01.031.

Fletcher, Kate (2010): "Slow Fashion: An Invitation for Systems Change." In: Fashion Practice 2/2, pp. 259–65. https://doi.org/10.2752/175693810X12774625387594.

Fletcher, Kate (2014 [2008]): Sustainable Fashion and Textiles: Design Journeys, London: Routledge. https://doi.org/10.4324/9781315857930.

Fletcher, Kate/Grose, Lynda (2012): Fashion and Sustainability: Design for Change, London: Laurence King Publishing.

Freudenreich, Birte/Schaltegger, Stefan (2020): "Developing sufficiency-oriented offerings for clothing users: Business approaches to support consumption reduction." In: Journal of Cleaner Production 247, 119589. https://doi.org/10.1016/j.jclepro.2019.119589.

Frick, Vivian/Gossen, Maike/Santarius, Tilman/Geiger, Sonja (2021): "When Your Shop Says #lessismore. Online Communication Interventions for Clothing Sufficiency." In: Journal of Environmental Psychology 75. https://doi.org/10.1016/j.jenvp.2021.101595.

Fuchs, Doris A./Lorek, Sylvia (2005): "Sustainable Consumption Governance: A History of Promises and Failures." In: Journal of Consumer Policy 28/3, pp. 261–288. https://doi.org/10.1007/s10603-005-8490-z.

Garcia-Ortega, Beatriz/Galan-Cubillo, Javier/Llorens-Montes, F. Javier/de-Miguel-Molina, Blanca (2023): "Sufficient Consumption as a Missing Link toward Sustainability: The Case of Fast Fashion." In: Journal of Cleaner Production 399, 136678. https://doi.org/10.1016/j.jclepro.2023.136678.

Gebauer, Jana (2018): "Towards Growth-Independent and Post-Growth-Oriented Entrepreneurship in the SME Sector." In: Management Revue 29/3, pp. 230–256. https://www.jstor.org/stable/26627699.

Gossen, Maike/Heinrich, Anneli (2021): "Encouraging Consumption Reduction: Findings of a Qualitative Study with Clothing Companies on Sufficiency-Promoting Communication." In: Cleaner and Responsible Consumption 3, 100028. https://doi.org/10.1016/j.clrc.2021.100028.

Gossen, Maike/Kropfeld, Maren Ingrid (2022): "'Choose Nature. Buy Less.' Exploring Sufficiency-Oriented Marketing and Consumption Practices in the Outdoor Industry." In: Sustainable Production and Consumption 30, pp. 720–736. https://doi.org/10.1016/j.spc.2022.01.005.

Gossen, Maike/Ziesemer, Florence/Schrader, Ulf (2019): "Why and How Commercial Marketing Should Promote Sufficient Consumption: A Systematic Literature Review." In: Journal of Macromarketing 39/3, pp. 252–269. https://doi.org/10.1177/0276146719866238.

Henninger, Claudia E./Alevizou, Panayiota J./Goworek, Helen/Ryding, Daniella (2017): Sustainability in Fashion: A Cradle to Upcycle Approach, Cham: Springer Nature. https://doi.org/10.1007/978-3-319-51253-2.

Hiller, Janine S. (2013): "The Benefit Corporation and Corporate Social Responsibility." In: Journal of Business Ethics 118, pp. 287–301. https://doi.org/10.1007/s10551-012-1580-3.

Katz, Robert/Page, Antony (2013): "Sustainable Business". Robert H. McKinney School of Law Legal Studies Research Paper No. 24, pp. 851–84.

Khmara, Yaryna/Kronenberg, Jakub (2018): "Degrowth in Business: An Oxymoron or a Viable Business Model for Sustainability?" In: Journal of Cleaner Production 177, pp. 721–731. https://doi.org/10.1016/j.jclepro.2017.12.182.

Kozlowski, Anika/Searcy, Cory/Bardecki, Michal (2016): "Innovation for a Sustainable Fashion Industry: A Design Focused Approach Toward the Development of New Business Models." In: Subramanian Senthilkannan Muthu/Miguel Angel Gardetti (eds.), Environmental Footprints and Eco-Design of Products and Processes, Singapore: Springer, pp. 151–169. https://doi.org/10.1007/978-981-10-0245-8_5.

Laitala, Kirsi Maria/Boks, Casper/Klepp, Ingun Grimstad (2015): "Making Clothing Last: A Design Approach for Reducing the Environmental Impacts." In: International Journal of Design 9/2, pp. 93–107. https://oda.oslomet.no/handle/10642/4920.

Lorek, Sylvia/Fuchs, Doris (2019): "Why Only Strong Sustainable Consumption Governance Will Make a Difference." In: Oksana Mont (eds.), A Research Agenda for Sustainable Consumption Governance, Cheltenham, Northhampton: Edward Elgar Publishing Ltd.

McKinsey & Company (2023): "The State of Fashion 2022," 7.12.2023 (https://www.mckinsey.com/~/media/mckinsey/industries/retail/our%20insights/state%20of%20fashion/2022/the-state-of-fashion-2022.pdf).

Millstone, Carina (2017): Frugal Value: Designing Business for a Crowded Planet, London: Routledge.

Mont, Oksana/Lehner, Matthias/Dalhammar, Carl (2022): "Sustainable Consumption through Policy Intervention – A Review of Research Themes." In: Frontiers in Sustainability 3. https://doi.org/10.3389/frsus.2022.921477.

Niessen, Laura/Bocken, Nancy M. P. (2021): "How Can Businesses Drive Sufficiency? The Business for Sufficiency Framework." In: Sustainable Production and Consumption 28, pp. 1090–1103. https://doi.org/10.1016/j.spc.2021.07.030.

Pal, Rudrajeet (2017): "Sustainable Design and Business Models in Textile and Fashion Industry." In: Subramanian Senthilkannan Muthu (eds.), Sustainability in the Textile Industry, Singapore: Springer, pp. 109–138. http://dx.doi.org/10.1007/978-981-10-2639-3_6.

Pedersen, Esben Rahbek Gjerdrum/Netter, Sarah (2015): "Collaborative Consumption: Business Model Opportunities and Barriers for Fashion Libraries." In: Journal of Fashion Marketing and Management 19/3, pp. 258–273. https://doi.org/10.1108/JFMM-05-2013-0073.

Princen, Thomas (2003): "Principles for Sustainability: From Cooperation and Efficiency to Sufficiency." In: Global Environmental Politics 3/1, pp. 33–50. https://doi.org/10.1162/152638003763336374.

Reichel, André (2018): "Sufficiency in Business Strategies." In: Leida Rijnhout/Riccardo Mastini (eds.), Sufficiency: Moving beyond the Gospel of Eco-Efficiency, Brussels: Friends of the Earth Europe, pp. 22–25, 7.12.2023 (https://www.foeeurope.org/sites/default/files/resource_use/2018/foee_sufficiency_booklet.pdf).

Sandberg, Maria (2021): "Sufficiency Transitions: A Review of Consumption Changes for Environmental Sustainability." In: Journal of Cleaner Production 293, 126097. https://doi.org/10.1016/j.jclepro.2021.126097.

Sandberg, Maria (2022): "Sufficiency Transitions: Realizing Consumption Changes for Environmental Sustainability." Doctoral Dissertation, Hanken School of Economics, Helsinki, 2022.

Schauman, Sebastian/Greene, Sharon/Korkman, Oskar (2023): "Sufficiency and the Dematerialization of Fashion: How Digital Substitutes Are Creating New Market Opportunities." In: Business Horizons 66/6, pp. 741–751. https://doi.org/10.1016/j.bushor.2023.03.003.

Schneidewind, Uwe/Palzkill-Vorbeck, Alexandra (2011): "Suffizienz Als Business Case: Nachhaltiges Ressourcenmanagement Als Gegenstand Einer Transdisziplinären Betriebswirtschaftslehre." In: Wuppertal Institut für Klima, Umwelt, Energie GmbH, Impulse Zur WachstumsWende 2, pp. 4–20, 30.10.2023 (http://nbn-resolving.de/urn:nbn:de:bsz:wup4-opus-39553www.econstor.eu).

Spangenberg, Joachim (2018): "Sufficiency: A Pragmatic, Radical Visionary Approach." In: Leida Rijnhout/Riccardo Mastini (eds.), Sufficiency: Moving beyond the Gospel of Eco-Efficiency, Brussels: Friends of the Earth Europe, p. 48, 7.12.2023 (https://www.foeeurope.org/sites/default/files/resource_use/2018/foee_sufficiency_booklet.pdf).

Stål, Herman I./Jansson, Johan (2017): "Sustainable Consumption and Value Propositions: Exploring Product – Service System Practices Among Swedish Fashion Firms." In: Sustainable Development 25/6, pp. 546–558. https://doi.org/10.1002/sd.1677.

Vesterinen, Essi/Syrjälä, Henna (2022): "Sustainable Anti-Consumption of Clothing: A Systematic Literature Review." In: Cleaner and Responsible Consumption 5, 100061. https://doi.org/10.1016/j.clrc.2022.100061.

Vita, Gibran/Lundström, Johan R./Hertwich, Edgar G./Quist, Jaco/Ivanova, Diana/Stadler, Konstantin/Wood, Richard (2019): "The Environmental Impact of Green Consumption and Sufficiency Lifestyles Scenarios in Europe: Connecting Local Sustainability Visions to Global Consequences." In: Ecological Economics 164, 106322. https://doi.org/10.1016/j.ecolecon.2019.05.002.

Wiefek, Jasmin/Heinitz, Kathrin (2018): "Common Good-Oriented Companies: Exploring Corporate Values, Characteristics and Practices That Could Support a Development Towards Degrowth." In: Management Revue 29/3, pp. 311–331. http://dx.doi.org/10.5771/0935-9915-2018-3-311.

The Paradox of Minimalism in the Field of Lifestyle Products

Uncovering How the Minimalism Business Impedes Sufficiency

Viola Muster and Marlene Münsch

Abstract *The commercialized manifestations of minimalism do not necessarily contribute to sufficiency-oriented consumption. Various minimalism business segments have emerged that are primarily based on selling dispensable, aesthetic lifestyle products. In this chapter, we analyze different business segments and discuss possible opportunities and risks for sufficiency-oriented consumption.*

1. Introduction

Since Marie Kondo's bestseller "The life-changing magic of tidying up" (2014) and uncounted subsequent books, magazine articles and videos, minimalism is regarded as a so-called lifestyle trend (Muster et al. 2022).

Minimalism and sufficiency-oriented consumption are related concepts. Both problematize overconsumption and the quantity of goods consumed. The concepts have a shared tradition in the voluntary simplicity movement (Elgin/Mitchell 1977; Etzioni 1999), which criticizes consumer society and advocates a fulfilling life with fewer consumption goods. Both sufficiency-oriented and minimalist consumption are facets of sustainable consumption (Elgin/Mitchell 1977; Gossen et al. 2019; Kang et al. 2021; Sandberg 2021).

However, the media and social reception, as well as the implementation, of these concepts differ significantly. While sufficiency-oriented consumption remains primarily an academic and political concept and – if at all – a niche movement, minimalism has become a commercially oriented, pop-cultural lifestyle trend emulated by people all over the world (Meissner 2019; Zavestoski/DeLaure 2022).

This chapter adopts a critical perspective on the lifestyle minimalism concept as a business. The main hypothesis of our contribution is that the commercialized, pop-cultural manifestations of minimalism risk sustaining consumerism, i.e. the widespread propensity in Western societies to consume and keep consuming. In turn, this support for consumerism could lead to minimalism offshoots not contributing to efforts of strong sustainable consumption and climate protection but rather harming them. We support our hypothesis by illustrating business segments that have only recently emerged through the minimalism trend and by enlightening sufficiency-inhibiting effects that minimalist principles can have on consumption behavior.

The chapter is structured as follows. In the next section, we trace the development of minimalism into a commercial lifestyle trend. Building on that, the following section focuses on the business of minimalism. We present and analyze various business segments that, at their core, address two questions: "How to become a minimalist?" and "What does a minimalist need?" Then, we discuss the opportunities and risks of minimalism business and prominent minimalist consumption principles for sufficiency-oriented consumption. Finally, we draw a conclusion.

2. The origins of lifestyle minimalism

There are two relevant streams that are significant in capturing the contemporary, pop-cultural minimalism trend in consumption. *First,* minimalism emerged as a design and art movement in the 1960s (VanEenoo 2011). At the heart of this movement was a new aesthetic of simplicity and plainness. Instead of exaggerated emotion and symbolism, it was now considered desirable to emphasize the essential (Wilson/Bellezza 2022). Through advertising, fashion and design, this "aesthetic minimalism" eventually found its way into consumer culture (Wilson/Bellezza 2022).

Second, in the late 1970s, Elgin and Mitchell described a lifestyle in the United States they termed "outwardly simple and inwardly rich" (1977: 13). They characterized voluntary simplicity as a frugal and contented way of living that stemmed from both ecological awareness and a strong interest in personal growth and psychological well-being (Elgin/Mitchell 1977). They extensively examined the market potential of the voluntary simplicity movement and concluded: "Although the demand for some types of products will be damped by VS [voluntary simplicity], the outlook for others will benefit" (Elgin/Mitchell 1977: 14). They listed numerous aspects of product categories and features that could interest people in the voluntary simplicity movement. Shama (1985) also builds on this concept and presents a "marketing guide" to effectively target the voluntary simplicity audience.

In the subsequent decades, especially in the last 10 years, both movements converged into a new form of "lifestyle minimalism". Recent publications and popular media on minimalism emphasize the individual and their psychological issues, such as stress and overload, and combine it with the aesthetics of simplicity (Ludwigsen 2019; Meissner 2019; Sandlin/Wallin 2022; Wilson/Bellezza 2022; Zavestoski/DeLaure 2022).

The increased popularity of lifestyle minimalism does not seem to be a coincidence. The minimalism trend can be attributed to consumerism reaching its peak over the past two decades due to digitalisation and globalisation. This culmination can be seen, for example, in the development of (ultra) fast fashion, which has contributed significantly to overcrowded closets. It is therefore hardly surprising that the minimalism trend is particularly evident in the fashion area (Vladimirova 2021). Moreover, an increasing number of people feel burdened by the multitude of belongings in their households (Ross et al. 2021; Roster/Ferrari 2023). Some authors argue that societal crises such as the global financial crisis in 2008 and the COVID-19 pandemic further intensified a shift away from the taken-for-granted nature of consumerism (Khamis 2019; Sandlin/Wallin 2022). The increased popularity and dissemination of minimalism in the past decade are also due to its transformation into marketable products, making the idea of simplicity catchier and consumable. This marketability and censurability of minimalism are closely linked to specific content-related features that characterize lifestyle minimalism.

3. Key features of commercialized lifestyle minimalism

3.1 Individualization

As criticized by Khamis (2019) and Meissner (2019), minimalism – and related concepts such as decluttering – are concepts that are apolitical and individualistic in their orientation. Consumption's impact on the environment and society plays a smaller role; instead, the focus is on a new consumer-oriented self-perception. Khamis states, "[d]e-cluttering – at least as popularized by Kondo – sees the removal of excess as less a commitment to social or environmental concerns than a testament to a new and improved consumer self" (2019: 524). This individual-oriented approach is accompanied by a focus on improving one's own life and well-being. While it is acknowledged that the modern consumer and work culture – i.e. systemic structures – contribute to stress, overload and dissatisfaction, the solution is primarily seen within the individual (and not in changing the system).

3.2 Aesthetics

The current understanding of minimalism has led to aesthetics becoming a central component of an entire lifestyle. In addition to reducing the existing belongings, lifestyle minimalism focuses on the deliberate selection of goods and their careful arrangement. Rooms, spaces and products should align with minimalist aesthetics. As Wilson and Bellezza illustrate, "minimalist spaces, collections, and items are usually composed of simple designs, clean lines, limited ornamentation, and monochromatic colours" (2022: 800). The design thus focuses on essential elements and thereby tries to emphasize a sense of calm, order and functionality (Chou 2011). Achieving a minimalist home that meets aesthetic standards often requires additional design and the acquisition of minimalist products.

3.3 Symbolism

For minimalists, the selection of products is not primarily based on their functional utility but on whether they are aesthetically pleasing and bring joy and happiness. The aim is to reflect on one's feelings towards belongings and their significance in one's life. Meissner writes, "[i]n so doing, minimalist narratives perpetuate consumerism's tendency to revolve around individuals' self-expression, rather than questions of need and/or functionality" (2019: 197). This focus maintains and even intensifies the quasi-religious relationship with possessions (Meissner 2019; Sandlin/Wallin 2022). Especially because many people struggle to navigate the complexity and confusion of the world, minimalism offers a central compensatory, symbolic function – namely, the ability to organize at least one's own home and life. Moreover, minimalism as a lifestyle tends to be a phenomenon among socioeconomically affluent groups (Ramchandani/Coste-Maniere 2018). It demonstrates sophistication, taste and exclusivity and thus serves particularly well as a means to distinguish oneself from the mass consumption of the less educated or less affluent.

4. Buy to have less: minimalism business segments

In the following, we outline the most important areas in which the "business of minimalism" can be observed from our perspective.

The minimalism business must be clearly distinguished from sufficiency-oriented business models that embody a "new understanding of corporate value creation" (Jungell-Michelsson/Heikkurinen 2022: 6) and aim to achieve an absolute reduction in resource consumption within their core business. Conversely, we understand the business of minimalism as a primarily profit-oriented, conventional business model that mainly markets (dispensable) lifestyle products or services.

At its core, the business of minimalism is based on two questions: "How does one become a minimalist?" and "What does a minimalist need?". The answers to both questions are provided for different business segments (see Table 1) that we present in the following sections.

Table 1: Overview of emerging minimalism business segments

How to become a minimalist			What a minimalist needs	
Books	Vlogs	Coaching	Aesthetic products	Accessories and tools

4.1 How to become a minimalist

In the following, we present books, vlogs and coaching as important business segments that aim to support the transition from a consumeristic to a minimalist lifestyle.

All three business segments offer advice and recommendations on how to become a minimalist. The focus is always on decluttering as a central method for achieving a minimalist lifestyle. The assumption is that minimalist living can only begin once the home is decluttered and released from unnecessary stuff. One's own possessions are described as the cause of dissatisfaction and frustration. Therefore, the minimalism guidebooks and vlogs are full of recommendations on how to declutter. Sometimes, even specific quantities or percentages are given to illustrate how much can be sorted out. While the goal certainly is to acquire fewer new things, most minimalism guides anticipate that new acquisitions are probably inevitable. Accordingly, minimalists have come up with a rule of thumb to avoid filling up the house again. As the name of the "one-in-one-out-rule" implies, with every purchase, another good shall leave. Ideally, goods are being exchanged within the same product category. All three segments, especially vlogs, also function as essential marketing channels for products and services that a minimalist is supposed to need.

Books

In the past ten years, an overwhelming number of books on minimalism and the related method of decluttering have been published (Meissner 2019; Ross et al. 2021; Sandlin/Wallin 2022; Zavestoski/DeLaure 2022). Both in the United States and in Europe, a separate genre has emerged. In an analysis of German exemplary guidebooks on minimalism, we found central commonalities. The guidebooks are application-oriented, give step-by-step instructions for the path to minimalist practices and contain practical exercises to help identify important life goals or to question consumption practices. They all promise the prospect of more freedom, clarity and well-being.

Data on the number of publications and sales figures are lacking. However, based on a Google books search, it can be assumed that, in Germany alone, several hundred books with the keyword minimalism in the title have been published in recent years. In English-speaking countries, the number is probably higher. Books on minimalism are in high demand and can be found on recent bestseller lists such as Amazon Bestsellers (e.g., more than 10 books on minimalism among the top 50 in the category "house & household" [Amazon 2023a]), and many books have been translated into various languages and distributed internationally.

Especially prominent examples of international bestsellers are the books by Marie Kondo. Her four most successful books, including the most well-known book "The life-changing magic of tidying up", have sold over 11 million copies in more than 40 countries (Foden 2020). These books may provide helpful suggestions and guidance on how to achieve a minimalist lifestyle. Yet, it is evident that the demand for books has been successfully stimulated and satisfied solely due to the vast number of different publications available.

Vlogs

Numerous minimalism influencers on social media use vlogs to demonstrate how minimalism can work in practice and report how it has transformed their own lives. They provide tips and tricks for all areas of life. Followers get to see a minimalist dream world – beautiful people in aesthetically curated homes leading fulfilling minimalist lives. The vlogs function in a similar way to the guidebooks. Packaged in personal stories, the influencers give step-by-step instructions on how minimalism can be realized in various areas. Influencers are known to often earn money by advertising products and services. Although minimalism influencers talk about a life with fewer belongings and reduced consumption, their business models are also based on advertising that stimulates consumption. The promoted products are characterized by minimalist aesthetics, and their necessity is often justified as essential for a slowed-down, minimalist lifestyle.

One example is the influencer MJ Gordon, who identifies herself as an influencer for minimalism, finance and health (MJ Gordon 2023). In her YouTube videos, she showcases her large, beautiful house and provides advice for a relaxed, stress-free, minimalist life. In the description of her videos, she includes links to her Amazon shop, where she sells various items such as supplements, natural cosmetics, pillows, planners, essential oils and light-blocking glasses (Amazon 2023b). In another example, influencer A to Zen Life shares her journey of decluttering and getting rid of debt to lead a happier, more liberated life. While she mentions second-hand products in the description below her YouTube videos, there are also numerous links to new clothing items and decluttering accessories such as boxes, glass jars or hangers (A to Zen Life 2023).

Coaching

Some influencers also earn money with their own consulting services or cooperation with other coaches. So-called minimalism coaches offer workshops, online courses, guidebooks, individual training or consulting and mentoring sessions. It is particularly noticeable that most coaches also offer their services digitally, which is certainly partly due to the aforementioned boom in the minimalism business during the pandemic. The prices for coaching correspond to standard market fees for counselling and coaching.

An important difference to other forms of coaching is that, to the best of our knowledge, there is currently no certified degree or training to qualify as a minimalism coach. Marie Kondo is an exception here. She not only offers her online tidying course for $39.99 on her website; she also offers training to become a certified KonMari consultant. These courses do not only qualify participants to become a tidying coach; as stated on the website: "Certified KonMari consultants don't just tidy homes, they change lives". According to Marie Kondo, there are already more than five hundred KonMari consultants worldwide (KonMari 2023).

Other coaches usually offer short counselling sessions (a few hours/one day) as well as in-depth courses (several weeks). For example, coach Regina Wong offers a 1-Day Mentoring Session for $100 on her website livewellwithless. This session includes consultation via email, a one-on-one mentoring session, an action plan and one post-session check-in via email two weeks after completion. Additionally, customers can book a one-month session for $400 (Wong 2023).

Furthermore, coaches often advertise additional support material such as plans and worksheets. The website simplehappyzen, for instance, offers monthly online programs and accompanying e-books. In a 20-week course with guided sessions, participants receive additional worksheets with instructions, audio files for replaying and weekly emails (Simplehappyzen 2021).

4.2 What a minimalist needs

Lifestyle minimalism does not only involve owning fewer of one's existing goods but also recommends owning the *right*, few goods. In addition, there are plenty of accessories and tools designed to make minimalist life succeed. In the following, we present two categories: (i) aesthetic products and (ii) accessories and tools for a minimalist lifestyle.

Aesthetic products

In recent years, products and styles in minimalist aesthetics have spread across almost all consumption areas. Although, especially in the origins of the voluntary simplicity movement, high quality and exclusivity of goods was particularly important, many minimalist products in the mass market are meanwhile primarily focused on aesthetics. Lamps without shades, bicycles without gears and lights, plain unicolor tops or wardrobes with clear shapes and without ornaments are just some examples of minimalist aesthetics. Our observations found that minimalist aesthetics is particularly widespread in fashion and furniture.

For example, a minimalist wardrobe does not seem to consist simply of fewer clothes. Quite the opposite, according to certain advertising statements, there are numerous recommendations for which pieces belong in a minimalist wardrobe, such as well-fitting jeans, a black dress, solid-colored tops, a black legging or a solid-colored blazer (Modern Minimalism 2023). The recommendations are so specific that the obvious suggestion for consumers is to start shopping for "capsule wardrobe" pieces. It is not surprising that major fast-fashion companies such as SHEIN or Primark offer capsule wardrobe outfits (Primark 2023; Shein 2023). Fashion magazines promote clothing for the seasonal capsule wardrobe (Vogue 2023).

Another area of a flourishing minimalist product palette is interior and especially minimalist furniture design. Again, recommendations for creating a minimalist living room are often not so much focused on integrating existing pieces of furniture. Rather, specific types of pieces are suggested to create a minimalist living room, such as angular furniture, a statement mirror or a linen sofa (BetterHomes&Gardens 2023). Further, several furniture companies have recently emerged that include minimalism as their unique selling point, such as The Minimalist (The Minimalist 2023) and Minimalist (Minimalist 2023); but existing manufacturers – from IKEA to Westwing or Home24 – also use minimalism as an advertising slogan.

Minimalist aesthetics imply owning few but carefully selected goods. The governing principle for selection is the distinction between things that give pleasure and things that do not: The focus is on the emotional relationship to individual objects in the present. The goal is to create spaces that are aesthetically pleasing. A few objects, carefully chosen and arranged, are supposed to promise clarity and peace.

Accessories and tools

As shown above, lifestyle minimalism emphasizes fostering well-being by reducing possessions, linking minimalism to mindfulness and wellness. We find that several accessories have emerged that are intended as complements to the minimalist lifestyle with a deeper connection with oneself. Examples include a minimalist meditation cushion sold at $145.00 (Amazema Interiors 2023) or a minimalist essential oil diffuser at $80.00 (Simons 2023). In addition, a wide range of minimalist beauty products and do-it-yourself sets are offered that promise consumers that they can buy fewer things. In practice, these offers often include countless different skincare products, for example, three different face serums on top of face cream and toner in a minimalist "skin care essential" set by the French brand Typology, sold at $208.20 (Typology Paris 2023).

Further, specific tools are marketed that supposedly help people maintain a minimalist lifestyle. Storage options play an important role in maintaining order and aesthetics in a minimalist space. Examples include storage boxes or containers to organize personal belongings but with a large variety of sizes and purposes. From drawer dividers made from bamboo, acrylic make-up organizers, a heatproof organizing station for hair styling tools, to food containers or wine racks in a geometric design – there seems to be practically no limit to new storage options (The Zoe Report 2023), always following the latest trend in material or shapes.

5. Discussion

In the previous sections, we have outlined key features and business segments of lifestyle minimalism. In the following, we discuss their potential in promoting sufficiency-oriented consumption and their drawbacks.

The pop-cultural, commercial manifestations of lifestyle minimalism have played an important role in mainstreaming the idea of "owning less". This mainstreaming is beneficial to the promotion of sufficiency-oriented consumption because it increases the potential audience. The integration of minimalism into the societal mainstream has been successful because the basic principles of lifestyle minimalism have been translated into marketable products, especially books, vlogs and coaching services, making the principles easy to understand and imitate.

Within lifestyle minimalism, simplicity and consumption reduction are exclusively communicated in association with positive effects, seen as liberation, relief and contribution to well-being. This communication also has substantial value in promoting sufficiency-oriented consumption as it fosters the acceptance of consumption reduction practices. Moreover, there are numerous empirical studies that also prove these positive effects (Kang et al. 2021). The emphasis on aesthetics also carries symbolic value. Consumption reduction does not simply mean leaving out; it involves deliberate selection and composition, through which status and distinction can be conveyed. As demonstrated, numerous products facilitate this approach and might attract consumers with conspicuous motives (Ramchandani/Coste-Maniere 2018).

As a central minimalist method, decluttering can also promote reflection and learning processes about one's own consumption behavior and possessions. First studies show that these reflection processes can have a positive effect on reduced acquisition behavior (Chamberlin/Callmer 2021; Muster et al. 2022). In summary, it can be concluded that lifestyle minimalism can indeed have positive effects on disseminating sufficiency-oriented consumption practices. From our perspective, however, there are central risks that might offset the opportunities.

Of Sandberg's (2021) four types of sufficiency-oriented practices (absolute reduction, sharing practices, product longevity, modal shifts), lifestyle minimalism initially only addresses one dimension: (absolute) reduction. This dimension is primarily achieved through decluttering possessions and, ideally, by limiting new purchases. Decluttering, however, might result in the disposal of items that are still usable and functional, rather than keeping them for potential future needs, repurposing or passing them on. Furthermore, the goal of actual limitation and reduction of new purchases is undermined by the frequently communicated "one-in-one-out" rule. Following the rule could imply disposing of goods regardless of their condition, age or quality simply because they are "too much". Since many consumers may not be able to resist the temptations of consumption, the one-in-one-out rule offers an easy relief principle that has the potential to maintain and even foster overconsumption.

Moreover, it appears questionable whether absolute reduction in consumption can be achieved at all when numerous new and often dispensable products are marketed as necessary tools for a minimalist lifestyle. Based on our observations, borrowing or sharing practices play a subordinate role in lifestyle minimalism. This subordination arises because, even in minimalism, thing culture and materialism are significant; while fewer, special possessions are aspired to, ownership of objects remains unquestioned (Meissner 2019; Sandlin/Wallin 2022). The emphasis on the aesthetic value of reduction actions can impede the focus on another crucial sufficiency dimension: extending product lifespans through maintenance and repair. However, because the recommendation is to discard items that do not bring joy or have no emotional value, "functionality" and "durability" as basic qualities of goods play subordinate roles. Moreover, new products marketed as minimalist are not necessarily high-quality and long-lasting but primarily aesthetically pleasing.

Lastly, the individualistic orientation of lifestyle minimalism, combined with the overemphasis on ego-driven motivations such as well-being and relief, can make it challenging to transfer and apply the reduction concept to other areas of life, such as political engagement for sufficiency policies or, especially, ecologically relevant consumption areas. From a sufficiency perspective, the resource intensity of goods is more important than their emotional value or potential to spark joy (Geiger et al. 2018). The sole focus on reducing the quantity of visible material goods in households carries the risk of overlooking individual goods that are especially resource-intensive. These goods include resource-intensive investment goods (such as cars, houses, heating systems), as well as resource-intensive services (such as air travel) and consumer goods (such as animal products). However, these consumption areas play a subordinate role within minimalism, which is inadequate from a sufficiency perspective.

6. Conclusion

In this chapter, we have presented minimalism as a commercialized lifestyle trend with its business fields and prevailing principles. While there is no empirical evidence – as far as we know – that the business of minimalism has actually contributed to lower consumption levels, one finding is particularly obvious: successful business fields have emerged, and many (dispensable) new products are being sold. Although pop-cultural commercial minimalism certainly holds opportunities for sufficiency, the risks appear to be significant.

It seems important for minimalist businesses to critically reflect on the principles currently in place and focus on values such as quality and longevity of goods and truly mindful and slow consumption, values that were in the roots of the minimalism movement but were lost in the path of commercialization. It is also important that consumers can clearly distinguish and recognize genuinely sufficiency-oriented business models. Therefore, education about misleading advertising campaigns that use minimalism as a "green claim" remains essential. Consumers need to understand that a sufficiency-oriented or truly minimalist lifestyle is never just about individual products or reducing possessions in the short term but rather about reducing consumption levels in the long term.

References

A to Zen Life (2023): "A simple path to living better," 7.12.2023 (https://www.youtube.com/c/atozenlife).

Amazema Interiors (2023): "Minimalist Meditation Cushion – Grey," 7.12.2023. https://www.amazema.com/cushions-throws/minimalist-meditation-cushion-grey.

Amazon (2023a): "Best Sellers in Home Improvement & Design Books," 26.7.2023 (https://www.amazon.com/-/de/Bestseller-Bcher-Haus-Haushalt/zgbs/books/6158312011/ref=zg_bs_nav_books_2_48?language=en_US).

Amazon (2023b): "MJ Favorites," 22.7.2023. https://www.amazon.com/shop/emjay.

BetterHomes&Gardens (2023): "11 Minimalist Living Room Ideas to Simplify Your Space," 26.7.2023. https://www.bhg.com/minimalist-living-rooms-7484011.

Chamberlin, Lucy/Callmer, Åsa (2021): "Spark Joy and Slow Consumption: An Empirical Study of the Impact of the KonMari Method on Acquisition and Wellbeing." In: Journal of Sustainability Research 3/1, e210007. https://doi.org/10.20900/jsr20210007.

Chou, Jyh-Rong (2011): "A Gestalt–Minimalism-based decision-making model for evaluating product form design." In: International Journal of Industrial Ergonomics, 41/6, pp. 607–616, https://doi.org/10.1016/j.ergon.2011.07.006.

Elgin, Duane/Mitchell, Arnold (1977): "Voluntary simplicity." In: Planning Review 5/6, pp. 13–15, https://doi.org/10.1108/eb053820.

Etzioni, Amitai (1999): "Voluntary simplicity: Characterization, select psychological implications, and societal consequences." In: Alexander Brink/Jacob Dahl Rendtorff, Ethical Economy. Studies in Economic Ethics and Philosophy, Berlin, Heidelberg: Springer, pp. 1–26. https://doi.org/10.1007/978-3-662-03900-7_1.

Foden, Jennifer (2020): "How Much Marie Kondo's Tidying Up Empire is Worth," 26.7.2023 (https://www.slice.ca/how-much-marie-kondos-tidying-up-empire-is-worth/#:~:text=The%20Japanese%20organizing%20consultant%20has,credentials%20don't%20end%20there).

Geiger, Sonja/Fischer, Daniel/Schrader, Ulf (2018): "Measuring what matters in sustainable consumption: an integrative framework for the selection of relevant behaviors." In: Sustainable Development 26/1, pp. 1–33, https://doi.org/10.1002/sd.1688/full.

Gossen, Maike/Ziesemer, Florence/Schrader, Ulf (2019): "Why and how commercial marketing should promote sufficient consumption: A systematic literature review." In: Journal of Macromarketing 39/3, pp. 252–269, https://doi.org/10.1177/0276146719866238.

Jungell-Michelsson, Jessica/Heikkurinen, Pasi (2022): "Sufficiency: A systematic literature review." In: Ecological Economics 195, 107380. https://doi.org/10.1016/j.ecolecon.2022.107380.

Kang, Jiyun/Martinez, Cosette M. Joyner/Johnson, Catherine (2021): "Minimalism as a sustainable lifestyle: Its behavioral representations and contributions to emotional well-being." In: Sustainable Production and Consumption 27, pp. 802–813, https://doi.org/10.1016/j.spc.2021.02.001.

Khamis, Susie (2019): "The aestheticization of restraint: The popular appeal of de-cluttering after the global financial crisis." In: Journal of Consumer Culture 19/4, pp. 513–531, https://doi.org/10.1177/1469540519872071.

Kondo, Marie (2014): The life-changing magic of tidying up: The Japanese art, New York: Random House.

KonMari (2023): "The KonMari approach to sentimental items," 27.7.2023 (https://konmari.com/how-to-konmari-sentimental-objects/).

Ludwigsen, Kristin (2019): "Marie Kondo and the New Self-Help." Book Publishing Final Research Paper, 45. https://archives.pdx.edu/ds/psu/29391.

Meissner, Miriam (2019): "Against accumulation: lifestyle minimalism, de-growth and the present post-ecological condition." In: Journal of Cultural Economy 12/3, pp. 185–200. https://doi.org/10.1080/17530350.2019.1570962.

The Minimalist (2023): "The Minimalist," 26.7.2023 (https://www.theminimalisthome.com.au/).

Minimalist (2023): "Minimalist" 23.7.2023 (https://beminimalist.co/).

MJ Gordon (2023): "Live your everyday vacation. Level up your energy, maximize your life," 22.7.2023 (https://www.mj-gordon.com/).

Modern Minimalism (2023): "The Ultimate Minimalist Wardrobe Checklist 2023," (https://modernminimalism.com/minimalist-wardrobe-checklist/).

Muster, Viola/Iran, Samira/Münsch, Marlene (2022): "The cultural practice of decluttering as household work and its potentials for sustainable consumption." In: Frontiers in Sustainability 3, 958538. https://doi.org/10.3389/frsus.2022.958538.

Primark (2023): "The A/W Capsule Wardrobe Items You Need," (https://www.primark.com/en-gb/a/inspiration/sustainability/the-aw-capsule-wardrobe-items-you-need).

Ramchandani, Mukta/Coste-Maniere, Ivan (2018): "Eco-conspicuous versus eco-conscious consumption: co-creating a new definition of luxury and fashion." In: Subramanian Senthilkannan Muthu (eds.), Models for Sustainable Framework in Luxury Fashion: Luxury and Models, Singapore: Springer, pp. 1–10. https://doi.org/10.1007/978-981-10-8285-6_1.

Ross, Gretchen R./Meloy, Margaret G./Bolton, Lisa E. (2021): "Disorder and downsizing." In: Journal of Consumer Research 47/6, pp. 959–977. https://doi.org/10.1093/jcr/ucaa051.

Roster, Catherine A./Ferrari, Joseph R. (2023): "Having less: A personal project taxonomy of consumers' decluttering orientations, motives and emotions." In: Journal of Consumer Affairs, 57/1, pp. 264–295. https://doi.org/10.1111/joca.12499.

Sandberg, Maria (2021): "Sufficiency transitions: A review of consumption changes for environmental sustainability." In: Journal of Cleaner Production 293, 126097. https://doi.org/10.1016/j.jclepro.2021.126097.

Sandlin, Jennifer A./Wallin, Jason James (2022): „Decluttering the pandemic: Marie Kondo, minimalism, and the "joy" of waste." In: Cultural Studies↔ Critical Methodologies 22/1, pp. 96–102. https://doi.org/10.1177/15327086211049703.

Shama, Avraham (1985): "The voluntary simplicity consumer." In: Journal of Consumer Marketing 2/4 pp. 57–63, https://doi.org/10.1108/eb008146.

Shein (2023): "8 minimalist outfits to wear when nothing else makes sense," 25.7.2023 (https://us.shein.com/campaign/premium-minimalism-us).

Simons (2023): "Minimalist ultrasonic diffuser," 26.7.2023 (https://www.simons.ca/en/decor/diffusers-home-fragrances/minimalist-ultrasonic-diffuser--20112-3231410).

Simplehappyzen (2021): "Hi, I'm Vera" 26.7.2023 (https://simplehappyzen.com).

Typology Paris (2023): "Facial Routine Daily skincare essentials for normal to combination skin," 26.7.2023 (https://uk.typology.com/products/face-routine-normal-to-combination-skin?utm_campaign=ggdes0001&utm_source=google&utm_medium=shopping&gclid=EAIaIQobChMI5NCg8b2sgAMVFpCDBx0gYAUtEAQYASABEgL3nvD_BwE).

VanEenoo, Cedric (2011): "Minimalism in Art and Design: Concept, influences, implications and perspectives." In: Journal of Fine and Studio Art 2/1, pp. 7–12. https://doi.org/10.5897/JFSA.9000002.

Vladimirova, Katia (2021): "Consumption corridors in fashion: deliberations on upper consumption limits in minimalist fashion challenges." In: Sustainability: Science, Practice and Policy 17/1, pp. 102–116. https://doi.org/10.1080/15487733.2021.1891673.

Vogue (2023): "A Quintessential Summer Capsule Wardrobe Starts With These 12 Essentials," 25.7.2023 (https://www.vogue.com/article/summer-capsule-wardrobe).

Wilson, Anne V./Bellezza, Silvia (2022): "Consumer minimalism." In: Journal of Consumer Research 48/5, pp. 796–816, https://doi.org/10.1093/jcr/ucab038.

Wong, Regina (2023): "Live well with less," 25.7.2023 (https://www.livewellwithless.com/).

Zavestoski, Stephen/DeLaure, Marilyn (2022): "The Evolution of Voluntary Simplicity: From Soulful Search for Meaning to Extreme Lifestyle Experiment." In: Hélène Cherrier/Michael S. W. Lee (eds.), Anti-Consumption. Exploring the Opposition to Consumer Culture, London: Routledge, pp. 28–44, https://doi.org/10.4324/9780367821586.

The Zoe Report (2023): "If You're An Aspiring Minimalist, These 40 Organization Products On Amazon Are Life-Changing," 26.7.2023 (https://www.thezoereport.com/living/if-youre-aspiring-minimalist-these-40-organization-products-on-amazon-are-life-changing-22605500).

Paving the Way towards Sufficiency in Mobility

Promoting Cycling Through a Bicycle Subscription Service

Laura Niessen, Nancy M. P. Bocken and Marc Dijk

Abstract *This chapter explores to what extent Swapfiets, a bicycle subscription provider, can promote sufficiency mobility practices among users. Through social practice theory, we trace mobility changes attributable to the subscription model and to determinants beyond the firm's reach: external factors and related practices. We conclude with business and policy recommendations.*

1. Changing mobility practices for sufficiency

The way we produce and consume is highly unsustainable, leading to adverse effects on the climate, biodiversity and societal well-being (Wiedmann et al. 2020). This requires a transition towards sustainable levels of production and consumption in all sectors. Some suggest the need for a de-transition, for example, shifting back to car-free cities (Taillandier et al. 2023) or simpler lifestyles (Osikominu/Bocken 2020) for sustainability. To tackle the excessive use of resources through consumption behavior and related production, sufficiency is an important leverage point. Sandberg (2021) lists four types of consumption changes that can promote sufficiency: reducing absolute amounts of consumption, shifting consumption modes, increasing product lifetimes and sharing products. These changes can be operationalized in all sectors. In this chapter, we look into an example from mobility. Here, sufficiency could mean to "create a transport system that facilitates the highest quality of life possible while staying within the capacity of the environment to handle emissions" (Waygood et al. 2019: 56). This sufficiency can be promoted by travelling less often and less far, through a modal shift away from fossil fuel-based private transport, through extending the lifetime of vehicles and through using vehicles more intensively by sharing (Heisserer/Rau 2015; Sandberg 2021). Cycling can be considered a sustainable mobility practice and can promote sufficiency if it replaces less sustainable mobility practices. Changing mobility practices is eminently necessary since the sector is estimated to cause around 24 per cent of global CO_2 emissions (Solaymani 2019).

Businesses can be key actors in driving sufficiency if they change their own production processes and influence their customers towards sustainable lifestyles (Bocken/Short 2016). To promote sufficiency in their customers' practices, they can implement sufficiency-enabling strategies, such as services to extend product lifetimes, reuse, sharing and leasing systems (Niessen/Bocken 2021), or actively promote sufficiency practices in their communications (Gossen et al. 2019; Niessen et al. 2023b). For mobility, businesses could promote less travel, a modal shift to low emission active transport, as well as increasing vehicle use through sharing and long lifetimes. However, despite the will of some businesses to promote sufficiency, it is unclear to what extent they can support such a shift.

In Niessen et al. (2023a), we collected customer data from Swapfiets, a bicycle-as-a-service business that encourages its customers to use cycling as a transport mode. This data was used to understand to what extent the service can bring about a modal shift to cycling and support long bike lifetimes through better care. It showed that the bicycle subscription can increase the uptake of cycling and can also support the continuation of the practice after the subscription is finished. While the service was able to recruit practitioners to the practice of cycling, it also lost some again after the subscription period was up. In interviews, it was highlighted that the practice of cycling is highly dependent on external factors and other practices. In this chapter, we delve deeper into these interview data to further tease out these processes of practice change and other influences. We aim to answer the following questions: *To what extent can a bicycle subscription business promote sufficiency mobility practices amongst its users? And to what extent are these practices influenced by determinants outside of the business' control?*

A practice theoretical lens will be used to understand changes in mobility patterns through the bicycle-as-a-service offer. Practice theory focuses on the practices that humans perform rather than on individuals or overarching societal structures (Evans 2018). Practices can be understood as "a routinized type of behaviour" (Reckwitz 2002: 249). Mobility choices are usually habitual (Javaid et al. 2020), with few people consciously choosing different forms of mobility every day. Therefore, practice theory lends itself to analyzing transport and mobility transitions. Shove et al. (2012) developed a simplified practice theory model that consists of three elements: materials, meanings and competences. In this model, materials refer to objects, physical entities and technologies; competences to knowledge and skills; and meanings to symbolic meaning and ideas. The model will be used in this research to understand and illustrate practice changes.

A bicycle-as-a-service subscription is broadly consistent with the practice of cycling but holds some distinct elements that make it different from cycling a bike that is owned. Spotswood et al. (2015) analyzed cycling in the United Kingdom as a social practice and identified relevant materials, meanings and competences. In Niessen et al. (2023a), we analyzed the practice of using a Swapfiets bicycle subscription through Shove et al.'s (2012) elements model (see Figure 1). While the materials were similar to conventional cycling practices, some were specific to the service, such as recognizable bicycle elements (e.g., blue tire) and business model structures (e.g., store). In terms of competences, users of the subscription did not see many requirements beyond being able to ride a bike. The meanings also largely focused on the perception of the business model (e.g., convenient) rather than cycling. There were some contested practice elements (marked with an asterix in Figure 1). For instance, interviewees disagreed on whether the bicycle subscription could be seen as sustainable. While some argued that any cycling was sustainable and that the business encouraged product longevity, others pointed out that owning a bike might be more sustainable. While the practice of using a bicycle-as-a-service is somewhat distinct from the practice of cycling, it is considered in the following as cycling to discuss the modal shift between different mobility practices.

*Figure 1: Practice elements of using a bicycle-as-a-service. * indicates disagreement among interviewees on item as part of the practice. (From Niessen et al. [2023a])*

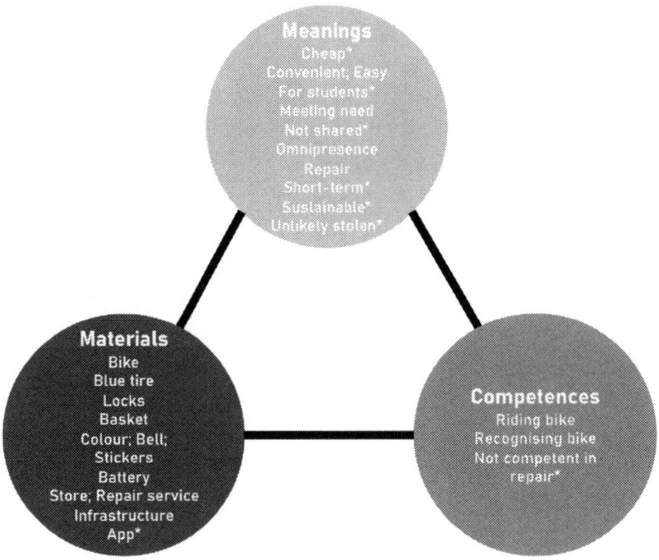

A practice can expand by "recruiting" more practitioners that perform it (Shove et al. 2012). In mobility, this recruitment can imply a modal shift: "We can think about practices as competing to recruit practitioners, or to encourage defection from rival practices – for example from commuter driving to cycling" (Spurling et al. 2013: 28). By recruiting practitioners to the practice of cycling, these people likely defect from other mobility practices which they performed before. The practice of cycling can replace other forms of mobility, such as cars, public transport or walking. For sustainability considerations, it is important to note that public transport and walking can also be considered as sustainable forms of transport (as opposed to car-based private transport), so the best modal shift for sufficiency is away from car use towards cycling. To what extent such practice change can be brought about by one business is not sufficiently studied (Niessen et al. 2023a) and will be further analyzed here.

In the following, the case and the methods of data collection are introduced. Building on the data from interviews, we then look at the role of the subscription business and to what extent it has the ability to promote sufficiency, as opposed to the influence of determinants beyond the firm's reach. We conclude with business recommendations and policy implications.

2. Method

Businesses can promote sufficiency practices through various strategies. From the four generic ways of sufficiency mentioned above, businesses in the mobility sector may be most inclined to the latter three, i.e. sufficiency changes through modal shift, long vehicle lifetimes and sharing, rather than promoting reduced travel frequency and distance. Bicycle subscription business Swapfiets was used as a case study, since it was identified as publicly promoting sufficiency (Niessen/Bocken 2022) and allowed access to users through its channels. The business operates in several European countries and customers can join a bicycle subscription service for regular or electric bicycles. The user pays a monthly fee and is given a bicycle for their exclusive use. While the business retains ownership of the bike, users receive repairs, maintenance and a replacement if the bike is stolen. Swapfiets actively advocates for more cycling and less overall consumption through its communication channels, for instance in their "Consume less, Enjoy more" campaign (Niessen et al. 2023a).

To better understand users' mobility practices and what impacted them before, during and after their membership with the subscription service, interviews with customers were analyzed. These interviews partly overlap with the data in Niessen et al. (2023a), but, here, we include more details into the practice change that had not yet been unpacked. In March to May 2022, the first author conducted semi-structured interviews with Swapfiets users. These interviews took place in the local Swapfiets stores in Cologne (Germany), Leuven (Belgium) and Maastricht (Netherlands), as well as remotely through online or telephone calls. A total of 66 interviews were conducted, ranging from 1 to 9 minutes (short in-store interviews) and 12 to 27 minutes (longer interviews). Table 1 provides interviewee details per location. The interviews included questions about demographics, use of the vehicle, mobility patterns and how the service was perceived[1]. Interviewees were also asked about their mobility modes before the subscription, during and, hypothetically, after they might leave the subscription. Participants for longer interviews were then recruited through a printed survey in Cologne, Leuven and Maastricht, and an online survey sent to Netherlands-based users in which they could volunteer to join further research. Longer interviews used the same interview guide as short interviews but further elaborated on participants' answers, asking for motivations behind travel practices and perceptions. Participants in longer interviews were reimbursed by Swapfiets with a one-month voucher for their subscription (value up to €20).

Table 1: Interview sample used for this chapter

Location	Gender	Age range
Amsterdam		
Short interviews: 0	/	/
Long interviews: 4	3 female, 1 male	25–39
Cologne		
Short interviews: 18	8 female, 10 male	22–65
Long interviews: 3	1 female, 2 male	25–30
Leuven		
Short interviews: 13	3 female, 10 male	19–42
Long interviews:1	1 male	26
Maastricht		
Short interviews: 23	7 female, 16 male	18–57
Long interviews: 4	3 female, 1 male	19–26

All interviews were coded using thematic coding and patterns. For this chapter's focus, interview transcripts were coded deductively along the three stages of potential modal shift: mobility before, during and after the subscription. We also coded for the uses of the bike and potential external factors that might influence mobility changes. While overarching categories had been determined beforehand, new themes inductively came to the fore, such as infrastructural or geographic factors.

1 The interview guide can be found in Appendix B of Niessen et al. 2023a.

3. Findings

In the following, we present the results of the data analysis, trying to differentiate between the potential impact of the business in driving change towards sufficiency mobility practices and the impact of determinants outside of the control of the business.

3.1 Joining the subscription

Recruiting people to the practice of cycling might entail a modal shift away from other mobility practices, such as cars, public transport or walking. Figure 2 shows the process flow of 51 of the interviewees in their cycling practices before, during and after the subscription.[2] Respondents were considered cyclists if they reported to cycle periodically (as opposed to rarely or never). As visible in Figure 2, all but one of the interviewees were active cyclists during their subscription[3], even if twelve of them did not actively cycle beforehand. Not all of these previous non-cyclists stated which form of transport they used instead but public transport and cars were common answers and also often combined. To better understand a potential modal shift from this to cycling, we can look at what recruited users to the practice.

2 While 66 people were interviewed, complete data for all three temporal stages was only obtained from 51 interviewees.

3 One subscription user did not actively use her bike while paying for the subscription because she found cycling inconvenient.

Figure 2: Sankey diagram of modal shift in cycling based on data from 51 interviewees. (Own illustration made with SankeyDiagram.net)

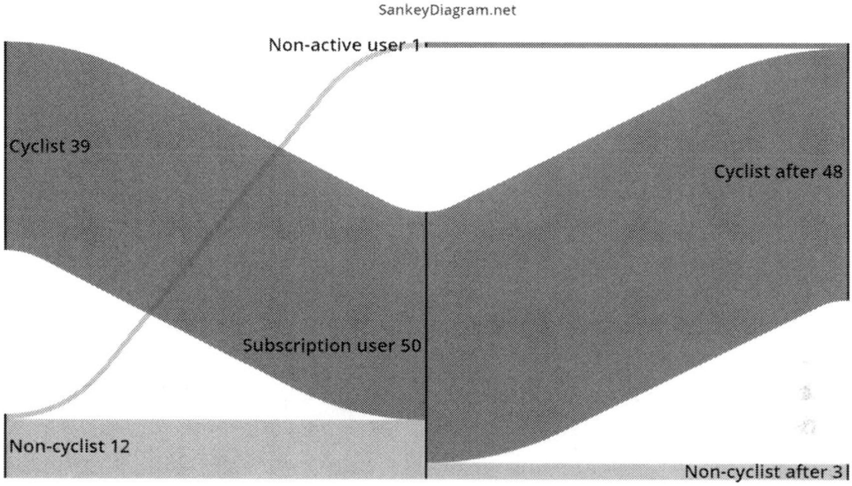

Interviewees were asked what made them join the subscription. In many instances, the subscription was taken up by people that had previously cycled but relocated to a new city. In those cases, the move to another place meant that it was more convenient to join the subscription than purchasing another (additional) bike: "My bike is in The Hague. So it's a bit too far to bring it to Maastricht. So we got a bike [subscription] here" (Maastricht, female, 18). These users did not experience a modal shift, since they moved from cycling with another bike to cycling with a Swapfiets.

Yet, there were also instances where the business offer brought about a modal shift to more cycling. Two of the interviewees that did not cycle regularly had owned bicycles but had not used them as a regular form of transport because their bicycles broke repeatedly or were difficult to ride: "I have a bike but it is relatively old and it is a relatively sluggish bike and it cannot get it to move. It is very annoying to ride it so I haven't used it much" (Translated from German[4], Cologne, female, 22). As such, these interviewees that did not relocate decided to take up cycling because of the provision of a well-functioning bicycle through the business.

However, for the ten other people that did not commonly cycle before, the move to another location made them take up cycling. This was mainly spurred by determinants beyond the Swapfiets offer, such as a new convenience for cycling and cycling

4 The interviews were conducted in English, German or Dutch. Where an original quote was translated into English, it is highlighted in the text.

being the norm. This interviewee had taken up cycling because distances were short compared to his home city: "[W]e have long distances there, so I use the car in Italy. I don't usually cycle" (Leuven, male, 30). Another incentive for change mentioned was the infrastructure for cycling that had not previously been available: "I didn't cycle at all because in my country, there's problem[s] with bike lanes. There is not enough of them, so I mainly use public transport [...] or cars" (Maastricht, male, 19). All of the interviewees that did not actively cycle before knew how to ride a bicycle. Still, they often mentioned that it was not as common to cycle in their previous home as it was in their new location: "I knew how to cycle but I wasn't cycling daily. It wasn't really a daily thing in my country. So when I came here, I saw it's like an everyday thing and you don't walk, you just bike" (Leuven, female, 19).

3.2 Mobility during the subscription

The vast majority of subscription users were active cyclists during the time of the contract (see Figure 2). Only one interviewee did not actively use her subscription bicycle. In that sense, we can surmise that the impact of Swapfiets in promoting cycling as a sufficiency mobility practice was quite successful during the subscription. However, another finding was that cycling was often not the only form of transport that interviewees used during the subscription. This combination of mobility modes was created by determinants beyond the business offer.

While using the Swapfiets bike, most interviewees combined it with walking, public transport and car use. Walking as an addition was used for shorter distances. Public transport was seen as a popular alternative when cycling was uncomfortable, for instance because of strong winds or heavy rain: "Sometimes you have to go for work – 40 minutes biking – and it's a lot of wind [...] or terrible weather, then I take once or twice the public transport" (Amsterdam, female, 27). Public transport also often complemented cycling for longer distances: "Normally, I use [the bike]. Sometimes I walk or go with [the] train if I am going far away" (Maastricht, female, 22).

During the time of the bicycle subscription, a considerable number of interviewees (almost a third) also owned cars or used cars they had access to through car sharing or borrowing. This would indicate that a potential modal shift to cycling did not always mean a shift away from cars. Cars were mainly used for the same reasons as public transport: for comfort and for longer distances. In terms of comfort, one car-driving interviewee describes the need to look fresh when arriving at important occasions: "Especially if I have something important to do, I take the car [so] that I'm not too sweaty because I get red very quickly" (Leuven, female, 21). For longer distances, interviewees also reported using cars, particularly when leaving the city. One recurrent reason for owning a car next to the bicycle subscription was if the interviewees had children. Taking them to childcare, school or other activities was not something that these interviewees felt could easily be done by bike: "Of course, I use a car. It's a bit difficult [to cycle] with my kids" (Maastricht, male, 48).

The interviewees were asked what activities they would use their subscription bicycle for. Activities that the interviewer suggested included cycling to work or study, to meet friends, for free time activities, to do (heavy) groceries or for weekend trips. Almost half of the interviewees responded that they would use the bicycle for everything, particularly within the city and at short distances. Less popular uses of the subscription bike were weekend trips and heavy groceries. Weekend trips were mainly considered to be longer distance and the interviewees did not consider the bicycle a good form of transportation for that, also because the bike models in the subscription are more convenient for city biking: "I did buy a good trekking bike. So if I would go somewhere far away, I would take that one because my [subscription bike] doesn't have any gears" (Amsterdam, female, 27). While many interviewees used the bike for grocery shopping, there were some concerns with the weight of the shopping: "Sometimes I get [groceries] delivered because it's heavy to go by bike" (Maastricht, female, 19). The bicycle was commonly used for free time activities, such as meeting friends, but also to go to study or work. Many interviewees used it to commute and some also used it for their work as bicycle delivery drivers: "So I work 20 hours with that bike, and I could keep it with me at home. So [...] I used it to go to university, to go around" (Leuven, male, 24).

Yet, cycling was rarely the sole means of transport and cars were often required for work purposes, as illustrated by this interviewee who owned two cars: "I need the cars for my work because I sometimes have to cover longer distances at 6am and I refuse to go by train" (translated from German, Cologne, female, 60). Sometimes, the materials required for other practices constrained cycling, for instance for one interviewee who had to transport work equipment: "But the problem remains that I have to transport things [for work]. Expensive equipment. And bike bags left and right would not be enough. I would need a real electronic cargo bike and that is not currently an option for me" (translated from German, Cologne, male, 30).

In addition, the interview data also brought up external determinants that influenced which mode of transport was preferred. Good cycling infrastructure, short distances and a cycling culture were named in 3.1 as enablers to joining the practice. There were also external barriers to cycling. Among these were topographical conditions (e.g., hilly terrain), long distances in widespread settlements and weather: "I specifically do not bike during the winters because it's too cold outside around that time and I don't want to take the headache. [...]. Uphill roads, cold winds and super cold temperature outside" (Leuven, male, 26). Another barrier was the lack of appropriate cycling infrastructure that made users feel that cycling was not a safe practice in some places: "But tomorrow, if I move to Madrid, [...] I don't think I would get [a bike] because it's not the main public transport. [...]. You're just going to get killed on the road" (Amsterdam, female, 25).

3.3 Mobility after the subscription

Interviewees were asked what hypothetical form of transport they would use in the future if they were to end their subscription. In most cases, ending the subscription did not mean stopping the practice of cycling. Many interviewees indicated that they would continue cycling and purchase a bike of their own. This was the case for both the interviewees that cycled before the subscription and some that had only started cycling with the subscription bike. Yet, it would be difficult to attribute long-term cycling to the Swapfiets business offer, since interviewees did not state this was explicitly caused by their experience with the subscription provider. Oftentimes, interviewees rather mentioned that their modal shift was influenced by determinants beyond Swapfiets. This interviewee had come to the shop to return his subscription bike: "I've already bought my own bike. So I think I'll just give the Swapfiets back" (Maastricht, male, 19). He had not been an active cyclist before the subscription and reported this was due to a lack of cycling lanes in his home city. Since coming to live in Maastricht, he had taken up cycling and decided to buy his own bike to continue cycling[5].

Several other interviewees that were non-cyclists before the subscription stated that they would continue the practice of cycling even if they went back home: "Cycling is just really great. [...]. I mean, depends really on the city. But I would say there's a pretty high likelihood I'd go back and cycle a lot. [Interviewer: Even in [your home country]?] I: Even in [my home country]" (Maastricht, male, 18). Before the subscription, this interviewee had used public transport because he found cycling in his hilly home city difficult. Therefore, he suggested that while he might cycle, he might get an electric bike. Similarly, another interviewee who had not cycled beforehand in his home city thought he might continue the practice if he went home but would have to adjust the bicycle to make it more convenient: "I'm going to see if I can put a motor in my bike over there. [Interviewer: An electric one?] Yeah." (Leuven, male, 29). Several interviewees that had been previous non-cyclists had joined the practice of cycling through the Swapfiets subscription and intended to bring it with them to other locations, even if sometimes in an altered form.

There were also interviewees that intended not to cycle in the future. Three of the interviewees that did not cycle before the subscription answered that they would probably not cycle regularly in the future. This was oftentimes related to cycling infrastructure: "It's about 15 kilometres or more and we haven't got many cycle lane[s]. So it would be also dangerous in some streets to go by bike" (Leuven, male, 30); and spatial planning: "Because of the rural location of my house, I will go back to driving a car" (Maastricht, female, 57). While only three interviewees stated they would not

5 The interviewee did not specify if he would continue cycling should he move to a city with less convenient cycling infrastructure, such as his home city.

cycle after the subscription (see also Figure 2), it is important to note that several others were planning to use the bicycle much less and only as an additional form of transport. Even some interviewees that had been cyclists before the subscription stated that they would move away from biking as their main form of transport: "[F]or longer distances, of course, I would get a car. But if I can cycle, I would still do it" (Maastricht, male, 20). Sometimes, cycling was seen as a sport or free time activity in the future rather than a form of transport: "I feel all of these modes of transport serve very different needs but for leisure activity, for just aimless wandering, I would probably bike" (Leuven, male, 26).

4. Discussion

In this book chapter, we aim to answer: *To what extent can a bicycle subscription business promote sufficiency mobility practices amongst its users? And to what extent are these practices influenced by determinants outside of the business' control?* The Swapfiets user data provided some insight into this, graphically represented in Figure 3. In the upper half, there are practice configurations for mobility outside of the bicycle subscription, before and after. Mobility practices could be cycling dominant (i.e. mainly moving around by bike), but interviewees combined this with car driving and public transport or walking. Other interviewees had previous mobility configurations in which the car or public transport and walking were dominant, while cycling was still present to a small extent, often as a leisure activity. Upon entering the bicycle subscription (bottom half of the picture), all but one interviewee became active cyclists. However, when ending the subscription, there was also a "bounce back" into previous mobility configurations.

This research set out to understand the impact of one business – Swapfiets – that wanted to promote the sufficiency mobility practice of cycling. Through enabling a modal shift away from car-driving to cycling, the business could potentially support sufficiency practices. Interviews with customers showed that users of the subscription mostly cycled while they had the contract. In a few cases, the convenience offered by the Swapfiets service can be assumed to have promoted a modal shift to more cycling. Yet, as visually represented in Figure 3, the influence of Swapfiets on user behavior is largely limited to the time of the subscription (illustrated as a dashed circle). Even during the subscription, users employed a mix of transport modes, with many still using cars. Therefore, it is important to look at the second research question and the determinants beyond the business that influence mobility practices.

Figure 3: Graphical representation of mobility practice changes (note: PT refers to public transport).

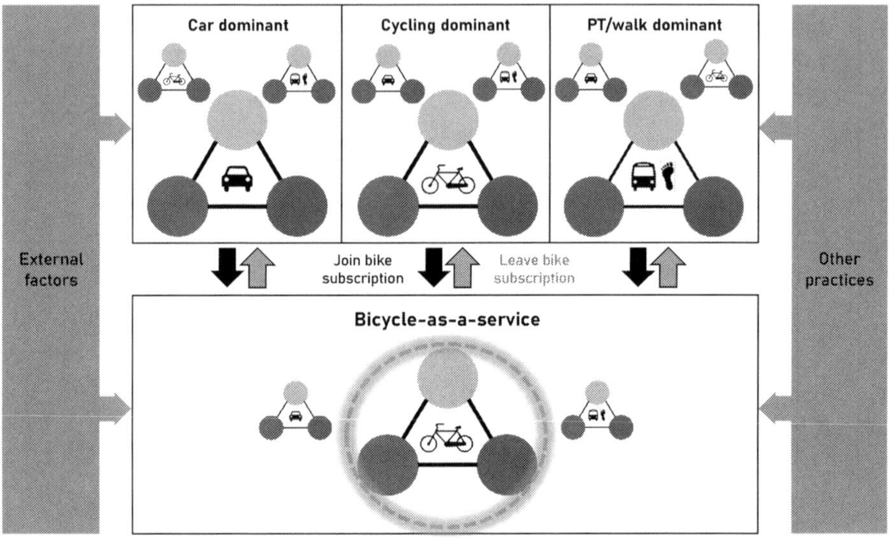

In the interviews, two main other influences were identified: related practices and external factors. These seemed to play a large role in determining the mobility mix of users, as well as what mode of transport was chosen before and after the subscription. This is visually represented in Figure 3 through the blocks on the sides influencing the mobility mix before, during and after the subscription. Dillman et al. (2021) suggest that mobility does not fulfil an immediate need but is rather a means to reach activities and relationships. Mobility practices are therefore always dependent on other practices that they help accomplish (Kent 2021), making it important to understand "why particular trips are made – what other practices (e.g., shopping, working, other leisure activities) [...] all these trips enable?" (Spurling et al. 2013: 29). The interview data showed that related practices, such as child-care, working or grocery shopping were sometimes seen as barriers to cycling.

The interviews also echo existing research on the factors that influence how high the modal share of cycling is in an urban area (Adam et al. 2020), here referred to as external factors, since they are external to the Swapfiets business offer. Adam et al. (2020) identified the following factors as influencing cycling: (1) cycle-conducive infrastructure, (2) policy programs to promote cycling, (3) an overall policy direction towards cycling, (4) exogenous factors (physical environment, spatial planning), (5) socio-cultural factors (cycling culture), (6) individual factors (attitudes and beliefs). The interview data reflected the importance of several of those when users decided whether to cycle or not, particularly (1) the infrastructure, (4) exogenous factors and (5) socio-cultural factors. Particularly, cycling infrastructure was often connected to feeling safe when cycling. Safety concerns are one of the major deterrents in making more people take up cycling, as are comfort and convenience (Hull/O'Holleran 2014). These factors are largely beyond the influence of one business.

4.1 Practice change through a business offering

Swapfiets plays a role in paving the way towards more cycling. As Spaargaren (2003) points out: "When there is a high level [...] of green provisioning, people are more or less brought into a position in which the greening of their corresponding lifestyle segment becomes a feasible option" (690). The business constitutes part of the provisioning in offering convenient access to cycling. An illustrative example of this was given by the two interviewees who had bicycles beforehand but did not cycle because the bikes were not well-functioning. Providing well-functioning, convenient access made cycling their dominant form of transport. Yet, the previous points in the discussion show clear limits to the influence that a business offer such as that of Swapfiets can have.

To extend its influence and promote sufficiency beyond its current reach, Swapfiets might be able to address some of the determinants beyond its control. Organizations that want to promote cycling need to understand interlinking practices, i.e. the practices that mobility is used for, to enable adoption (Hesselgren et al. 2020). The interviews showed that some activities were less frequently undertaken with the bike, for instance grocery shopping or longer distance journeys. The business could amend its offer to add bike storage bags to its subscription offer (currently, customers can add a basket for an additional fee). These would hold a larger quantity of groceries. For longer journeys, bicycles with gears are more comfortable. Swapfiets already offers these but at an increased price, which often makes users decide for the cheaper model. The price for these models could be adjusted, potentially seasonally, so that good weather cycling over longer distances can be done with a gear-model subscription bike. Another linked practice that stopped users from cycling was childcare. In the Netherlands, a common way of transporting children by bicycle is the "bakfiets", the Dutch cargo bike with space for seating in the front (te Brömmelstroet et al. 2020). Swapfiets might add this to their subscription offer in order to facilitate users cycling even if they have to take care of children. Similarly, electric bicycles might have a higher potential to replace cars (Bourne et al. 2020) and could be suitable for longer distances. Electric bakfiets or cargo bikes might also facilitate some practices that other bicycles would not, for instance carrying work equipment. Such diverse forms of cycling could be included in the Swapfiets subscription offer. Another potential way to support moving away from cars as a share of users' mobility mix might be to promote sustainable inter- or multimodal journeys, where several modes of transport are combined (Jonuschat et al. 2015). Combinations with public transport, such as bike-train trips, could replace car trips and seem mostly successful if they are perceived as the best available option (Nello-Deakin/te Brömmelstroet 2021). Swapfiets could collaborate with public transport providers, for instance on ticketing, to make such combinations more attractive than car-based trips.

Even with these possible changes by the business, the practice of cycling is influenced by not just one actor (i.e. the bike subscription business) but also by other actors in the system, such as public bodies (e.g., roads, signage, rules of traffic) and wider society (e.g., a culture giving cyclists safe space on the road). Therefore, we provide some brief policy reflections below.

4.2 Practice change through policy

While the subscription business provides one entry point for cycling as a common practice, other parts are still missing. Policy can play an important role in (also literally) paving the way for more cycling. In Adam et al.'s (2020) assessment of the factors that influence cycling, infrastructure was identified as the most important leverage point. This includes both safe cycling infrastructure (pull factor), as well as infrastructure interventions that deter other forms of transport (push factors), specifically cars. Taillandier et al. (2023) similarly found that push and pull factors need to be combined to decrease car dependence in cities. As Shove et al. (2015) point out: "infrastructures embody and carry historically specific ideas about normal and appropriate ways of living, effectively transporting these from one generation to the next" (280). Therefore, building bicycle infrastructure cannot only foster a better system of provision but also influence cultural perceptions (especially because it reduces the association of cycling being unsafe). Cultural norms towards cycling are difficult to shake. In certain contexts, cycling is considered a form of mobility for the poor, while driving cars represents status (Steinbach et al. 2011). Policy interventions could target the perception of cycling to make active transport a desirable and easy choice, building up a cycling culture akin to the one in the Netherlands (Te Brömmelstroet et al. 2020), where even some prime ministers are fond of cycling to work (Whiting/Knowles 2019).

Other relevant policy measures include spatial planning interventions to increase population density, constrain car access and improve connections to public transport, as well as programs to promote cycling at different scales (Adam et al. 2020). Examples of these could be cycle training for schoolchildren or all new drivers (Hull/O'Holleran 2014). As pointed out by Hull and O'Holleran (2014): "promotion of cycling must involve more than physical infrastructure, it must integrate across policy delivery areas including spatial planning, transport, health and education" (385).

5. Conclusion

We need to transform societal practices towards more sustainable alternatives in order to stay within the boundaries of the planet. Sufficiency alternatives to the currently dominant car mobility include public transport and active transport, such as walking and cycling. In the case of Swapfiets, the business tried to promote cycling amongst its customers to reduce the use of less sustainable forms of mobility. This research highlighted the limited reach a business has in influencing its users' mobility practices. The subscription bicycle was used as the main form of transport by both previous cyclists and non-cyclists because it was considered convenient and easy. Yet, despite using a subscription bike, users often also used other forms of mobility, such as public transport, walking or cars. Therefore, the company's offering could not fully replace other mobility practices, including unsustainable ones. Furthermore, some users expected to move (back) to car use in the future. This expectation and the mobility mix of users were mainly influenced by determinants outside of the business offer, namely external factors (e.g., weather or cycling infrastructure) and related practices (e.g., travel for work or childcare).

Even though Swapfiets offers its services and uses its communications to promote cycling, there are factors that cannot be influenced by one company. We suggested potential avenues for the business to expand its influence beyond current reach. Still, policy intervention is required to promote cycling as the main form of transport. Variables such as local weather or topography cannot be changed by policy but the availability of cycling infrastructure, spatial planning and cycling culture can be targeted. While cycling might not be able to replace car use in all contexts, policy can help to build a supportive context that makes cycling the easy choice.

This research was subject to several limitations. Data was collected from users of only one business, which allowed for more depth, but limits the transferability of the results to other businesses. Future research could investigate different businesses, other sectors and localities. Another limitation was the hypothetical nature of future transport. Users were asked what form of transport they think they would use if they left the subscription. This could not be confirmed within the scope of this research, so future research could usefully employ a longitudinal approach or experimental design to support users' assessments of their future transport.

References

Adam, Lukas/Jones, Tim/Te Brömmelstroet, Marco (2020): "Planning for cycling in the dispersed city: establishing a hierarchy of effectiveness of municipal cycling policies." In Transportation 47, pp. 503–527. https://doi.org/10.1007/s11116-018-9878-3.

Bocken, Nancy M. P./Short, Samuel W. (2016): "Towards a sufficiency-driven business Model: Experiences and opportunities." In: Environmental Innovation and Societal Transitions 18, pp. 41–61. https://doi.org/10.1016/j.eist.2015.07.010.

Bourne, Jessica E./Cooper, Ashley R./Kelly, Paul/Kinnear, Fiona J./England, Clare/Leary, Sam/Page, Angie (2020): "The impact of e-cycling on travel behaviour: a scoping review." In: Journal of Transport & Health 19, 100910. https://doi.org/10.1016/j.jth.2020.100910.

Dillman, Kevin Joseph/Czepkiewicz, Michal/Heinonen, Jukka/Davíðsdóttir, Brynhildur (2021): "A safe and just space for urban mobility: a framework for sector-based sustainable consumption corridor development." In: Global Sustainability 4/e28, pp. 1–17. https://doi.org/10.1017/sus.2021.28.

Evans, David M. (2018): "What is consumption, where has it been going, and does it still matter?" In: The Sociological Review 67/3, pp. 499–517. https://doi.org/10.1177/0038026118764028.

Gossen, Maike/Ziesemer, Florence/Schrader, Ulf (2019): "Why and How Commercial Marketing Should Promote Sufficient Consumption: A Systematic Literature Review." In: Journal of Macromarketing 39/3, pp. 252–269. https://doi.org/10.1177/0276146719866238

Heisserer, Barbara/Rau, Henrike (2015): "Capturing the consumption of distance? A practice-theoretical investigation of everyday travel." In: Journal of Consumer Culture 17/3, pp. 579–599. https://doi.org/10.1177/1469540515602304.

Hesselgren, Mia/Sjöman, Martin/Pernestål, Anna (2020): "Understanding user practices in mobility service systems: Results from studying large scale corporate MaaS in practice." In: Travel Behaviour and Society 21, pp. 318–327. https://doi.org/10.1016/j.tbs.2018.12.005.

Hull, Angela/O'Holleran, Craig (2014): "Bicycle infrastructure: can good design encourage cycling?" In: Urban, Planning and Transport Research 2/1, pp. 369–406. https://doi.org/10.1080/21650020.2014.955210.

Javaid, Aneeque/Creutzig, Felix/Bamberg, Sebastian (2020): "Determinants of low-carbon transport mode adoption: systematic review of reviews." In: Environmental Research Letters, 15/10, 103002. https://doi.org/10.1088/1748-9326/aba032.

Jonuschat, Helga/Stephan, Korinna/Schelewsky, Marc (2015): "Understanding Multimodal and Intermodal Mobility." In: Sustainable Urban Transport 7, pp. 149–176. http://dx.doi.org/10.1108/S2044-994120150000007018.

Kent, Jennifer Lee (2021): "The use of practice theory in transport research." In: Transport Reviews 42/2, pp. 222–244. https://doi.org/10.1080/01441647.2021.1961918.

Nello-Deakin, Samuel/te Brömmelstroet, Marco (2021): "Scaling up cycling or replacing driving? Triggers and trajectories of bike–train uptake in the Randstad area." In: Transportation 48, pp. 3239–3267. https://doi.org/10.1007/s11116-021-10165-9.

Niessen, Laura/Bocken, Nancy M. P. (2021): "How Can Businesses Drive Sufficiency? The Business for Sufficiency Framework." In: Sustainable Production and Consumption 28, pp. 1090–1103. https://doi.org/10.1016/j.spc.2021.07.030.

Niessen, Laura/Bocken, Nancy M. P. (2022): "A Sufficiency Database as a Tool to Drive Sustainable Business Models." Presented at: New Business Models 2022, Rome, Italy.

Niessen, Laura/Bocken, Nancy M. P./Dijk, Marc (2023a): "The impact of business sufficiency strategies on consumer practices: The case of bicycle subscription." In: Sustainable Production and Consumption 35, pp. 576–591. https://doi.org/10.1016/j.spc.2022.12.007.

Niessen, Laura/Bocken, Nancy M. P./Dijk, Marc (2023b): "Sufficiency as trend or tradition? – Uncovering business pathways to sufficiency through historical advertisements." In: Frontiers in Sustainability 4, 1165682. https://doi.org/10.3389/frsus.2023.1165682.

Osikominu, Jessica/Bocken, Nancy (2020): "A voluntary simplicity lifestyle: Values, adoption, practices and effects." In: Sustainability 12/5, 1903. https://doi.org/10.3390/su12051903.

Reckwitz, Andreas (2002): "Toward a Theory of Social Practices: a Development in Culturalist Theorizing." In: European Journal of Social Theory 5/2, pp. 243–263. https://doi.org/10.1177/13684310222225432.

Sandberg, Maria (2021): "Sufficiency transitions: A review of consumption changes for environmental sustainability." In: Journal of Cleaner Production 293/126097. https://doi.org/10.1016/j.jclepro.2021.126097

Shove, Elizabeth/Pantzar, Mika/Watson, Matt (2012): The Dynamics of Social Practice: Everyday Life and how it Changes, London: Sage Publications

Shove, Elizabeth/Watson, Matt/Spurling, Nicola (2015): "Conceptualizing connections: Energy demand, infrastructures and social practices." In: European Journal of Social Theory 18/3, pp. 274–287. https://doi.org/10.1177/1368431015579964.

Solaymani, Saeed (2019): "CO_2 emissions patterns in 7 top carbon emitter economies: The case of transport sector." In: Energy 168, pp. 989–1001. https://doi.org/10.1016/j.energy.2018.11.145.

Spaargaren, Gert (2003): "Sustainable Consumption: A Theoretical and Environmental Policy Perspective." In: Society & Natural Resources 16/8, pp. 687–701. https://doi.org/10.1080/08941920309192.

Spotswood, Fiona/Chatterton, Tim/Tapp, Alan/Williams, David (2015): "Analysing cycling as a social practice: An empirical grounding for behaviour change." In: Transportation Research Part F: Traffic Psychology and Behaviour 29, pp. 22–33. https://doi.org/10.1016/j.trf.2014.12.001.

Spurling, Nicola/McMeekin, Andrew/Shove, Elizabeth/Southerton, Dale/Welch, Daniel (2013): "Interventions in practice: re-framing policy approaches to consumer behaviour." Sustainable Practices Research Group Report, 25.7.2023 (https://pure.manchester.ac.uk/ws/portalfiles/portal/32468813/FULL_TEXT.PDF).

Steinbach, Rebecca/Green, Judith/Datta, Jessica/Edwards, Phil (2011): "Cycling and the city: A case study of how gendered, ethnic and class identities can shape healthy transport choices." In: Social Science & Medicine 72/7, pp. 1123–1130. https://doi.org/10.1016/j.socscimed.2011.01.033

Taillandier, Chloe/Dijk, Marc/Vialleix, Martial (2023): "Back to the Future: "De-Transition" to Low-Car Cities." In: Future Transportation, 3/2, pp. 808–839. https://doi.org/10.3390/futuretransp3020046.

te Brömmelstroet, Marco/Boterman, William/Kuipers, Giselinde (2020): "How culture shapes-and is shaped by-mobility: cycling transitions in The Netherlands." In: Carey Curtis (eds.), Handbook of Sustainable Transport, Cheltenham: Edward Elgar Publishing, pp. 109–118. https://doi.org/10.4337/9781789900477.00023.

Waygood, E. Owen D./Sun, Yilin/Schmöcker, Jan-Dirk (2019): "Transport sufficiency: Introduction & case study." In: Travel Behaviour and Society 15, pp. 54–62. https://doi.org/10.1016/j.tbs.2018.12.002.

Whiting, Kate/Knowles, David (2019): "Why I ride my bike to work, by the Prime Minister of the Netherlands." In: World Economic Forum, 26.9.2019 (https://www.weforum.org/agenda/2019/09/why-i-ride-my-bike-to-work-by-the-prime-minister-of-the-netherlands/).

Wiedmann, Thomas/Lenzen, Manfred/Keysser, Lorenz T./Steinberger, Julia K. (2020): "Scientists' warning on affluence." In: Nature Communications 11, 3107. https://doi.org/10.1038/s41467-020-16941-y.

From Efficiency to Sufficiency in the ICT Sector

Reflecting on Fifteen Years of Trial and Error

Isabelle Dabadie

Abstract *This chapter draws on fifteen years of personal experience acquired at the interface between business and academic research, dedicated to steering the telecoms industry towards sustainability. From eco-design to sufficiency, it recounts the progress made, the disappointments encountered and the questions that remain unanswered in relation to a task whose immensity is matched by its urgency and criticality.*

1. Introduction

The worsening ecological crisis and growing public concern with ecological issues has led to more and more companies taking action to reduce their environmental impact. Yet, few of them have really started to question in depth the way they do business (Niessen/Bocken 2021). Such a shift seems even more unlikely in the Information and Communication Technology (ICT) sector, in which business models are still largely based on ever more use and on ever more powerful technological solutions for consumers (Jardim 2017). Although ICT firms do seek to reduce their environmental impact (with "green IT" initiatives) and try to offer technology that supports the ecological transition ("IT for Green"), the sector's ecological footprint continues to grow and it is still a very long way from a sustainable model (Ferreboeuf et al. 2021).

The literature extensively documents the environmental consequences associated with the ICT sector, encompassing telecommunications activities. According to the European Commission's evaluation (European Commission 2020), the sector's energy and environmental effects account for approximately five to nine per cent of global electricity consumption and over two per cent of total emissions. This figure of two per cent is comparable to the worldwide carbon dioxide emissions generated by the civil aviation industry. It is important to note that ICT operates interdependently with other sectors and, due to its pervasive nature, also has an impact on them. ICT plays a role in various aspects of our daily lives, both professionally and personally.

Considering the medium-term perspective, specifically until around 2030, the ICT industry represents a rapidly growing sector that will significantly contribute to addressing environmental challenges such as CO_2 emissions, raw material consumption and pollution, among others. The literature highlights rebound effects and the need for sufficiency policies to complement consistency and efficiency efforts in the ICT sector (e.g., Santarius et al. 2022). While the latter are not yet widespread, sufficiency policies are still in their infancy or even taboo, as we were able to observe in the field.

After having worked for fifteen years – from 2008 to 2023 – on projects at the intersection of business and academic research, seeking to steer the telecoms industry towards sustainability (understood as a development compatible with planetary boundaries), now seems a good time to take stock of my actions, which unfortunately appear to have had a limited impact. While previous research has studied "exemplary companies" (e.g., Gossen/Kropfeld 2022), I suggest looking back at an experience of "trial and error" in order for us to be able to learn lessons, question the course of action for the coming years and help implement the changes that are becoming increasingly vital in the short term. This is precisely the goal of this chapter, which aims to draw on the account of a personal experience, in order to shed light on the progress made and the setbacks encountered, and identify the challenges for academics and practitioners in the coming years.

This chapter aims to provide an original, authentic, sincere account that shares the efforts and mistakes made, and mistakes that will doubtless be made again. It retraces various stages in my career, from my position as program manager in an ICT firm from 2008 to 2012, where I was involved in setting up eco-design programs, to my role as doctoral student, then assistant professor, associate professor and researcher from 2013 to 2023, studying from an academic point of view, in close cooperation with business partners, the different paths that will lead from efficiency to sufficiency policies. This story reveals doubts and questions that are still open. It also illustrates the need for more radical changes: faced with the urgency of the climate situation, we can no longer afford any further digressions.

2. From efficiency to sufficiency: eco-design as a starting point

This story starts in 2008. Back then, I worked for Technicolor, a manufacturing firm in the IT sector, which provides network infrastructure and end-user equipment to service operators (telcos, cable, terrestrial or satellite operators). These operators provide voice, data and video services to customers who access them through devices usually composed of a box for internet access and a set-top box for television services. This equipment is traditionally sold by the manufacturer to the operator who in turn rents it to end-users as part of their monthly subscription to the services.

My company had launched CSR initiatives, which included the implementation of an eco-design program. The objective of these programs was to integrate a method in the product and services development process aiming to control and reduce their environmental impact along their entire lifecycle, with a multi-criteria approach to avoid transfers of impact from one phase of the life cycle to the other or of one type of impact to another.

2.1 Implementing eco-design: the first success stories

The eco-design program, led by the Quality Department, started with the implementation of a process and the training of R&D teams. On the business side, however, no precise objectives had been defined. Concerned with the environmental impact of an activity whose main purpose (entertainment, mainly via television) invites us to question its social utility, I decided to take up this issue. At the time, I was Program Manager in the Marketing & Sales Department. My role was to manage the development of a product on behalf of a customer (which was to be manufactured in tens or even hundreds of thousands of units over several years), from the signing of the contract (sometimes earlier) through to delivery of the finished product and its deployment. I was therefore at the interface of all the company's functions. My mission was to meet the project's objectives and to build a lasting relationship with the customer.

In this position, I was able to play a facilitating role in implementing eco-design. In 2010, a Life Cycle Assessment (LCA) was carried out for one of my products, which identified its main environmental impacts and led to the identification of areas for improvement. I asked the R&D teams to study the possibility of replacing PVC parts with recycled plastic. A multidisciplinary task force was set up. The mechanical engineers were not convinced, and neither was sourcing. Doubts were expressed as to the aesthetics of the final product and its acceptability to the customer, its solidity, the ability to source recycled material and the likely additional cost of this material. Despite these resistances, tests were launched. The results were surprisingly good: the difference was undetectable to the naked eye, the product passed all resistance tests, the material was available and its cost lower than that of virgin plastic. And to complete the picture, this positive experience helped to build new bridges between experts who had little opportunity to rub shoulders on a daily basis and gave new meaning to an industry going through difficult times (relocation, etc.). This first experience was a success and encouraged us to continue in this direction.

I was convinced, however, that in order to expand the scope of this endeavor, marketing would need to be more directly involved. Indeed, as long as the eco-design approach remained associated solely with a "quality" approach and without a clear directive from management indicating that it should imperatively be implemented in product development processes, or a clear perception of the competitive advantage it could bring, it ran the risk of being perceived as an additional constraint and cost that would complicate an already difficult context, with strong pressure on costs, in particular. On the other hand, I was also convinced that eco-design could help create value, and that the efforts associated with its implementation could be a profitable investment for the company. These possible sources of value were manifold (e.g., cost reduction or creation of a competitive advantage).

In 2011, I therefore suggested developing an activity within the Marketing & Sales Department aimed at promoting eco-design, both through internal training efforts and external communication. Two thorny issues needed to be resolved: 1) How to make the improvements achieved through eco-design visible to our customer (service operators) and to their own customers?; 2) How to communicate on this subject without risking accusations of greenwashing? As regards the second point, claims of providing "eco-friendly" products could easily be attacked by those who considered that these "non-essential" products should not be manufactured at all. What was more, although this was first and foremost an improvement initiative, it was still difficult to justify the fact that our products were far from perfect in environmental terms, given that there was still a great deal of room for improvement. One main lever was therefore mobilized: cooperation with our customers who were also committed to a similar approach.

2.2 Disappointments and first steps towards sufficiency

In the early 2010's, eco-design was progressively being implemented but still lacked managerial support. No objectives were set in terms of the number of products to be evaluated by means of an LCA nor in terms of reduction of environmental impact from one product generation to the next. When the eco-design method was implemented, it led to improvements, but these remained marginal: e.g., eco-design of packaging, choice of more environmentally-friendly plastic materials, but these weighed little against the impact of the product over its entire life cycle (the most significant aspect of the impact being related to energy consumption during the use phase). Another challenge was linked to the difficulty of creating value in a B2B model in which the benefits of the approach accrue solely to the end-user, who attaches little importance to them. Indeed, in the case of manufactured products (set-top boxes, sold to an operator who rents them to the end-user), the eco-designed nature of the equipment (use of recycled materials, for example) is not a criterion considered by the customer when choosing their service operator. Energy savings are of little importance to most customers, who are not really aware of the energy consumption of this type of equipment, nor of the savings they can make. The environmental benefit is also difficult to communicate and promote.

Nevertheless, we continued our efforts to reduce the environmental impact of our activities. On the manufacturing side, hand in hand with our customer, we continued to focus on reducing the energy consumption of the set-top boxes, which had so far been characterized by the fact they consume almost as much energy on standby as they do when in use. There are two main reasons for this. Firstly, operators need to be able to access equipment during standby phases (to send information, updates, etc.). Secondly, the deeper the equipment is in standby mode, the longer it takes to restart when the user wants to access services. The configuration of equipment is based on a strong presupposition: customers do not want to wait. When they press the button on the remote control, the picture must appear immediately on the TV, a function they have always been used to. Old-fashioned analogue TV did not require a set-top box with a start-up time or the loading of information that is necessary today to display program guides, and so on.

Three areas for improvement were identified. The first was technical. Equipment manufacturers and operators were engaged in research and development programs aimed at creating more efficient standby modes (with faster box wake-up) and more intelligent standby modes (incorporating a range of possible standby modes). The second was regulatory. The European Commission had proposed that players in the sector drew up "voluntary regulations", a "code of conduct", which would subsequently define obligations concerning box consumption in operation and standby, with a "true" standby at 1W. Not all players were playing the same game. While some argued for a soft form of regulation, we pushed for more stringent rules. As a matter of fact, we were resolutely committed to drastically reducing the standby power consumption of set-top boxes and providing advanced functions to minimize the inconvenience for both operators and end-users. The third area requiring attention was a consideration of the acceptability of such measures for both operators and their customers. The risk was that, if the constraint was perceived as too strong, set-top boxes would be delivered with an energy-saving standby mode by default, and this mode would be deactivated by users at first installation.

This was the beginning of the reflection on a form of "sufficiency" that did not yet dare to speak its name. A number of pertinent questions emerged: Did customers really need their set-top box to wake up instantly? How long were they prepared to wait? What risk, in terms of customer satisfaction, was the operator prepared to accept on this point? How could we explain to customers the environmental and economic benefits of using a deep sleep mode? Avenues were being explored around nudge, for example, or nurturing the feeling of participating in a collective action that makes a significant impact on a large scale. For example, by communicating an aggregate figure to users who would set their set-top box to an energy-saving mode, informing them of the level of savings achieved by all users who would have made the same gesture. The user might then have been likely to accept a slower restart and find value in this option offered by the operator.

2.3 Intermediate stage: PSS and circular economy

The eco-design track and the exploration of different paths to reduce the environmental impact of products and services led us to take a closer look at the possibilities offered by Product Service Systems (PSS). Service operators, for their part, are already a step ahead on this subject: the boxes used to access the Internet and digital television services are in fact leased to end customers. The operator retains ownership of these boxes and therefore retains an interest in optimizing product design and the entire supply chain (including the reverse logistics process) to ensure that they last as long as possible. This means, for example, designing products that can be repaired, upgraded and easily refurbished. Indeed, when a customer changes their equipment, it is systematically "refurbished" for deployment with another customer. As products must always be as good as new, this means, for example, providing a shell and front panel that can easily be replaced if scratched or manufacturing them from a more resistant material to prevent this problem from occurring.

This logic enables a shift into another area, that of the circular economy. As the operator has a "deposit" of material when they recover end-of-life products, it seems possible to work on reducing the impact of the end-of-life phase and to re-inject as much material as possible into the manufacture of new products. However, since the operator is not the manufacturer, it is not easy to close this loop.

In 2012, as part of a restructuring of my company, the eco-design function I had held in the marketing and sales department disappeared from the organizational chart, which prompted me to pursue this work outside the organization, as I shall explain in the following section.

3. Eco-design: an essential step but one that must be surpassed

Looking back on this experience, which lasted from 2008 to 2012, I asked myself several questions. The first related to the rebound effect, a concept which I was not aware of at the time. When measuring the results obtained, not only do our past efforts now seem derisory in relation to the issues of the time, and even more so in relation to today's challenges, but it also seems that we sometimes missed our target. Should we therefore admit failure, and make amends for having felt that we were among the forerunners in our field? Have our attempts to reach sustainability through efficiency masked the need for sufficiency? Or can we find reasons for satisfaction in the work we have accomplished? What lessons can we draw from these experiences? In an attempt to answer these questions, I interviewed a few former colleagues from my company, as well as from the operator with whom we carried out joint work. A few verbatims reflect the testimonies of two of them, E*, who was one of the pioneers on these subjects in his company and continues to push these questions on a daily basis, and P*, who joined more recently. This reflective work is also an opportunity to evoke the emotions felt along the way.

3.1 The rebound effect: a statement of failure?

While we initially noted the limits of eco-design, which only provides marginal improvements, we progressively realized that our actions may have adverse consequences: as they become more efficient, our products enable new services to be offered to consumers which leads to an increase in consumption. As a result, the environmental impacts of our activity increase instead of being lessened. Without knowing it, we contributed to the rebound effect theorized by Jevons (1865) and blatantly observed in the IT sector (Gossart 2014; Santarius et al. 2022).

Our work on the energy efficiency of set-top boxes is a good illustration of this phenomenon. We worked hard on both the equipment manufacturer and the operator side to develop intelligent set-top box standby modes to reduce energy consumption without inconveniencing the user. However, the results did not always live up to expectations. Reflecting on the irony of the situation, E* explains:

> We had wake-up times. The dilemma was that we needed 45 seconds to wake up from standby mode. The customer couldn't stand waiting 45 seconds before accessing the TV. He'd leave his box ON. We fought to reduce the standby time. [...] I remember a guy in the technical department saying to me: E*, do not worry, for the next generation, we are going to upgrade to two Gigas of RAM, so your problem will be solved. [...] Instead of going from 45 seconds to 20, we went from 45 seconds to 1 minute 30. In fact, we had more memory, so we made a nice portal, adding complexity. On the one hand, the guys added RAM, and some of them thought: let's load it up to make a nice portal. That's the way it is. In fact, we are getting a little better. You play a bit with technique here and there. (E*)

However, these efforts were not completely useless. For example, this point has improved over time:

> Now it is quite a bit of time to get out of standby on small boxes, because they've improved the architecture. That means we need a new generation of boxes, so we will need more time. (E*)

While this example may seem anecdotal, we are well aware of the wider problem to which it gives rise. Is this a failure or an incomplete success? We cannot really answer that question, but we have learned a few lessons from these experiences.

3.2 Lessons learned: eco-design - a potential blind alley but a necessary stage

Do not bury your head in the sand. The road to hell is paved with good intentions. Eco-design, PSS and circular economy were all started with the objective of reducing environmental impacts in order to make products and services more sustainable. The observation of rebound effects shows that, while improvement is possible on a unitary basis, the objective is often not achieved overall. And yet, the eco-design approach has been put in place precisely to ensure, by scrupulous measurement of impacts on numerous criteria (water, air and soil pollution, resource consumption, etc.) throughout the product lifecycle (from the extraction of raw materials to the end of life) that there is no uncontrolled transfer of impact from one criterion to another or from one phase of the lifecycle to another. In other words, we make sure that we do not contribute to further degradation while thinking we are doing the right thing. The Achilles heel of eco-design, however, is consumption, a variable over which product or service designers have little or no control. An eco-designed product whose impact is halved and consumption multiplied by four does not solve the problem. It would be tempting to give in to discouragement. On the contrary, it seems preferable to pursue these efforts, which are necessary, while being realistic about the limits of these approaches. To do this, we need to take a systemic approach. We need to look not just at the impact of our own activity but also at the wider impact of the ecosystem in which we operate. For example, we might ask what new uses are facilitated by increased network performance. But we also need to take a broader time perspective. Some rebound effects are only visible in the medium or long term. This means we need to remain vigilant over the long term. We must also be vigilant as to the risk of moral licensing (cf. Blanken et al. 2015) in our professional activity. By giving us a clear conscience, eco-design allows us to continue business as usual. We have the feeling that we are doing things right, or the best we can, and do not feel a need for a more profound questioning of the way we do business.

Do not throw the baby out with the bathwater. It would be all too easy to say that eco-design does not solve any environmental problems. While it could well be used as part of a greenwashing strategy, we believe that it is also the starting point to think about a firm's environmental impact and explore avenues for its reduction. We have experienced rebound effects. A growing body of literature has described it in detail. However, we should not give in to "eco-design bashing", which some promoters of alternative models (such as low-tech, frugal innovation or sufficiency, which we also support) might be tempted to instil in people's minds. Instead, we should continue our efforts, offer massive training (not necessarily to train experts but at least to understand the ins and outs of this approach) and also inform about the limits.

P* provides a particularly useful reminder when, discouraged by this unfortunate rebound, we could be tempted to give up on methods, which are not sufficient but are still very much needed:

> "If you do eco-design, it is better than not doing it at all. On the other hand, you really shouldn't think that it is a big factor in changing the model. All we know is that it is essential. It is kind of the basic thing to do." (P*)

This is also something to bear in mind with late adopters of the method. The proverbial "better late than never" applies here. Even if we are further along the learning curve, we should inform newcomers of the pitfalls but not set out to daunt them.

3.3 Dealing with emotions in order to move forward

If doubt is the driving force behind our research, both in industry and academia, it is also the dominant feeling we have experienced, more or less painfully, over the years. If the implementation of eco-design helped me to restore a sense of direction in an industry that had lost its bearings, this moment of enlightenment was short-lived. I realized how difficult it was to give real scope to the efforts undertaken. Today, given the insignificant nature of the progress made, I cannot help questioning the legitimacy of our actions.

Are our efforts really worthwhile, or are they just a way of "saving our jobs"? How sincere are we when we think we can (must) change things from within?

The feeling that things are not going fast enough dominates. I often tend to see the glass as half empty. Progress is being made, but rebound effects limit its scope. We are looking for more radical solutions, we are hoping to find a solution to the "impossible decoupling" of growth and resource consumption, and we have the impression that there are far more problems than solutions in this area. We have the feeling that we are perpetually lagging behind the issues at stake, particularly in the current period of accelerating disasters linked to climate change, which are making the latter more visible. At the same time, we regularly observe that many players are still far removed from these concerns. For some, awareness is still in its infancy, while for others, there is considerable perplexity as to how to tackle the problem, and how to identify courses of action to get started. So, finally, are we too early or too late? How can we share our progress and setbacks without sounding judgmental or pessimistic?

We are well aware of the limits of our efforts. So, when I ask E* if everything we have done in the last 15 years has been for nothing, and if it would be worse if we had done nothing, the answer is yes, but mixed:

> Yes, I think it would be worse. But the trends are still there. I do not regret what I've done. I am really happy with what I am doing. But you realize that in the end, it is a drop in the ocean. And I think we have even been... We have been a lever for growth. And yet, we have contributed to... [...] I haven't thrown in the towel. But there are not many signs. (E*)

A circular economy expert, who has recently started work on these issues, acknowledges that it is difficult for those who have been exploring these subjects for years to remain optimistic.

> I think it takes a lot of resilience. When you've been working on a subject for a long time and you've been pushing it for a long time, but you haven't managed to motivate many people, [the risk is] to say, 'But there are too many things to do, there are too many problems to solve.' I think it takes a lot, a lot, a lot of resilience. (P*)

The challenge is huge, and we need to speed things up, but we have also got to hang in there.

> "There are always people who are not convinced, but more and more people see that there are problems, think it is important, want to change things. There's a solid basis for change. After that, I would like things to move a lot faster." (P*)

Things are changing. Even if those who have been involved for a long time are going through moments of doubt, newcomers, like P*, are instilling new hope:

> "I feel I've come at the right time, a time that's relatively easy for me, easier than it was for you, I think, 15 years ago. In that sense, I have the impression that [the company] is moving in the right direction." (P*)

This is too little, too slow, but change is in progress:

> I've been working on it with the team for six months now. Are we moving fast enough? No. Do people notice? No, and I wasn't necessarily aware of it before. What we need to do from an environmental point of view in a company like [ours] to try and align ourselves with the objectives we want to achieve over time, is to acquire more knowledge, so the more we train people, the more they'll realize that we are not moving fast enough. (P*)

4. The path towards sufficiency

4.1 From business practice to academia

In 2012, the project to promote eco-design within the Marketing & Sales department of my company was put on hold. This marked a turning point in my career, as well seeing a shift in research interests towards exploring new avenues to reduce the environmental impact of products and services. The eco-design track had already led me to study PSS alternatives. I decided to pursue research in this domain by leaving the industry for the academic world and embarking on a doctoral thesis on collaborative consumption. As a matter of fact, this phenomenon appeared an interesting way to look at PSS from a consumer perspective. The partnerships forged with a number of industry players, either through commercial relationships or independent working groups while I was in the industry, continued, notably with the operator with whom I had worked on various eco-design and energy efficiency issues. This enabled me to develop numerous teaching and research partnerships, both during my PhD (from 2013 to 2017) and in my subsequent position as associate professor in Management Science at the university (starting in 2018).

4.2 Research projects at a crossroads

Discussions between the university and industry players started mainly through educational projects including lectures on eco-design based on feedback from experience. In 2018, the combined awareness of the deceptive nature of collaborative consumption studied during my PhD – a "revolution" touted by its promoters as a solution to the environmental, social and economic problems posed by traditional models, which in fact turned out to be a way of reinforcing them and maintaining consumption levels – and of the disappointments of my experience of eco-design in the industry led me to turn to the study of sufficiency. Faced with various forms of rebound effects in both fields, sufficiency appeared as an unavoidable path. In a rather disruptive way, some of my colleagues in the industry had already started the debate in their company. In 2019, we participated in the organization of a research day on the theme of digital sufficiency in which we jointly presented a paper around the following questions: How can value creation and sufficiency be reconciled in a telecoms sector that is culturally very far removed from such considerations? And how can marketing contribute to this? As a matter of fact, sufficiency seems to be a particularly difficult path to follow in the ICT sector, where belief in technological progress as a solution to environmental problems seems hard to shake, and where the very essence of technological progress seems unstoppable (Dabadie/Vautier/Bertin 2021). Furthermore, in the particular case of telecom operators, while it is possible with a modicum of R&D effort to increase the energy efficiency of their infrastructure, it is more difficult to limit the amount of traffic going through their network – and as a result the total energy consumption of their activity. As a matter of fact, telecom operators have little or no control of the services developed and promoted by content providers which take advantage of increased capacity of networks (e.g., larger bandwidth, decreased latency, etc.) to encourage unbridled consumption of services like video streaming or online gaming. If they sought to encourage a more responsible use of networks, this would result in a decrease in their average revenue per user (ARPU) and a subsequent decrease in company profitability, which might in turn not be acceptable for shareholders. In a highly competitive market, pursuing such a strategy is no small feat.

From 2018 onwards, several types of projects were launched. On the teaching side, student projects in partnership with a telecom operator were initiated to study various issues. For instance, students analyzed consumer perceptions of a new sufficient telecom service devised by the operator, and its implications in terms of advertising. On the research side, several collaborative projects followed, notably within a larger collective, EcoSD,[11] an association composed of academics and practitioners founded in 2012, to promote design for sustainability. In 2020, I participated in a project centered on frugal innovation. In 2021, work continued as part of a project in which we studied low-tech viability. The idea behind these projects was that eco-design alone is not sufficient in itself to really have an impact, that a change of model is necessary and that needs have to be questioned. In 2022, a three-year project supported by EcoSD was started specifically on this issue and that of the discrepancy between consumer needs, market offers and the effective use of products and services. Looking at this question from different angles within a multidisciplinary team (a mix of practitioners and academics in engineering and social sciences), the first results allowed us to measure intended and unintended deviations. The next steps will consist of identifying ways to improve design for sustainability methods in order to limit the rebound effects that these deviations generate.

While they bring useful insights, these projects also bring questions, which remain unanswered. Among them, we wonder whether initiatives such as frugal innovation or low-tech are compatible with large corporations. We also question the role of marketing and its ability to contribute to a change in the value creation model, a topic also currently addressed in partnership between academia and practitioners as part of ongoing doctoral dissertations and research contracts on sufficiency marketing and business models.

---

1 www.ecosd.fr

5. Conclusion

As I write this chapter, along with a growing community of researchers and practitioners, I am continuing my work to better understand how sufficiency can be put into practice, based on the assumption that it is necessary to curb environmental impacts. Many questions remain open as to how to implement it and how to avoid encountering rebound effects yet again. Mixed feelings of doubt and hope still prevail. Are we too optimistic when we attempt to change the model from inside? Mixed feelings of satisfaction and skepticism also arise when the issue of sufficiency suddenly became a national concern in France in September 2022, thanks to the acute energy and ecological crisis that France is experiencing as a result of geopolitical events (for instance, war in Ukraine and threats to fossil fuel supplies) and climatic events (repeated disasters in the summer of 2022, including mega-fires in Southern France). The term sufficiency, hitherto seen as particularly incongruous when associated with marketing, and deemed unpronounceable within certain companies where disruptive discourses have opened up the debate, is suddenly becoming the focus of attention. While I am delighted about this, it is hard to suppress my doubts as regards this sudden turnaround. Are we really talking about the same thing? Who is really prepared to promote a reduction in consumption when, at the same time, the question of growth and purchasing power remains at the heart of public debate and company strategies?

Other questions beset me. Is sufficiency simply yet another blind alley? Are we going fast enough? Taking this retrospective angle on fifteen years of work leads me to make a few calculations and realize that 2030, the date set for many programs aimed at limiting the effects of climate change, is almost visible on the horizon. We will be there in less than seven years... What have we achieved in double that time? What can we hope to change in such a short space of time? Is the pace of academic research adapted to the urgency of the situation? Am I in the right place to change things?

This introspective work leads me to make a few very humble recommendations. Firstly, we should be very realistic and develop awareness with regard to the limits of our attempts to contribute to reducing the environmental impact on the production side. The rebound effects pointed out by Santarius (2016) are difficult to escape. But at the same time, we must not give in to discouragement and should instead help build momentum around these issues. Secondly, in order to make progress, it seems essential to continue to work hand in hand with practitioners who are faced with the difficulty of changing the way of doing business and are the driving force to make the necessary changes happen. Finally, we need to question our priorities in light of the urgency of the situation, which leads to another question: How can we accelerate this topic when we should simultaneously decelerate to limit the negative impacts of social acceleration both at personal and macro-ecological level, as highlighted by Hollstein/Rosa (2023)? This collective work provides an invaluable opportunity to collect and share thoughts on these pivotal issues and can hopefully act as a springboard for debate, reflection and further action.

References

Blanken, Irene/van de Ven, Niels/Zeelenberg, Marcel (2015): "A Meta-Analytic Review of Moral Licensing" In: Personality and Social Psychology Bulletin 41/4, pp. 540–558. https://doi.org/10.1177/0146167215572134.

Dabadie, Isabelle/Vautier, Marc/Bertin, Emmanuel (2021): "'Your 6G or Your Life': How Can Another G Be Sustainable?" In: Emmanuel Bertin/Noël Crespi/Thomas Magedanz (eds.), Shaping Future 6G Networks: Needs, Impacts and Technologies, Hoboken: John Wiley & Sons Ltd, pp. 55–67. https://doi.org/10.1002/9781119765554.ch5.

European Commission (2020): "Communication from the Commission to the European Parliament, the Council, the European Economic and Social Committee and the Committee of the Regions. Shaping Europe's digital future." Brussels, 19.2.2020, COM (2020) 67 final, 25.7.2023 (https://eur-lex.europa.eu/legal-content/en/TXT/?uri=CELEX%3A52020DC0067).

Ferreboeuf, Hugues/Efoui-Hess, Maxime/Verne, Xavier (2021): "Impact environnemental du numérique: Tendances à 5 ans et gouvernance de la 5G." 25.7.2023 (https://theshiftproject.org/article/impact-environnemental-du-numerique-5g-nouvelle-etude-du-shift/).

Gossart, Cédric (2014): "Rebound Effects and ICT: A Review of the Literature." In: Lorenz M. Hilty/Bernard Aebischer (eds.), ICT Innovations for Sustainability. Advances in Intelligent Systems and Computing, Cham: Springer, pp 435–448. https://doi.org/10.1007/978-3-319-09228-7_26.

Gossen, Maike/Kropfeld, Maren Ingrid (2022): ""Choose nature. Buy less." Exploring sufficiency-oriented marketing and consumption practices in the outdoor industry." In: Sustainable Production and Consumption 30, pp. 720–736. https://doi.org/10.1016/j.spc.2022.01.005.

Hollstein, Bettina/Rosa, Hartmut (2023): "Social Acceleration: A Challenge for Companies? Insights for Business Ethics from Resonance Theory." In: Journal of Business Ethics 188, 709–723. https://doi.org/10.1007/s10551-023-05506-w.

Jardim, Elizabeth (2017): "From Smart to Senseless: The Global Impact of Ten Years of Smartphones." 8.12.2023 (https://www.greenpeace.org/usa/research/from-smart-to-senseless-the-global-impact-of-ten-years-of-smartphones/).

Jevons, William Stanley (1865): The Coal Question; an Inquiry Concerning the Progress of the Nation, and the Probable Exhaustion of Our Coal-Mines, London, New York: The Macmillan Company.

Niessen, Laura/Bocken, Nancy M. P. (2021): "How Can Businesses Drive Sufficiency? The Business for Sufficiency Framework." In: Sustainable Production and Consumption 28, pp. 1090–1103. https://doi.org/10.1016/j.spc.2021.07.030.

Santarius, Tilman (2016): "Investigating Meso-Economic Rebound Effects: Production-Side Effects and Feedback Loops between the Micro and Macro Level." In: Journal of Cleaner Production, Special Volume: Transitions to Sustainable Consumption and Production in Cities 134/A, pp. 406–413. https://doi.org/10.1016/j.jclepro.2015.09.055.

Santarius, Tilman/Bieser, Jan C. T./Frick, Vivian/Höjer, Mattias/Gossen, Maike/Hilty, Lorenz M./Kern, Eva/Pohl, Johanna/Rohde, Friederike/Lange, Steffen (2022): "Digital Sufficiency: Conceptual Considerations for ICTs on a Finite Planet." In: Annals of Telecommunications 78, pp. 277–295. https://doi.org/10.1007/s12243-022-00914-x.

Self-Restraint and Sufficiency of a Steel Processor
Countering the Corporate Rebound Effect

Jana Gebauer, Laura Niessen and Maike Gossen

Abstract *Based on an in-depth case study analysis, the chapter discusses whether and to what extent companies that limit their growth and resource use through sufficiency can avoid rebound effects at the firm level. It also identifies entry points for companies and policy makers on how efficiency measures can contribute to absolute resource reductions rather than accelerating growth.*

1. Introduction

The growth economies of the global North are failing to reduce their environmental impacts and consumption to the extent that would be ecologically necessary and globally equitable (Parrique et al. 2019). Technical efficiency and consistency measures are proposed to achieve the necessary reductions by dematerializing and ecologizing economic activity. However, as long as growth- and profit-driven exploitation interests determine the use of nature, the gains often flow back to other uses in so-called "rebound effects" (Herring/Sorrell 2009). Rebound effects in a micro-economic context (as opposed to on the scale of the national economy) can take different forms, including economic or psychological (Santarius/Soland 2018). For economic rebound effects, an increase in efficiency might lead to lower costs, thus the consumer might use the additional money for further consumption. For psychological rebound effects, the more efficient product might be perceived as less harmful to the environment and may be used more intensively. Consumers may also feel that they can act in a less environmentally responsible way. As a result, resource consumption may ultimately increase.

How can this be understood at the firm level? The problem of rebound effects has been primarily located in household consumption (Greening et al. 2000; Sorrell 2007; Santarius 2015). Research analyzing production-side rebounds, their manifestations and causal relationships has been limited (Figge et al. 2014). However, the literature suggests that companies are far from realizing their full efficiency potential: They do not identify or implement possible measures – the so-called "efficiency gap" (Solnørdal/Foss 2018). Alternatively, when efficiency measures are implemented, they often do not have the desired effect: the environmental impact is instead shifted to upstream or downstream stages of the value chain (burden shifting); producing the equipment for the efficiency measures is itself resource-intensive (embodied energy); and the planning and implementation of the measures are flawed (Schöpflin/Lautermann submitted). Wüst et al. (2023) developed a typology for rebound effects in firms based on the existing literature (e.g. Jenkins et al. 2011; Santarius 2015; 2016):

- Output effects, which result from increasing production and sales to penetrate and develop markets;
- Factor substitution effects, which result from the replacement of production processes and the associated increase in the use of energy services;
- Re-utilization effects resulting from performance-enhancing changes in production processes and production organization;
- Re-design effects resulting from performance-enhancing changes in product design;
- Re-spending effects resulting from the use of saved additional financial resources for regular current expenditures;
- Reinvestment effects resulting from the use of accumulated financial savings for product development, product differentiation or diversification;
- "Frontier" effects resulting from the development of entirely new products and services.

These rebound effects can occur due to (i) strategic priorities, (ii) cognitive and institutional factors and (iii) psychological factors.

Firstly, in terms of strategic priorities, environmental resource savings are often not the focus of efficiency measures but rather a means to other ends. Efficiency gains are then partly or fully diverted to these other uses (Schöpflin/Lautermann submitted). In doing so, companies often follow norms and routines of competition and growth, especially if they perceive high productivity and cost pressures in their industries (Wüst et al. 2023). Ecological problems, on the other hand, are seen as subordinate or even conflictual. This gives rise to a strategic rationale for companies to invest efficiency gains in the expansion and differentiation of production, in automation, performance enhancement or process quality improvements (Gebauer 2022).

Secondly, rebound effects also arise from deficits in knowledge and information management (Wüst et al. 2023). Rebound risks cannot be identified and countered if information is lacking on consumption data, life cycle costs or the extent of material and financial gains from an efficiency measure. Environmental management and financial controlling tools to provide this information are rarely implemented and used with the required level of detail (Lautermann/Schöpflin 2021).

Thirdly, similarly to psychological rebound amongst consumers, rebound effects also occur in companies as a result of psychological reassessment and relief (Wüst et al. 2023). With an efficiency measure, the technology, process or overall behavior in the company may be considered less harmful to the environment. This may lead employees and customers to use the technology more intensively or to question their own responsibility for energy- and material-saving behavior. If they change their behavior as a result, resource consumption could ultimately increase.

The rebound effect caused by strategic priorities, in particular, is seldom given a critical reflection. On the contrary, (intended) growth made possible by increased efficiency is seen as a success and not as a negative impact of the measure (Behrendt et al. 2018). This framing neglects the environmental impacts of expanding production and sales and is a barrier to closing the gap between required absolute resource reductions and the delivered relative solutions. Rebound effects characterize (business decisions in) growth economies and systematically prevent decoupling of economic growth from environmental pollution and consumption, a prerequisite for green growth (Parrique et al. 2019; Hickel/Kallis 2019).

With few exceptions, there is little data on the micro-economic rebound effect of energy efficiency programs in a single company. Konash and Nasr's (2022) calculations of the rebound effect in a single firm suggest that energy efficiency programs have limited ability to realize their full energy savings potential and reduce energy use over time. It is therefore considered crucial to look beyond efficiency measures and selectively reduce production and consumption levels through sufficiency, a concept of absolute "enough" that aims to prevent rebound effects (Schneider et al. 2010; Herring/Sorrell 2009; Best et al. 2022) and that complements the weaknesses of efficiency approaches (Dyllick/Hockerts 2002).

In this chapter, we discuss whether companies that limit their growth and resource consumption through sufficiency can avoid rebound effects at the company level: To what extent can a sufficiency-orientation in a firm avoid micro-level rebound effects? To answer this question, we discuss the case of Richard Henkel GmbH, a small manufacturing firm that combines a strong efficiency orientation with self-restraint and sufficiency in the setting of a resource-intensive and competitive sector. We use three efficiency measures to show how it deals with efficiency gains and associated rebound effects. The example shows the potential for absolute savings when environmental benefits are prioritized and growth is subordinated. However, it also shows the limits of micro-level agency and effectiveness within the growth economy. In the conclusion, we draw lessons and recommendations for companies, multipliers and policy makers.

2. Rebound prevention through corporate self-restraint and sufficiency?

Generally speaking, sufficiency, as a "principle of self-restraint" ("Prinzip der Selbstbeschränkung", Sachs 2015: 2), means reducing resource and energy demand and finding a measure of "enough" that ensures what is needed. It thus aims to avoid both over-consumption and under-provision (Fuchs et al. 2021). To achieve this, sufficiency relies on an institutional change (Kropfeld/Reichel 2021) and a fundamental change in values and behavior. Other strategies, such as efficiency and consistency require this only to a limited extent, so that only a sufficiency shift can break with the paradigm of exploitation and growth still inherent in the other two (Martínez-Alier et al. 2010). Sufficiency is therefore often seen as the least relatable, represented and implemented of the three sustainability strategies: it appears fundamentally at odds with consumer, political and corporate interests. It is also still less present in policy debates (Zell-Ziegler et al. 2021), even though it is gaining visibility (e.g., the 2022 French Energy sobriety plan). Sufficiency is also increasingly discussed in research (Sandberg 2021) and has been presented as a business strategy to promote and enable sustainable consumption (Niessen/Bocken 2021).

Sufficiency at the business level is understood as companies not only promoting sufficiency-oriented lifestyles but also reducing or limiting their own resource consumption and production volumes (Jungell-Michelsson/Heikkurinen 2022). While most current research investigates the role of businesses in promoting sufficiency (Bocken/Short 2016; Niessen/Bocken 2021), mainly by marketing means (Gossen et al. 2019b; Gossen/Kropfeld 2022; Kelleci/Yildiz 2021), research on sufficiency in production is still rare. Instead of striving for growth, firms can strive to maintain their productive capacity and become non-growing firms (Liesen et al. 2015). Beyeler and Jaeger-Erben (2022) look into the practices of businesses that are willing to operate at smaller organizational scales and pursue sufficiency. Bärnthaler and Gough (2023) conceptualize production corridors, which meet essential needs without excess production. Degrowth advocates even call for a renunciation of sales, profit maximization and market power (Deimling 2016; Khmara/Kronenberg 2018; Nesterova 2020). The importance here is not on limits and savings per se but rather on a new perception of values and well-being, human needs and natural resources, and the pursuit of qualitative change. A redefinition of business values would be moving from the primacy of profit to the primacy of purpose (Mayer 2020). Moreover, degrowth-oriented companies emphasize their attitude, ability and willingness to reflect and to learn to change (Froese et al. 2023). They develop and reinforce a qualitative understanding of success with ideas about an appropriate size (usually a corridor) and growth rate. In order to achieve and maintain their appropriate size, the entrepreneurs examine their decisions in terms of the growth effects they generate (Gebauer 2018). A deliberate decision to forgo growth is not necessarily aimed at improving environmental performance (Liesen et al. 2015). However, when land and building space, machine capacity, suppliers, investment, customers, sales, distribution channels, transport routes, etc. are constrained, limits for environmental impacts and consumption emerge 'naturally' (Gebauer 2018). Entrepreneurs who explicitly justify their self-restraint with societal embeddedness evaluate decision options in terms of social and environmental costs. They may refrain from financially promising actions that would have a negative impact on others or invest in precautionary measures (Deimling 2017).

Therefore, an orientation towards sufficiency and self-restraint in a business could change the context of efficiency improvements. Savings from efficiency measures are not (automatically) invested in expanding capacity, performance, automation or output but rather in reinforcing impact through more eco-effective use of the savings (Gebauer 2022). Sufficiency-oriented business might therefore be better able to avoid rebound effects of efficiency measures, by reinvesting savings in impact instead. To support these thoughts empirically, we turn to the case study.

3. Case Study: Richard Henkel GmbH

The case study was part of the German research project "Holistic Management of Energy and Resource Efficiency in Companies".[1] The project investigated rebound effects in companies both conceptually and empirically. In addition to a baseline survey of medium-sized to large companies and company workshops, practical insights were gained through in-depth case studies in ten companies from different sectors. Based on the findings, recommendations for action were developed for companies, multipliers and policy makers (Wolff et al. 2022; 2023).

While the case studies were comparative, this chapter focuses on Richard Henkel GmbH (referred to as Henkel in the following). From November 2019 to July 2021, the first author conducted three rounds of on-site and online interviews with Henkel, with a total of five interviews. In the first round, preliminary research and a site visit informed the selection and analysis of efficiency measures; in the second round, potentials and drivers for rebound and reinforcement effects were explored. In the third round, supplemented by written and telephone follow-ups with the business owners in 2022, the findings and recommendations for rebound management were

1 The project was funded by the German Federal Ministry of Education and Research (BMBF) as part of its programme "Research for Sustainability" (FONA). Project partners included Oeko Institut, Institute for Ecological Economy Research (IÖW), Leuphana University (Centre for Sustainability Management), Data Center Group (DCG) and the business association B.A.U.M. e.V.

discussed. Interviews were conducted in German and quotes were translated into English by the first author.

The interviews followed semi-structured questionnaires and were recorded and analyzed in accordance with the templates developed by the project. At Henkel, the interviewees were the two managing owners (MO 2019, MO 2020, MO 2021, MO 2022) and the heads of the two business units (HF 2021, HC 2021). Other sources included the company's Sustainability Reports (SR), EMAS Environmental Statements (ES) and existing research on the business (Deimling 2016; Gebauer et al. 2015). The descriptions are based on the interviews and sources provided by Henkel, unless stated otherwise.

3.1 The company

Henkel is a small owner-managed German steel and metal processing company, established in 1922. Its first business unit manufactures and sells tubular steel furniture such as chairs, stools, tables and medical furniture to consumers and commercial customers, such as care homes for the elderly, clinics and wellness facilities. Its second business unit offers surface treatment services to industrial customers in aviation, automotive, medical and climate-tech industries. Finishing metal surfaces by grinding, blasting and powder coating accounts for around two thirds of Henkel's sales. Henkel's main suppliers are regional or European companies in the steel and plastics industries, as well as manufacturers of powder coatings, washing chemicals and packaging. The company has constantly retained a workforce of around 50, down to 45 in recent years, mainly due to a shortage of skilled workers. The annual turnover is relatively stable between €2.5 and €3.5 million, the annual income is about €250,000 before investments.

Richard Henkel, the founder of the company, focused on aligning the company's services with customer needs for functional and durable products. This included reducing the use of resources and making production as environmentally friendly as possible. Transparency and environmental protection have been explicitly anchored in the company since the 1950s (Deimling 2016). Henkel has been validated according to the Eco-Management and Audit Scheme since 1998 and has been a signatory to the Charter of the Business Sustainability Initiative of the State of Baden-Württemberg since 2015. Henkel aims to achieve an overall positive record across all areas of life cycle management and has received several awards for its environmental commitment.

Over the past twenty years, a wide range of energy efficiency measures and a switch to renewable energy have more than halved the company's energy consumption and CO_2 emissions, both in absolute terms and relative to sales. In addition to electricity and heat, the company has drastically reduced its material consumption. It has introduced closed loops and recycling systems in all its processes, from rinsing baths to scrap metal and packaging. In its furniture unit, repair and refurbishment are increasingly replacing new production.

When Susanne Henkel took over the company lead in the 1990s, she sharpened the firm's environmental profile and not only set further limits on environmental impact and consumption but also on corporate growth itself (Deimling 2016; Gebauer et al. 2015). The latter was a particular response to the 2008/09 financial crisis and to the industry's strong market and price dynamics and dependencies. Susanne Henkel has since focused on what she calls 'inner growth', keeping capacities, employment and sales stable while constantly decreasing resource use and increasing circularity in all areas of the business. As such, and despite the fact that this is termed life-cycle management and efficiency within the company, Henkel could be seen as being guided by ideas of sufficiency or self-restraint: forgoing growth in favor of absolutely reducing environmental consumption.

3.2 Energy efficiency measures

Henkel's energy-intensive processes depend on the efficiency and stability of its production systems. Since 2005, three measures have been particularly relevant: the new insulation of the paint ovens, the renewal of the conveyor system and the replacement of the automatic powder booth. All were accompanied by substantial energy savings – reductions in actual or projected consumption increases – and represent Henkel's way of thinking: a consistent focus on savings and an unconventional search for solutions. The measures were necessary because of an actual or imminent deterioration in resource consumption data or because of an additional reduction opportunity in the course of replacement investments. All measures were implemented on the company's own initiative, explicitly going beyond the market standard.

Insulating the painting ovens (2005/2006)

Henkel constantly reviews data to determine saving opportunities: Where is the greatest consumption, unexpected deterioration or heavy wear and tear? Increased temperatures in the hall and frequent motor wear pointed to a problem in the walls of the ovens; thermal imaging cameras revealed the crumbling of the polystyrene insulation. As it could not be replaced, the oven manufacturer offered to demolish and rebuild the ovens or walls. To avoid this, Susanne Henkel used her network to find an insulation from the nuclear power plant sector and applied it to the outside of the ovens. This reduced heat radiation by almost 60 per cent, cut energy consumption by at least 30 per cent and extended the life of the motors. Lowering the temperature in the hall also improved working conditions for the employees. The €20,000 investment amortized in less than 1.5 years.

Improving the conveyor belt (2012)

The conveyor in the powder coating line needed to be replaced due to wear and tear. According to the company's internal guidelines, a new conveyor would have to use less energy. This was achieved through a redesign: products move through the system on supports to which they are attached. By using a high-strength but thinner material, the weight of the supports could be reduced, thereby reducing the energy required to move, heat and cool them. However, the conveyor manufacturer was reluctant to use the new material. Henkel decided to have the steel parts specially made and installed without the manufacturer. The extra cost of €4,000 was recouped in one year through savings in energy costs. The new conveyor, with lighter parts, uses 8 per cent less electricity and 12 per cent less process heat, which has also improved the working environment. The material will be used exclusively in both business units in the future.

Replacement of the automatic powder booth (2014/2015)

After 25 years, the powder booth needed to be replaced as spare parts were no longer available from the equipment manufacturer. Henkel realized that the current market standard would increase energy consumption by 60 per cent compared to the old booth due to increased automation. When the usual equipment manufacturers could not provide a solution, Henkel commissioned an SME to build a new powder booth that increased energy consumption by only 24 per cent. However, this smaller increase still worsened Henkel's energy-related productivity metric: the improvement is only relative to the projected deterioration. The investment cost was around €450,000 with an expected payback period of up to seven years.

(Rebound) effects of energy efficiency measures

All three efficiency measures resulted in significant reductions: either in actual or in anticipated increases of energy consumption and other parameters. However, lacking experience with the new solutions and data from the manufacturers, it was not possible to set specific targets beforehand – improvements were to be made "as far as possible" (MO 2019). It is therefore not possible to determine whether the reductions actually occurred to the extent expected or if the efficiency measures resulted in a rebound effect. However, rebound risks were clearly present: data from the environmental declarations show that the actual efficiency gains from the first two measures did not fully translate into corresponding and sustained reductions in total consumption. In its B2B coating business, Henkel has to process a fluctuating but increasing proportion of heavier parts. The interviewees pointed out that the increased need for process heat eats up the savings from the efficiency measures. This can be seen as an output effect that is triggered further down the value chain: the rebound effect results from Henkel processing more product mass due to changes by industrial customers. In the case of the conveyor, for example, this means that although the supports are lighter and save energy compared to the old technology, the products transported are heavier and literally outweigh the improvements. Additionally, the use of high-strength steel in the conveyor means that it can handle heavier products. This could be described as a reutilization effect: with the efficiency measure, Henkel has also increased the performance, enabling changing customer requirements. Finally, the financial efficiency gains (such as reduced expenditure on electricity, process heat and motors) will feed into Henkel's investment budget. This could trigger a re-investment effect, where the accumulated savings finance medium- to long-term investments that in turn trigger resource consumption. In the case of the booth replacement, for example, the reinvestment of previous efficiency gains indirectly led to deteriorating consumption data, despite Henkel's efficiency targets.

4. Findings

In order to determine whether and which rebound effects occurred, we will interpret Henkel's practice against the background of the rebound drivers presented at the beginning.

4.1 Managing rebound risks

As outlined in the introduction, rebound risks increase due to strategic priorities, cognitive and institutional factors, as well as psychological factors. In this context, how can Henkel's approach to efficiency gains be qualified? And how does a sufficiency orientation influence potential rebound?

Strategic priorities

Henkel has a *non-growth, eco-oriented corporate strategy and culture*, prioritizing savings in resource consumption and costs over growth, as described by interviewees and in several reports. A broad concept of "enough" is pursued, and working hours, machinery and production facilities are reduced rather than expanded. With sales stable, profits increase through reduced resource costs and process optimization and are reinvested in the company and its employees while the employer's remuneration is kept stable: "These are also limits to growth: What is contentment? [...] [Y]ou can say: That's enough. I would rather go for a walk with my children" (MO 2021).

Improving efficiency does *not aim at expanding production*. Instead, it aims to minimize the use of resources, reduce negative impacts and control costs. Innovative solutions and their effects in terms of efficiency gains are replicated and reinvested throughout the company to reinforce their positive impact. Interviewees confirmed that efficiency measures do not lead to more growth but rather that "each action has made [them] aware of even more to-dos" (MO 2020).

For the same reason, the *variety of materials and products is reduced* rather than increased, e.g., by standardizing processing through standardized steel grades and higher quality materials, which can support longevity of the products. Standardization and process optimization also make it possible to reduce the number of machines and the size of production halls whose sites are then converted into green areas.

Machines and equipment are used, updated, maintained and repaired for as long as possible. For Henkel, becoming more efficient does not necessarily mean switching to modern machinery – quite the opposite. Henkel uses some machines that are many decades old, and the interviewees stated that they prefer the older ones as they are "much more efficient than the new machines [...], they are more stable, maintenance is very easy" (HF 2021).

Annual action plans set *priorities for (replacement) investments*. These are financed through accumulated efficiency gains and follow clear guidelines: they should deliver further resource savings or otherwise enable social and environmental improvements. Solutions are preferably low-tech and low-energy and are often adapted from other applications. For example, spaghetti strainers are used for rainwater filtration, milk filters replace large filter systems in the production water cycle, and the cooling of the production halls is modelled on the ventilation principle of termite mounds. Manual labor is constantly improved but explicitly preserved.

In addition, *potential co-benefits* are identified and incorporated into the planning process to find the measure that will deliver the greatest efficiency gains with the least risk of rebound. For example, a planned modification of the supply air system was combined with heat recovery for the high-power coating systems and an improved transport process for faster cooling of parts, resulting in less extra cooling. Additionally, it presented an improvement for the workplace as parts were less hot when handled by employees.

The furniture unit became *less manufacturing-oriented and more service-oriented:* Henkel's aim is to provide high-quality, durable furniture that could withstand intensive use and adapt to changing physical needs. To support their longevity, products can be refurbished, and components are standardized and replaceable. Commercial and private customers are strongly encouraged to refurbish rather than buy new.

Henkel does not use the term "sufficiency". However, all three principles of "less, better and enough" guide its life cycle management and are strongly reflected in the strategic prioritization within the company, influencing and potentially reducing rebound effects in various sufficiency-related ways.

Cognitive and institutional factors: knowledge, tools, structures

As Henkel's resource consumption data shows, focusing on absolute reductions and non-growth is not only crucial to limit, reduce and avoid possible rebound effects but also reinforces the positive effects of efficiency measures by focusing attention on the necessary knowledge base and structures for learning. Continuous data collection is necessary to reduce or avoid possible rebounds. Henkel attaches great importance to creating this information base. As part of its *energy and material flow management system,* consumption data for products, machines, systems and processes are collected and aggregated on a regular basis.

Major energy consumers are prioritized as a basis for decisions on replacement or investment measures. *Measures are planned in detail* and their success is *closely monitored.* In addition, *employees are systematically involved* in measuring and recording and are strongly encouraged to develop solutions: "It comes from the 'smallest' employee: if there is an idea, it is addressed and [...] that's how everything is initiated and that's how solutions are sought" (HF 2021).

All *employees are also trained* on quality and energy management to raise awareness, "so that if an employee walks past a compressed air leak and hears it, they will report it" (MO 2021). This awareness could also be used by employees in their own homes and other surroundings to improve efficiency and energy management.

Learnings are transferred directly and systematically to other use cases. Improvements are automatically checked for their relevance in other areas, "and then they are always transferred in full" (HF 2021). This may involve a new approach to identifying a problem, a better material, a more convivial technology or more like-minded business partners.

Collaboration with research institutions is used to fill knowledge gaps and develop missing tools and assessment methods. Such collaboration includes an "active exchange with scientists on the topics of resources [and] climate change: what is necessary, what [is] to do?" (SR 2018) through research projects and lectures.

Consolidation and institutionalization take place through procurement specifications, such as purchasing criteria and routines, as well as contractually regulated individual responsibility for environmental performance. In procurement, product data sheets are required and, e.g., life cycle consumption data is strongly requested while employees' contracts include environmental guidelines.

Knowledge sharing and an institutional orientation towards absolute reductions and non-growth can therefore help to reduce potential rebound risks.

Psychological factors: moral justification, perceived self-efficacy and diffusion of accountability

Not only the tools and structures but also the culture of the company is geared towards making everyone co-responsible. The company's *non-growth eco-positioning is lived and communicated to employees,* reinforcing that every single action of every employee counts: "[...] [A]t Henkel it's normal, I tell you, it's already in your head that you're always thinking about efficiency and resources." (HC 2021)

Henkel is very active in disseminating its view of environmental and economic problems and the solutions it has developed. In its *reports and communication*, Henkel emphasizes the urgency of political, corporate and individual action in the face of the climate emergency, the loss of biodiversity or the depletion of resources. Internally, the "Effie Bird", an efficiency mascot, is a tongue-in-cheek but constant reminder in the workplace. Interviewees stated that "this [eco-thinking] is already a principle in the company [...] and that it's fun to implement it" (HC 2021). Behavioral changes during or after the measures, which could increase resource consumption, are not considered conceivable – which Susanne Henkel doubles down on: "That doesn't fit in with environmentally compliant behavior" (MO 2020).

Henkel's *management also communicates and appeals strongly to suppliers, customers and corporate networks* in order to strengthen their perception of self-efficacy, (personal) responsibility, moral obligation and economic rationality. This includes informing their customers about better materials or less environmentally damaging processes, such as foregoing chemical pre-treatment that can be replaced by other means.

Given Henkel's non-growth strategic priorities and practices, management systems and corporate culture, it can be argued that the lower than possible efficiency gains are neither an outcome nor a re-utilization or reinvestment effect at the company level. Rather, it supports the assumption that rebound risks lie upstream and downstream in the value chain. The accounts presented show that Henkel not only proactively seeks to avoid rebound effects but also to achieve reinforcement effects, i.e. to increase the impact of its efficiency measures.

4.2 Opportunities and limits of corporate action and impact

The focus on sufficiency and self-restraint means that material efficiency gains are not spent expansively and some rebound risks can be reduced. The company's long-term analysis of environmental data shows that resource consumption is decreasing in both absolute and relative terms, albeit with fluctuations. The financial data, however, show that the financial efficiency gains are also partly eaten up by *rising costs*, in particular due to developments in prices, for example for steel or electricity. This also lowers Henkel's rebound risks: with their raw materials becoming more expensive, monetary savings from efficiency cannot be used to buy more material. Thus, by saving resources in absolute terms, Henkel also "simply become[s] a little more resistant to price increases" (MO 2020), which leads to an even more conscious use of materials and energy. However, there are also limitations to how much the business can influence rebound and several external factors are at play.

In terms of resource savings and efficiency measures, internal efforts are partly counteracted by *deteriorating market standards* for replacement investments by equipment manufacturers or by market trends towards heavier products of B2B customers. In the furniture sector, the idea of high-quality, durable, modular and repairable products has been very successful with customers (B2B, B2C). Services that accompany and replace production account for an increasing share of sales. However, Henkel is too small to actually enforce major changes and performance requirements (or transparency requirements) on suppliers and manufacturers: "[I]t's out of our hands to influence people like that. But, unfortunately that's the way it is: The demand is the market, and [...] if only ten per cent of all customers want something, then it's not a priority for the manufacturers" (HF 2021).

The situation is similar with large B2B customers in the surface coating service. As *one supplier among many*, Henkel positions itself as a sustainable, carbon-neutral supplier but can only communicate its own positions and innovations to a limited extent – as in the case of the thinner steel. Despite the many benefits of the material, which Henkel emphasizes, B2B customers are reluctant to make the necessary changes to their products, machines and processes, probably "until the cost pressure really increases dramatically for them" (MO 2020). In this context, both *machine manufacturers and large industrial customers focus on value propositions other than environmental improvements* and show less awareness of resource issues. The main reasons for this are expansionary market trends, distorted factor prices, wrong or missing financial incentives and a lack of awareness among customers and manufacturers alike of the running costs of resource use in machinery.

Also within the company itself, some factors make it difficult to identify and avoid rebound effects or to reinforce the positive effect of an efficiency improvement: even though the company attaches great importance to continuous data collection, this is not always specific and comparable enough to track rebounds. Furthermore, although employees strongly identify with Henkel's sustainability positioning, the commitment of the company depends heavily on the activities of its owner-managers, and it is a constant challenge to keep the "management issue" of resource conservation present as an "employee issue". Therefore, both external and internal factors beyond the sufficiency orientation influence to what extent efficiency measures can be implemented and rebound effects can be avoided.

5. Discussion and practical recommendations

Rebound effects in resource use often stem from an unquestioned and enforced economic growth orientation, as material and financial gains from efficiency measures are typically reinvested without reflection in growth steps at the firm level and in the economy as a whole (Wüst et al. 2023). The economic motivation and narrative with which increasing resource efficiency is usually pursued creates a gap between the absolute need for and the path to a solution. To narrow this gap, sufficiency is increasingly linked to corporate action and discussed in terms of sufficiency-oriented and self-restraining business practices by companies (Niessen/Bocken 2021; Jungell-Michelsson/Heikkurinen 2022). However, single-company case studies on this topic reveal that there is a lack of clear sufficiency orientation at the organizational level to prevent the rebound effect (Robra et al. 2020). This draws attention to companies as consumers: Do they recognize the notion of "enough" for their resource-consuming activities and develop strategies of (selective) self-restraint to avoid further increases in negative environmental and social impacts? And to what extent can companies that limit their growth and resource consumption through sufficiency avoid rebound effects at the company level?

Companies such as Richard Henkel GmbH demonstrate the potential for avoiding rebound effects and strengthening efficiency measures by limiting corporate growth and promoting sufficiency. This case study underlines the importance of a different approach to efficiency improvement, one in which companies reflect on the environmental impacts of growth decisions and systematically place greater emphasis on resource conservation and the notion of enough with regard to both inputs and outputs. A strategic reprioritization toward sufficiency reduces the risk that efficiency gains will be automatically or intentionally re-spent directly. It helps to ensure that the cost savings from efficiency measures are used in an eco-effective manner. The fundamental strategic decision to view resource efficiency as a contribution to absolute reduction rather than as a growth accelerator can therefore be seen as a prerequisite for successful – low-rebound – resource management. This requires environmental awareness and recognition of environmental problems, so that conflicting goals are not resolved "by default" in favor of economic expectations. It also requires a stronger purpose orientation of entrepreneurial action, a reflection on the social costs of a corporate growth orientation (Mayer 2020) and sustained efforts and environmental values of the business owners (Nesterova 2021).

A rebound avoidance approach also requires that companies give high priority to knowledge building, monitoring and reporting in a way that systematically supports the identification of rebound effects. Key to this would be absolute and long-term consumption targets and data at the company, division and activity levels that go well beyond the usual relative and short-term perspective (Lautermann/Schöpflin 2021). This would provide evidence for monitoring efficiency measures and their effects and for identifying factors affecting data trends. However, management systems and tools in companies are often inadequate (ibid.). Henkel continuously monitors and records data trends with the overall goal of achieving "the greatest possible reduction" in resource consumption and environmental costs. While it has been difficult to calculate rebound effects due to the lack of data specificity, the management's knowledge of all operational processes, resource consumers and potential (cross) influencing factors can nevertheless enable sound planning and decision-making. Incorporating consumption data requirements into procurement criteria and routines to improve the database can raise resource awareness on all sides and ultimately free up capacity, especially in smaller companies, that would otherwise be tied up in lengthy data research. In addition, cross-departmental teams and dedicated resource scouts can raise awareness throughout the organization and generate valuable knowledge about efficiency potentials and losses, as well as about sufficiency measures.

In this context, employees should be involved in strategic decision-making processes (Beyeler/Jaeger-Erben 2022) and be assured that their own actions make a difference. Henkel is an example of how the employees' identification with the strategic positioning of the company and their participation in efficiency measures can keep awareness high so that individual co-responsibility does not diminish. On the contrary, motivation and opportunities to further reduce resource consumption and environmental impact tend to increase over time. However, there are limits to how much employees feel encouraged and empowered to save resources if policy, decision-making and communication remain a matter of management and company ownership.

Furthermore, companies should be aware of the potential rebound effects of their sufficiency-oriented measures. This effect, which has been demonstrated for individual households, offsets the expected energy and emissions savings from sufficiency measures (Sorrell et al. 2020) and limits their effectiveness. In the case of a firm, too, sufficiency can only be determined by looking at its overall behavior. In this sense, the business sufficiency perspective argues against both growth-oriented efficiency measures and isolated sufficiency-oriented value propositions that are primarily intended to contribute to company growth.

The Henkel case study emphasizes the constraints and external factors influencing corporate decisions: The absolute savings achieved by Henkel's reduction efforts are at risk because the company is dependent on market developments in equipment manufacturing and from industrial customers. While Henkel focuses not only on efficiency and consistency measures but also on sufficiency-driven self-restraint, the ecological parameters of the machines as well as the products of the industrial customers often deteriorate at the same time. Therefore, Henkel's measures to increase efficiency are often measures to avoid deterioration.

As Henkel's market power is too small to influence major manufacturers and customers, the company relies on a general change in awareness and values and a coherent policy framework. A substantial increase in a CO_2 tax, for example, could change the ratio of factor prices in favor of labor and make the excess use of resources more expensive (Zell-Ziegler et al. 2021). Currently, exemptions for large consumers from energy taxes and levies prevent action precisely where the relevance and potential for absolute reductions is greatest. In this context, energy labelling or other information requirements for machinery and equipment manufacturers would make it easier for small companies to obtain relevant information on consumption data and running costs.

In promoting sufficiency to address the (un)intended consequences of efficiency measures, business-related actors and institutions such as industry associations, standardization bodies, consultants, energy agencies, business networks and others play a crucial role. They can enable companies to identify, recognize and reduce rebound risks through training and education formats for various professional groups. Emphasis should be placed on absolute savings targets and on ensuring that achieved efficiency gains are not primarily translated into further consumption elsewhere, making sufficiency a holistic corporate responsibility. In this context, the (rising) running costs of inefficient machinery and their impact on the amortisation period of investments should also be addressed to highlight the economic rationale. Last but not least, multipliers can support the collection of information and the dissemination of solutions through information platforms, networking, exchange and consulting.

References

Bärnthaler, Richard/Gough, Ian (2023): "Provisioning for Sufficiency: Envisaging Production Corridors." In: Sustainability: Science, Practice and Policy 19/1, 2218690. https://doi.org/10.1080/15487733.2023.2218690.

Behrendt, Siegfried/Göll, Edgar/Korte, Friederike (2018): "Effizienz, Konsistenz, Suffizienz: Strategieanalytische Betrachtung für eine Green Economy," Institut für Zukunftsstudien und Technologiebewertung, 5.10.2023 (https://www.izt.de/media/2022/10/IZT_Text_1-2018_EKS.pdf).

Best, Benjamin/Christ, Michaela/Santarius, Tilman/Wiese, Frauke (2022): "Exploring Energy Sufficiency: New Challenges and Options in Times of Crisis." In: TATuP – Zeitschrift für Technikfolgenabschätzung in Theorie Und Praxis 31/2, pp. 11–17. https://nbn-resolving.org/urn:nbn:de:0168-ssoar-80332-3.

Beyeler, Laura/Jaeger-Erben, Melanie (2022): "How to Make More of Less: Characteristics of Sufficiency in Business Practices." In: Frontiers in Sustainability 3, 949710. https://doi.org/10.3389/frsus.2022.949710.

Bocken, Nancy/Short, Samuel W. (2016): "Towards a Sufficiency-Driven Business Model: Experiences and Opportunities." In: Environmental Innovation and Societal Transitions 18, pp. 41–61. https://doi.org/10.1016/j.eist.2015.07.010.

Deimling, Daniel (2017): Wertesystem, unternehmerische Verantwortung und Wachstumsneutralität. In: Irene López (eds.), Management-Reihe Corporate Social Responsibility. CSR und Wirtschaftspsychologie, Berlin, Heidelberg: Springer Gabler, pp. 31–46, https://doi.org/10.1007/978-3-662-52746-7_3.

Deimling, Daniel (2016): Sinnstrukturen und Muster nachhaltiger Unternehmen im Kontext der Wachstumskritik: eine Untersuchung unter Einsatz einer Systemaufstellung, Münster: LIT.

Dyllick, Thomas/Hockerts, Kai (2002): "Beyond the Business Case for Corporate Sustainability." In: Business Strategy and the Environment 11/2, pp. 130–141. https://doi.org/10.1002/bse.323.

Figge, Frank/Young, William/Barkemeyer, Ralf (2014): "Sufficiency or Efficiency to Achieve Lower Resource Consumption and Emissions? The Role of the Rebound Effect." In: Journal of Cleaner Production 69, pp. 216–224. https://doi.org/10.1016/j.jclepro.2014.01.031.

Froese, Tobias/Richter, Markus/Hofmann, Florian/Lüdeke-Freund, Florian (2023): "Degrowth-Oriented Organisational Value Creation: A Systematic Literature Review of Case Studies." In: Ecological Economics 207, 107765. https://doi.org/10.1016/j.ecolecon.2023.107765.

Fuchs, Doris/Sahakian, Marlyne/Gumbert, Tobias/Di Giulio, Antonietta/Maniates, Michael/Lorek, Sylvia/Graf, Antonia (2021): Consumption Corridors: Living a Good Life within Sustainable Limits, New York: Routledge, 1.12.2023 (https://www.taylorfrancis.com/books/9781000389432).

Gebauer, Jana (2022): "Unternehmensbezogene Rebound-Effekte: Rebound-Vermeidung durch unternehmerische Selbstbegrenzung und Suffizienz," 1.12.2023 (https://www.meru-projekt.de/fileadmin/meru-projekt/user_upload/publikationen/Gebauer_2022_Unternehmensbezogene_Rebound-Effekte.pdf).

Gebauer, Jana (2018): "Towards Growth-Independent and Post-Growth-Oriented Entrepreneurship in the SME Sector." In: Management Revue 29/3, pp. 230–256. https://www.jstor.org/stable/26627699.

Gebauer, Jana/Mewes, Heike/Dietsche, Christian (2015): "Wir Sind so Frei. Elf Unternehmen Lösen Sich Vom Wachstumspfad," Berlin: Institut für ökologische Wirtschaftsforschung, 1.12.2023 (https://www.ioew.de/fileadmin/user_upload/BILDER_und_Downloaddateien/Publikationen/2015/Wir_sind_so_frei_-_Elf_Postwachstumspioniere.pdf).

Gossen, Maike/Kropfeld, Maren Ingrid (2022): ""Choose nature. Buy less." Exploring sufficiency-oriented marketing and consumption practices in the outdoor industry." In: Sustainable Production and Consumption 30, pp. 720–736. https://doi.org/10.1016/j.spc.2022.01.005.

Gossen, Maike/Pentzien, Jonas/Peuckert, Jan (2019a): "What Use Is It Really for Sustainability? Potentials and Impacts of Peer-to-Peer Sharing in the Domains of Accommodation and Mobility." In: Sustainability Management Forum 27, pp. 125–138. What Use Is It Really for Sustainability? Potentials and Impacts of Peer-to-Peer Sharing in the Domains of Accommodation and Mobility.

Gossen, Maike/Ziesemer, Florence/Schrader, Ulf (2019b): "Why and How Commercial Marketing Should Promote Sufficient Consumption: A Systematic Literature Review." In: Journal of Macromarketing 39/3, pp. 252–269. https://doi.org/10.1177/0276146719866238.

Greening, Lorna/Greene, David L./Difiglio, Carmen (2000): "Energy efficiency and consumption – the rebound effect – a survey." In: Energy Policy 28/6-7, pp. 389–401. https://doi.org/10.1016/S0301-4215(00)00021-5.

Heikkurinen, Pasi/Young, William/Morgan, Elizabeth (2019): "Business for Sustainable Change: Extending Eco-Efficiency and Eco-Sufficiency Strategies to Consumers." In: Journal of Cleaner Production 218, pp. 656–664. https://doi.org/10.1016/j.jclepro.2019.02.053.

Herring, Horace/Sorrell, Steve (eds.) (2009): Energy Efficiency and Sustainable Consumption: The Rebound Effect. Basingstoke and New York: Palgrave Macmillan.

Hickel, Jason/Kallis, Giorgos (2019): "Is Green Growth Possible?" In: New Political Economy 25/4, pp. 1–18. https://doi.org/10.1080/13563467.2019.1598964.

Jenkins, Jesse/Nordhaus, Ted/Shellenberger, Michael (2011): "Energy Emergence: Rebound and Back-fire as Emergent Phenomena," Breakthrough Institute, 1.12.2023 (https://s3.us-east-2.amazonaws.com/uploads.thebreakthrough.org/legacy/blog/Energy_Emergence.pdf).

Jungell-Michelsson, Jessica/Heikkurinen, Pasi (2022): "Sufficiency: A systematic literature review." In: Ecological Economics 195, 107380. https://doi.org/10.1016/j.ecolecon.2022.107380.

Kelleci, Alpaslan/Yildiz, Oğuz (2021): "A Guiding Framework for Levels of Sustainability in Marketing." In: Sustainability 13/4, 1644. https://doi.org/10.3390/su13041644.

Khmara, Yaryna/Kronenberg, Jakub (2018): "Degrowth in Business: An Oxymoron or a Viable Business Model for Sustainability?" In: Journal of Cleaner Production 177, pp. 721–731. https://doi.org/10.1016/j.jclepro.2017.12.182.

Konash, Anastassija/Nasr, Nabil (2022): "The Circular Economy and Resource Use Reduction: A Case Study of Long-Term Resource Efficiency Measures in a Medium Manufacturing Company." In: Cleaner Production Letters 3, 100025. https://doi.org/10.1016/j.clpl.2022.100025.

Kropfeld, Maren Ingrid/Reichel, André (2021): "The Business Model of Enough: Value Creation for Sufficiency-Oriented Businesses." In: Annabeth Aagaard/Florian Lüdeke-Freund/Peter Wells (eds.), Business Models for Sustainability Transitions, Cham: Springer International Publishing, pp. 163–189. https://doi.org/10.1007/978-3-030-77580-3_6.

Lautermann, Christian/Schöpflin, Patrick (2021): "Unternehmensbezogene Rebound-Effekte: Welche Anhaltspunkte liefern Nachhaltigkeitsberichte?" 1.12.2023 (https://www.meru-projekt.de/fileadmin/meru-projekt/user_upload/publikationen/MERU_Diskussionspapier_Effizienz-Reporting_2021-10-04.pdf).

Liesen, Andrea/Dietsche, Christian/Gebauer, Jana (2015): "Successful Non-Growing Companies." In: Humanistic Management Network Research Paper 25/15, 18.4.2017 (http://dx.doi.org/10.2139/ssrn.2623920).

Martínez-Alier, Joan/Pascual, Unai/Vivien, Franck-Dominique/Zaccai, Edwin (2010): "Sustainable De-Growth: Mapping the Context, Criticisms and Future Prospects of an Emergent Paradigm." In: Ecological Economics 69/9, pp. 1741–1747. https://doi.org/10.1016/j.ecolecon.2010.04.017.

Mayer, Colin (2020): "The Future of the Corporation and the Economics of Purpose." In: Journal of Management Studies 58/3, pp. 887–901. https://doi.org/10.1111/joms.12660.

Nesterova, Iana (2020): "Degrowth Business Framework: Implications for Sustainable Development." In: Journal of Cleaner Production 262, 121382. https://doi.org/10.1016/j.jclepro.2020.121382.

Nesterova, Iana (2021): "Addressing the Obscurity of Change in Values in Degrowth Business." In: Journal of Cleaner Production 315, 128152. https://doi.org/10.1016/j.jclepro.2021.128152.

Niessen, Laura/Bocken, Nancy M. P. (2021): "How Can Businesses Drive Sufficiency? The Business for Sufficiency Framework." In: Sustainable Production and Consumption 28, pp. 1090–1103. https://doi.org/10.1016/j.spc.2021.07.030.

Parrique, Timothée/Barth, Jonathan/Briens, François/Kerschner, Christian/Kraus-Polk, Alejo/Kuokkanen, Anna/Spangenberg, Joachim H. (2019): "Decoupling Debunked – Evidence and Arguments against Green Growth as a Sole Strategy for Sustainability," Brussels: European Environmental Bureau, 9.7.2019 (https://eeb.org/wp-content/uploads/2019/07/Decoupling-Debunked.pdf).

Robra, Ben/Heikkurinen, Pasi/Nesterova, Iana (2020): "Commons-Based Peer Production for Degrowth? – The Case for Eco-Sufficiency in Economic Organisations." In: Sustainable Futures 2, 100035. https://doi.org/10.1016/j.sftr.2020.100035.

Sachs, Wolfgang (2015): "Suffizienz. Umrisse Einer Ökonomie Des Genug." In: Uwf UmweltWirtschaftsForum 23/1–2, pp. 3–9. https://doi.org/10.1007/s00550-015-0350-y.

Sandberg, Maria (2021): "Sufficiency Transitions: A Review of Consumption Changes for Environmental Sustainability." In: Journal of Cleaner Production 293, 126097. https://doi.org/10.1016/j.jclepro.2021.126097.

Santarius, Tilman (2015): Der Rebound-Effekt. Ökonomische, psychische und soziale Herausforderungen für die Entkopplung von Wirtschaftswachstum und Energieverbrauch, Marburg: Metropolis.

Santarius, Tilman (2016): "Investigating meso-economic rebound effects: production-side effects and feedback loops between the micro and macro level." In: Journal of Cleaner Production 134, pp. 406–413. https://doi.org/10.1016/j.jclepro.2015.09.055.

Santarius, Tilman/Soland, Martin (2018): "How Technological Efficiency Improvements Change Consumer Preferences: Towards a Psychological Theory of Rebound Effects." In: Ecological Economics 146, pp. 414–424. https://doi.org/10.1016/j.ecolecon.2017.12.009.

Schöpflin, Patrick/Lautermann, Christian (submitted): Resource efficiency management in companies: Multiple benefits and rebound effects.

Schneider, François/Kallis, Giorgos/Martinez-Alier, Joan (2010): "Crisis or Opportunity? Economic Degrowth for Social Equity and Ecological Sustainability. Introduction to This Special Issue." In: Journal of Cleaner Production 18/6, pp. 511–518. https://doi.org/10.1016/j.jclepro.2010.01.014.

Solnørdal, Mette Talseth/Foss, Lene (2018): "Closing the Energy Efficiency Gap – A Systematic Review of Empirical Articles on Drivers to Energy Efficiency in Manufacturing Firms." In: Energies 11/3, 518. https://doi.org/10.3390/en11030518.

Sorrell, Steve (2007): "The Rebound Effect: An assessment of the evidence for economy-wide energy savings from improved energy efficiency. A report produced by the Sussex Energy Group for the Technology and Policy Assessment function of the UK Energy Research Centre," London, 5.10.2023 (https://d2e1qxpsswcpgz.cloudfront.net/uploads/2020/03/the-rebound-effect-an-assessment-of-the-evidence-for-economy-wide-energy-savings-from-improved-energy-efficiency.pdf).

Sorrell, Steve/Gatersleben, Birgitta/Druckman, Angela (2020): "The Limits of Energy Sufficiency: A Review of the Evidence for Rebound Effects and Negative Spillovers from Behavioural Change." In: Energy Research & Social Science 64, 101439. https://doi.org/10.1016/j.erss.2020.101439.

Wolff, Franziska/Gensch, Carl-Otto/Kampffmeyer, Nele/Schöpflin, Patrick/Lautermann, Christian/Gebauer, Jana/Schaltegger, Stefan/Norris, Simon/Wüst, Sebastian/Thiel, Dieter/Buda, Fabian (2023): "Rebound Effects – Management and Prevention. Guideline for Companies," 5.10.2023 (https://www.meru-projekt.de/fileadmin/meru-projekt/user_upload/publikationen/MERU_2023_Company_guide_on_managing_rebounds.pdf).

Wolff, Franziska/Gensch, Carl-Otto/Kampffmeyer, Nele/Schöpflin, Patrick/Lautermann, Christian/Gebauer, Jana/Schaltegger, Stefan/Norris, Simon/Wüst, Sebastian/Thiel, Dieter/Buda, Fabian (2022): "Ganzheitliches Management von Energie- und Ressourceneffizienz in Unternehmen: Wie können Rebound-Effekte vermindert werden? Handlungsoptionen für die Politik," 5.10.2023 (https://www.meru-projekt.de/fileadmin/meru-projekt/user_upload/publikationen/MERU_Politikoptionen_2022-06.pdf).

Wüst, Sebastian/Schaltegger, Stefan/Wolff, Franziska/Lautermann, Christian/Schöpflin, Patrick (2023): "Conceptual framework for exploring company-level rebound effects," 5.10.2023 (https://www.meru-projekt.de/fileadmin/meru-pr

ojekt/user_upload/publikationen/Wuest_et_al_2022_-_MERU_Conceptual_Paper_en.pdf).

Zell-Ziegler, Carina/Thema, Johannes/Best, Benjamin/Wiese, Frauke/Lage, Jonas/Schmidt, Annika/Toulouse, Edouard/Stagl, Sigrid (2021): "Enough? The Role of Sufficiency in European Energy and Climate Plans." In: Energy Policy 157, 112483. https://doi.org/10.1016/j.enpol.2021.112483.

Part C –

Transformative Changes for Sufficiency on Political and Societal Levels

(In)Compatibility of the Market with Sufficiency

Applying a Systemic Lens on Markets

Isaac Arturo Ortega Alvarado

Abstract *This chapter considers sufficiency as a call for reductions in consumption and production. Markets are addressed as a site for knowledge and intervention that present incompatibilities with sufficiency – by embedding social life into economic activity. A move beyond markets toward extensive social transformations could change what businesses are and do.*

1. Introduction

This chapter builds on the relationship between sufficiency and market roles, looking at their compatibility in light of The Great Acceleration (cf. Steffen et al. 2015) – of production, consumption and environmental degradation.

The core idea of sufficiency is reducing production and consumption to defined levels (cf. Alcott 2008) – for example, aimed at decent living (Millward-Hopkins et al. 2020). Those sufficiency levels require aligning human activity – its impacts – to the safe space of Earth's carrying capacity (cf. Li et al. 2021). It may be challenging to operationalize sufficiency – as Jungell-Michelsson and Heikkurinen's (2022) review of the concept shows. The challenges increase due to concerns that link the reductions of matter-energy throughput to human-need satisfaction that considers social and distributive justice. As Steinberger and Roberts have suggested, "… with thoughtful restructuring, highly developed countries could use a fraction of their current energy without any measurable loss in human development" (2010: 432).

The review by Jungell-Michelsson and Heikkurinen (2022) addresses the challenges for the objective definition of sufficiency, considering consumption and production as sites for intervention or empirical sources, where missing an objective definition of sufficiency is seen as a research gap. As sites of intervention for sustainability research, the positions about production and consumption are also intrinsically related to markets – as a third site.

Geels et al. (2015) discuss three positions to understand the relations between production, consumption and markets: the reformist puts markets as mediators of consumption and production, the revolutionary puts markets as the system that drives consumption and production, and the reconfiguration puts markets as a result of the practical and infrastructural entanglement of production and consumption. How markets are put in relation to consumption and production might be essential to introducing and enacting sufficiency.

Influence on consumption is central in market interventions that introduce sufficiency as a principle for business innovation (cf. Bocken/Short 2016). According to Bocken and Short (2016), business model innovation is compatible with, and possible by, introducing the most desirable options in the waste hierarchy as part of how businesses work –limiting overconsumption and unnecessary resource use. However, the compatibility proposed by Bocken and Short (2016) relies on changing some of the fundamental aspects that animate the existence of business by turning towards education and consumer engagement for sustainable consumption but not mentioning the essential factor that most companies are profit-oriented as a result of their embeddedness in a market logic. Moreover, Bocken and Short's (2016) perspective is positioned in businesses as mediators of consumption.

This chapter revises sufficiency in the relation between production and consumption by looking at markets from the revolutionary and reconfiguration perspectives offered by Geels et al. (2015). Thus, the market is discussed here as the system that drives – over – consumption and – over – production and as a set of infrastructures that support a social structuration. The central assumption is that the overlapping of these two positions provides a necessary framing to understand how markets' functions drive overconsumption and may not be compatible with sufficiency.

The crises of environmental degradation that motivate the introduction of sufficiency are linked to the process known as The Great Acceleration (cf. Figueiredo et al. 2020; Head et al. 2022). The Great Acceleration concept describes the increase in resource use – material and energy – since the Second World War, mobilizing changes worldwide and affecting how humans relate to and understand each other and their consumption patterns (cf. Shoshitaishvili 2021).

The liberalization of markets can also explain The Great Acceleration. The institutional changes through the liberalization of markets can be explained from a political perspective as a form of distribution of power in an economic system, from landowners that centralized the distribution of wealth to an open system of wealth distribution through free market participants – for example, in the case of Britain (cf. Mokyr/Nye 2007). Social relations also became embedded in market activity as markets rose to be the central institution that structures social life. Polanyi (2001) put forward this argument about the rise to power by markets in his book "The Great Transformation":

> Ultimately, that is why the control of the economic system by the market is of overwhelming consequence to the whole organization of society: it means no less than the running of society as an adjunct to the market. Instead of economy being embedded in social relations, social relations are embedded in the economic system. (Polanyi 2001: 60).

The inclusion of sufficiency may quarrel with the basic institutional setup of markets, as it would – normatively – require re-embedding economic activity to socio-ecological reasons beyond the market's institutional setup – and the agencies it enables.

2. The market as site

This section works on the market as a third site – complementing production and consumption. Market activity can be modelled by measuring and aggregating discrete value transactions – what Callon (2021) calls the interface model of markets. The interface model of markets is the most commonly used by economists and distinguishes between supply and demand categories. Still, it is only one way to understand markets. Although market activity is based on transactions of something for another thing, markets' social role means more than discrete transactions as markets function as infrastructure that animates social life. For instance, markets accomplish a distributive role, which means that people who participate in the market are motivated by access to resources beyond their means of production.

Callon (2021) also points out a flaw in understanding markets as an interface of supply and demand. In this understanding, there is a lack of acknowledgement of markets as social sites, which means that markets are also a result of social relations. Callon (2021) offers the agentic model to understand markets as social relations. In the agentic model, the focus is given to agencies in markets. For Callon (2021), the agencies of markets are primarily related to increasing transactions by attracting possible buyers and incentivizing the desire to buy. In this model, markets produce the conditions for sales, which drive up demand and supply. Instead of an interface of supply and demand, in the agentic model, markets are understood as the grounding reason for acts of acquisition and sales. In other words, as long as there is agency in the markets, it will require the production and reproduction of agencies of transaction – in acts of sale and buying.

The two models presented (Callon 2021) reflect two understandings of the relationship between production, consumption and market. These two models also position transactions in two ways: as the point of encounter between supply and demand and as the agencies that sustain markets as social institutions. These two models formulate markets as a site of transactions. However, the agentic model better explains how markets structure social life. Transactions in the agentic model are the primary social reason to participate in markets. Thus, to extrapolate it to Polanyi's (2001) concept of embeddedness, transactions take the central role of structuring society by disembedding economic activity from other social reasons and embedding society in the market.

The embedding of society in the market – through specific agencies for transactions– does not answer to demand or supply for the satisfaction of needs. Instead, it responds to the double movement argued by Polanyi (2001), where more supply and demand are required in answer to transactions. In contradiction to the agencies of the market, sufficiency intends to serve as the principle that limits production and consumption, which necessarily means focusing on agencies different to the ones of transactions – and may not be found through market interventions.

For example, mobility between places, which could be free by moving one's body – walking, running, rolling with a wheelchair, among others – is subsumed to the capacity of individuals to pay for their right to be transported, whether by the purchase of passes for collective means or through the direct purchase of transport means (e.g., cars, bicycles, among others). In the hyper-commodification of everyday life, through embedding society in markets, even mobility and location data become a product to be transacted (cf. Thatcher 2017).

The embeddedness of social relations in economic activity through market mechanisms cannot go unacknowledged by anyone proposing sufficiency or the reduction of consumption and production as a principle for sustainability. In particular, sufficiency would require re-embedding economic activity to other socio-ecological reasons not mediated by transactions – or at least to some socially defined sets of limits to how material resources can be used. Such limits signal a return to a political economy or, in other terms, economic models that do not formulate social life under commercial considerations (cf. Robinson 2017).

3. Market-embedded insufficiency

Using Polanyi's (2001) concept of market embeddedness, one must assume that sufficiency implies embedding economic activity into specific socio-ecological reasons – this is probably the reason why Jungell-Michelsson and Heikkurinen (2022) could not identify an objective definition of sufficiency. In Polanyi's (2001) perspective, economic activity can be embedded in social relations, and social relations can also be embedded into economic activity – an opposite movement that Polanyi (2001) calls market disembeddedness. Under this perspective, most current societies are arranged under economistic principles, particularly market liberalization, which means that market activities drive social relations.

As Polanyi (2001) argued, economic activity can be embedded in social relations, which means that social relations and cultural aspects are the main reasons people participate in the economy – the transactions and gatherings to circulate resources for particular needs. However, economic activity can also be disembedded from social relations and become the reason for production and consumption – usually mediated by markets – and without limits from social relations or contexts (cf. Stones 2012). The main point here is that economic activity can be enacted for the sake of socio-ecological reasons or economic activity itself.

Sufficiency supposes limits to the use of resources in economic activity – reduction of materials and energy sources for production and consumption (cf. Bocken/Short 2016). However, weaknesses of sufficiency may come from what becomes embedded. On the one hand, economic activity could be embedded through some socio-ecological reasons, such as addressing well-being (cf. Hayden/Dasilva 2022). On the other hand, socio-ecological reasons could be embedded in economic activity – a priority given to economic outputs, such as economic growth or private profit-making (cf. Hayden/Dasilva 2022)

In a liberal market economy, the rate and pace of replacing material resources (in the form of products and services that use energy) would be defined by market self-regulation through consumption – the consumer sovereignty exposed by Princen et al. (2002). However, as argued by Bocken and Short (2016), the consumer can be aided by businesses following sufficiency as their primary goal (other than profits). Yet, the socio-ecological groundings of some other business goals for sufficiency are weak if the solutions remain embedded in the agencies enabled through markets.

4. Embedding economic activity in socio-ecological reasons

This section conveys a counterpoint to the market agencies by grounding ways to re-embed economic activity into socio-ecological reasons. This counterpoint focuses on the possibility of bounding economic activity to socio-ecological reasons – for example, through the definition of sufficiency by people in collective rule-making (e.g. Princen et al. 2002). The arguments for a counterpoint are constructed in opposition to the embeddedness of society in market agencies.

In embedding economic activity (Polanyi 2001) to socio-ecological reasons fitting sufficiency, one must assume that these social reasons will not expand overproduction and overconsumption. The fulfilment of this assumption could require grounding these reasons in an ecological understanding that properly integrates human activity with that of the rest of the natural world (cf. Enzensburger 1976). Furthermore, sufficiency as a means to embed economic activity may require facing a contradiction to the dominant social paradigm – for example, in dealing with individuality and the notions of having (Gorge et al. 2015).

There is an empirical question about the definition of the socio-ecological reasons that would be effective in re-embedding economic activity – and if this is a question about an objective definition, as Jungell-Michelsson and Heikkurinen (2022) discuss. Elsewhere, the study of Gorge et al. (2015) positions sufficiency and its definition from the position of individuals –in isolation or groups – with arguments for sufficiency as a concertation of collective action that reconciles human needs and environmental protection – favoring being over having.

The reconciliation of economic activity and socio-ecological limits is present in The Doughnut Economy by Raworth (2017). The Doughnut Economy is an example of an economic model that embeds economic activity to thresholds defined through environmental and social limits. In this model, the distribution and redistribution of value rely on public and collective infrastructure – known as the commons.

The Doughnut Economy model represents an understanding of economic activity that takes sufficiency as a principle to ground economic activity. In Raworth's (2018: 233–236) perspective, sufficiency comes in opposition to the aspiration to grow –in possessions as in consumerism and in the flux of market transactions as required by economic growth. To Raworth (2018: 235), a lack of sufficiency connects to "... neglected relationships with each other and the living world." These neglected relationships can be interpreted as the socio-ecological reasons that should embed economic activity.

Furthermore, the basics of this model are echoed in the work of Bärnthaler and Gough (2023), which proposes that some of the production for commodities should be limited by and transferred to public and communal ownership, creating a corridor for provision that operates between a threshold of sufficiency – a ceiling limit before excess production and a floor limit above deprivation. In these two examples, exchanges through market means are not dismissed but adapted within the established thresholds.

This grounding of sufficiency as a principle that embeds economic activity into socio-ecological reasons will require specific processes of decision for policy-making and policy-enacting based on democratic processes for the definition of what is necessary production and consumption but also about the mechanisms to allow or disallow the enaction of production and consumption as processes mediated by provision processes – a function commonly addressed by market mechanisms (Bärnthaler/Gough 2023). These mechanisms are impossible to establish today because of the existing infrastructures, meanings and values that focus on market liberalization as a proxy for general freedom – as Robinson (2017) and Raworth (2018) have argued.

A question here is whether the possibility of sufficiency limits is to be decided by groups in specific productive sectors – the reformists identified by Geels et al. (2015) – or if the limits to productive sectors should be determined in collective by the general population – as argued by Princen (2005) as a function of democracy.

Furthermore, the position that productive sectors can decide when to produce and when not to in the best interests of people and the environment presents us with the typical formulation of sustainability as a matter of prioritizations and assessments of three dimensions – people, planet, profit (cf. Hammer/Pivo 2017). However, embedding these dimensions into market mechanisms – that enable agencies through transactions – presents the risk of favoring a unilateral decision based on the success of particular business sectors – creating an offer that may not be ruled by sufficiency but sustained through the promotion and creation of demand.

In contrast, policies with specific political mandates that seek to restrict production or create new infrastructures for sharing and commoning resources could better impact the grounding of a sufficiency model that would still require markets but not to the same scale and geographical coverage of today's markets – for example, sufficiency put as requiring a cultural shift to support political change (Alexander/Gleeson 2022). However, most claims about sufficiency are hypothetical and require testing about what roles markets would play, for example, in promoting cooperation across different countries and populations – and also about the value chains that can be localized against those that cannot.

Furthermore, these questions extend to the possibility of local and regional markets that use and share resources already available within geographical limits – as circulation networks – and that resort to markets as a means to replenish resources that are not locally available. A research program that investigates collective sufficiencies with worldwide impacts that consider the role of markets should consider exchanges between regions as a mechanism for cooperation – even more the ending of extractivist relations that sustain inequalities in production and consumption – for example, in the context of the circular economy (e.g., Barrie et al. 2022; Jaeger-Erben et al. 2021).

5. Sufficiency and the market dilemma

The contingencies for sufficiency – as a means – to embed economic activity into socio-ecological reasons – instead of the market agencies – present a problem to businesses as their room for action or social reason is conventionally based on market agencies.

Although there are proposals to focus on use-value as access to products and services – for example, in suggestions of a service or access economy as part of a circular economy (cf. Stahel 2016) – most of these still focus on exchange-value, which means a centralization of market mechanisms for distribution and redistribution – without decentering the agencies that put accumulation and competence as the primary purposes and goals of economic activity. These two aspects, accumulation and competence, are not intrinsic traits of markets but result from capitalism as a system without coercions (cf. Sternberg 2015). Moreover, markets within capitalist models have usually been shaped around these two objectives – some of the evils pointed out by Polanyi (2001).

Focusing on sufficiency would mean establishing some coercion – at least coercion from a capitalist perspective on market regulations (cf. Sternberg 2015). This coercion contradicts capitalistic notions of freedom – invoked in liberal economic theory. Another understanding that would benefit the application of sufficiency through market interventions is in the organizational and institutional aspects that reveal the market as a social structure – with agencies (Callon 2021) and organizational challenges in value, competition and cooperation (Beckert 2009). The roles of markets are not limited to the production of sales points or profit maximization. Markets also have the social role of facilitating the distribution of existing value and its movement from those with that value to others who may need it. And it also grounds a set of challenges for sufficiency-oriented research and practices. So the question is whether markets can be the main institutional setup for societies with material sufficiency.

In extension, market agencies as individual choices are also incompatible with sufficiency –similarly pointed out by Bocken and Short (2016) as the argument to include sufficiency as a principle for business intervention, which would require some self-imposed regulations by businesses. Whether the regulations are cultural, government or supply-side driven, they represent the kind of interventions that market-embedded societies would, in principle, reject. The central dilemma is the misalignment between conventional market roles – as a means for freedom in provision – and sufficiency. The push for material sufficiency through businesses could be considered a case of moralizing production and consumption.

A focus on collective needs as a means to guide responsibility – concerning socio-ecological reasons – may also be beyond the function of businesses. Companies can be rethought through sufficiency as part of the infrastructures and practices that support social life (cf. Rinkinen/Shove 2023). However, the social construction of what a business is and does is also weakened without the centrality of the market. In a way, embedding economic activity in socio-ecological reasons may reveal a double movement in transforming businesses and societies, where companies alone cannot change unless collective needs change.

In addition to market, consumption and production, the definition of sufficiency must be elucidated from other sources – as both epistemic and intervention sites. My central claim is that embedding economic activity to socio-ecological reasons would require looking beyond businesses and focusing on shared understandings of what it means to be part of society and what society should allow for each of its members. In this sense, there must be a more extensive societal transformation before calling for companies' unilateral definitions of production and consumption thresholds. Otherwise, any business that implements sufficiency without looking to be transformative is at risk of failing.

Furthermore, aligning economic activity and sufficiency requires a complete rethinking of the roles of markets, particularly as a social site and infrastructure – with physical spaces and means – that sustain the distribution and circulation of materials and products. Embeddedness of economic activity into social relations – and reasons – leading to sound ecological limits can be promoted by support to practices that do not take the market as its site of intervention. Thus, policymakers or other actors interested in promoting sufficiency should start by looking at possibilities outside the market and how to enable them through value distribution. However, there is always a risk that looking beyond markets could result in pulling solutions towards market agencies – for example, by offering public services that drive up consumption and production through a convenience gained by facilitating transactions.

6. Conclusion

The grounding of sufficiency requires acknowledging the market as a social site – a source of knowledge and interventions. Markets can be understood socially in the production of particular agencies (Callon 2021); in this understanding, a market exists in the interactions that lead to fulfilling transactions involving selling and buying. Markets are, therefore, a force driving up consumption and production.

This chapter elucidates the question of whether markets are compatible with material sufficiency. Markets are considered a site of intervention by those proposing material sufficiency – reduction of production and consumption – through business innovation. However, Polany"s (2001) concept of embeddedness is invoked in this chapter to support the claim that sufficiency for businesses cannot look only at market interventions as it requires the socio-ecological reasons for sufficiency to be grounded in a more extensive social transformation – which in turn would transform businesses.

Grounding the socio-ecological reasons for sufficiency in a more extensive social transformation does not mean businesses should not aim for change and be drivers of social shifts. This question and move beyond markets could result in restructurations – and even revolutions – that challenge the centrality of markets in social life. In extension, a business contribution to sufficiency could also require disembedding their activity from market institutions and agencies – to which one could question what a business outside market agencies is.

The question here is not if markets will still be necessary or if the market agencies can be replaced, but instead, if markets as an institution can aid in fulfilling the functions of other social institutions without increasing production and consumption. On the one hand, if the answer is positive, then the task remains to reduce the role of markets and their pervasiveness in all aspects of life. On the other hand, if the answer is negative, the task is to find the mechanisms and proper institutions that allow the distribution of goods and social functions –as value – to those who need them, for example, in exploring the commons.

References

Alcott, Blake (2008): "The sufficiency strategy: Would rich-world frugality lower environmental impact?" In: Ecological Economics 64/4, pp. 770–786. https://doi.org/10.1016/j.ecolecon.2007.04.015.

Alexander, Samuel/Gleeson, Brendan (2022): "Collective Sufficiency: Degrowth as a Political Project." In: Samuel Alexander/Sangeetha Chandrashekeran/Brendan Gleeson (eds.), Post-Capitalist Futures, Singapore: Springer, pp. 53–64. https://doi.org/10.1007/978-981-16-6530-1_5.

Bärnthaler, Richard/Gough, Ian (2023): "Provisioning for sufficiency: Envisaging production corridors." In: Sustainability: Science, Practice and Policy 19/1, 2218690. https://doi.org/10.1080/15487733.2023.2218690.

Barrie, Jack/Anantharaman, Manisha/Oyinlola, Muyiwa/Schröder, Patrick (2022): "The circularity divide: What is it? And how do we avoid it?" In: Resources, Conservation and Recycling 180, 106208. https://doi.org/10.1016/j.resconrec.2022.106208

Beckert, Jens (2009): "The social order of markets." In: Theory and Society 38/3, pp. 245–269. https://doi.org/10.1007/s11186-008-9082-0.

Bocken, Nancy M. P./Short, Samuel W. (2016): "Towards a sufficiency-driven business Model: Experiences and opportunities." In: Environmental Innovation and Societal Transitions 18, pp. 41–61. https://doi.org/10.1016/j.eist.2015.07.010.

Callon, Michel (2021): Markets in the Making. Rethinking Competition, Goods, and Innovation, Princeton: Princeton University Press.

Enzensburger, Hans Magnus (1976): "A Critique of Political Ecology." In: Hilary Rose/Steven Rose (eds.), The Political Economy of Science. Ideology of/in the Natural Sciences, London: Palgrave, pp. 161–195. https://doi.org/10.1007/978-1-349-15725-9_9.

Figueiredo, Marina Dantas de/Marquesan, Fábio Freitas Schilling/Imas, José Miguel (2020): "Anthropocene and "Development": Intertwined Trajectories Since the Beginning of The Great Acceleration." In: Revista de Administração Contemporânea 24/5, pp. 400–413. https://doi.org/10.1590/1982-7849rac2020190400.

Geels, Frank W./McMeekin, Andy/Mylan, Josephine/Southerton, Dale (2015): "A critical appraisal of Sustainable Consumption and Production research: The reformist, revolutionary and reconfiguration positions." In: Global Environmental Change 34, pp. 1–12. https://doi.org/10.1016/j.gloenvcha.2015.04.013.

Gorge, Helene/Herbert, Maud/Özçağlar-Toulouse, Nil/Robert, Isabelle (2015): "What Do We Really Need? Questioning Consumption Through Sufficiency." In: Journal of Macromarketing 35/1, pp. 11–22. https://doi.org/10.1177/0276146714553935.

Hammer, Janet/Pivo, Gary (2017): "The Triple Bottom Line and Sustainable Economic Development Theory and Practice." In: Economic Development Quarterly 31/1, pp. 25–36. https://doi.org/10.1177/0891242416674808.

Hayden, Anderd/Dasilva, Clay (2022): "The wellbeing economy: Possibilities and limits in bringing sufficiency from the margins into the mainstream." In: Frontiers in Sustainability 3, 966876. https://doi.org/10.3389/frsus.2022.966876.

Head, Martin J./Steffen, Will/Fagerlind, David/Waters, Carolin N./Poirier, Clement/Syvitski, Jaia/Zalasiewicz, Jan A./Barnosky, Anthony D./Cearreta, Alejandro/Jeandel, Catherine/Leinfelder, Reinhold/McNeill, J. R./Rose, Neil L./Summerhayes, Colin/Wagreich, Michael/Zinke, Jens (2022): "The Great Acceleration is real and provides a quantitative basis for the proposed Anthropocene Series/Epoch." In: Episodes Journal of International Geoscience 45/4, pp. 359–376. https://doi.org/10.18814/epiiugs/2021/021031.

Jaeger-Erben, Melanie/Jensen, Charlotte/Hofmann, Florian/Zwiers, Jakob (2021): "There is no sustainable circular economy without a circular society." In Resources, Conservation and Recycling 168, 105476. https://doi.org/10.1016/j.resconrec.2021.105476.

Jungell-Michelsson, Jessica/Heikkurinen, Pasi (2022): "Sufficiency: A Systematic Literature Review." In: Ecological Economics 195, 107380. https://doi.org/10.1016/J.ECOLECON.2022.107380.

Li, Mo/Wiedmann, Thomas/Fang, Kai/Hadjikakou, Michalis (2021): "The role of planetary boundaries in assessing absolute environmental sustainability across scales." In: Environment International 152, 106475. https://doi.org/10.1016/j.envint.2021.106475

Millward-Hopkins, Joel/Steinberger, Julia K./Rao, Narasimha D./Oswald, Yannick (2020): "Providing decent living with minimum energy: A global scenario." In: Global Environmental Change 65, 102168. https://doi.org/10.1016/j.gloenvcha.2020.102168.

Mokyr, Joel/Nye, John V. C. (2007): "Distributional Coalitions, the Industrial Revolution, and the Origins of Economic Growth in Britain." In: Southern Economic Journal 74/1, pp. 50–70. https://doi.org/10.1002/j.2325-8012.2007.tb00826.x.

Polanyi, Karl (2001 [1944]): The Great Transformation, Boston: Beacon Press.

Princen, Thomas (2005): The logic of sufficiency, Cambridge: MIT Press.

Princen, Thomas/Maniates, Michael/Conca, Ken (2002): "14: Conclusion: To Confront Consumption." In: Thomas Princen/Michael Maniates/Ken Conca (eds.), Confronting Consumption, Cambridge: MIT Press, pp. 317–328. https://doi.org/10.7551/mitpress/2097.003.0018.

Raworth, Kate (2017): "Why it's time for Doughnut Economics." In: IPPR Progressive Review 24/3, pp. 216–222. https://doi.org/10.1111/newe.12058.

Raworth, Kate (2017): Doughnut Economics: Seven Ways to Think Like a 21st-Century Economist, London: Random House Business Books.

Rinkinen, Jenny/Shove, Elizabeth (2023): "Material culture and the circular economy." In: Frontiers in Sustainability 4, 1158079. https://doi.org/10.3389/frsus.2023.1158079.

Robinson, Joan (2017 [1970]): In Freedom and Necessity. An Introduction to the Study of Society, London: Routledge, pp. 13–19.

Shoshitaishvili, Boris (2021): "From Anthropocene to Noosphere: The Great Acceleration." In: Earth's Future 9/2, e2020EF001917. https://doi.org/10.1029/2020EF001917.

Stahel, Walter R. (2016): "The circular economy." In: Nature 531/7595, pp. 435–438. https://doi.org/10.1038/531435a.

Steffen, Will/Broadgate, Wendy/Deutsch, Lisa/Gaffney, Owen/Ludwig, Cornelia (2015): "The trajectory of the Anthropocene: The Great Acceleration." In: The Anthropocene Review 2/1, pp. 81–98. https://doi.org/10.1177/2053019614564785.

Steinberger, Julia K./Roberts, J. Timmons (2010): "From constraint to sufficiency: The decoupling of energy and carbon from human needs, 1975–2005." In: Ecological Economics 70/2, pp. 425–433. https://doi.org/10.1016/j.ecolecon.2010.09.014.

Sternberg, Elaine (2015): "Defining Capitalism." In: Economic Affairs 35/3, pp. 380–396. https://doi.org/10.1111/ecaf.12141.

Stones, Rob (2012): "Disembedding." In: George Ritzer (eds.), The Wiley-Blackwell Encyclopedia of Globalization, Hoboken: John Wiley & Sons, Ltd. https://doi.org/10.1002/9780470670590.wbeog154.

Thatcher, Jim (2017): "You are where you go, the commodification of daily life through 'location.'" In: Environment and Planning A: Economy and Space 49/12, pp. 2702–2717. https://doi.org/10.1177/0308518X17730580.

Limits of Sufficiency Strategies in Business Practices

Overcoming Business-Related Boundaries for a Transition Towards Sufficiency

Maike Gossen, Josephine Tröger and Vivian Frick

Abstract *This chapter discusses the limited effectiveness of sufficiency-promoting communications as a result of larger structural causes that prevent companies from implementing effective sufficiency approaches in their communications as well as in their overarching business strategies – namely, pro-consumption advertising and the growth-oriented economy.*

1. Introduction

A socio-ecological transformation towards sustainability requires structural changes in all areas of the society and economy; changes that simultaneously enable the pursuit of social justice and promote long-term individual and societal well-being within planetary boundaries. This implies an overall reduction in consumption and production in line with the concept of sufficiency.

Recent research indicates that interventions targeting individuals by providing information, increasing awareness and fostering personal responsibility have shown limited effectiveness in altering overall consumption patterns (Hirth et al. 2023). These approaches are often not successful enough to reach beyond a small sustainability-oriented niche segment of consumers. Apart from limited pro-environmental motivation, one reason is that individuals have limited capacity to absorb and process an overwhelming volume of information (Oehler/Wendt 2017). It is clear that in order to achieve real change towards sufficiency, we need to broaden the scope and look beyond individual decision-making to collective decision-making processes and the role of governments and businesses (e.g., Whitmarsh et al. 2021).

Moving beyond individuals, one approach that businesses could pursue to address the impacts of overconsumption is to advocate for sufficiency. Due to their strategic position in the supply chain, their decisions, orientations or activities influence both upstream production and downstream consumption towards a slower, local and socially just economy (Heikkurinen et al. 2019; Jungell-Michelsson/Heikkurinen 2022). So far, research has identified two main approaches on how exactly this transformation might occur: the adoption of business models that prioritize the reduction of overall consumption (Niessen/Bocken 2021) and the use of marketing strategies that promote sufficiency-oriented consumption (Gossen et al. 2019) and elicit social action aimed at preventing and addressing the root causes of the unsustainable economy. Perhaps unsurprisingly, research also suggests that most of the strategies implemented to enable sufficiency-oriented consumption can be categorized as "shallow", as they focus primarily on knowledge and support, such as communication campaigns (e.g., Gossen/Kropfeld 2022; Svenfelt et al. 2022). These strategies have been shown to be inadequate in influencing intentions and decisions towards sufficiency-oriented behaviors, for example in online environments, where they are overshadowed by frequent pro-consumption advertisements (e.g., Frick et al. 2021a; Tröger et al. 2021).

The reasons why current approaches often fail to effectively realize their potential to drive behavior change toward sufficiency are, we argue, both structural and self-inflicted: First, businesses are embedded in a growth-based economic system. The logic of capitalism means that profit-seeking firms and unsustainable demand from households are institutionalized through private ownership and capital accumulation (Gunderson et al. 2018). As a result of this path dependency, companies have limited capacity to change the underlying "structural forces" of exponential growth and excessive consumption (Beyeler/Jaeger-Erben 2022). This conflict of interest can create tensions within companies and discourage them from adopting sufficiency strategies (Gossen/Heinrich 2021). Second, despite their limited effectiveness in guiding consumer choices in the long term (Frick et al. 2021a; Tröger et al. 2021; Gossen et al. 2023), one of the most common strategies used by companies to promote sufficiency-oriented consumption are communication and information campaigns.

In what follows, we discuss the limitations of consumer-centered communication approaches that focus on individual behavior change and absolve other actors of their responsibilities. We then explain the challenges and limitations of sufficiency-promoting messaging, followed by an analysis of the main barriers that prevent companies from implementing effective sufficiency approaches in their communications as well as in their overarching business strategies. In analyzing the causes and interdependencies, it becomes clear that they are mutually reinforcing. We conclude by pointing to opportunities for political support that are essential for a profound transformation of the economy and society.

2. Limitations of consumer-centered approaches

In promoting sufficiency, companies often rely on marketing campaigns or communication efforts to encourage behavior change at the consumer level. However, such campaigns often fall short of their intended outcomes. One potential reason for this ineffectiveness is the intention-behavior gap. Prior research has extensively studied this gap, which suggests that even when individuals have strong intentions or a high willingness to change, these intentions do not always translate into actual behavior (Bamberg/Möser 2007). Everyone knows from their own experience how difficult it is to change a certain habit from one day to the next, such as giving up sweets or exercising for 10 minutes in the morning. This is of particular relevance in the context of environmental behavior, as many people have a high awareness of the problem and express the intention to behave in an environmentally friendly way but often do not succeed due to adverse circumstances (Bamberg/Möser 2007; ElHaffar et al. 2020). In the behavioral sciences and psychology, there are countless studies on bridging the gap between intention and behavior, often focusing on motivational processes (Sheeran/Webb 2016). Structural barriers are integrated in the form of social norms.

However, the focus on individuals leads to an individualization of societal problems and absolves other critical and influential actors, such as companies and governments, from their share of responsibility in driving large-scale change towards sufficiency and sustainability (Chater/Loewenstein 2022). Grunwald (2010) called this allocation of responsibility the privatization of sustainability, Akenji (2014) described it as consumer scapegoats. Both authors agree that focusing solely on consumers as agents of change can have detrimental effects: If sufficiency depends on consumer choice, then companies and legislators do not share this responsibility and may fail to take the necessary action. In other words, the focus on the individual legitimizes companies to follow the rules of the free market and pursue the goal of corporate growth and accumulation rather than sufficiency. This coincides with neoliberal thinking and the prevailing "dictatorship of consumption" (Lepenies 2022: 225), in which personal purchasing decisions are misunderstood as the exercise of subjective freedoms.

In summary, the embeddedness of human behavior or thinking in social systems is often underestimated and the responsibility of actors beyond individual consumers is not adequately addressed. The focus on the consumer has promoted the trend towards individualization and privatization of sustainability and sufficiency – a narrative that many companies have been happy to support – but which, as described in the next chapter, has led to limited results.

3. Limitations and obstacles of sufficiency-promoting communication

Current business strategies to promote sufficiency focus on product design and include, for example, developing durable, high-quality and repairable alternatives to conventional products, as well as extending the usual warranty period and offering repair services (Bocken et al. 2014; Bocken/Short 2016; Kropfeld/Reichel 2021). These strategies are often complemented by communication measures such as the use of anti-consumerist messages that aim to raise awareness of the impact of consumption on the environment and human well-being and to challenge the materialistic norms of consumer society. It seems that companies find it easier to implement sufficiency strategies at the level of marketing and customer communications than at the level of other business practices because these measures create less tension and require fewer changes in the design of business practices and models. However, their effectiveness has not yet been proven because it is not clear whether communications promoting sufficiency actually reduce consumption. The much-discussed case of Patagonia's 2011 Black Friday campaign "Don't buy this jacket" serves as a vivid example of this ambiguity. Although the provocative campaign aimed to critically reflect on consumption (Patagonia Inc. 2021), it ultimately led to an increase in sales for the outdoor brand.

Consequently, studies that use methods to directly measure the impact of sufficiency messaging on behavior yield less conclusive results. For example, Frick et al. (2021) conducted two experiments with sufficiency-promoting social media communications from companies aimed at reducing consumption and extending the lifetime of clothing. In their real-world social media intervention, both the experimental and control groups showed reduced clothing consumption over time. Thus, the intervention itself did not reduce clothing consumption. However, in their laboratory experiment, sufficiency-promoting social media communication led to stronger sufficiency behavior, as measured by choosing a coupon for a second-hand store or making a donation, compared to neutral and consumption-promoting communication. In a similar study, Gossen et al. (2023) examined the potentially positive effects of sufficiency messages based on dynamic norms on mobile phone usage intentions and purchasing decisions. Dynamic norms communicate a continuous shift in behavioral tendencies relevant to the target behavior – in this case, the growing interest of people in repairing and prolonging the life of mobile phones. The results showed that a sufficiency message emphasizing a dynamic norm had no particularly significant effects compared to the two other conditions. Furthermore, in a diary intervention study that aimed at increasing sufficiency orientation and consumption, it was shown that simply being part of the experiment increased participants' pro-sufficiency attitudes after a one-week diary intervention and remained at that level for four weeks thereafter (Tröger et al. 2021). These studies indicate that businesses, which decide to promote sufficiency to their customers through advertising and communication efforts, might have only a limited impact on customer behavior.

From a methodological perspective, it is challenging to operationalize the concept of sufficiency and accurately measure sufficiency-oriented behavior change in real-world settings. These limitations affect the reliability and validity of the studies' results and contribute to their mixed results, which are still few in number. Furthermore, the design and practical implementation of interventions to promote sufficiency-oriented consumption play a crucial role. Habit formation requires repeated performance of desired actions in stable contexts, followed by a desirable reward. Therefore, sustained communication over time – as opposed to shallow, one-time information-based interventions – is required to have a meaningful impact (Nielsen et al. 2020).

4. Key barriers for business approaches promoting sufficiency-oriented lifestyles

Even if we know about the limitations of consumer-centered approaches and the effectiveness of sufficiency-promoting communication from businesses is uncertain, there is a need for more businesses to take up sufficiency strategies. This, however, is obstructed by the dominance of pro-consumption advertising and the growth paradigm in the current economic system that works against an overall sufficiency orientation in businesses.

4.1 Dominance of pro-consumption advertising as a barrier to sufficiency-promoting communication

Sufficiency-oriented communication is still a niche activity compared to conventional advertising that is disseminated online as well as in print media, on billboards, radio or TV. Accordingly, expenditure on advertising has steadily increased – while in 2000 more than $300 billion was spent on advertising worldwide, by 2020 it was more than $600 billion (Statista 2023a). In recent decades, online advertising in search engines, social media or on displays has become by far the most attractive form of advertising and the main driver of growth in advertising spending, with an annual growth rate of around 10 per cent worldwide (Statista 2023b). As a result, a German survey, for example, found that internet users see significantly more consumption-promoting advertising than sufficiency-oriented content (Frick et al. 2021b). This predominance of the traditional, consumption-promoting form of advertising has several adverse effects on sufficiency:

- Environmental impact of the advertising sector: Online advertising and the production of advertising and media campaigns have a significant impact on the environment, e.g., through resource and energy consumption or CO_2 emissions (Pärssinen et al. 2018; Hartmann et al. 2022).
- Misleading information for sufficiency-oriented consumption choices: Advertising can spread misinformation and greenwashing. Greenwashing can occur when the environmental benefits of products are overstated. It is widely used in online retail (Gossen et al. 2022a) and leads consumers to choose less sustainable products than intended. When greenwashing is exposed, it also reduces the trustworthiness of sustainable products (Hartmann et al. 2022). Further, online services based on advertising revenue disseminate misinformation on environmental topics such as climate change more intensively and quickly than scientifically-based information (Kingaby 2021; Vosoughi et al. 2018); this may counteract environmental concerns that motivate sufficiency-oriented behavior.
- Increased consumption levels: Advertising can increase the amount of goods and services consumed and, thus, the environmental impact in other sectors.

Especially this last aspect of increasing consumption levels poses a serious threat to sufficiency-oriented lifestyles and business practices. It remains a challenge for empirical studies to definitively prove whether advertising actually increases consumption and the mediated effect of advertising is still under investigation (Gossen et al. 2022b, Frick et al. 2021b). From a broader economic perspective, it is unclear whether advertising solely redistributes a fixed amount of consumption from one company or provider to another, or if it genuinely enhances overall consumption levels based on the success of advertising (Gossen et al. 2022b). Yet, studies from diverse disciplinary and methodological backgrounds suggest that advertising does contribute to increased consumption. On a macro-level, there is evidence of a correlation between advertising expenditure and economic growth or increased spending (e.g., Brulle/Young 2007; Molinari/Turino 2018). From a household perspective, regular exposure to media content is associated with higher product sales (e.g., Rubinson 2009) and increased material aspirations (e.g., Shrum et al. 2005). In the field of marketing research, numerous authors criticize the primary use of marketing to generate additional consumer demands, leading to unsustainable production and consumption escalation (e.g., Key et al. 2020). The advent of online marketing exacerbates the risks of overconsumption. For instance, Dinner et al. (2013) found that online advertising is even more effective than traditional advertising in increasing sales. Recent digital developments such as personalization, instant shopping or influencer marketing further contribute to this detrimental trend. Correspondingly, Kasser and Kanner (2004) explored how advertising stimulates consumption, fosters consumerist attitudes and influences overall well-being. Advertising often cultivates a desire for novelty, which has been shown to contribute to the shortened lifespan of smartphones (Jaeger-Erben et al. 2021). Furthermore, advertising can lead to a rise in materialistic values, escalating levels of consumption and ecological burdens (Kasser 2020).

The dominance of pro-consumption advertising also has a structural cause, which is particularly visible in the digital markets. The internet is largely dependent on advertising as its main source of revenue (Kingaby 2021) and the most visited search engines, online news media and social media, are owned and designed by profit-driven platform companies whose financing models are based on advertising and the collection of personal data (Lewandowsky et al. 2020). They collect data from users to personalize information, services and advertising to their individual interests and sell advertising space to companies in real-time bidding.

All in all, not only the relationship between advertising and overconsumption, the ubiquity of commercial and pro-consumption content in the consumer environment but also the design and funding models of companies pose major obstacles to sufficiency strategies. As the next chapter shows, the obstacles described are symptoms of the current market system.

4.2 Growth-oriented economy and neoliberal market systems as barriers for sufficiency-oriented strategies in businesses

The current economic thinking is dominated by growth orientation and the optimization of economic indicators as the central goal rather than societal well-being (Raworth 2017). The relentless pursuit of economic growth is seen as essential for societal progress and prosperity. In this paradigm, with few exceptions, most businesses encourage individuals to continuously acquire and consume more goods and services as a means of achieving these goals. In such growth-oriented institutional settings, alternative businesses – businesses which are willing to operate at smaller organizational scales and pursue sufficiency rather than growth – struggle to thrive (Beyeler/Jaeger-Erben 2022; Lloveras et al. 2022) and may even refrain from pursuing strategies that support sufficiency, both in their own organizational operations and in their offerings to consumers as a result (Gossen/Heinrich 2021). Taken together, the dominant growth orientation of the current economic paradigm seems to prevent most organizations from adopting sufficiency strategies. Below, we highlight four aspects that we have identified as particularly important.

First, there is a lack of access to finance and investment for sufficiency-oriented businesses, especially compared to conventional businesses that promise higher returns to their investors. Organizations that need capital to start their sufficiency-oriented business rely on conventional financial investment as well as own savings, state subsidies or purpose-oriented financial investment strategies such as crowdfunding, impact investors or private donations (Bocken et al. 2022). And although control over financial investments and financial ownership seems to be essential for sufficiency-oriented companies (Beyeler/Jaeger-Erben 2022), the limited access to funding capital at the same time is a disadvantage in the market. As long as most investors seek profit maximization and high financial returns, companies that find ways to create value that are independent of growth (Banerjee et al. 2021) or that turn away from the principle of profit maximization altogether (Nesterova 2020) are not attractive investments for them.

Second, the growth dependency inherent in the economic system de-incentivizes businesses from reducing production or encouraging customers to consume less. The current business environment – characterized by competitive conditions, demand effects and business ownership – reinforces the benefits of growth and scale (Gebauer et al. 2017). Furthermore, quantitative growth in business activity is typically accompanied by increased complexity in terms of financial obligations, competitive pressures and infrastructure. The result is a growth spiral in which increasing complexity and growth dependency drive each other (Froese et al. 2023). Existing companies are often caught in these dynamics, and it takes knowledge, capacity and a willingness to experiment – often with unpredictable consequences – to overcome these lock-ins and path dependencies. As an example, consider the Swedish second-hand clothing market, which is dominated by for-profit organizations that prevent non-profits from operating more sustainably (Persson/Hinton 2023).

Third, powerful actors shape demands and desires, pushing sufficiency to the periphery. The current economic system is stabilized by a variety of settings, including power constellations. In the current asymmetric market, a powerful consumer culture industry shapes desires and market-driven forces shape demand. As a result, sufficiency advocates are a minority in their institutions and sufficiency-oriented businesses are a niche phenomenon. At the same time, political decision-making continues to be constrained by the power of interest groups such as industrial lobby groups or multinational corporations, which reinforces the power imbalance in the current economic system. These power asymmetries need to be taken into account in order to realize the shift towards sufficiency in the economy (Fuchs et al. 2016; Avelino 2017).

Fourth, purpose-oriented businesses that value sufficiency and care over self-interest are at odds in the current extractivist, capitalist system. Values shape the behavior of actors in the economic system and influence decision-making in companies. A redefinition of business values would be moving from the primacy of shareholders to the primacy of purpose (Mayer 2020). So-called purpose-driven companies create both wealth and social well-being, are a source of social change and contribute to the common good (European Parliamentary Research Service 2023). An example could be companies which pursue a perspective of caring that prioritizes the well-being of all living beings, including humans, nonhumans and nature (Beyeler/Jaeger-Erben 2022; Jungell-Michelsson/Heikkurinen 2022; Lorek et al. 2023). A care-centred perspective challenges the current paradigm of constant economic growth and competition and seeks a fair and equitable distribution of resources, the elimination of systems of oppression and the reduction of carbon emissions and resource consumption (Lorek et al. 2023). However, such alternative businesses are disadvantaged in the existing economic system. Because the time and financial costs of operating in a system that targets opposed values are often high, imitators are discouraged. Therefore, the question arises how we can create more favorable conditions for sufficiency-oriented businesses.

5. The time is ripe for systemic change in policy-making and business

Political institutions from the supranational (e.g., EU) to the local level must introduce policies that help sufficiency-oriented business succeed and at the same time abolish subsidies for unsustainable forms of production and consumption. Examples of policy support for sufficiency strategies can be found in legislation to facilitate repairs, such as in Sweden with a VAT reduction for repair services (Dalhammar et al. 2020) or in France, where repair scores have been made mandatory for certain electronic appliances (Ministère de la transition écologique 2021).

In order to introduce such policies, political actors often argue that broad public acceptance is required. Current research shows that such acceptance can be assumed at least to some degree. The majority of people want fair and equitable policies that secure the future of our planet and are willing to accept strong regulatory measures to this end (e.g., Fabre et al. 2023). Communicating the impact of such measures plays a crucial role in acceptance. According to Dütschke et al. (2023), people want to be informed about how policy measures affect themselves and society, and they also want to know that potential savings for the state, for example, are passed back to society. This is also true vice versa: if people are misinformed, there can be a lack of political support, which can prevent systemic changes that are urgently needed for the transition. So, when it comes to system change, including change in businesses, social acceptance is needed, but it also needs to be fostered through communication from key stakeholders.

We have shown that companies aiming to drive sustainability and sufficiency prefer consumer-oriented communication interventions, probably because they do not require a profound change in management or production processes, which would often be considered costly and effortful. Garcia-Ortega et al. (2023) introduced the term "anti-consumerist washing" to describe the phenomenon that companies only symbolically engage in sufficiency-promoting communication to give the appearance of social responsibility. Instead, they use misleading advertising to create an overly positive image, gain legitimacy and maintain "business as usual". But for sufficiency to become a common practice, a deep transition of management is needed. Some companies have already started to experiment with sufficiency-oriented business models (e.g., Niessen/Bocken 2021; Bocken et al. 2022). Changes at the business level may include, for example, changing the form of organization to a cooperative. Due to their organizational form, cooperatives are characterized by the commoditization of ownership and property as well as the co-determination and self-determination of their members and can thus largely escape the growth pressure of the economic market (e.g., Lautermann/Pfriem 2018). Moreover, equivalent to the consumption corridor that determines sufficient consumption as a level at which planetary boundaries are respected and human needs are met, a "production corridor" (Bärnthaler/Gough 2023) needs to be defined for businesses. It exists in a sphere between essential production to meet basic needs within planetary boundaries and excess production that is detrimental to the environment and does not contribute to need satisfaction.

Ultimately, sufficiency should not be regarded as a mystical standard to be attained within the economy and society but a way of aligning resources to meet the needs of both humans and non-humans alike.

References

Akenji, Lewis (2014): "Consumer scapegoatism and limits to green consumerism." In: Journal of Cleaner Production 63, pp. 13–23. https://doi.org/10.1016/j.jclepro.2013.05.022.

Avelino, Flor (2017): "Power in Sustainability Transitions: Analysing power and (dis)empowerment in transformative change towards sustainability." In: Environmental Policy and Governance 27/6, pp. 505–520. https://doi.org/10.1002/eet.1777.

Bamberg, Sebastian/Möser, Guido (2007): "Twenty years after Hines, Hungerford, and Tomera: A new meta-analysis of psycho-social determinants of pro-environmental behaviour." In: Journal of Environmental Psychology 27/1, pp. 14–25. https://doi.org/10.1016/j.jenvp.2006.12.002.

Banerjee, Subhabrata Bobby/Jermier, John M./Peredo, Ana Maria/Perey, Robert/Reichel, André (2021): "Theoretical Perspectives on Organizations and Organizing in a Post-Growth Era." In: Organization 28/3, pp. 337–357. https://doi.org/10.1177/1350508420973629.

Bärnthaler, Richard/Gough, Ian (2023): "Provisioning for sufficiency: envisaging production corridors." In: Sustainability: Science, Practice and Policy 19/1. https://doi.org/10.1080/15487733.2023.2218690.

Beyeler, Laura/Jaeger-Erben, Melanie (2022): "How to Make More of Less: Characteristics of Sufficiency in Business Practices." In: Frontiers in Sustainability 3, 949710. https://doi.org/10.3389/frsus.2022.949710.

Bocken, Nancy/Short, Samuel William (2016): "Towards a Sufficiency-Driven Business Model: Experiences and Opportunities." In: Environmental Innovation and Societal Transitions 18, pp. 41–61. https://doi.org/10.1016/j.eist.2015.07.010.

Bocken, Nancy/Short, Samuel William/Rana, Padmakshi/Evans, Steve (2014): "A Literature and Practice Review to Develop Sustainable Business Model Archetypes." In: Journal of Cleaner Production 65, pp. 42–56. https://doi.org/10.1016/j.jclepro.2013.11.039.

Brulle, Robert. J./Young, Lindsay E. (2007): "Advertising, individual consumption levels, and the natural environment, 1900–2000." In: Sociological Inquiry 77/4, pp. 522–542. https://doi.org/10.1111/j.1475-682X.2007.00208.x.

Chater, Nick/Loewenstein, George (2022): "The i-frame and the s-frame: How focusing on individual-level solutions has led behavioral public policy astray." In: Behavioral and Brain Sciences, pp. 1–60. https://doi.org/10.1017/S0140525X22002023.

Dalhammar, Cornelia (eds.)/Richter, Jessika Luth (eds.)/Almén, Josefina/Anehagen, Maja/Engström, Emma/Hartman, Cornelia/Jonsson, Clara/Lindbladh, Frida/Ohlsson, Jonna (2020): "Promoting the Repair Sector in Sweden." International Institute for Industrial Environmental Economics, Lund University, Lund, Sweden.

Dinner, Isaac M./Van Heerde, Harald J./Neslin, Scott A. (2013): "Driving Online and Offline Sales: The Cross-Channel Effects of Traditional, Online Display, and Paid Search Advertising." In: Journal of Marketing Research 51/5, pp. 527–545. https://doi.org/10.1509/jmr.11.0466.

Dütschke, Elisabeth/Preuß, Sabine/Brunzema, Iska/Piria, Raffaele (2023): "Using the revenues from carbon pricing – Insights into the acceptance and perceptions of particularly burdened groups." In: Energy Policy 175, 113468. https://doi.org/10.1016/j.enpol.2023.113468.

ElHaffar, Ghina/Durif, Fabien/Dubé, Laurette (2020): "Towards closing the attitude-intention-behavior gap in green consumption: A narrative review of the literature and an overview of future research directions." In: Journal of Cleaner Production 275, 122556. https://doi.org/10.1016/j.jclepro.2020.122556.

European Parliamentary Research Service (2023): "Beyond Growth: Pathways towards Sustainable Prosperity in the EU." Brussels.

Fabre, Adrien/Douenne, Thomas/Mattauch, Linus (2023): "International attitudes toward global policies." In: Social Science Research Network. https://doi.org/10.2139/ssrn.4448523.

Frick, Vivian/Gossen, Maike/Santarius, Tilman/Geiger, Sonja (2021a): "When Your Shop Says #lessismore. A Field and Laboratory Intervention on Online Communication for Clothing Sufficiency." In: Journal of Environmental Psychology 75, 101595. https://doi.org/10.1016/j.jenvp.2021.101595.

Frick, Vivian/Matthies, Ellen/Thøgersen, John/Santarius, Tilman (2021b): "Do online environments promote sufficiency or overconsumption? Online advertisement and social media effects on clothing, digital devices, and air travel consumption." In: Journal of Consumer Behaviour 20/2, pp. 288–308. https://doi.org/10.1002/cb.1855

Froese, Tobias/Richter, Markus/Hofmann, Florian/Lüdeke-Freund, Florian (2023): "Degrowth-Oriented Organisational Value Creation: A Systematic Literature Review of Case Studies." In: Ecological Economics 207, 107765. https://doi.org/10.1016/j.ecolecon.2023.107765.

Fuchs, Doris/Di Giulio, Antonietta/Glaab, Katharina/Lorek, Sylvia/Maniates, Michael/Princen, Thomas/Røpke, Inge (2016): "Power: The Missing Element in Sustainable Consumption and Absolute Reductions Research and Action." In: Journal of Cleaner Production 132, pp. 298–307. https://doi.org/10.1016/j.jclepro.2015.02.006.

Garcia-Ortega, Beatriz/Galan-Cubillo, Javier/Llorens-Montes, F. Javier/De-Miguel-Molina, Blanca (2023): "Sufficient consumption as a missing link toward sustainability: The case of fast fashion." In: Journal of Cleaner Production 399, 136678. https://doi.org/10.1016/j.jclepro.2023.136678

Gebauer, Jana/Lange, Steffen/Posse, Dirk (2017): "Wirtschaftspolitik für Postwachstum auf Unternehmensebene. Drei Ansätze zur Gestaltung." In: Frank Adler/Ulrich Schachtschneider (eds.), Postwachstumspolitiken. Wege zur wachstumsunabhängigen Gesellschaft, München: oekom, pp. 239–252.

Gossen, Maike/Heinrich, Anneli (2021): "Encouraging Consumption Reduction: Findings of a Qualitative Study with Clothing Companies on Sufficiency-Promoting Communication." In: Cleaner and Responsible Consumption 3, 100028. https://doi.org/10.1016/j.clrc.2021.100028.

Gossen, Maike/Kropfeld, Maren Ingrid (2022): "'Choose Nature. Buy Less.' Exploring Sufficiency-Oriented Marketing and Consumption Practices in the Outdoor Industry." In: Sustainable Production and Consumption 30, pp. 720–736. https://doi.org/10.1016/j.spc.2022.01.005.

Gossen, Maike/Ziesemer, Florence/Schrader, Ulf (2019): "Why and How Commercial Marketing Should Promote Sufficient Consumption: A Systematic Literature Review." In: Journal of Macromarketing 39/3, pp. 252–269. https://doi.org/10.1177/0276146719866238.

Gossen, Maike/Tröger, Josephine/Veneny, Marek/Eichhorn, Henriette/Bergener, Jens (2023): "Do people make sufficiency-oriented mobile phone choices based on dynamic norms? The perception and effectiveness of sufficiency-promoting messages in online media." In: Frontiers in Sustainability, 4. https://doi.org/10.3389/frsus.2023.1145243

Gossen, Maike/Jäger, Sebastian/Hoffmann, Marja Lena/Bießmann, Felix/Korenke, Ruben/Santarius, Tilman (2022a): "Nudging Sustainable Consumption: A

Large-Scale Data Analysis of Sustainability Labels for Fashion in German Online Retail." In: Frontiers in Sustainability, 3. https://doi.org/10.3389/frsus.2022.922984.

Gossen, Maike/Frick, Vivian/Kettner, Sara Elisa (2022b): "Digitale Vermarktungsstrategien – Relevanz und Einfluss auf nachhaltigen Konsum." UBA-Texte 41/2022.

Grunwald, Armin (2010): "Wider die Privatisierung der Nachhaltigkeit – Warum ökologisch korrekter Konsum die Umwelt nicht retten kann." In: GAIA – Ecological Perspectives for Science and Society 19/3, pp. 178–182. https://doi.org/10.14512/gaia.19.3.6.

Gunderson, Ryan/Stuart, Diana/Petersen, Diana/Yun, Sun-Jin (2018): "Social Conditions to Better Realize the Environmental Gains of Alternative Energy: Degrowth and Collective Ownership." In: Futures 99, pp. 36–44. https://doi.org/10.1016/j.futures.2018.03.016.

Hartmann, Patrick/Marcos, Aitor/Castro, Juana/Apaolaza, Vanessa (2022): "Perspectives: Advertising and climate change – Part of the problem or part of the solution?" In: International Journal of Advertising 42/2, pp. 430–457. https://doi.org/10.1080/02650487.2022.2140963.

Heikkurinen, Pasi/Young, C. William/Morgan, Elizabeth (2019): "Business for Sustainable Change: Extending Eco-Efficiency and Eco-Sufficiency Strategies to Consumers." In: Journal of Cleaner Production 218, pp. 656–664. https://doi.org/10.1016/j.jclepro.2019.02.053.

Hirth, Steffen/Kreinin, Halliki/Fuchs, Doris/Blossey, Nils/Mamut, Pia/Philipp, Jeremy/Radovan, Isabelle (2023): "Barriers and Enablers of 1.5° Lifestyles: Shallow and Deep Structural Factors Shaping the Potential for Sustainable Consumption." In: Frontiers in Sustainability 4, 1014662. https://doi.org/10.3389/frsus.2023.1014662.

Jaeger-Erben, Melanie/Frick, Vivian/Hipp, Tamina (2021): "Why do users (not) repair their devices? A study of the predictors of repair practices." In: Journal of Cleaner Production 286, 125382. https://doi.org/10.1016/j.jclepro.2020.125382.

Jungell-Michelsson, Jessica/Heikkurinen, Pasi (2022): "Sufficiency: A Systematic Literature Review." In: Ecological Economics 195, 107380. https://doi.org/10.1016/j.ecolecon.2022.107380.

Kasser, Tim. E./Kanner, Allen D. (2004): Psychology and consumer culture: The struggle for a good life in a materialistic world, Washington, D. C.: American Psychological Association.

Kasser, Tim (2020): "Advertising's role in climate and ecological degradation." 8.12.2023 (https://static1.squarespace.com/static/5ebd0080238e863d04911b51/t/5fbfcb1408845d09248d4e6e/1606404891491/Advertising%E2%80%99s+role+in+climate+and+ecological+degradation.pdf).

Key, Thomas M./Clark, Terry/Ferrell, O. C./Stewart, David W./Pitt, Leyland (2020): “Marketing’s theoretical and conceptual value proposition: Opportunities to address marketing’s influence.” In: AMS Review 10/3–4, pp. 151–167. https://doi.org/10.1007/s13162-020-00176-7.

Kingaby, Harriet (2021): “Promises and environmental risks of digital advertising.” In: Ökologisches Wirtschaften 36/1, pp. 15–19. https://doi.org/10.14512/oew0360115.

Kropfeld, Maren I./Reichel, André (2021): “The Business Model of Enough: Value Creation for Sufficiency-Oriented Businesses.” In: Annabeth Aagaard/Florian Lüdeke-Freund/Peter Wells (eds.), Business Models for Sustainability Transitions, Springer eBooks: pp. 163–189. https://doi.org/10.1007/978-3-030-77580-3_6.

Lautermann, Christian/Pfriem, Reinhard (2018): „Transformationspotenziale von Energiegenossenschaften.“ In: Christian Lautermann (eds.), Die Energiewende der Bürger stärken, Metropolis: pp. 65–99.

Lepenies, Philipp (2022): Verbot und Verzicht: Politik aus dem Geiste des Unterlassens, Berlin: Suhrkamp Verlag.

Lewandowsky, Stephan/Smillie, Laura/Garcia, David/Hertwig, Ralph/Weatherall, Jim/Egidy, Stefanie/Robertson, Ronald E./O’Connor, Cailin/Kozyreva, Anastasia/Lorenz-Spreen, Philipp/Blaschke, Yannic/Leiser, Mark (2020): “Technology and democracy: Understanding the influence of online technologies on political behaviour and decision-making.” Publications Office of the European Union, Luxembourg. https://doi.org/10.2760/709177.

Lloveras, Javier/Marshall, Adam P./Vandeventer, James S./Pansera, Mario (2022): “Sustainability Marketing beyond Sustainable Development: Towards a Degrowth Agenda.” In: Journal of Marketing Management 38/17–18, pp. 2055–2077. https://doi.org/10.1080/0267257X.2022.2084443.

Lorek, Sylvia/Power, Kate/Parker, Natasha (2023): “Economies that Dare to Care – Achieving social justice and preventing ecological breakdown by putting care at the heart of our societies.” Hot or Cool Institute, Berlin., Germany.

Mayer, Colin (2020): “The Future of the Corporation and the Economics of Purpose.” In: Journal of Management Studies 58/3, pp. 887–901. https://doi.org/10.1111/joms.12660.

Ministère de la transition écologique (2021): “Indice de réparabilité,” 28.6.2023 (https://www.ecologie.gouv.fr/indice-reparabilite).

Molinari, Benedetto/Turino, Francesco (2018): “Advertising and Aggregate Consumption: A Bayesian DSGE Assessment.” In: The Economic Journal 128/613, pp. 2106–2130. https://doi.org/10.1111/ecoj.12514.

Nesterova, Iana (2020): “Degrowth Business Framework: Implications for Sustainable Development.” In: Journal of Cleaner Production 262, 121382. https://doi.org/10.1016/j.jclepro.2020.121382.

Nielsen, Kristian S./van der Linden, Sander/Stern, Paul C. (2020): "How Behavioral Interventions Can Reduce the Climate Impact of Energy Use." In: Joule 4/8, pp. 1613–1616. https://doi.org/10.1016/j.joule.2020.07.008.

Niessen, Laura/Bocken, Nancy M. P. (2021): "How Can Businesses Drive Sufficiency? The Business for Sufficiency Framework." In: Sustainable Production and Consumption 28/6, pp. 1090–1103. https://doi.org/10.1016/j.spc.2021.07.030.

Oehler, Andreas/Wendt, Stefan (2017): "Good Consumer Information: The Information Paradigm at Its (Dead) End?" In: Journal of Consumer Policy 40/2, pp. 179–191. https://doi.org/10.1007/s10603-016-9337-5.

Patagonia Inc. (2021): "Don't Buy This Jacket, Black Friday and the New York Times." 8.12.2023 (https://www.patagonia.com/stories/dont-buy-this-jacket-black-friday-and-the-new-york- times/story-18615.html).

Pärssinen, Matti/Kotila, Mikko/Cuevas, Ruben/Phansalkar, Amit/Manner, Jukka (2018): "Environmental impact assessment of online advertising." In: Environmental Impact Assessment Review 73, pp. 177–200. https://doi.org/10.1016/j.eiar.2018.08.004.

Persson, Ola/Hinton, Jennifer B. (2023): "Second-hand clothing markets and a just circular economy? Exploring the role of business forms and profit." In: Journal of Cleaner Production, 390, 136139. https://doi.org/10.1016/j.jclepro.2023.136139.

Raworth, Kate (2017): Doughnut Economics: Seven Ways to Think Like a 21st-Century Economist, London: Random House Business Books.

Rubinson, Joel (2009): "Empirical evidence of TV advertising effectiveness." In: Journal of Advertising Research 49/2, pp. 220–226. https://doi.org/10.2501/s0021849909090321.

Sheeran, Paschal/Webb, Thomas L. (2016): "The intention-behavior gap." In: Social and Personality Psychology Compass 10/9, pp. 503–518. https://doi.org/10.1111/spc3.12265.

Shrum, L. J./Burroughs, James E./Rindfleisch, Aric (2005): "Television's cultivation of material values." In: Journal of Consumer Research 32/3, pp. 473–479. https://doi.org/10.1086/497559.

Statista (2023a): "Prognose der Werbeausgaben weltweit," 28.6.2023 (https://de.statista.com/statistik/daten/studie/74622/umfrage/prognose-der-werbeausgaben-weltweit/).

Statista (2023b): "Digital Advertising – Worldwide," 28.6.2023 (https://www.statista.com/outlook/dmo/digital-advertising/worldwide).

Svenfelt, Åsa/Engström, Eskil/Eggestrand Vaughan, Hanna/Gerdin Emma (2022): "62 Ways of Enabling Sustainable Consumption. A Collection of Examples from Research in Mistra Sustainable Consumption." Mistra Sustainable Consumption/Stockholm KTH, Stockholm, Sweden.

Tröger, Josephine/Wullenkord, Marlis C./Barthels, Clara/Steller, Rubina (2021): "Can Reflective Diary-Writing Increase Sufficiency-Oriented Consumption? A Longitudinal Intervention Addressing the Role of Basic Psychological Needs, Subjective Well-Being, and Time Affluence." In: Sustainability 13/9, 4885. https://doi.org/10.3390/su13094885.

Vosoughi, Soroush/Roy, Deb/Aral, Sinan (2018): "The spread of true and false news online." In: Science 359/6380, pp. 1146–1151. https://doi.org/10.1126/science.aap9559.

Whitmarsh, Lorraine/Poortinga, Wouter/Capstick, Stuart (2021): "Behaviour Change to Address Climate Change." In: Current Opinion in Psychology 42, pp. 76–81. https://doi.org/10.1016/j.copsyc.2021.04.002.

Policy-Making as a Crucial Element for Sufficiency on the Business Level

Discussing the Role of Policies to Push Sufficiency beyond Pioneers

Jonas Lage, Benjamin Best, Tobias Froese and Carina Zell-Ziegler

Abstract *Research into sufficiency at business level often focuses on pioneers and a bottom-up approach to transformation. However, business activities are shaped and limited by political framework conditions. We analyze the interdependent relationships between business and policy making, arguing for greater emphasis on the structural perspective to foster sufficiency-oriented shifts in business.*

1. Introduction

Evidence supporting the notion that sustainability goals cannot be achieved solely through technological innovations but rather by incorporating sufficiency strategies grows year on year (Haberl et al. 2020). The Intergovernmental Panel on Climate Change now recognizes sufficiency as a crucial strategy for achieving climate goals (IPCC 2022) and an increasing number of energy scenarios integrate sufficiency approaches, acknowledging their significant potential (Wiese et al. 2022). However, the implementation of a sufficiency strategy remains unusual at all levels of society, including in business and policy making.

Building on a growing body of sufficiency definitions (Sandberg 2021; Lage 2022; Jungell-Michelsson/Heikkurinen 2022), we define sufficiency as *a strategy for reducing the consumption and production of end-use products and services through changes in social practices in order to comply with environmental sustainability while ensuring an adequate social foundation for all people*. In this chapter, we focus specifically on the production side. For business, this means that sufficiency encompasses limits on absolute production levels of end-use products and services, aiming to stabilize or even reduce production levels in certain areas or countries and to influence consumers accordingly (Lage 2022; Niessen/Bocken 2021). Additionally, sufficiency entails changes in the nature of the goods produced. For instance, a sufficiency-oriented approach in the automotive industry could mean producing significantly fewer cars and instead prioritizing the production of trams and buses, which would help reduce the need for private vehicles while ensuring basic mobility for a large part of the population. Similarly, the construction industry would shift from new construction to renovation and refurbishment, and the clothing industry would significantly reduce the amount of material produced, while supporting the reuse and repair of clothing. Thus, adopting a sufficiency perspective in business strategies entails a fundamental shift in business activities, with the overall aim of reducing production and consumption. Therefore, it is not surprising that sufficiency-oriented business strategies and corresponding business models are rare when it comes to downsizing, shifting or reducing production (Niessen/Bocken 2021).

Research into sufficiency and businesses often focuses on the activities of first-movers, examining their potentials, practices and obstacles regarding sufficiency-oriented production (Bocken et al. 2020; Gossen/Kropfeld 2022). Such studies frequently analyze best practice examples, where niche actors develop new practices and make them viable. Many studies on sufficiency-oriented business activities seem to adopt a strong bottom-up approach, relying on the diffusion of sufficiency-oriented business practices from the niche to move the production side towards sufficiency. This research is significant as it provides crucial insights into the transferability and limitations of sufficiency-oriented entrepreneurial actions. However, it neglects the effect of political framework conditions on sufficiency-oriented business strategies and their mainstreaming. Business activities always occur within politically shaped frameworks, while simultaneously directly or indirectly influencing political conditions. These interrelated and diverse relationships between sufficiency in business and policy making are rarely explored.

In this chapter, we examine this relationship between business and policy making on sufficiency and argue for a shift in the focus of sufficiency-related business research from the analysis of pioneers towards a more structural perspective. First, we analyze the relationships between business and policy making on sufficiency, focusing not only on pioneer businesses but also on businesses that hinder the implementation of sufficiency policies. Then, we analyze the role that policy making can play in influencing businesses to adopt sufficiency and explore sufficiency policies in different dimensions.

2. The influence of business on policy making on sufficiency

2.1 Pioneering businesses as drivers of sufficiency policies

Business can stimulate sufficiency policies and influence public debate, societal culture and market structures by successfully implementing sufficiency-oriented business models and showcasing sufficiency as a current possibility. Businesses can support sufficiency-oriented consumer practices and shifts in business culture, as well as reshape market structures in ways that can eventually instigate policy changes. Thus, following Palzkill and Schneidewind (2014), the basic assumption is that while businesses are exposed to market pressures and structural constraints (as explained below), they do have the potential to act as agents of change in several ways.

Firstly, pioneering businesses are instrumental in changing public discourse and common practice by initiating changes in consumer behavior, actively sharing knowledge through peer learning activities and providing replicable templates for other businesses (Froese et al. 2023). By way of illustration, PREMIUM, a German beverage producer, renounces profit and advertising and openly shares its business model with peers (e.g., through advisory services). PREMIUM's ambition is to promote its business logic in order to showcase and mainstream their approach to doing business (Edinger-Schons et al. 2019). Furthermore, in France, Murfy, a business offering professional repair services for home appliances, launched a marketing campaign featuring slogans, such as "The best value fridge is already in your kitchen", to promote product repairs (Munten/Vanhamme 2023: 14). Other businesses operating in France, such as Spareka and iFixit, also offer repair guides, repair services and spare parts, demonstrating the feasibility of repair-oriented business models. iFixit, in particular, is known for rating the repairability of laptops, smartphones and tablets. Against this background (although there is no proof of direct causality) it is worth noting that France introduced a ban on planned obsolescence in 2015 and the repairability index law for certain electrical devices in 2019 (Légifrance 2021; Ministère de la transition écologique 2021). The latter now mandates producers to provide repairability scores to consumers. Subsequently, in April 2022, the European Parliament demanded a legislative proposal for a 'right to repair' to ensure, among other things, that products are easier to repair, contain replaceable parts and are more durable (EUR-Lex 2022). Consequently, in line with Bidmon and Knab (2018), we argue that successful, sufficiency-oriented business models can influence the discourse and practices of consumption and production and, eventually, contribute to a socio-economic environment that makes it easier for policymakers to implement sufficiency policies.

Secondly, businesses that are pioneers of sufficiency can join forces to gain political power and proactively influence political actors. As Beyeler and Jaeger-Erben (2022: 21) highlight in their study on fourteen sufficiency pioneers, "sufficiency practitioners turn to their peers to collaborate for a sufficiency-oriented ecosystem and lobby for legislation that supports sufficiency practices". For example, Too Good To Go, together with other businesses, is campaigning for labels on food products to indicate that food is often still edible after the best-before date (Too Good To Go 2023). This initiative represents an effort to build on and change established policies, encouraging responsible consumption and reducing food waste.

However, the food industry also highlights how the relationship between pioneering businesses and policy decisions is dynamic, complex and anything but univocal. The spread of vegetarian and vegan diets around the world is an example of this. This cultural shift has not been driven solely by business. Social movements and non-governmental organizations, such as ProVeg and PETA (People for the Ethical Treatment of Animals), play a pivotal role (Whelan/Gond 2017). Nevertheless, Oatly (a producer of plant-based dairy alternatives) and Beyond Meat (a producer of plant-based meat alternatives) have responded to this movement very successfully. Along with similar businesses, they have contributed to the normalization of plant-based diets and the availability of associated products in supermarkets (Bocken et al. 2020). As outlined above, such changes in public perception can lead to supportive policy measures. They can, however, also cause incumbent and powerful businesses to respond with counter-measures as happened in 2020 when, under pressure from agricultural associations, the EU Parliament decided that plant-based dairy alternatives could not be referred to as 'milk' or 'cheese', etc. (Beret 2019). In summary, the adoption of sufficiency into the mainstream and policy making is a complex and conflicted process, which in many cases is actively hindered by incumbent businesses.

To conclude, pioneering businesses can contribute to a shift in discourse, power structures and socio-economic conditions and thus influence policy making on sufficiency. However, while these pioneers exhibit the potential for radical and authentic sufficiency strategies, they are usually small businesses operating in market niches. While there are attempts to join forces, such niche businesses do not generally have the same influence as larger businesses (e.g., corporations) to drive widespread policy change. The subsequent sections will explore how businesses may both inhibit and be influenced by policy change, shedding further light on the complex interplay between business practices and sufficiency policies.

2.2 Businesses as inhibitors of sufficiency policies

In numerous instances, businesses actively inhibit the development of policies geared towards sufficiency. When the aim of a sufficiency policy is to decrease the volume of cars, meat, dairy products, clothes or appliances produced and consumed, it has the potential to threaten the fundamental income models of some businesses. Therefore, it is likely that while certain businesses will experiment with sufficiency-oriented business models (as mentioned above), others will oppose sufficiency policies. Following the literature on climate action delay and denial, we identify four different ways in which businesses might hinder sufficiency-oriented policy making.

As outlined above in the case of sufficiency-oriented businesses, one way in which businesses can influence policy making on sufficiency is via direct lobbying. In contrast to many sufficiency-oriented businesses, companies whose business models would be endangered by sufficiency policies tend to be economically and politically powerful and influential. According to an analysis by the NGO LobbyControl, for every meeting with environmental associations between 2018 and 2021, the transport minister of Germany had 80 meetings with the automotive industry (Deckwirth 2021). The car industry in Germany donates millions of euros to the political parties in government and especially to those known for their car-friendly policies (LobbyControl 2017). Moreover, many politicians start working in high positions in businesses directly after resigning from the political sphere, known as the "revolving door" effect (Blanes i Vidal et al. 2010). A similarly strong connection between policy making and businesses opposed to sufficiency can be found in several industries.

A second way in which businesses use their economic and political power to hinder the implementation of sufficiency policies is by influencing the public discourse. Think tanks and industrial associations, such as the *Heartland Institute* in the USA or the Institute *Neue Soziale Marktwirtschaft* in Germany, run campaigns against well-established and well-researched phenomena such as the negative health impact of tobacco consumption or global warming. They fund thousands of fabricated studies to disrupt scientific evidence (as is well-documented for the tobacco industry), speak on talk shows, provide teaching materials for schools and roll out big campaigns in the media (Götze/Joeres 2020; Oreskes/Conway 2010). Such campaigns are used to erode the legitimacy of health protection or climate mitigation policies in the public discourse.

A third way in which businesses delay policy making on climate change mitigation is by voluntarily committing to develop sustainable business strategies and by pushing "pseudo-solutions" (Götze/Joeres 2020; I.L.A. Kollektiv 2017). These technical innovations (such as electric cars, synthetic fuels for aeroplanes or net zero campaigns) are necessary and indispensable as part of a socio-ecological transformation. However, they become a climate delay strategy when they are used to suggest that no big changes in modes of living are necessary, that endless growth can continue and that businesses are part of the solution and do not need further regulations (Bragg et al. 2021). Many of these "solutions" are criticized as being unfeasible and only possible on a small-scale because of a lack of resources, because they involve other ecological burdens (e.g., mining or land use change), or because they externalize costs to poorer regions (I.L.A. Kollektiv 2017).

Finally, businesses indirectly hinder the implementation of substantial sufficiency policies due to their structural entrenchment. Regions and nations depend to some extent on their key industries and businesses thriving. These dependencies comprise a material dimension, such as tax revenues or jobs, and a cultural dimension, such as the identities connected to the specific industry, as it can be noticed for example in regions where the coal mining or automobile industry dominates. Sufficiency policies, including both further environmental regulations on the production process and an absolute reduction in production levels, conflict with these dependencies. From the perspective of business, these dependencies are a source of power that can be used to effectively hinder sufficiency policy. From the perspective of policy making and research on sufficiency, these dependencies emphasize the importance of developing structures of growth independence.

The arguments outlined above hold true for many forms of climate protection policies. However, what makes these points sufficiency-specific is that sufficiency often poses a fundamental challenge to business models. Firstly, at the level of products and services, sufficiency questions conventional business models by emphasizing the need for fundamental changes, such as the construction of trams or cargo bicycles, or transitioning towards mobility service providers rather than producing electric cars. Secondly, sufficiency challenges the growth paradigm of businesses and the economy. As sufficiency entails setting absolute limits on the production and consumption of consumer goods, business models must shift away from growth-oriented approaches. Therefore, sufficiency policies are expected to face even greater resistance from influential businesses than climate protection policies. Consequently, it is unlikely that businesses alone will play a major part in the mainstreaming of sufficiency-oriented business models. Pioneer businesses are likely to remain a niche phenomenon. In contrast, it is important to acknowledge the primacy of policy making, which needs to set the framework conditions and guide business in a sufficiency-oriented direction. In the following, we therefore outline the dimensions of business-related sufficiency policies.

3. Sufficiency policies for sufficiency-oriented business strategies

3.1 Sufficiency-oriented framework conditions for business

Policies to incentivize and encourage the adoption of sufficiency at business level need to address framework conditions at both the macro- and meso-economic level. At the macro level, sufficiency policies entail changes to the current structures of the prevailing economic system in which businesses operate. The liberalized and globalized market is generally characterized by cheap resources, low cost energy and transport possibilities, prevailing weak environmental and social standards and large gaps between labor costs in the Global North and the Global South (Hickel et al. 2022; SERI et al. 2009). Consequently, production constantly moves to those countries (mostly in the Global South) where standards are lowest and labor is cheapest, so supply chains become excessively long and complex. Scholars describe this system as externalizing and imperial because it is based on discrimination and exploitation of people (especially in the Global South) and nature, while material wealth is primarily generated in the Global North (Brand et al. 2021). Sufficiency policies would address this externalization and the long supply chains by internalizing environmental and social costs through regulations and incentives aimed at changing the purpose of businesses from maximizing profit to maximizing the common good (Salleh 2010). Such policies may entail redistribution of material wealth, focus on the quality rather than quantity of products and emphasize a regional production

Another dimension of the prevailing system that impedes a sufficiency orientation at business level is the growth imperative driven by competitive framework conditions and market pressure. In competitive markets, businesses are driven to secure and increase their market share in order to survive and avoid bankruptcy (Richters/Siemoneit 2019). Businesses may try to maintain their competitiveness by increasing their productivity capacities or by lowering wages. This growth orientation is also driven by the businesses themselves through an artificial increase of the "needs" (probably better described as "wants") of consumers, e.g., through advertisements or the creation of ever-shorter fashion cycles (Mahmood 2022).

In recent years, some laws have been implemented (or discussed) that aim to change framework conditions on the macro level in a sufficiency-oriented way (even though sufficiency might not have been the starting point for these laws). The Supply Chain Act (EP 2023) and the Critical Raw Materials Act (EC 2023a), which are under discussion at EU level, and the German Act on Corporate Due Diligence Obligations in Supply Chains (BMAS 2023), intend to secure supply chains (e.g., in the textile industry) without the use of child labor, environmental destruction and with fair wages. In general, these regulations are intended to make businesses take more responsibility for their whole supply chain. Such measures are called "push-measures" and they intend to guarantee social and environmental standards. These regulations are likely to reduce exploitative fast fashion practices because cheap unsustainable products that incentivize overconsumption will no longer be available. At regional level, we tend to see "pull-measures" aiming to reduce externalization such as regional labels intended to shorten supply chains, bring value creation back into the regions and connect consumers to the producers (e.g., the label "Regionalfenster" in Germany).

These examples are starting points for policy to reshape the macro-economic framework conditions in order to support businesses to move towards sufficiency. There are, however, no explicit regulations on overconsumption or on the reduction of production – most of the existing policies focus on buying different products that are less ecologically and socially problematic. Therefore, to make a significant transformation towards sufficiency at business level possible, it is necessary to introduce more policies at the macro level. Such policies could entail a tax system that not only taxes the profit or turnover of a business but also takes its contribution to the common good into account such as in the approaches put forward by the Economy for the Common Good (Felber et al. 2015). This could change framework conditions and make sufficiency-oriented business models more profitable. Import taxes in proportion to the distance travelled by a product could incentivize more localized production. We identified about 300 policies in the "European Sufficiency Policy Database" on different levels and with different transformative potential to show that policy can support sufficiency in many ways – also beyond the business level (cf. Zell-Ziegler et al. 2023).

On the meso level, there are many incentives that impede sufficiency-oriented business models (Bocken/Short 2016). Examples include low standards for the repairability of products and reusability of primary materials, a lack of restrictions on advertisements (for specific products) and the absence of financial incentives to sell and drive adequately-sized cars. The relevance of such framework conditions on the meso level can be observed in the field of energy efficiency. Without the European Emission Trading System (ETS) (with its associated carbon costs), businesses would not have had an incentive to invest in energy efficiency technologies (Elmer et al. 2016)[1]. Moreover, without the EU's Ecodesign and Energy Labelling Framework Directives, producers of electrical devices would not have had such an incentive to invest in efficiency improvements and high-consuming devices would not have been banned from the market (EC 2023b).

In the field of sufficiency, alternative framework conditions for product design, such as repairability and longevity (as described above for France) would be desirable. Financial bonus systems for repair, such as in the German federal state of Thuringia (Verbraucherzentrale Thüringen 2023) or in Austria (BMK 2023) are good approaches, but are only a patch as opposed to being systemic solutions to the problem. Repairing is much more expensive and time-consuming for consumers than buying a new product, and it is often impossible due to the lack of spare parts or design that does not lend itself to being repaired. Regulations for longer warranties covering more aspects of a product and mandatory affordable repair services could increase the lifecycle and repairability of products and decrease the growth in production. Despite the fact that pioneer businesses continue to demonstrate sufficiency business cases, the current political framework conditions contain disincentives that cannot be overcome (especially not at the required pace)

---

1 It should be noted, however, that the ETS is also criticised because it could stimulate greater energy efficiency (Elmer et al. 2016).

by individual pioneer businesses. Timely and collective change cannot be achieved without political regulation and targeted incentive structures.

3.2 Structural policy enables sufficiency-oriented business strategies

In addition to policies directly addressing business, as described above, an orientation towards sufficiency also depends on structural policies. Businesses are often deeply connected with the regions in which they are located (Bracyzk et al. 2004). This interconnection of business and region, on different levels and in both directions, impedes the implementation of sufficiency policies. Therefore, sufficiency as a strategy for reducing production and consumption poses a challenge not only for businesses but also for industrial regions, which are partly dependent on key export industries. It is an open question which regions and sectors would be most affected by sufficiency policies. The most obvious examples in Germany are the automotive, dairy and construction sectors. Such industries are of high economic importance: for example, the automotive sector employed 786,000 workers in 2022 in Germany, according to the "German Association of the Automotive Industry" (BDA). Therefore, sectoral sufficiency policies (as proposed in 3.1) need to be complemented by structural policy (Marks 1992) in order to develop future-proof visions and imaginaries (Marquardt/Nasiritousi 2022) for the sustainable transformation of both industries and regions.

This must happen faster and more 'preventatively' than in the past. Traditional structural policy has been 'aftercare', only implemented after significant policy delay and sheltering of old industries. However, sufficiency demands proactive regional structural change in industrial regions – long before the respective business models become uneconomic (Gärtner/Frenzel 2014). At the same time, it should be avoided to put the system we live in at risk, by eradicating system-relevant industries in an uncontrolled way. Therefore, sufficiency policies must include structural policies for a stepwise transformation towards sufficiency-oriented modes of working and doing business, addressing also the embeddedness in the region (Princen 2005). The interconnectedness of regions and business entails different dimensions. We distinguish material, institutional and cultural dimensions.

The *material* dimension relates to assets, jobs and fiscal revenues. The economic impact that regions could experience when large industries reduce, shift or even stop their production needs to be softened by structural policies as part of a sufficiency program. The classic toolbox of structural policies includes early retirements, short-term allowances and the settlement of government institutions, as well as the promotion of education, art, culture and science. Interestingly, many promising business models, such as bus and train construction, will also expand due to sufficiency-mainstreaming and may allow for new jobs using similar skillsets to some traditional industries. Traditional structural policy aims to push regional clusters, businesses and technologies in order to generate growth and exports. Future-proof and sufficiency-oriented programs, however, should refrain from material growth orientation. Repurposing, recycling, repairing and reusing are the economic models of the future, which include many opportunities for civil society, research and business.

The *institutional* dimension refers to the underlying norms, rules and processes of policy making. In regions that are highly dependent on certain businesses, such as in the German city Wolfsburg where Volkswagen is located, the political and business decision makers are closely connected (see section 2.1). In order to loosen this connection, participatory decision-making should be strengthened – although this will not necessarily lead to a stronger sufficiency orientation. Participatory governance of this sectoral and regional structural change should involve actors from policy, business, associations and non-governmental organisations (environmental and other), following the framework of the Quadruple Helix (Carayannis/Campbell 2012).

On a *cultural* level, a region's identity (especially in industrial regions) is often connected to its predominant businesses and industries. These cultures need to be addressed by sufficiency policies in order to render a major transformation towards sufficiency possible at business level. New visions and knowledge about socio-spatial development plays an important role in small-scale regional transitions. The seminal example for a successful cultural change is the IBA Emscher Park (Ganser 1999). Located in the northern Ruhr area, it is nowadays a destination for recreational trips and a venue for major art fairs; however, until the 1980s, it was a structurally weak region, polluted by industrial waste and open sewage canals. The IBA Emscher Park did not aim to build new housing or develop new growth pathways, but to foster "change without growth", by including art in landscape design and through regenerating the natural environment (Best 2019: 214). However, culture, art, bottom-up initiatives and civic actors are often neglected or ignored in structural policies. These agents should be included in sufficiency-oriented structural policies through participatory processes. Culture and the arts can facilitate the reflection and transformation of imaginaries, visions and power structures to support sustainable development and the escape from high-energy and high-carbon lock-ins (Marquardt/Nasiritousi 2022).

4. Conclusion

In conclusion, we find that the focus on individual business models remains limiting and should be complemented by a perspective on the interrelationships between policy making and business. Sufficiency policies are needed to push sufficiency on the production side out of the niche. We identify various relevant linkages that exist between sufficiency policy and sufficiency at business level: how policies can hinder, enable and cushion sufficiency in businesses, but also how businesses hinder sufficiency policy. These linkages have so far received little attention in business-related sufficiency research.

It could be argued that our critique of the predominant focus on pioneer businesses in sufficiency-related business research derives from a different approach to socio-ecological transformation, which focuses on structural change instead of bottom-up activity (Lage 2022; Hirth et al. 2023). However, from research into socio-ecological transformation, we know that both approaches are needed. We do not argue that the focus on pioneer businesses is wrong, but rather that it should be complemented by a focus on the relationship between policy making and business activities. This would include a shift in the research object and research questions. Instead of pioneer businesses, the analysis of power structures in the context of policy making on sufficiency and the role of businesses within these power structures could become a central research object. Main research questions might focus on the effects of business-related sufficiency policies, what kind of conflicts arise around the implementation of these policies and how business-related sufficiency policies can gain leverage. A crucial research question, not only connected to business research but also to sufficiency policy research in general, is how to put sufficiency policies into practice.

On the level of policy making, we conclude that business models and economic sectors need an orientation towards sustainability criteria (e.g., planetary boundaries, Sustainable Development Goals). Linking social and ecological perspectives instead of playing them against each other would enforce long-term thinking on the business side. Businesses require a stringent policy framework; otherwise, sufficiency-orientation at business level will lead only to shifts in consumption, rather than to absolute reductions in consumption and production. Sufficiency policy also needs to include structural policies in order to create viable economic visions for the fossil industries and associated regions. Policy must expect resistance from companies against the mainstreaming of sufficiency, which can be particularly interesting for researchers.

References

Beret, Caroline (2019): "Soy Milk vs. E.U. Law: Who's Really Harmed by Labeling Bans?", 19.9.2023 (https://medium.com/@animalcharityev/soy-milk-vs-e-u-law-whos-really-harmed-by-labeling-bans-1d8cd05b595c).

Best, Benjamin (2019): Energiewende und Bürgerbeteiligung – Multi Level-Konstellationsanalysen des Beteiligungsprozesses der InnovationCity Ruhr – Modellstadt Bottrop, Wiesbaden: SpringerVS. https://doi.org/10.1007/978-3-658-26184-9.

Beyeler, Laura/Jaeger-Erben, Melanie (2022): "How to make more of less: Characteristics of sufficiency in business practices." In: Frontiers in Sustainability 3, pp. 1–25. https://doi.org/10.3389/frsus.2022.949710.

Bidmon, Christina M./Knab, Sebastian F. (2018): "The three roles of business models in societal transitions: New linkages between business model and transition research." In: Journal of Cleaner Production 178, pp. 903–916. https://doi.org/10.1016/j.jclepro.2017.12.198.

Blanes i Vidal, Jordi/Draca, Mirko/Fons-Rosen, Christian (2010): "Revolving Door Lobbyists." In: American Economic Review 102/7, pp. 3731–3748. http://dx.doi.org/10.2139/ssrn.1641217.

BMAS (2023): "Supply Chain Act," 1.9.2023 (https://www.bmas.de/EN/Europe-and-the-World/International/Supply-Chain-Act/supply-chain-act.html).

BMK (2023): "Reparaturbonus," 1.9.2023 (https://www.reparaturbonus.at/).

Bocken, Nancy M. P./Short, Samuel W. (2016): "Towards a sufficiency-driven business Model: Experiences and opportunities." In: Environmental Innovation and Societal Transitions 18, pp. 41–61. https://doi.org/10.1016/j.eist.2015.07.010.

Bocken, Nancy M. P./Morales, Lisa Smeke/Lehner, Matthias (2020): "Sufficiency Business Strategies in the Food Industry – The Case of Oatly." In: Sustainability 12/3, 824. https://doi.org/10.3390/su12030824.

Bracyzk, Hans -Joachim/Cooke, Philip/Heidenreich, Martin (2004): Regional Innovation Systems: The Role of Governances in a Globalized World, London: Routledge.

Bragg, Jesse/Jackson, Rachel Rose/Lahiri, Souparna (2021): "How Big Polluters are advancing a "net zero" climate agenda to delay, deceive, and deny," 1.9.2023 (https://corporateaccountability.org/wp-content/uploads/2021/06/The-Big-Con_EN.pdf).

Brand, Ulrich/Wissen, Markus/Jungwirth, Barbara (2021): The imperial mode of living: Everyday life and the ecological crisis of capitalism, London, New York: Verso.

Carayannis, Elias G./Campbell, David F. J. (2012): Mode 3 Knowledge Production in Quadruple Helix Innovation Systems: 21st-Century Democracy, Innovation, and Entrepreneurship for Development, New York: Springer. https://doi.org/10.1007/978-1-4614-2062-0.

Deckwirth, Christina (2021): "Lobbyismus bremst Klimaschutz: Problematische Nähe zwischen fossiler Industrie und Politik," 1.9.2023 (https://www.lobbycontrol.de/lobbyismus-und-klima/lobbyismus-bremst-klimaschutz-problematische-naehe-zwischen-fossiler-industrie-und-politik-92893/).

EC (2023a): Proposal for a Regulation of the European Parliament and of the Council establishing a framework for ensuring a secure and sustainable supply of critical raw materials and amending Regulations (EU) 168/2013, (EU) 2018/858, 2018/1724 and (EU) 2019/1020, Brussels: European Comission.

EC (2023b): "Electronic displays including televisions—Energy labelling and ecodesign requirements apply to this product," Brussels: European Comission.

Edinger-Schons, Laura-Marie/Lübbermann, Uwe/Kaya, Bienja (2019): "Premium Cola – Wir hacken die Wirtschaft: Veränderung aus dem System heraus." In: Alexander Kraemer/Laura-Marie Edinger-Schons (eds.), CSR und Social Enterprise, Berlin, Heidelberg: Springer Gabler, pp. 203–210. https://doi.org/10.1007/978-3-662-55591-0_22.

Elmer, Carl-Friedrich/Bradke, Harald/Faulstich, Martin/Nabitz, Lisa (2016): "Klimaschutz und industrielle Wettbewerbsfähigkeit – Synergien nutzen, Konflikte entschärfen." In: Wirtschaftsdienst 9, pp. 667–673. https://doi.org/10.1007/s10273-016-2032-y.

EP (2023): "Unternehmen sollen Menschenrechte und Umweltnormen in Lieferketten berücksichtigen," 1.6.2023 (https://www.europarl.europa.eu/news/de/press-room/20230524IPR91907/lieferketten-unternehmen-sollen-menschenrechte-und-umweltnormen-berucksichtigen).

EUR-Lex (2022): "European Parliament resolution of 7 April 2022 on the right to repair (2022/2515(RSP))," 19.9.2023 (https://eur-lex.europa.eu/legal-content/EN/TXT/?uri=CELEX:52022IP0126).

Felber, Christian (2015): "Change everything: Creating an economy for the common good." London: Zed Books.

Froese, Tobias/Richter, Markus/Hofmann, Florian/Lüdeke-Freund, Florian (2023): "Degrowth-oriented organisational value creation: A systematic literature review of case studies." In: Ecological Economics 207, 107765. https://doi.org/10.1016/j.ecolecon.2023.107765.

Ganser, Karl (1999): "Nachhaltige Regionalentwicklung durch die IBA Emscher Park." In: Dieter Kurth, Rudolf Scheuvens/Peter Zlonicky (eds.), Laboratorium Emscher Park, Dortmund: Institut für Raumplanung, pp. 14–19.

Gärtner, Stefan/Frenzel, Adeline (2014): Präventiver Strukturwandel – Strukturpolitische Möglichkeiten für die Innovationsregion Rheinisches Revier: IAT – Institut Arbeit und Technik.

Gossen, Maike/Kropfeld, Maren Ingrid (2022): ""Choose nature. Buy less." Exploring sufficiency-oriented marketing and consumption practices in the outdoor industry." In: Sustainable Production and Consumption 30, pp. 720–736. https://doi.org/10.1016/j.spc.2022.01.005.

Götze, Susanne/Joeres, Annika (2020): Die Klimaschmutzlobby: Wie Politiker und Wirtschaftslenker die Zukunft unseres Planeten verkaufen, München: Piper.

Haberl, Helmut/Wiedenhofer, Dominik/Virag, Doris/Kalt, Gerald/Plank, Barbara/Brockway, Paul/Fishman, Tomer/Hausknost, Daniel/Krausmann, Fridolin/Leon-Gruchalski, Bartholomäus/Mayer, Andreas/Pichler, Melanie/Schaffartzik,

Anke/Sousa, Tânia/Streeck, Jan/Creutzig, Felix (2020): "A systematic review of the evidence on decoupling of GDP, resource use and GHG emissions, part II: synthesizing the insights." In: Environmental Research Letters 15/6, pp. 1–42. https://doi.org/10.1088/1748-9326/ab842a.

Hickel, Jason/Dorninger, Christian/Wieland, Hanspeter/Suwandi, Intan (2022): "Imperialist appropriation in the world economy: Drain from the global South through unequal exchange." In: Global Environmental Change 73, 102467. https://doi.org/10.1016/j.gloenvcha.2022.102467.

Hirth, Steffen/Kreinin, Halliki/Fuchs, Doris/Blossey, Nils/Mamut, Pia/Philipp, Jeremy/Radovan, Isabelle/The EU1.5°Lifestyles Consortium (2023): "Barriers and enablers of 1.5° lifestyles: Shallow and deep structural factors shaping the potential for sustainable consumption." In: Frontiers in Sustainability 4, 1014662. https://doi.org/10.3389/frsus.2023.1014662.

I.L.A. Kollektiv (2017): Auf Kosten Anderer? Wie die imperiale Lebensweise ein gutes Leben für alle verhindert, München: oekom.

IPCC [P.R. Shukla, J. Skea, R. Slade, A. Al Khourdajie, R. van Diemen, D. McCollum, M. Pathak, S. Some, P. Vyas, R. Fradera, M. Belkacemi, A. Hasija, G. Lisboa, S. Luz, J. Malley, (eds.)] (2022): Summary for Policymakers. In: Climate Change 2022: Mitigation of Climate Change. Contribution of Working Group III to the Sixth Assessment Report of the Intergovernmental Panel on Climate Change," Cambridge, New York: Cambridge University Press. https://doi.org/10.1017/9781009157926.001.

Jungell-Michelsson, Jessica/Heikkurinen, Pasi (2022): "Sufficiency: A Systematic Literature Review." In: Ecological Economics 195, 107380. https://doi.org/10.1016/J.ECOLECON.2022.107380.

Lage, Jonas (2022): "Sufficiency and transformation – A semi-systematic literature review of notions of social change in different concepts of sufficiency." In: Frontiers in Sustainability 3. https://doi.org/10.3389/frsus.2022.954660.

Légifrance (2021): "Article L441-2 – Code de la consummation," 19.9.2023 (https://www.legifrance.gouv.fr/codes/article_lc/LEGIARTI000044330817).

LobbyControl (2017): "Auto-Lobby spendete 17 Millionen an Parteien," 1.9.2023 (https://www.lobbycontrol.de/pressemitteilung/auto-lobby-spendete-17-millionen-an-parteien-36317/).

Mahmood, Zainab (2022): "Ultra-fast fashion is taking over – and using every trick in the book to get us addicted," 1.9. 2023 (https://www.theguardian.com/commentisfree/2022/apr/18/ultra-fast-fashion-retail-sites-shein).

Marks, Gary (1992): "Structural policy in the European Community." In: Alberta Sbragia (eds.), Europolitics: Institutions and Policy Making in the 'New' European Community, Washington D.C: The Brookings Institution, pp. 191–224.

Marquardt, Jens/Nasiritousi, Naghmeh (2022): "Imaginary lock-ins in climate change politics: The challenge to envision a fossil-free future." In: Environmental Politics 31/4, pp. 621–642. https://doi.org/10.1080/09644016.2021.1951479.
Ministère de la transition écologique (2021): "Indice de réparabilité," 28.6.2023 (https://www.ecologie.gouv.fr/indice-reparabilite).
Munten, Pauline/Vanhamme, Joëlle (2023): "To reduce waste, have it repaired! The quality signaling effect of product repairability." In: Journal of Business Research 156, 113457. https://doi.org/10.1016/j.jbusres.2022.113457.
Niessen, Laura/Bocken, Nancy M. P. (2021): "How Can Businesses Drive Sufficiency? The Business for Sufficiency Framework." In: Sustainable Production and Consumption 28, pp. 1090–1103. https://doi.org/10.1016/j.spc.2021.07.030.
Oreskes, Naomi/Conway, Erik M. (2010): Merchants of doubt: How a handful of scientists obscured the truth on issues from tobacco smoke to global warming, New York: Bloomsbury Press.
Palzkill, Alexandra/Schneidewind, Uwe (2014): "Managementwissenschaften – Geschäftsmodelle – Kritik: Business Model Resilienz als Perspektive in einer fragilen Moderne." In: Camilo von Müller/Claas-Philip Zinth (eds.), Managementperspektiven für die Zivilgesellschaft des 21. Jahrhunderts, Wiesbaden: Springer Gabler, pp. 27–43. https://doi.org/10.1007/978-3-658-02523-6_3.
Princen, Thomas (2005): The logic of sufficiency, Cambridge: MIT Press.
Richters, Oliver/Siemoneit, Andreas (2019): "Growth imperatives: Substantiating a contested concept." In: Structural Change and Economic Dynamics 51, pp. 126–137. https://doi.org/10.1016/j.strueco.2019.07.012.
Salleh, Ariel (2010): "From Metabolic Rift to "Metabolic Value": Reflections on Environmental Sociology and the Alternative Globalization Movement." In: Organization & Environment 23/2, pp. 205–219. https://doi.org/10.1177/1086026610372134.
Sandberg, Maria (2021): "Sufficiency Transitions: A Review of Consumption Changes for Environmental Sustainability." In: Journal of Cleaner Production 293, 126097. https://doi.org/10.1016/j.jclepro.2021.126097.
SERI/GLOBAL 2000/Friends of the Earth Europe (2009): "Ohne Maß und Ziel? Über unseren Umgang mit den natürlichen Ressourcen der Erde," 19.9.2023 (https://www.bund.net/fileadmin/user_upload_bund/publikationen/ressourcen_und_technik/ressourcen_natuerliche_ressourcen_foee_bericht.pdf).
Too Good To Go (2023): "Impact Report 2022 – Gemeinsam gegen Lebensmittelverschwendung," 19.9.2023 (https://www.toogoodtogo.com/de/download/impact-report-2022).
Verbraucherzentrale Thüringen (2023): "Reparaturbonus 3.0." 1.9.2023 (https://www.reparaturbonus-thueringen.de/).

Whelan, Glen/Gond, Jean-Pascal (2017): "Meat Your Enemy: Animal Rights, Alignment, and Radical Change." In: Journal of Management Inquiry 26/2, pp.123–138. https://doi.org/10.1177/1056492616671828.

Wiese, Frauke/Thema, Johannes/Cordroch, Luisa (2022): "Strategies for climate neutrality. Lessons from a meta-analysis of German energy scenarios." In: Renewable and Sustainable Energy Transition 2, 100015. https://doi.org/10.1016/j.rset.2021.100015.

Zell-Ziegler, Carina/Best, Benjamin/Thema, Johannes/Wiese, Frauke/Vogel, Bendix/Cordroch, Luisa (2023): "European Sufficiency Policy Database [Data set]: Energy Sufficiency Research Group," 1.9.2023 (https://energysufficiency.de/policy-database/).

Appendix

Authors

Benjamin Best is a senior researcher at the Wuppertal Institute, Germany, where he leads the Research Group Energy Sufficiency and works on energy sufficiency policy, citizen participation and sustainable territorial development.

Laura Beyeler is a doctoral candidate at Brandenburg University of Technology Cottbus – Senftenberg, Cottbus, Germany, in the chair of Sociology of Technology and the Environment. With her research in sufficiency, Laura explores the role businesses and their ecosystem play for the absolute reduction of production and consumption volumes.

Nancy M. P. Bocken is professor in Sustainable Business at the Maastricht Sustainability Institute at Maastricht University, the Netherlands, and Fellow at the Cambridge Institute for Sustainability Leadership, the UK. Nancy focuses on topics like sufficiency, regeneration, experimentation and scaling up impact in a business context.

Julia Bruckner is a doctoral researcher at the Institute for Sustainable Management, University of Ulm, Germany. Julia focuses on sufficiency in the business sphere and explores how businesses can effectively promote sufficiency on a larger scale.

Hubert Buch-Hansen is an associate professor at Roskilde University, Denmark. Hubert's research focuses on the political economy of degrowth transformations.

Isabelle Dabadie is an associate professor of marketing and information systems at Université Bretagne Sud, Vannes, France, after an initial career in the telecoms industry. Isabelle's research focuses on corporate strategy and consumer behavior in response to climate change. She is particularly interested in the relationships between sufficiency and technology.

Blanca de-Miguel-Molina is a professor and researcher at the Universitat Politècnica de València. Spain. Blanca's research areas include management, competitiveness, innovation, corporate community involvement, sustainability, ethics and creative industries.

Marc Dijk is assistant professor and research coordinator at the Maastricht Sustainability Institute at Maastricht University, the Netherlands. Marc's research focuses on innovation and innovation policy, sustainability assessment, societal transformations, experimentation, learning and upscaling.

Vivian Frick is a sustainability researcher at the Institute for Ecological Economy Research in Berlin, Germany. Vivian's research topics include behavior change, sufficiency and civic engagement in the fields of socio-ecological transformation, digital transformation, mobility and energy transition.

Tobias Froese is a research assistant and doctoral candidate at the Chair for Corporate Sustainability at ESCP Business School's Berlin Campus, Germany, where he conducts research into degrowth and sustainability in the context of organizations, as well as on underlying value theories.

Javier Galan-Cubillo is pursuing a PhD degree in business administration and is a part-time professor at Universitat Politècnica de València, Spain. Javier is conducting research in business communication and ethics, digitization and sustainability.

Beatriz Garcia-Ortega is an associate professor and researcher at Universitat Politècnica de València, Spain. Her research areas encompass management, business ethics, digitization, corporate social responsibility and sustainability.

Jana Gebauer is an independent researcher based in Berlin, Germany, working on topics such as degrowth/post-growth and sufficiency approaches of transformative businesses that contribute to eco-solidary and diverse economies beyond growth. Jana is fellow at the Institute for Ecological Economy Research (IÖW), Berlin, Germany.

Maike Gossen is a post-doc researcher at Technical University Berlin, Germany. Maike's research centers around sustainable consumption, sufficiency, sufficiency-promoting marketing and digitalisation.

Michaela Hausdorf is a doctoral researcher at Hamburg University, Germany. Passionate about fueling a mind-shift in human-animal-nature relationships, Michaela explores transformative and post-anthropocentric business models in theory and practice.

Pasi Heikkurinen is research director in the Department of Economics and Management at the University of Helsinki and professor of Sustainable Business at the LUT Business School, Finland. Pasi's research focuses on sustainable organizations, the phenomenology of sustainability and degrowth.

Joshua Hurtado Hurtado is a doctoral researcher at the Department of Economics and Management, Process Studies on Sustainable Economy (PROSE) Research Group, University of Helsinki, Finland, focusing on the ideological and strategic dimensions of degrowth.

Jessica Jungell-Michelsson is a doctoral researcher in the Process Studies on Sustainable Economy Research Group (PROSE) at the University of Helsinki, Finland. Jessica's research centres around strongly sustainable food systems and business organisations.

Maren Ingrid Kropfeld is a professor for Sustainability & Entrepreneurship at Tomorrow University of Applied Sciences and Program Director for the Impact MBA in Sustainability, Innovation and Leadership. Maren's key research topics include sustainable business model design and sustainable business strategies.

Jonas Lage works at the Norbert Elias Center for Transformation Design and Research at the Europa-Universität Flensburg, Germany, on questions of sufficiency, socio-ecological transformation and urban development and is doing his PhD at TU Dortmund, Germany.

F. Javier Llorens-Montes is a professor and researcher at the University of Granada, Spain. His extensive research is centered around subjects such as innovation and operations management, among others.

Christel Maurer is a management consultant and coach with her own company that supports businesses and entrepreneurs to contribute to a more purpose-driven and social economy (MCC Maurer Consulting & Coaching). Christel is also co-founder of the event series "Teil der Lösung" in Zurich, Switzerland, which focuses on sustainable lifestyles and business management.

Oksana Mont is a professor in Sustainable Consumption Governance at the International Institute for Industrial Environmental Economics at Lund University, Sweden. Oksana works with sustainable business models, sustainable consumption and lifestyles, and policies.

Marlene Münsch is a project manager at ConPolicy Institute, Berlin, Germany. Marlene works on sustainable consumption and sufficiency practices and is interested in developing effective tools and communication for consumers.

Viola Muster is a research assistant at the Technical University Berlin, and project manager at ConPolicy Institute, Berlin, Germany. Viola's research focuses on sustainable consumption, consumer behavior and consumer policy.

Iana Nesterova is a visiting researcher at Roskilde University, Denmark. Iana's research focuses on the role of business in degrowth transformations.

Laura Niessen is a doctoral researcher at the Maastricht Sustainability Institute at Maastricht University, the Netherlands. Laura works on sufficiency-based business models and on how companies can promote sufficiency practices amongst their customers.

Tina Nyfors is a doctoral researcher at the Department of Economics and Management, Process Studies on Sustainable Economy (PROSE) Research Group, University of Helsinki, Finland, studying how the concept of ecological sufficiency could be applied in climate policy.

Isaac Arturo Ortega Alvarado is a post-doc researcher at the Norwegian University of Science and Technology, Trondheim, holding a PhD in Design. Isaac's research focus is on socio-material systems.

André Reichel is a professor for International Management & Sustainability at International School of Management Stuttgart, Germany, and Program Director for the MA Sustainability Management. Key research topics include sustainability transformation in business and society, as well as the political economy of degrowth.

Heini Salonen is a doctoral researcher at the Department of Economics and Management, Process Studies on Sustainable Economy (PROSE) Research Group, University of Helsinki, Finland, focusing on understanding organizational cultures in the context of sustainability transitions.

Maëlle Soulis recently graduated from Lund University's Master's Program in Environmental Management and Policy. Her 2023 master's thesis delves into sufficiency-oriented business models in the fashion sector, examining their financial viability and impact on growth and profit.

Jana-Michaela Timm is an assistant professor at Hamburg University, Germany. She strives for meaningful contributions in three research fields: transformational sustainability entrepreneurship, sustainable business models, and sustainability entrepreneurship education.

Josephine Tröger is a senior researcher at Fraunhofer Institute for Systems and Innovation Research ISI in Karlsruhe, Germany. Josephine's research is on attitude and behavior change in favor of sufficiency in various fields of action related to the energy transition. Her current focus is on mobility.

Kristoffer Wilén is a doctoral researcher at the Department of Economics and Management, Process Studies on Sustainable Economy (PROSE) Research Group, University of Helsinki, and Hanken School of Economics, Department of Marketing, Finland, studying political ecology, socio-ecological economics and sustainable consumption.

Carina Zell-Ziegler is a researcher within the Energy and Climate Division of the Oeko-Institute, Germany, and a doctoral candidate at Technical University Berlin working on energy sufficiency and sufficiency policy.